T0393145

KGB Operations against the USA and Canada in Soviet Ukraine, 1953–1991

Oriented for a general reading audience, this book gives a unique and rare perspective on the KGB "special operations" in Soviet Ukraine, which targeted especially the USA and Canada, using issues related to Soviet Ukrainian identity and cultural diplomacy of Soviet Ukraine after Stalin's death in 1953 until the perestroika of the 1980s.

Concentrating on the period of the Cold War after Stalin and combining the counterintelligence documents from the KGB archive in Kyiv, Ukraine, with the official KGB correspondence and reports to the political leadership of Soviet Ukraine, this book offers an experimental view of the political and cultural history of relations between Soviet Ukraine and "capitalist America" through the prism of KGB operations against the US and Canada. Written from a "hidden" perspective of KGB operations from 1953 to the end of the 1980s, this book covers intelligence and counter-intelligence operations and the active measures of the KGB, but also various problems of anti-American cultural campaigns in Soviet Ukraine, sponsored by the KGB, involving the issues of cultural consumption, knowledge production, youth culture and national identity.

Using carefully researched archive materials, this is an invaluable resource for scholars and advanced students of KGB operations, the Cold War, counterintelligence and political and cultural history of the relations between Soviet Ukraine and the United States and Canada, and a role of cultural consumption in this history.

Sergei I. Zhuk is Professor of History at Ball State University, USA. Since 1997 he has taught American colonial history and Russian/Soviet and Ukrainian history at Ball State University, the University of Pennsylvania, Johns Hopkins University and Columbia University. His research interests are international relations, knowledge production, cultural consumption, religion, popular culture and identity in the history of imperial Russia, Ukraine and the Soviet Union.

Routledge Histories of Central and Eastern Europe

The nations of Central and Eastern Europe experienced a time of momentous change in the period following the Second World War. The vast majority were subject to Communism and central planning while events such as the Hungarian uprising and Prague Spring stood out as key watershed moments against a distinct social, cultural and political backcloth. With the fall of the Berlin Wall, German reunification and the break-up of the Soviet Union, changes from the 1990s onward have also been momentous with countries adjusting to various capitalist realities. The volumes in this series will help shine a light on the experiences of this key geopolitical zone with many lessons to be learned for the future.

Czechoslovakism
Edited by Adam Hudek, Michal Kopeček, Jan Mervart

Poland in a Colonial World Order
Adjustments and Aspirations, 1918–1939
Piotr Puchalski

The Nation's Gratitude
World War I and Citizenship Rights in Interwar Romania
Maria Bucur

KGB Operations against the USA and Canada in Soviet Ukraine, 1953–1991
Sergei I. Zhuk

Tracing the Atom
Nuclear Legacies in Russia and Central Asia
Edited by Susanne Bauer and Tanja Penter

For more information about this series, please visit: https://www.routledge.com/Routledge-Histories-of-Central-and-Eastern-Europe/book-series/CEE

KGB Operations against the USA and Canada in Soviet Ukraine, 1953–1991

Sergei I. Zhuk

Routledge
Taylor & Francis Group

LONDON AND NEW YORK

First published 2022
by Routledge
4 Park Square, Milton Park, Abingdon, Oxon OX14 4RN

and by Routledge
605 Third Avenue, New York, NY 10158

Routledge is an imprint of the Taylor & Francis Group, an informa business

© 2022 Sergei I. Zhuk

British Library Cataloguing-in-Publication Data
A catalogue record for this book is available from the British Library

Library of Congress Cataloging-in-Publication Data
A catalog record has been requested for this book

ISBN: 978-1-032-08012-3 (hbk)
ISBN: 978-1-032-08014-7 (pbk)
ISBN: 978-1-003-21252-2 (ebk)

DOI: 10.4324/9781003212522

Typeset in Times New Roman
by MPS Limited, Dehradun

Contents

Introduction: Rise and Fall of the KGB in Soviet Ukraine after Stalin

Sergei I. Zhuk

In his very personal reaction to the news about the attempts by the Russian intelligence to influence the US President Donald Trump, a retired KGB officer noted,

> Today journalists and scholars suddenly discovered that the KGB and its successor organizations from the post-Soviet space interfered in domestic politics of the USA and meddled with the careers of the American politicians, such as Donald Trump. But they forgot that the similar KGB operations were part of the wider and more traditional old domestic front of the KGB: the fight against any American influence in various domestic aspects of the Soviet life. To understand the international operations of the KGB in America, scholars need to find how this American threat inside of the Soviet society was connected by the KGB operatives to the international dimensions of the KGB intelligence work. For the KGB in Soviet Ukraine, not one, but two North American nations, the USA and Canada, represented the common threat of Ukrainian nationalism from the Ukrainian diaspora in America, which challenged the Soviet vision of independent socialist Ukrainian nation. Another aspect of the KGB operations, which is ignored by the scholars, was related to a ubiquity of the KGB presence in the everyday life of Soviet society; it influenced every detail of this life. The KGB operations could be considered as the quintessential source material for our understanding of the Soviet history, and especially of the Soviet-American relations during the Cold War. Historians could use this KGB material [about its operations] as a peculiar encyclopedia of the Soviet history.[1]

Paradoxically, these observations, made by a professional KGB operative, who was a very loyal representative of his organization, repeated almost word by word the recommendations made to me more than fifteen years before by my dissertation adviser and a close friend, Nikolai N. Bolkhovitinov (1930–2008), a Russian (former Soviet) historian-Americanist, a world known expert on a history of Russia-American relations. Knowing about my plans to study the Soviet-American relations in the Cold War through a consumption of the products of American popular culture by the Soviet youth and through a knowledge production about the North American civilization by Soviet Americanists, Bolkhovitinov suggested me in January of 2004 to start my research with the KGB reports to the Communist political leadership, which became available to researchers in the former Communist party archives all over the post-Soviet space in those days. It is noteworthy that his argumentation (circa 2004) was very close to the former KGB officer's logic in 2019. Bolkhovitinov recommended me to "begin the research, first, with the Ukrainian materials about the KGB operations in Soviet Ukraine against the Ukrainian 'nationalistic' diaspora in the US and Canada, and then to concentrate on how these KGB actions affected all other problems of the Ukrainian national identity in cultural Cold War."[2]

So, I tried to follow the suggestions of my former mentor, and I visited the archives in my hometown Dnipropetrovsk (now Dnipro), and found what I was looking for – the regular monthly KGB reports to the Communist leadership of Dnipropetrovsk Region of Ukraine. These documents became the basis for a research of my two previous books.[3] But when I went to Kyiv in the summer of 2008 to get the documents from a former KGB archive there, I was stopped by the former KGB/now SBU officials, who denied my access to their material. Only many years after, in 2015, a Ukrainian successor of the KGB, the SBU (*Sluzhba bezpeku Ukrainy*), the Service of Security of Ukraine, opened its archive to everybody. As a result, in January of 2019, I returned to the same archive of SBU in Kyiv and spent almost a year there, following Bolkhovitinov's suggestions to write a book, using the material of KGB operations as a tool for understanding of various (sometime hidden) aspects of Soviet-American relations during the Cold War, concentrating on the available Ukrainian archival documents. The more I studied the SBU documents, concentrating on the SBU fund 16, featuring the KGB correspondence, reports, information presentations to the political leadership of Soviet Ukraine, and the SBU fund 1 with the files about counterintelligence work of the Ukrainian KGB, the more my book manuscript grew. Eventually, I realized that my material about the KGB operations against the Ukrainian diaspora in America would require the separate book project, which would cover in detail the period from 1945 until the 1980s and would involve the documents from the American archives as well. Meanwhile, in this given book, I decided to concentrate ONLY on the major topics of the KGB operations against the "capitalist America," originating in Soviet Ukraine, during the period from the opening of the USSR to the Western influences after Stalin's death in 1953 until the perestroika of the 1980s.

The KGB vs. the "Main Adversary"

After the Second World War, during the Cold War, Soviet political police and major intelligence agency, the KGB, targeted the US of America (the United States of America) as the "main enemy in the world" for the Soviet Union. According to Christopher Andrew, "throughout the Cold

War, Soviet intelligence regarded the United States as its 'main adversary.' In second place at the beginning of the Cold War was the US' (the United States's [in an original]) closest ally, the United Kingdom. In third position came France."[4] But, according to the experts, for the KGB of Soviet Ukraine, and their "special operations," another "'main adversary', besides the US, was Canada, a close US ally."[5] As a former KGB general, Oleg Kalugin, noted, the KGB always targeted the Ukrainian diaspora in America (in both the US and Canada), and the KGB "had a good network of agents among the Ukrainian émigrés, particularly in Canada, where several million Ukrainians had settled."[6] The KGB "carried on a low-level campaign to infiltrate numerous anti-Soviet émigré organizations, as well as so-called centers of ideological diversion. Virtually all of the large national groups in the Soviet Union – Ukrainians, Armenians, Lithuanians, Latvians and Estonians – had vocal émigré organizations abroad that fought for independence of their countrymen at home." And he continued,

> [Our] job in KGB foreign counterintelligence was to insinuate agents into these groups who would keep abreast of émigré activities, let us know which leaders were likely targets for recruitment, and, if possible, soften the anti-Soviet thrust of these usually rabid anti-Communist organizations. Our ultimate goal in working with these groups was to find agents who might eventually go to work for Western intelligence and security services.[7]

In their everyday counterintelligence activities in Soviet Ukraine, through the entire period of post-Stalin socialism, the KGB operatives still dealt mainly with the intelligence from the "main adversary," the US. According to the official counter-intelligence research of KGB in Kyiv, a number of the spies from the USA always dominated over number of the spies from other capitalist countries. Thus, in January–August of 1969, there were 133 cases of espionage in Soviet Ukraine, committed by foreigners. 74 of them were committed by Americans, 12 – by Englishmen, 19 – by French and 11 – by West Germans.[8] This was typical ratio for the KGB operations in Ukraine. During the 1970s and the 1980s more than 60% of all recorded and reported KGB counter-intelligence operations in Soviet Ukraine targeted the US and Canada only.

KGB Operations and Active Measures

This book will focus on a controversial character of the KGB "special operations," including "KGB active measures" in Soviet Ukraine, which targeted especially the USA and Canada, using the issues related to Soviet Ukrainian identity and cultural diplomacy of Soviet Ukraine after Stalin. Over several decades of late socialism, KGB operatives developed and enhanced their tactics, strategies, and practices of ideological and political control over Soviet citizens, creating the most enduring tradition of regimentation and manipulation in the Soviet ideological space. This tradition survived the crises of post-Soviet developments and solidified its dominance under the current political administration in the Russian Federation.

The major topics of this book will include the stories of both (1) the regular, "more traditional for the spying agency" espionage (collecting the intelligence information and analyzing it) and counterintelligence activities by the KGB, (2) and the so-called KGB active measures (*aktivnye meropriiatiia* in Russian). As early as 1980s, the CIA documents had already addressed some of the KGB "active measures" as "Soviet covert operations."[9] In 1992, Vladimir Bukovsky, a famous Soviet dissident and civil rights activist, was invited by the Russian President Boris Yeltsin to analyze the recently opened KGB documents in Moscow. Eventually, Bukovsky copied and published them in 1995, exposing to the world the KGB activities, which were called in those documents the "active measures." Bukovsky defined these KGB activities as the "actions of political warfare conducted by the Soviet and Russian security services (Cheka, OGPU, NKVD, KGB, FSB) ranging from media manipulation to outright violence."[10] Among many definitions of this term, which appeared after 1995, Seth G. Jones, in 2018, offered the most inclusive and shortest description of such KGB activities. According to him,

> During the Cold War, the Soviet Union developed a broad campaign to influence populations across the globe, which was best captured in the phrase ... "active measures." Active measures encompassed a range of activities, which were different from typical espionage and counterespionage activities. Examples included: written and oral disinformation (or *dezinformatsiya*); forgeries and false rumors; "gray" (unattributed) and "black" (falsely attributed) propaganda; manipulation and control of foreign media assets; political action and the use of agents-of-influence operations; clandestine radio stations; use of foreign Communist Parties and international front groups for pursuing Soviet foreign policy objectives; support for international revolutionary and terrorist organizations, including national liberation movements; political blackmail and kidnapping; targeted assassinations, including the killing of defectors.[11]

The main important target of the KGB active measures was the US. The most famous anti-American KGB operations, which were defined as active measures by former KGB operatives, such as Vasili Mitrokhin, who fled to the West, included the following: "operation Cedar" of disrupting power supply of both the US and Canada in 1959–1973; discrediting of the CIA in 1973–1978, using a historian Philip Agee, who was codenamed Pont (in

1974, according to KGB statistics, over 250 active measures were targeted against the CIA alone, leading to denunciations of Agency abuses); "operation Pandora," which planned to stir up racial tensions in the US between Afro-Americans and Jews in 1971 by mailing bogus letters from the Ku Klux Klan, placing an explosive package in "the Negro section" of New York City; planting and promoting claims that both John Kennedy and Martin Luther King Jr. had been assassinated by the CIA; discrediting US military aid to the El Salvador government in 1981–1984, trying to make it so unpopular within the US that public opinion would demand that it be halted (as a result, 150 committees were created in the USA, which spoke out against US interference in El Salvador, and the direct contacts were made with US Senators); starting rumors that fluoridated drinking water was in fact a plot by the US government to affect population control; fabrication of the story that AIDS virus was manufactured by US scientists at Fort Detrick in Frederick, Maryland.[12]

Many scholars had already described various aspects of KGB active measures. As Thomas Rid noted, "Spreading anarchy and chaos and disrupting order have long been a strategy embedded in active measures."[13] In 2017 a group of the Ukrainian political scientists and politicians even prepared a special pamphlet about the USSR active measures against the USA. Unfortunately, this document quoted only the most famous cases without a referral to the collection of the KGB archive in Kyiv. The major emphasis of this document was on using "the active measures" by Russia against Ukraine after the Maidan Revolution.[14] Recently, Olga Bertelsen emphasized another important aspect of active measures. According to her,

> They [active measures] had two dimensions, domestic and foreign. Their task was to enforce and reinforce a Soviet version of the story, a discourse, and rhetoric across geographical and political lines. During the Cold War, the stability and omnipresence of the chekist narrative and discourse guaranteed change in public opinion, and this change had to be universal. The prevalence of this discourse ultimately suppressed and marginalized other voices, truths, or discourses (domestically and overseas) that were inadmissible for the Soviet regime.[15]

Overall, active measures were interwoven into the regular KGB operations on retrieving and analyzing the intelligence information, which involved traditional spying activities.[16] As a result, the archival material on the KGB operations offers sometimes the cases, which combined the different strategies and tactics, presenting a confusing picture of the historical events. Therefore, this book will analyze the stories of the KGB archival documents, trying not to concentrate on the typology of the KGB operations, but rather on the sequence of historical events presented in those documents.

Discovery of the "Capitalist Seductive" America through KGB Operations in Soviet Ukraine

The "capitalist America" became not only the "main," but also "seductive" "adversary" of the KGB, creating the attractive cultural products and practices for Soviet consumers. Paradoxically, the KGB operatives were also attracted to various "material and cultural items" they associated with the "seductive America." As one retired KGB officer recalled, "despite all our ideological communist upbringing, we, young KGB officers, still dreamed about the products 'made in the USA,' about a possibility to get a special assignment involving a 'business trip' to America, which would allow us to bring the desired items from America to Ukraine."[17] Former KGB officers, like Oleg Kalugin, recalled how the KGB agents, living in the USA on the intelligence assignment, enjoyed a consumption of the American products and services, literally "falling in love with America" and American way of life. As Kalugin (who was sent officially to the US as an exchange student of journalism) described his own fascination with America in his memoirs, "I was twenty-four and had been turned loose in New York City with the princely sum of $250 a month in Fulbright spending money." "I was living for free in Columbia's John Jay Hall, – he continued, – taking journalism courses, and being encouraged by the school newspaper – and the KGB – to sniff around New York and get acquainted with American life... I visited scores of neighborhoods and all the major museums. I saw ball games and went to the Metropolitan Opera. I rode buses and subways for hours and saw more than one hundred films. I went to a strip club in Greenwich Village, shelling out $40 for a drink with one of the dancers..."[18] According to contemporaries, all "KGB people" after visiting America on the intelligence assignment developed a psychological phenomenon, which was known as "a fondness of America and its people."[19]

This hidden curiosity and fascination about "capitalist America" were obviously present in all individual KGB reports (including the counterintelligence ones), which were submitted to their administration by the KGB operatives, who worked with the American visitors in Soviet Ukraine. Those KGB officers, who "worked" with the American tourists in Kyiv, recalled, that "after a long communication with an American visitor, besides the classified intelligence information, a KGB agent usually reported the numerous details of everyday life in America of his visitor: about American cars, education, food, fashions, even films and television shows."[20] As KGB operatives joked, by participating in those anti-American operations, the KGB officers "discovered the various details of everyday life in American civilization: it was a peculiar process of the 'discovery of America/the American Other' by struggling not only with the alleged American intelligence agents, but also with American propaganda during consumption of the 'seductive American products'."[21]

According to the KGB statistics, the overwhelming majority of criminal cases involving the American influences in Soviet Ukraine were not related directly to the US intelligence, but rather to the consumption of cultural products, produced in the US. Massive consumption of American jazz and rock music by Soviet youth produced not only a massive phenomenon of the black market and *fartsovshchiks* (black marketers) in every Soviet city, but also the youth subcultures of *stiliagi*, hippies and punks, which were considered by the KGB administration to be "the alternative political culture to Komsomol."[22] All those subcultures used a variety of the American cultural practices and models of behavior. Therefore, the KGB interpreted those subcultures as the "anti-Soviet American threat" and organized the special KGB operations, especially against the subcultures of hippies and punks during the 1970s and the 1980s. This book will cover also the story of the KGB anti-American operations against the youth culture in Soviet Ukraine, especially against the youth subcultures, such as hippies and punks and various non-traditional religions, practiced by Soviet young people.

Historiography, Sources and Structure of the Book

Numerous studies were published on the CIA-KGB confrontation during the Cold War. Majority of these publications used mainly the CIA documents, and those rare KGB files, which were copied by the former KGB officers, like a KGB archivist Vasili Mitrokhin, who fled to the West with those copies, made sometime by hand.[23] Chronologically, the first experience of working with the real classified KGB documents was recorded by a famous Soviet dissident Vladimir Bukovsky in 1995. Using an access to the KGB documents provided by the Russian President Yeltsin, Bukovsky not only made copies of those rare documents, but also tried to analyze them as a source for understanding of the Soviet international and domestic policy during the Cold War.[24] After 1995, some scholars used occasionally the regular KGB reports to the Communist party leadership. But only after 2015, with opening of the Ukrainian archive of the KGB in Kyiv to all researchers, more the Cold War historians had begun using the KGB documents in their research.[25] The best and the more efficient engagement of the KGB documents from Kyiv archive was done in the fascinating analysis of the Soviet youth subculture of hippies by Juliane Fürst, especially, in its well-written, but incomplete, parts, dealing with Soviet Ukraine.[26] Recently, using the SBU/KGB archival materials, Olga Bertelsen prepared a series of the interesting publications about the KGB operations, targeting the Ukrainian and Jewish international communities.[27] Concentrating on a variety of sources, including the rare SBU/KGB archival documents, Serhii Plokhy published three captivating monographs about various problems of the Cold War history, ranging from the collapse of the "Grand Alliance" of WWII in 1945–1946, to the Cuban missile crisis, and to the Chernobyl catastrophe of 1986.[28]

Despite the growing number of the recent publications, based on the KGB documents from the SBU archive in Kyiv, the topic of the KGB special operations against two countries of "capitalist America" – the US and Canada – during the Cold War needs more archival research and analysis. Concentrating on the period of the Cold War after Stalin, when Soviet Ukraine became gradually opened to American and Canadian visitors, and combining the counterintelligence documents from fund 1 of the SBU archive with the official KGB correspondence and reports to the political leadership of Soviet Ukraine from fund 16 of the same archive, my book offers the experimental view of political and cultural history of the relations between Soviet Ukraine and "capitalist America" through a prism of the KGB operations against the US and Canada. As the participants of this history noted, "the organs of the KGB always played a role of the political, but secretly hidden, weapon of the Communist party leadership in the USSR; therefore, to understand the hidden side of the Soviet history, including the Soviet diplomacy, we need to explore the KGB stories of the Cold War."[29] So, this book became a peculiar experiment in writing a history of Soviet-American relations "from a hidden/secret" point of view of the KGB operations from 1953 to the end of the 1980s. As a result, this book will cover not only the most typical intelligence and counter-intelligence operations and the active measures of the KGB, but also various problems of anti-American cultural campaigns in Soviet Ukraine, sponsored by the KGB, involving the issues of cultural consumption, knowledge production, youth culture and national identity. Therefore, this book became also a special extension of my previous books' material on the youth culture in the closed city of Soviet Ukraine and on the cultural history of Soviet Americanists in Russia and Ukraine, which were written between 2004 and 2016.[30]

The first and major historic source for the book is a variety of the KGB agents' reports, who participated in the different KGB counterintelligence operations of the ongoing Cold War. These reports offer us not only the precious "spy stories" about the hidden secret Soviet diplomacy with the US and Canada, but also give us a unique opportunity to explore a mindset and mentality of the KGB operatives and of their "targets" – Americans and Canadians – during this period from 1953 until 1980. Other important KGB files of the counterintelligence documents cover a period of the 1950s and 1960s for the special anti-American operations (against the alleged US spies) in the separate regions (*oblast'*) of Soviet Ukraine. In addition, this book used a unique file of the KGB documents, which summarized the counterintelligence operations against the US exhibitions, which were organized by the US government on the territory of Soviet Ukraine. The KGB correspondence with the political leadership of Soviet Ukraine also offer the precious information, and often the very good sociological analysis and statistics of various social and political developments in Soviet Ukraine, which included the honest professional conclusions and recommendations, covering the different issues – from the "Americanization" and commercialization of the Soviet youth to the failure of communist indoctrination of the Ukrainian society and to the catastrophe of Soviet Ukraine's economy by the beginning of the 1980s.[31]

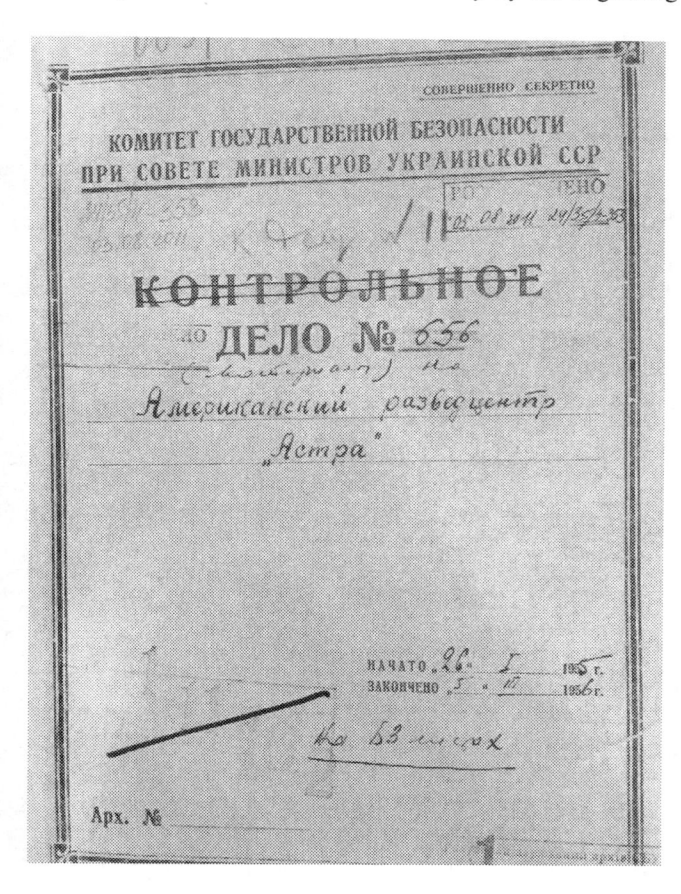

Figure 0.1 US spy center ASTRA file.

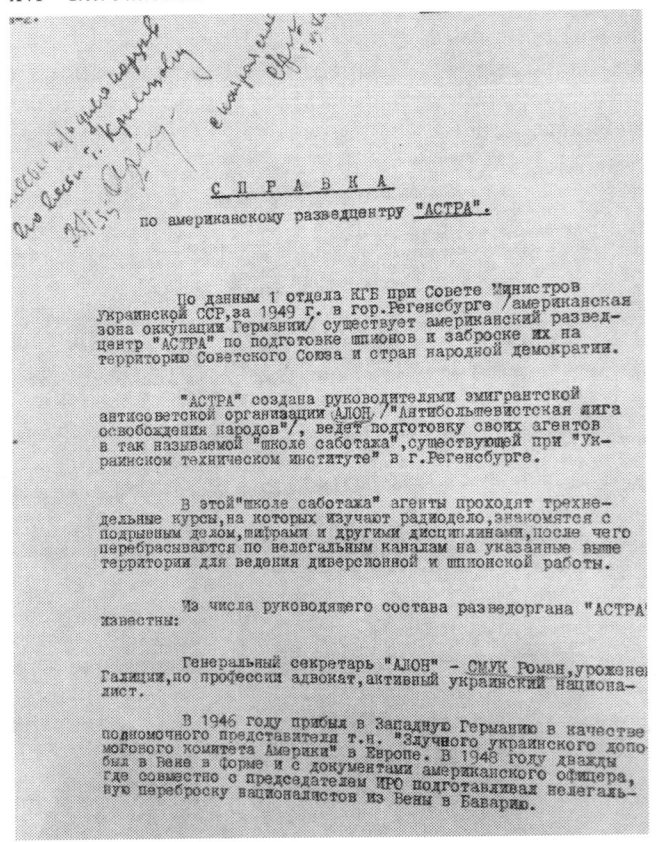

Figure 0.2 Page document of Astra spy center.

The second group of "unexpected" sources for this book consists of my recorded conversations/interviews with the retired KGB officers in Kyiv and Dnipro during the period from 1991 to 2019. In June of 2012, Leonid Leshchenko (1931–2013), Ukrainian Americanist and my colleague, introduced me in Kyiv to three former KGB officers, who were engaged in various KGB operations, including those, which were connected to the US President Nixon's visit to Kyiv in 1972 and the opening of US Consulate in Kyiv afterward. Frankly speaking, after those meetings with Leshchenko's friends, I decided to engage those interviews in my research. Therefore, later on, in 2019, while doing my research in Kyiv archives, I interviewed Leshchenko's friends and used their notes and observations in my analysis of the real archival documents about the same events they had covered in our conversations. I promised to my interviewees that I would use only their first names in my publication, and that I would not reveal their real officer rank and position during their service in my book.

The last group of sources for this book are the published memoirs of the contemporaries of the events, covered by the book. Among many books of memoirs, the best sources of the information for my research were memoirs of the Soviet Ambassador to the US, Anatoly Dobrynin, and a book, written by a former General of the KGB Oleg Kalugin, a head of the KGB political operations in the US. Besides memoirs, this book uses various contemporary periodicals, a few personal diaries, and the published collections of the KGB documents, such as "Mitrokhin Archive."

The structure of this book follows the chronological and thematical order, reflecting the major topics of the Cold War after Stalin, and a story of the special KGB operations from 1953 until 1991. The first part of the book deals with the creating of the models for the special KGB operations against the US and Canada after WWII. The first chapter focuses on the KGB targeting the Ukrainian diaspora in America and the American "spy schools" in West Germany. The second chapter deals with the problems of the "double" agents among the "displaced persons" in Europe, who became recruited by both the American intelligence officers and the KGB operatives. Another topic of this chapter is the special KGB operations against the "Jewish nationalism/Zionism," and the operations, which were connected to the KGB attempts to involve the Soviet Jews in various active measures against the US. Using stories of two Canadian Communists and one Soviet Ukrainian Americanist, the third and fourth chapters explore how in its struggle against Ukrainian nationalists ("*banderovtsy*" in the official documents) in America, the Ukrainian KGB tried to use the American Ukrainian Left Pro-Communist activists. Ukrainian Canadians, members of the Communist Party of Canada, became the "useful tools" of Soviet KGB meddling in the Ukrainian Diaspora affairs in America through the entire 1960s and the 1980s.

The main focus of the second part of this book is on the counterintelligence operations and active measures, targeting the US officials and American and Canadian tourists. The fifth chapter analyzes how 1960 U-2 incident triggered a "spy hysteria" in Soviet Ukraine, affecting both US officials and Western tourists, who visited Ukrainian republic after 1953, and producing the public trials of the "American spies" in Kyiv. The sixth chapter of this book deals with the counterintelligence operations targeting the US exhibitions in Soviet Ukraine and it also explores the problems of industrial and technological espionage, performed by the KGB during the Khrushchev's and Brezhnev's eras. The seventh chapter explores the cases of the collaboration between the KGB and the CIA in the planning and organizing visits of two US Presidents to Kyiv (in 1960 and 1972), and the KGB attempts of meddling in the US and Canadian politics, using American and Canadian politicians and tourists, who visited Soviet Ukraine, and the US Consulate in Kyiv during 1974–1982.

The final, third, part of my book is devoted to the KGB struggle with American cultural influences in Soviet Ukrainian society, and to the KGB role in the cultural Cold War. The chapter 8th is about the KGB operations against the consumption of American rock music and Western films, which triggered the birth of the new youth "Americanized" subcultures of hippies and punks and the rise of neo-Fascism among the youth of Soviet Ukraine. The 9th chapter deals with a variety of forms of cultural consumption – from the erotic "forbidden" literature to the exotic religions, such as Krishnaism, to disco music and video tapes – which had the direct American influences on the Soviet youth. Eventually, all these American influences led to the massive commercialization of not only the Soviet youth, but also of the KGB operatives and Soviet ideologists, responsible for the fight against American ideology and culture. At the end of perestroika, by 1991, it became obvious that the KGB failed and lost its position in the Cold War against the US and Canada on both the international and domestic fronts.

Notes

1 Interview with Ivan Grigorovich K., a retired KGB officer, February 3, 2019, Kyiv, Ukraine.
2 Interview with Nikolai N. Bolkhovitinov, January 4, 2004, Moscow, Russian Federation.
3 Sergei I. Zhuk, *Rock and Roll in the Rocket City: The West, Identity, and Ideology in Soviet Dniepropetrovsk, 1960–1985* (Baltimore, MD: Johns Hopkins University Press & Washington, D.C.: Woodrow Wilson Center Press, 2010), and idem, *Soviet Americana: The Cultural History of Russian and Ukrainian Americanists* (London and New York: I.B. Tauris, 2018).
4 Christopher Andrew and Vasili Mitrokhin, *The Sword and the Shield: The Mitrokhin Archive and the Secret History of the KGB* (New York: Basic Books, 1999), 150. See also John Earl Haynes, Harvey Klehr, and Alexander Vassiliev, *Spies: The Rise and Fall of the KGB in America* (New Haven: Yale University Press, 2009), esp. 293–481.
5 Interview with Leonid Leshchenko, June 25, 2013, Kyiv, Ukraine. Many years ago, one retired KGB officer told me the same. I used his interviews in my book about Soviet Dnipropetrovsk (Interview with Igor T., a retired KGB officer, May 15–18, 1991). See in Sergei I. Zhuk, *Rock and Roll in the Rocket City*.
6 Oleg D. Kalugin, *Spymaster: My Thirty-Two Years in Intelligence and Espionage Against the West* (New York, NY: Basic Books, 2009), 221.
7 Oleg D. Kalugin, *Spymaster*, 221. See also Serhii Plokhy, *The Man with the Poison Gun: A Cold War Spy Story* (New York: Basic Books, 2016), esp. 222, 223ff.
8 Galuzevyi Derzhavnyi Arkhiv Sluzhby Bezpeky Ukrainy (hereafter – SBU), f. 16, op. 1, spr. 988, ark. 138.
9 See especially Richard H. Shultz, and Roy Godson, *Dezinformatsia: Active Measures in Soviet Strategy* (New York, NY: Pergamon-Brassey's International Defense Publishers, 1984).

10 See the recent English translation of the original book, published in Russian in 1996 as *Moskovskii protsess*: Vladimir Bukovsky, *Judgment in Moscow: Soviet Crimes and Western Complicity*, trans. Alyona Kojevnikov (Westlake Village, CA: Ninth of November Press, 2019), 629.

11 Seth G. Jones, "Going on the Offensive: A U.S. Strategy to Combat Russian Information Warfare," Quoted from: https://www.csis.org/analysis/going-offensive-us-strategy-combat-russian-information-warfare. See also his book, *A Covert Action: Reagan, the CIA, and the Cold War Struggle in Poland* (New York: W.W. Norton, 2018).

12 Christopher Andrew and Vasili Mitrokhin, *The Sword and the Shield*; Thomas Rid, *Active Measures: The Secret History of Disinformation and Political Warfare* (New York: Farrar, Straus and Giroux, 2020), 263–277, 278–287, 288–297, see especially a chapter 22: "AIDS Made in the USA": 298–311. See also a link: https://en.wikipedia.org/wiki/Active_measures#cite_note-g-30

13 Thomas Rid, *Active Measures*, 9, 11.

14 D. Dubov, A. Barovska, T. Isakova, I. Koval, V. Horbulin; General editorship by D. Dubov. *"Active Measures" of USSR against USA: Preface to Hybrid War. Analytical Report* (Kyiv: The National Institute for Strategic Studies, 2017).

15 Olga Bertelsen, "Introduction: A Blind Spot of Active Measures," in *Russian Active Measures: Yesterday, Today and Tomorrow*, Edited by Olga Bertelsen (New York: ibidem Press and Columbia University Press, 2021), 15–35, citation is from p. 2. She also described how Soviet traditions still affected post-Soviet Russian intelligence: "First, they cast challenges to their narratives and alternative narratives as actions on the "extreme end of the Cold War spectrum." Second, any critique of Russian foreign policy or Russia's encroachments into other states' political and cultural spheres are identified as nationalistic manifestations of ultra-right neo-fascist governments or groups that have an ax to grind with Russia." Op. cit., 18.

16 See more information about the KGB active measures in detail in: Edward Mickolus, *The Counterintelligence Chronology: Spying By and Against the United States From the 1700s Through 2014* (Jefferson, NC: McFarland & Company, Inc., 2015); Kevin N. McCauley, *Russian Influence Campaigns Against the West: From the Cold War to Putin* (North Charleston, SC: CreateSpace Independent Publishing Platform, 2016); Jolanta Darczewska, Piotr Żochowski, "ACTIVE MEASURES: Russia's key export," *Point of View*, June 2017, Number 64 (Warsaw: Center for Eastern Studies), pp. 5-71; Richard Stengel, *Information Wars: How We Lost the Global Battle against Disinformation & What We Can Do About It* (New York: Atlantic Monthly Press, 2019).

17 Interview with Leonid K., a retired KGB officer, March 3, 2019, Kyiv, Ukraine. Leonid was a personal friend of the Soviet Ukrainian Americanists, such as Arnold Shlepakov and Leonid Leshchenko, who introduced me to this officer in 1992.

18 Oleg D. Kalugin, *Spymaster*, 27, 29.

19 Pavel Palazchenko, *My Years with Gorbachev and Shevardnadze: The Memoir of a Soviet Interpreter* (University Park, Pa.: The Pennsylvania State University

Press, 1997), p. 95. *Compare with* Allen H. Kassof, "Scholarly Exchanges and the Collapse of Communism," *The Soviet and Post-Soviet Review*, 1995, Vol. 22, No. 3, 263–274.

20 Interview with Leonid K.

21 Interview with Igor T., a retired KGB officer, May 18, 1991, Dnipropetrovsk, Soviet Ukraine. This vision of America as "the cultural Other" of Russia became a conceptual tool for the recent research of my Russian colleagues, Americanist-historians, Ivan Kurilla and Victoria Zhuravleva.

22 I quote my interview with Igor T. See also my book, *Rock and Roll in the Rocket City*.

23 Among the numerous studies of CIA operations against the USSR during the Cold War, see especially the best archival research by Benjamin Tromly, *Cold War Exiles and the CIA: Plotting to Free Russia* (New York: Oxford University Press, 2019). I refer to the publications of "Mitrokhin Archive," such as Christopher Andrew and Vasili Mitrokhin, *The Sword and the Shield*.

24 Vladimir Bukovsky, *Judgment in Moscow.*

25 Among many of publications, based on the SBU archival documents, see publications of the Ukrainian scholar Dmitrii Vedeneiev, *Ateisty v mundirakh: Sovetskie spetssluzhby i religioznaia sfera Ukrainy* (Moscow: Algoritm, 2016).

26 Juliane Fürst, *Flowers through Concrete: Explorations in Soviet Hippieland* (New York: Oxford University Press, 2021).

27 See her edited collection of essays: *Russian Active Measures: Yesterday, Today and Tomorrow,* Edited by Olga Bertelsen (New York: ibidem Press and Columbia University Press, 2021), and her monograph: Olga Bertelsen, *In the Labyrinth of the KGB: Ukraine's Intelligentsia in the 1960s–1970s* (Lanham, MD and Boulder, CO: Rowman and Littlefield's Lexington Press, 2022)

28 Serhii Plokhy, *Chernobyl: History of a Tragedy* (New York: Penguin, 2019); idem, *Forgotten Bastards of the Eastern Front: American Airmen behind the Soviet Lines and the Collapse of the Grand Alliance* (New York: Oxford University Press, 2019), idem, *Nuclear Folly: A History of the Cuban Missile Crisis* (New York: W.W. Norton, 2021).

29 Interview with Leonid Leshchenko, June 23, 2012, Kyiv, Ukraine.

30 I refer to Sergei I. Zhuk, *Rock and Roll in the Rocket City*, and idem, *Soviet Americana.*

31 The officials of SBU archive in Kyiv not only allowed the researchers to make photo pictures of the rare original documents from a fund 1 for free, but also permitted to download to researchers' computers the digital copies of the important documents from a fund 16 free of charge as well.

Acknowledgments

First, my words of gratitude go to a love of my life, my dear friend and wife, Irinushka (Irina M. Kozintseva), who patiently supported all my efforts to collect the archival material and write my book both in Ukraine and the US through all these years.

It would have been impossible for me to finish this book without support from various people and organizations. First of all, Ball State University granted me Special Assigned Leave with pay in 2019, and I spent the very productive time in Kyiv, Ukraine, at the State Archive of the Service of Security of Ukraine (SBU), searching for the important KGB documents there, being helped by the very friendly librarians and archivists there, and in Washington, DC, the United States, at the Kennan Institute of Woodrow Wilson International Center for Scholars, which awarded me with a couple of very important research grants, which allowed me to finish a systematization of my KGB archival files for my book project. I am also grateful to the Fulbright Program which awarded me with a grant to teach in Estonia and finish this book project there. Due to my health problems, I had to decline this Fulbright award in 2021. Still, my connections in East Europe and Estonia helped me to clear some important details of my book.

I also want to express my gratitude to those people who supported me and helped me during my research travels in 2018–2019 in Ukraine, Italy, Germany and Austria. I am much indebted to the staff of the State Archive of the Service of Security of Ukraine, especially Mariia Panova and Andrii Kohut, and four former KGB retired officers from Kyiv and Dnipro, for directing me to particularly useful material and for their tireless and good-natured assistance.

The suggestions and critical comments made by Olga Bertelsen, late Leonid Leshchenko, late Allen H. Kassof, Hiroaki Kuromyia, Taras Kuzio, Serhii Plokhy, Christopher Ward and Denise Youngblood, improved my manuscript. Many thanks go to the last reader of my manuscript,

Cory D. Balkenbusch, my graduate assistant at the Department of History of Ball State University

I am especially grateful to my editors from Routledge, whose editing made my prose more lucid, and who helped guide the book through the editorial process.

Part I

Creating the Models for the Special KGB Operations against the USA and Canada after WWII

"All KGB operations against the United States and Canada were influenced directly by Stalin's politics during and immediately after the Great Patriotic War," noted one retired KGB officer. "How to deal with the displaced people (many of whom were the residents of Soviet Ukraine) in Europe, how to trace and punish the Nazi collaborators and war criminals," he continued, "these were major problems for Stalin's administration, which became his legacy for the organs [KGB] work through the entire 1950s."[1]

After Stalin's death in 1953, the KGB of Soviet Ukraine still continued working with the criminal cases, related to this legacy of WWII: the problems of displaced people after the war, collaboration with Nazis of some residents of Ukraine. At the same time, the old problems took the new forms, such as Ukrainian and Jewish nationalism, and the dangerous American influences inside the Soviet geo-political space shaped the entire framework of Soviet intelligence practices during the beginning of the Cold War, as early as 1945. During this early Cold War, under Stalin, the United States, the former major Soviet political ally in the war against Nazi Germany, gradually had become a main political and ideological enemy of the Soviet Union by the end of 1947.[2]

In this new geo-political confrontation, the most important target (#1) of the KGB was Ukrainian nationalism, connected to and funded by the Americans. For the Ukrainian KGB (according to the archival materials), from 1953 until 1991, almost 50% of all criminal cases were devoted to this topic of "dangerous" Ukrainian nationalism. The second target of the Ukrainian KGB was another type of nationalism, Jewish one: Judaism and Zionism (more than 30% of all criminal cases). The third target of the Ukrainian KGB was religious sects (10%). American espionage and foreign visitors as agents of Western intelligence took fourth place as a threat for the KGB (almost 10%). As a general-major V. Nikitchenko, a head of the Ukrainian KGB, noted on March 12, 1954, "the major threat for Soviet Ukraine consists of Ukrainian bourgeois nationalists, Zionists, and religious sectarians, – all of them are funded and organized by intelligence services of the United States and England ... Many of these people belong to 16,000 suspected foreign spies, who still live in Soviet Ukraine."[3]

DOI: 10.4324/9781003212522-1

1 Legacy of the World War II: Ukrainian Nationalists in Diaspora and the Spy Schools in West Germany

The First Target of the KGB – The Ukrainian Nationalism

According to the KGB official reports, the so-called Ukrainian nationalist "*Banderovite* underground" (OUN-UPA, etc.), based in West Germany, with its connections to the American intelligence and to the Ukrainian diaspora in the United States and Canada, was a major concern of the Ukrainian KGB through the entire 1950s and the 1960s.[4] Almost every year the KGB reported to the Soviet Ukrainian political leadership about "a usage by American and British intelligence of the organizations of Ukrainian nationalists in the conspiratorial anti-Soviet activities against the Ukrainian SSR." In August 1952, the KGB analysts explained that

> The leaders of Ukrainian nationalist organizations in West Germany try to activate anti-Soviet activities, popularizing the actions of Banderovite underground in Ukraine. Relying on a possible rebellion in Ukraine against the Soviet Army in a case of the possible military conflict between the USSR and the USA, [the Ukrainian immigrant nationalist organization] intended to publish a special appeal to the population of Ukraine to begin the rebellious actions in the rear against the Soviet Army, if the war will start between the USSR and the USA. The Americans continue recruiting the Ukrainian nationalists for using them in the acts of subversion against the Soviet Union. The recruited nationalists were sent to the USA, and now around 300 of those emigrants returned to West Germany ready for the anti-Soviet actions, sponsored by the Americans.[5]

Moreover, the KGB officials discovered the CIA plans to use the Ukrainian emigrants, recruited by US intelligence for the spy operations in the industrial areas of Eastern Ukraine. The overwhelming majority of those spies of Ukrainian origin were trained in the special US "spy schools" in West Germany.[6]

As early as 1953–1954, the KGB leadership worried about a creation of a new Ukrainian nationalistic organization in the US, a replacement of the old

DOI: 10.4324/9781003212522-2

"nationalist leader" Stepan Bandera (1909–1959) with the new "more energetic and dangerous for Soviet Ukraine" leaders and "the Ukrainian nationalist center's moving from Europe, Munich, into the US and, especially,
about a total control by the US intelligence over this Ukrainian nationalistic
organization – "*Soyuz uchastnikov ukrainskoi vyzvol'noi borot'by*" [The
Union of the Participants of the Ukrainian Struggle for Liberation] (in
the KGB officer's wording). According to the KGB reports, in the
summer of 1953 Stepan Bandera, a legendary leader of the Ukrainian
diaspora in Europe, was replaced with the new Ukrainian emigrants from
Germany (Munich), where they were recruited by the US intelligence.[7]
For the KGB agents, who worked abroad (in Germany and the US), a
major goal was to "compromise and discredit" those pro-American
Ukrainian nationalists. They built the "special plans of discrediting of
them" with various strategies of developing of the "convincing *kompromat*
against each of those leaders."[8]

According to the first Ukrainian KGB report after Stalin, its operatives
tried to use various counter-intelligence actions to prevent recruiting the
Ukrainian nationalists in Europe by the American intelligence against not
only Soviet Ukraine, but also against the countries of the Soviet bloc, such
as Poland. At the end of 1953, the KGB sent their own agents to study the
Ukrainian nationalist connections with the US spies in Poland and West
Germany, trying to divide Ukrainian nationalist groups, used by Americans,
and eventually to "discredit those Ukrainian agents or even to re-recruit
them for the needs of Soviet Ukraine." The KGB agents planned to establish
their connections to and tried to control of Maksim Skorupskii, a former
OUN member, an agent of German intelligence, who was hired by the
American intelligence in Munich and pursued the active intelligence actions
(*razvedrabota*) in Soviet Ukraine. As it turned out, in 1946–1948, Skorupskii
had already brought a special group of the "trained US spies" into Poland,
helping them in their intelligence activities, establishing connections with
Ukrainians who lived there.[9] In 1950 he visited the United States, and in
June 1952 he returned to Munich, where he established connections with
another activist of PUN (*Provod ukrainskikh natsionalistov*) [The Leadership
of Ukrainian Nationalists] Stepan Suliatitskii, who was also involved in
instructing the American agents and sending them to other countries of
"people's democracy" (socialist countries). The KGB used their own agents
among the Ukrainians and Poles to infiltrate Skorupskii's and Suliatitskii's
spy groups. The major goal of the KGB counter-intelligence operations was
to create the special *"perepravochnye punkty"* (locations of transfer) on the
border of Poland and Ukraine for arrest, liquidation and *"pereverbovka"*
(re-recruiting) of the American agents, for capture of their material and
technical tools and to "play a 'game'" against US intelligence, "by giving them
falsified information." Soviet agents were infiltrated into a spy net, created by
Skorupskii and Suliatitskii, for spreading misinformation, monitoring and
controlling their actions in Ukraine.[10]

The KGB always monitored a situation in the Ukrainian emigrants' centers abroad. The KGB agents tried to use their active measures to prevent any serious effort to unite the Ukrainian emigrant groups against Soviet Ukraine.[11] They always supported those Ukrainian leaders who demonstrated in public their loyalty to the Ukrainian SSR. For example, in 1959, the KGB agents organized "the positive reaction in the foreign press" to the election of Anton Melnyk (nephew of Andrii Melnyk) as a new PUN secretary, explaining that "despite his position for Ukrainian independence from the Soviet Union, Melnyk was always loyal to and supportive of Soviet Ukraine."[12]

Since 1946 the KGB had been collecting the data about the Ukrainian immigration abroad. Every month the KGB officers in Kyiv analyzed this information and reported it to the political leadership of Soviet Ukraine. According to this information, by 1957, there were 18,000 ethnic Ukrainians in West Germany, 2,500 of whom lived in the city of Munich and its neighborhood, the less numerous groups of Ukrainian immigrants lived in other West German cities such as New Ulm, Augsburg, Regensburg, Stuttgart, and Hannover. As the KGB agent reported, "the overwhelming majority of Ukrainians lived miserably, having a support that could only compensate their unemployment. Only those, who had a job, could manage to survive. Only those Ukrainians, who worked for the Ukrainian Anti-Soviet nationalistic organizations had the best way of living there."[13]

According to the KGB estimates, another foreign Ukrainian "nationalist center for the anti-Soviet activities" was located in British Columbia, Canada, especially in the city of Vancouver, "where 10,000–12,000 Ukrainians resided." KGB analysts had calculated, that one-third of them were representatives of the so-called new post-war emigration from European countries.[14] The KGB officials complained that they had no the detailed information about the Ukrainian organizations in Vancouver and their leaders. But they noted that the main centers of the Ukrainian nationalistic organizations, besides Vancouver, were located in the major cities of Canada, such as Toronto, Winnipeg and Edmonton. They reported that these nationalistic centers triggered their activities among the Ukrainian emigration living in Canada "using their connections to the foreign intelligence in their hostile actions against the USSR." As a result, a leadership of the KGB in Soviet Ukraine ordered "(1) to implement the active measures about organizing of the special study of the persons [of Soviet citizens], who are in correspondence with Ukrainians, residing in Canada and (2) to pay a special attention to revealing of those who used their addresses for such a correspondence and (3) to activate our pre-war agents' infrastructure in Canada and (4) to work actively with those persons who prepared their documents to travel to Canada and returning to the USSR."[15]

At the same time, the KGB officers emphasized that their major goal was to monitor the creation and development of the organization of the "Ukrainian nationalists in the USA," SUUVB *"Soyuz uchastnikov ukrainskoi vyzvol'noi borot'by*," which was publicly announced at "*Ukrainskii narodnyi dim*" [The Ukrainian People's House] in New York City on November 6, 1954.[16] As KGB report noted, "the main goal of this organization [was] an active involvement into the nationalistic activities of those American Ukrainians who used to distance themselves from the nationalistic work, transforming nationalistic activities in the USA into anti-Soviet acts of liberation of Soviet Ukraine [from Russian oppression], maintaining their connections with the nationalistic underground in Soviet Ukraine and activation of its anti-Soviet work, composing the goals of the political platform of the so-called liberation movement [in Soviet Ukraine]."[17] The KGB leadership noted that American intelligence not only tried to weaken the position of Bandera and his followers in the Ukrainian emigration, moving its center of anti-Soviet action from Europe to the USA after 1954, but also to conceal the facts of the collaboration with the Nazi of the new leaders of this emigration. The KGB administration's major recommendation for the new KGB active measures was "the necessity of revealing and working out of the relatives' and other connections of the above-mentioned members of the SUUVB preparing committee [in Ukraine], to use these connections for influencing [the Ukrainian emigrants] abroad."[18]

These recommendations worked: all family connections of the Ukrainian diaspora and its American organizations in Soviet Ukraine were under the KGB surveillance and were "compromised" after 1954. By 1958, almost all the major groups of Ukrainian nationalists, employed as American spies, were "destroyed" by the special KGB measures in Ukraine and abroad. Soviet counter-agents were recruited among local Soviet Ukrainians, who tried to "compromise and discredit" Ukrainian ("Banderite") leaders and instructors of those American spy groups, who worked against Soviet Ukraine. Those KGB agents were sent to Poland and Germany and succeeded in undermining of the Ukrainian anti-Soviet groups from inside. After 1954, until the perestroika of the 1980s, the KGB had used the same strategy against the Ukrainian national centers in the USA and Canada: "compromise, divide, and weaken from inside."[19] In 1975–1976, the KGB organized 4 operations against those centers, and "implanted" 28 agents in various centers of the Ukrainian diaspora abroad, including 4 in the USA and 7 in Canada.[20] Among the numerous operations, organized by the KGB agents in America, the most successful was the KGB operation *Kaskad* (*Cascade*) in 1978–1979 against the OUN leadership abroad. The KGB agent *Marta* became close to OUN leaders, such as Ya. Stetsko and his wife S. Stetsko-Muzyka, and she obtained a lot of "the compromising materials," which the KGB used against "the Ukrainian nationalists" abroad until the end of the 1980s.[21]

KGB Operations against US "Spy Schools"

Another object of the KGB operations in Soviet Ukraine was the American intelligence (spy) centers in Western Germany. According to KGB documents, after WWII those centers were used by Americans for instructing and preparing the Russian, and especially, the Ukrainian, emigrants for their spying activities inside the Soviet Union after 1946. The CIA began funding and organizing various "spy anti-Soviet centers" in West Germany after WWII, recruiting former OUN-UPA activists, ROA soldiers and numerous former Soviet citizens, who were captured by Germans or fled with Nazis to Germany from Ukraine.[22] By 1954, the overwhelming majority of these recruits were Ukrainians. Since 1949, in the city of Regensburg (in the American zone of occupation of Germany), the KGB surveillance had noticed a special American intelligence center "entitled as ASTRA," which was organized "for recruiting, instructing former Soviet citizens and training them as the spies, for sending them inside the Soviet Union and the countries of people's democracy." According to the KGB analysts, ASTRA was created by the leaders of an emigrant anti-Soviet organization ALON («*Антибольшевистская лига освобождения народов*» [Anti-Bolshevik Bloc of Nations]), who were involved in a preparation of its agents in the so-called sabotage school, which had already existed at the "Ukrainian technical institute" in a city of Regensburg, Bavaria. In this "sabotage school" the agents took three-week courses, where they studied explosives, espionage actions, ciphering/deciphering and other subjects; "after finishing their preparation they were sent, by using the illegal channels on the territories [of the socialist countries] for performing sabotage and spying (*для ведения диверсионной и шпионской работы*)." Meanwhile, the KGB agents reported the detailed information about the leaders of this spy center, "the Ukrainian nationalists" such as "Roman Smuk from Galicia, who lived in Germany and the US; an agent of English intelligence Makogon Yakov (known also as Poltava-Razumovskii Nikolai, resident of a town of Stanislav); and Kul'chitskii Aleksandr, Ukrainian, a professor, a former instructor of psychology at Munich University of UNRRA (United Nations Relief and Rehabilitation Administration), who lived in Munich, had numerous connections with Ukrainians, especially those who resided in the region of river San and Lemkovshchina (Poland)."[23] Eventually, all these people became targets of the KGB active measures. The KGB officials were especially concerned about one member of this group, a priest, who was a main vicar of "the spy center," Petro Golynskii.[24] According to the KGB agents, Golynskii provided an important link between the spy center ASTRA and Greek-Catholic priests and their followers in Western Ukraine. The KGB organized a series of the special operations against the Ukrainian Greek-Catholics in Soviet Ukraine, blaming them not only with the connections to "the Banderite underground", but also with links to the CIA, through an American spy, a priest Golynskii from the spy center ASTRA in West Germany, who had the connections with his co-religionists all over Ukraine[25] (Figures 1.1 and 1.2).

For many years, the major object of the KGB studies of US intelligence centers in Europe was the US "spy school" in the city of Regensburg in West Germany. According to the KGB analysts, in this school, the prevailing

Figure 1.1 American agents from Ukraine.

majority of students consisted of the American military officers with a rank of captain and higher.

> The main themes for teaching of this school's students "were related to the studies of economic problems of the USSR and to the strategic and political issues of Soviet realities. Despite the fact that the American military officers, this school's students, are relatively fluent in Russian, the major emphasis in teaching there, still, is on the studies of Russian language. All teaching and pedagogical material used in school were in Russian language only. Teachers and students of this school do not speak English inside the school."[26]

There was a large library of materials in Russian, including the books representing the recent Soviet literature, and numerous newspapers and magazines, published recently in the Soviet Union. The school's teaching curriculum was divided into two levels of study – low and high levels (courses). The students of the low level studied for one year, and the students of the high level studied for two years. The complete cycle of study in this school lasted three years. According to the intelligence information, 80 intelligence officers had already graduated from this American spy school in Regensburg in 1954. After their graduation American officers usually visited the USSR, using "various diplomatic and other covers." [27]

Figure 1.2 American agents of Ukrainian dissent.

According to the KGB reports, the school administration consisted of mainly American officers: 6–7 people. One of them, a school's director, was a colonel in the US Army. This school in Regensburg, and, in particular, its "deputy director and 'rector' Mikhail Vasiliev, had the close contacts with American territorial counter-intelligence service, located in Western Germany and Austria. The deserters and refugees from the USSR [were] directed to Regensburg school, where they prepared and delivered the reports on the present situation in the Soviet Union, and especially about its economy, industry, conditions of kolkhozes etc., in the regions which [were] familiar to them." During this period of reports' presentation, Soviet refugees were given an invented name, ID and they were under complete surveillance of American counterintelligence. The length of time that they stayed in the school depended on their knowledge, expertise and ability to be helpful to the students of the school. At the same time, "American counter-intelligence was checking those refugees very closely."[28]

Another US "spy school" from the same German land of Bavaria, which was connected to one in Regensburg, became a new object of the KGB studies. It was an American spy school in the city of Oberammergau, Bavaria. According to the KGB, the head of the school was a colonel Muris Tsikharis, a former head of the 2nd department of the 13th corps of the US Army. His deputy was a colonel Arthur Roth. In the school there were 40 teachers, representing Americans, Germans and the people of Slavic origins, who collaborated with Germans during WWII.[29] This spy school had the following departments: training specialists-intelligence agents, experts on Russia, Czechoslovakia, Germany; training specialists-counter-intelligence agents on Germany; of military intelligence for the officers and the sergeants; for deciphering of photo shoots; for instruction of the officers of reserve; for instruction of the officers of commanding staff and staff officers; of the repeated teaching of Russian and Czech languages; military assistance; criminal investigations; repeated training for the officers of military police; military clerical workers; and "the special armament." Various departments had differing numbers of students and different times for graduation: intelligence-experts in Russia had 30 students, on Czechoslovakia – 15; each department required 6 months to finish. All students that entered the school were checked for their reliability by marking their files with "permitted for a secret work" and all of them were checked regarding their linguistic abilities.[30] Students at the department of "intelligence officers-experts on Russia" studied the Russian language, history, economics, geography, political system, armed forces and state institutions of the Soviet Union. Instructions in the Russian language included spoken Russian, reading and writing. According to the KGB agents, "the goal of this education was to teach the students to interrogate, orally and in writing to translate military and technical materials, to categorize and analyze the documents from a point of view of their value for intelligence, to train in the techniques of intelligence work." But overall, the major purpose was "to prepare American officers to rule the various regions of the USSR in case of American occupation."[31] One of the most prominent Russian teachers of that school was Aleksandr Avtorkhanov, who became "the intellectual and analytical center" of the entire teaching personnel there.[32]

Another spy school was organized exclusively for the "displaced persons of Ukrainian dissent" in the city of Mittenwald, Bavaria, under supervision of an American 7712 spy school of the European command in the city of Oberammergau.[33] According to the KGB data, this school was founded in 1948 by "the famous Ukrainian nationalist Kapustianskii Nikolai Aleksandrovich," who took the office of "the military minister of the so-called Ukrainian National Rada" abroad. As the KGB noted, a composition of this school's students was selected from mainly those "young displaced persons known as Plastuns," who graduated from the special courses, offered by the

Ukrainian youth organization of "Plast," which existed abroad, and, "moreover, from the immigrants from predominantly the western regions of Ukraine," who were drafted into this school from the American and British "displaced persons camps" in Western Europe. After graduating from this school, these graduates were sent to other special schools, which were located at the city of Weilheim, 55 kilometers to the south-west of Munich, and which had already existed under a cover of the seminary of the Ukrainian Autocephalous Orthodox Church, and also in the city of Stuttgart, under a cover of the school of the Ukrainian police in a displaced persons camp. According to the information, the US intelligence service financed all the anti-Soviet activities of the Ukrainian National Guard (UNG) and used those "guards" for spying in the countries of people's democracy and sending them as the agents into the Soviet Union. Those who were selected for spying cadres of the "guards" were trained in all branches of US spy schools under control of the commanding officers of UNG. Eventually, by 1956, all those schools (including the Ukrainian one) were merged in one US spy school No. 7712 in Bavaria, West Germany.[34]

The KGB administration tried to figure out how to use, compromise and re-recruit some of the teachers of this school, who still had relatives in Soviet Ukraine. One of those targets for the KGB special operations in the US spy school was Nikolai (Mykola) Mikhailovich Vasiliev. Vasiliev was a professor, "a rector and a deputy school director. He also composed the teaching plans for school and the instructions and teaching methods for teachers. He taught Russian grammar and the economics of Ukraine."[35] According to the KGB information Vasiliev was born in 1901 in the Kyiv region, had a Soviet college degree, was not a member of the Communist party and resided earlier on Tarasovskaia Street No. 9 in Kyiv. In 1933–1941, he worked in Kyiv as a scientific secretary at the All-Union Research Institute of Fruit and Vegetable Farming, which was included in a system of the former Narkomat (Ministry) of the USSR Food Industry. The KGB agents and former colleagues characterized Vasiliev as "all-around competent, politically developed, cultured scientific fellow, who knew a few foreign languages. While working at the institute, Vasiliev frequently delivered the reports during the ceremonial meetings, participated actively in social life of institute." (Figures 1.3 and 1.4).

Staying in Kiev, occupied by the German troops during WWII in the fall of 1941, Vasiliev joined the institute of economic studies, created by the occupants, submitting to the German administration the economic information about the different industrial regions of the USSR. During the same period of time, Vasiliev collaborated with a newspaper "New Ukrainian Word" (*Novoe Ukrainskoe slovo*), which was established by the Germans, "where he published the anti-Soviet articles on the economic themes, signing them in Ukrainian – Vasiliev M. (i.e., Mykola – Nikolai)." In the summer of 1943, Vasiliev, together with his colleagues from the above-mentioned institute, went to the city of Konigsberg, and then to

Figure 1.3 Mikhail Vasiliev in the Soviet times.

Kraftborn (near Breslavl), where he systematized the economic library, which was brought by Germans from the occupied areas of the USSR. When the Soviet army approached, the families of all German institute's officials from Kyiv, including Vasiliev's family (his Russian wife and mother-in-law), "fled into a depth of Germany."[36] The KGB agents noted that Vasiliev started his collaboration with Germans under the influence of his wife, and he always regretted this.[37] That is why the KGB administration decided to re-recruit him, using this information. Moreover, they decided to use his sisters, who still lived in Kyiv, Irina (born in 1895), and Ekaterina (born in 1898), as a "special emotional pressure" on him, to "persuade him to collaborate" with the KGB.[38] As early as December 1955, the KGB sent the special agents to approach Vasiliev and recruit him as a KGB agent in Germany.[39] Using the personal connections of Vasiliev in Kyiv, in February 1956 the KGB recruited the special agent with a nickname of *Nikolaev*. This agent was born in 1930 in Kyiv; he had a college education and was fluent in English and German. *Nikolaev* and his father lived in Western Germany in 1943–1945 together with the Vasiliev family in the same building and had very close good relations. The KGB used this agent as a link to Vasiliev's sisters, and simultaneously, the KGB established a special surveillance over them in Kyiv. Eventually, using his sisters' influence on Vasiliev and blackmailing him, the KGB successfully re-recruited Vasiliev as a new KGB agent.[40]

At the same time, the KGB operatives realized that another teacher at the same American spy school, who looked like "the best candidate to become a KGB double agent," was related to Vasiliev as well. This teacher was

Figure 1.4 Mikhail Vasiliev an instructor in US spy school.

Vsevolod Mikhailovich Grechko. In the spy school he taught classes on the foreign and domestic policy of the USSR, the structure of the Soviet Army and about the Soviet intelligence. The KGB agent provided a portrayal of this candidate:

> Grechko, who was "an officer of the US secret service," and lived in Munich, looked very old like "60 years old man. He is bold, face is plump, his teeth are very yellow, he is unmarried; he loves wine and women, drug addicted; he knows Russian, French and German languages."[41]

According to KGB agents, Grechko was born in 1908 in Kyiv; he received a college degree in the USSR, was a former Soviet associate professor (*dotsent*) of history, teaching Soviet and world history in various colleges and secondary schools in Kyiv before 1941. During the German occupation of Soviet Ukraine, Grechko lived in Kyiv with his wife Eri, who was Jewish. In the fall of 1941 Grechko's wife and her parents were arrested as Jews, and her parents were eventually executed by Germans. Using his personal connections, "especially his pre-war friend Kandiev," who worked as a head of the department of information and propaganda in the Kyiv city council (*goruprava*), created by Nazi, he managed to release his wife from the German prison. Afterward, trying to protect his wife, and following Kandiev's advice, Grechko began to work in *goruprava* "as a deputy of Kandiev, collaborating with Nazi, and engaging in the special anti-Soviet actions." According to the KGB investigations, despite all public demonstrations of his pro-Nazi feelings, eventually, in 1942, Grechko was arrested by the Germans and sent to Gestapo. After long interrogations by Germans and being afraid for the future of his Jewish wife, Grechko agreed to serve as a new Gestapo agent, and, as a result, he was released from Kyiv prison by his new Gestapo supervisors. Until 1943, Grechko had worked as a Gestapo agent in the Kyiv city council, and also collaborated in the editorial board of the newspaper "New Ukrainian Word." [42]

Facing an approaching Soviet Army, Grechko fled with his wife to Berlin, where he worked at the propagandist center "Vineta" (an organ of the Eastern department of the German Ministry of Propaganda).[43] Simultaneously, he worked as a teacher at the school of propagandists of ROA in Dabendorf, and from December 1943 he worked as an officer of German counter-intelligence organ "Zondenschtab-R." From July 1944 he worked in Berlin Gestapo. In December of 1944 he was included as a member of the anti-Soviet organization KONR (Committee for Liberation of the Peoples of Russia [*Комитет освобождения народов России*]) as a representative of the so-called Ukrainian People's Rada. After Germany's capitulation, he walked in the US zone of occupation, and got in a camp of Landau, where he became a member of the so-called Russian committee, sponsored by the US intelligence. During his staying in this camp, Grechko also became a member of NTS (*Народно-трудовой союз*) [the National Alliance of Russian Solidarists] and KOV (Committee of the United Vlasovtsy).[44]

The KGB investigators realized that in the fall of 1943, together with Grechko, his sister, Natalia Nikolaevna Bunge, went to Germany to bring her son Nikolai. Since August 1942, she worked for the Germans as a district inspector of propaganda, and then at the German general-commissariat of Kyiv, openly collaborating with the Nazi occupational regime in Soviet Ukraine. So the KGB agents discovered that a former husband of Grechko's sister still lived in Kyiv, and the KGB decided to use this man in their attempt to recruit Grechko as a new KGB agent in the special secret operation against the US "spy" school in West Germany.[45] The name of this former husband was Vasilii Konstantinovich Pekorin. Pekorin was born in 1901 in the city of Penza in Russia, he had a college degree in civil engineering, and worked as a deputy of the head of the department of survey of

Ukrgiprokommunenergo, an organization responsible for distribution of electricity in Soviet Ukraine. According to the KGB special investigation, before WWII, in 1938, Pekorin married Natalia Bunge, whose mother was arrested by NKVD the same year. Vsevolod Grechko had a common mother with Bunge, but different fathers. From 1941 to 1946, Pekorin served in the Soviet army, at the Headquarters of the 2nd Ukrainian Front, working in its topographical department. In a conversation with the KGB representatives, Pekorin characterized Grechko and Bunge positively, but noted how Grechko strived for material prosperity and "loved money very much." When the KGB explained that his former wife Bunge and his son were alive, residing in Germany, Pekorin immediately declared that he would do everything to bring his son back to the USSR, but he would not restore his marital relations with Bunge, because he was married to another woman in Kyiv. Pekorin agreed to perform the KGB assignment "if it would be necessary for the USSR and would help him to bring his son back."[46]

The KGB officials decided to recruit Pekorin as a KGB agent for the contacts with Grechko, using the new connections of his administration of *Ukrgiprokommunenergo* in Kyiv with foreign countries, including East Germany. As a KGB officer reported, "according to his personal qualities, Pekorin produced an impression of being a clever, all-around erudite man, he was quick to catch the thought of his interlocutor and he gave the convincing and very clever answers to the questions, he is energetic, he knows and understands the elements of secrecy." After conversation with a KGB representative, Pekorin "agreed willingly" to meet again the KGB people when he signed an agreement about *nerazglashenie* (non-disclosure of the state secrets). A KGB representative described Pekorin as an agent "suitable for recruitment, according to his personal and business qualities, abilities, and the state of his health, and according to the real pretext of the establishing connections with Grechko," Pekorin was, "overall, very good for counter-intelligence measures [in Germany]."[47]

The KGB officer, who worked with Pekorin, reported to his supervisors that on April 25, 1956, Pekorin was officially recruited as an agent of KGB with pseudonym *Dobrovol'skii,* "using as a real pretext his personal interest and desire to establish the personal contacts with his former wife Bunge and his son." The officer explained that *Dobrovol'skii* "willingly became the KGB agent," who "fitted the requirements for all the operative measures," and recently the KGB "worked to educate him, train him and cultivate the necessary skills, which were important for a KGB agent." In May–June 1956, the KGB administration began planning to use GDR (Eastern Germany) to send *Dobrovol'skii* there for establishing his contacts with Grechko in Western Germany. On June 20, 1956, the KGB officers organized the new operation of sending the letters from *Dobrovol'skii* to Grechko, inviting Grechko to visit GDR and meet *Dobrovol'skii* in person there. *Dobrovol'skii* had to explain Grechko that he was on business trip in East Germany and "he was eager to know about the life of his wife and son" in West Germany. Eventually, the KGB used their own East German agent *Mejer* (a German citizen Herbert Shultz), who not only arranged the meeting of Grechko with his relative in East Berlin, but also assisted *Dobrovol'skii* in recruiting Grechko as "a double agent." By the end of 1956, Grechko began working for the KGB.[48]

The last (#3) candidate for recruitment by the KGB was a teacher from the same US spy school with the last name of Krylov. The KGB investigation revealed that Krylov, who lived in Munich, was a former officer of the Vlasov army (ROA) during WWII. In the spy school he taught subjects on the Soviet agriculture and collectivization, and wrote many textbooks, which were widely used for the studies in the school. He was also one of the leaders of the anti-Soviet organization SBONR (the Union for the Struggle for the Liberation of the Peoples of Russia [*Союз Борьбы за Освобождение Народов России*]). According to KGB investigation, this teacher's full name was Konstantin Arkadievich Krylov. He was born in 1914 in Leningrad, was a former resident of Kyiv, with a college degree. After his graduation from Kyiv engineer-construction institute (KISI), Krylov worked in the system of Narkomat of Education of the Ukrainian SSR (Figure 1.5).

During WWII, Krylov had served in the Soviet army until 1942 when he was captured as POW by Germans and was imprisoned in the German POW camp in the city of Vladimir-Volynskii in Ukraine. There he entered ROA in the rank of *podporuchik* (a junior rank of military officer in the Russian tsarist army, used by the Vlasov army as well) and entered the anti-Soviet organization NTS. In 1943 Krylov worked as a teacher at Dabendorf School of Propagandists in Nazi Germany. In December of 1943, he was sent to France, where he worked as an editor of the anti-Soviet newspaper, which was published by the department of propaganda of the 7th German army. At the end of 1944, Krylov worked at the youth department of KONR and then moved to Innsbruck (Austria). In January 1945 Krylov returned to Dabendorf and worked in the department of propaganda of KONR. In 1947 he lived in Munich and worked as a head of human resources in the Russian-German construction firm "Algau." In 1950 he moved to Regensburg, where he worked as a teacher at the spy school. In Western Germany, Krylov resided together with his wife Krylova-Naumova Valentina Nikolaevna, her mother and Krylov's brother. All of them fled to the West after Germans retreated at the end of WWII. According to the KGB information, Krylova-Naumova was also an active participant of SBONR and an editor of the anti-Soviet journal of this organization *A Woman of Russia*.[49]

According to the KGB investigation, Krylov's anti-Soviet feelings were the result of his personal tragedy. Krylov's father was arrested in 1937 as "an enemy of the people" by OGPU, and on October 6, 1941 he was executed. KGB agents also discovered that after living in West Germany for many years, Krylov was disappointed in "the Western style of life" and tried

Figure 1.5 Krylov's photo (another instructor in US spy school).

to find the advantages in the classical model of Marxist socialism before Stalin. The KGB analysts realized that their agents could use these Krylov's frustrations by convincing him that the recent post-Stalin developments and public criticism of Stalin's atrocities in the USSR, including a rehabilitation of the innocent victims of Stalinist repressions, like Krylov's father, was an attempt to restore the very classical Marxism Krylov liked. Such approach could be helpful for recruitment of Krylov as a new KGB agent.[50]

A person, who could convince Krylov and explain to him the essence of post-Stalin developments, was a very close old Krylov's friend from his institute's years (1933–1939) in Kyiv. Fortunately for the KGB, it turned out that this man, whom Krylov trusted and relied on since his college days, had been already recruited as a KGB agent under a nickname *Smirnov*. A real name of this agent was Vlaikov Georgii Georgievich. He was born in 1914 in Kyiv; he joined the Communist party while in a college in Kyiv, where he befriended Krylov. After WWII he defended his Ph.D. dissertation in civil engineering in KISI and became the Soviet "candidate of technical sciences and afterwards worked as a chair of the construction department there." *Smirnov* was recruited by the KGB in 1932, but due to his serious engagement in the scientific research and college teaching, his collaboration with the KGB had been postponed until 1948. During WWII, he was drafted into the Soviet army, demobilized with a rank of a major as a military officer in reserve in 1945. In July 1948, the KGB restored the relations with him because his close relatives, sister and niece collaborated with the Nazis, during the German occupation of Kyiv, and were recruited as the active members of NTS. The KGB officers used this situation and Vlaikov's close relations with Krylov, to resume *Smirnov*'s status of "an active KGB agent." As the KGB supervisor of *Smirnov* explained in his official report,

> Due to the close relations between *Smirnov* and Krylov and the *Smirnov*'s family connections, who were well known to the leaders of NTS, we decided to use an agent *Smirnov* for a counter-intelligence work with Krylov ... According to his personal qualities, *Smirnov* [is] well developed intellectually, energetic, willful man, with the great organizational abilities ... *Smirnov* has a family: a wife and two children of the preschool age, whom he loves very much; and this factor will work for us very well, while he would be on his [KGB] assignment, traveling abroad![51]

Eventually, *Smirnov* re-established his relations with Krylov, traveled to Germany and participated in recruiting Krylov as a new "double KGB agent," persuading him during their conversations that Khrushchev brought back Lenin's model of Marxism to the Soviet Union after 1953.[52]

As we see, the KGB managed not only to infiltrate their agents through the students of this spy school, but also to influence and control at least three teachers of this school – Vasiliev, Grechko and Krylov. They used the relatives of those teachers in Soviet Ukraine as a very important leverage on them. The KGB also noted that all three teachers, who were recruited as the double KGB agents, had "tremendous idealization of the United States as a model for the new developments of humankind" after WWII, which the Soviet Union missed during Stalin's rule. Therefore, the KGB recruiting agents used the new discursive strategy in convincing Vasiliev, Grechko and Krylov to collaborate with the KGB. These recruiting agents tried to explain to all those teachers the new post-Stalin reality in the USSR as "modernization and (even) Americanization" of the Soviet way of life under Khrushchev. Overall, this argument of the "American influences" in "de-Stalinization" of Soviet life played a very important role in persuading Vasiliev, Grechko and Krylov to change their attitude toward the USSR.[53]

The last "unreliable" and "tentative" candidate for recruitment/or "neutralizing" by the KGB was Popluiko Anatolii Ivanovich, another teacher of Russian language in the US spy school in the city of Oberammergau, Bavaria. According to the KGB investigation, he arrived in Munich with his wife, Popluiko Nadezhda Anatolievna, in the beginning of 1955. Initially, they were invited to work in the Liberty Radio Station; he – as a political adviser, she – as a literary corrector. According to the KGB information, they were the "American intelligence agents": they both served as the officials at the Institute for the studies of the USSR history and culture at their school, he – as an economist, she – as a literary critic.[54]

As the KGB investigation discovered, Anatolii Popluiko was born in 1902 in the city of Ekaterinolav/Dnipropetrovsk, in the family of the local Ukrainian intellectuals. After graduating from the local university, he worked as a teacher at Dnipropetrovsk metallurgical institute. During WWII and Nazi occupation of Dnipropetrovsk, Popluiko was an active collaborator with Germans (he worked an assistant to the director of polytechnic institute created by Germans), afterward he fled with Germans and stayed in Germany, where he worked as a teacher at the German Ministry of Propaganda (in the Berlin school of ROA). According to the KGB agents, he and his wife were recruited by the US intelligence service, to use them against the USSR. The KGB tried to use Popluiko's family in Dnipropetrovsk, and his numerous relatives there. They even recruited his sister A.I. Zhulina and his niece as the new KGB agents to use them for creating "a special emotional pressure on him." But they were too late: Popluiko and his wife immigrated to the US and became the American citizens, pursuing their new careers there, which had nothing to do with the intelligence anymore.[55]

Despite the KGB failure with Popluiko, the KGB supervisors still succeeded in their major "active measures" against the US spy schools in West Germany. Eventually, they obtained not only the important information about the special "spying" assignments for the graduates of the US spy schools in West Germany, but could prevent and "neutralize" in Soviet Ukraine any CIA "spy operations," which initiated from those schools during the 1950s. The KGB also used the former Soviet citizens, who married American officials from US spy schools in Germany, trying to recruit them and utilize them against the US intelligence.[56] Overall, the KGB counter-intelligence active measures in both West Germany and Ukraine produced a positive result for the KGB. All CIA spies, sent to Ukraine, were arrested and some of them re-recruited as the double agents. Almost every year, the KGB reported about such operations, starting with June–July 1953 reports about how "the American intelligence sent three spies *"radisty"* (radio operators/radiomen): *Sergei, Vladimir,* and *Nikolai* to Ukraine, to Kyiv, who studied in the intelligence school in German city Rottach-Egern." As it turned out, that school was affiliated with the "main" US "spy" school # 7712 as well.[57]

The most important element of the KGB counter-intelligence active measures was using the Ukrainian and Russian displaced people, who had already been recruited by the British and US intelligence service, as the double KGB agents. Besides the Russian and Ukrainian officials from the

US spy schools in West Germany, hundreds of the ordinary Russians and Ukrainians, who officially belonged to the social category of the "displaced persons" (DP) and who were captives in numerous DP camps under US/British supervision, became an object of the KGB special operations as well.

Notes

1 Interview with Ivan Grigorovich K., a retired KGB officer, February 3, 2019, Kyiv, Ukraine.
2 See about this transformation of an image of the United States during Stalin and Khrushchev rule in: Rósa Magnúsdóttir, *Enemy Number One: The United States of America in Soviet Ideology and Propaganda, 1945–1959.* (New York: Oxford University Press. 2019), esp. 73, 151.
3 Galuzevyi Derzhavnyi Arkhiv Sluzhby Bezpeky Ukrainy (hereafter – SBU), f. 16, op. 1, spr. 902, ark. 142, 35.
4 OUN-UPA is an abbreviation for *Organizatsia ukrains'kykh natsionalistiv-Ukrains'ka povstans'ka armia* – the Organization of the Ukrainian Nationalists-Ukrainian Insurgent Army, associated by the KGB with the Ukrainian nationalist movement, and ROA is an abbreviation for *Russkai osvoboditel'naia armia* – the Russian Liberation Army, associated by the KGB with the Russian nationalist movement. Historically, OUN was divided in OUNb (*banderivtsi*) and OUNm (*mel'nikivtsi*), after WWII OUNb became leader of the anti-Soviet resistance in the Ukrainian Diaspora; it called itself ZChOUN (*Zakordonni chastyny OUN*).
5 SBU, f. 1, op. 1, spr. 842, ark. 202.
6 Ibid., 36–37, 367–370.
7 See about the KGB operations against Stepan Bandera in Serhii Plokhy, *The Man with the Poison Gun: A Cold War Spy Story* (New York: Basic Books, 2016), 101–103,117, 200–202.
8 These "Ukrainian nationalists on the American payroll" were Kononenko Konstantin S., Matla Zinovii A., Prokop Miroslav V., Matsik Yurii, Maslovich Kiril. The members of the organizing committee also included Dombrovskii Yurii, Barkovskii Roman, Moroz Iosif, Salii Zinovii. See in SBU, f. 16, op. 1, spr. 912, ark. 20–25. See in details about the divisions among the Ukrainian diaspora in the West, especially in the North America, after WWII in Taras Kuzio, "U.S. Support for Ukraine's Liberation during the Cold War: A Study of Prolog Research and Publishing Corporation," *Communist and Post-Communist Studies*, Vol. 45 (2012), 51–64.
9 SBU, f. 16, op. 1, spr. 882, ark. 124-130, esp. 125.
10 SBU, f. 16, op. 1, spr. 882, ark. 127, 129.
11 SBU, f. 1, op. 1, spr. 843, ark. 1.
12 Ibid., ark. 2–4. Historically, the KGB always prefer the moderate part of Andrii Melnyk's OUN to more radical Stepan Bandera's part of OUN.
13 Ibid., ark. 25. This report provided the names for 30 Ukrainian organizations in West Germany, such as "Zakordonnye chasti Organizatsii ukrainskikh natsionalistov-revoliutsionerov (banderovtsy)", "Zakordonnoe predstavitel'stvo Ukrainskogo Glavnogo Osvoboditel'nogo soveta," "Organizatsiia ukrainskikh natsionalistov za kordonom" (so-called "dvoikari"), "Organizatsiia ukrainskikh natsionalistov – solidaristov" (mel'nikovtsy), "Ukrainskaia natsional'naia rada," "Ukrainskaia revoliutsionno-demokraticheskaia partiia," etc.
14 Ibid., ark. 60. According to the KGB data in 1958, in Vancouver, there were the branches of such "active Ukrainian nationalistic" organizations: Branch (otdel) of LVU (Liga vyzvolennia Ukrainy), organized in 1954, its chair – V. Dmitrenko,

members of leading board – O. Orisiuk, M. Chuiko, V. Kashinskii, M. Sidorovich; Branch of SUM (Souz Ukrainskoi molodezhi); Branch of MUN (Molodye ukrainskie natsionalisty). In March of 1957, in Vancouver there was organized a branch of TUS (Tovarishchestvo ukraintsev samostiinikov). "Leaders (glavari) of the branch were I. Polonich, I. Rybak, E. Pelekh and Reshetnik." "Besides this, a nationalistic work is pursued on the basis of "The Ukrainian People's (narodnyi) House," at the Ukrainian Orthodox Church, located at 154 East 10 Ave., where is located a local branch of KUK – "Komitet ukraintsev Kanady." Ibid., ark. 61.

15 Ibid., ark. 61.
16 Ibid., ark. 147–151, 152–154 [I use the original KGB spelling of the name of this organization].
17 Ibid., ark.148. See the detailed biographies of the new leaders of the preparing committee of this new organization: Kononenko Konstantin Semenovich, Matla, Prokop, Matsik, Maslovich, etc. in SBU, f. 1, op.1, spr. 883, ark. 149–150.
18 Ibid., ark.151, 152–154.
19 SBU, f. 1, op. 1, spr. 1220, ark. 56-95.
20 SBU, f. 16, op. 1, spr. 1118, ark. 26–37, citation is from ark. 33.
21 SBU, f. 16, op. 1, spr. 1151, ark. 307-312. This KGB agent *Marta* pretended to represent a special "Ukrainian nationalistic center" in Soviet Ukraine. The KGB planned to use *Marta* and infiltrate OUN groups in Canada and the US during 1979 and 1980. See SBU, f. 16, op. 1, spr. 1171, ark. 39–44.
22 See about Anglo-American efforts to use the refugees from the Soviet space after WWII for intelligence work in Francesco Alexander Cacciatore, "Their Need Was Great": Émigrés and Anglo-American Intelligence Operations in the Early Cold War. Ph. D. dissertation, University of Westminster, March 2018, pp. 142–183.
23 SBU, f. 1, op. 1, spr. 1092, ark. 1–5.
24 SBU, f. 1, op. 1, spr. 1092, ark. 56–95. According to the KGB report, Golynski was "born in 1892, in a village Goshany, Rudkovskii district, region of Drogobych; he had a college education, graduated from the theological seminaries in the city of Peremyshl (Poland) and Innsbruk (Austria), before 1939 he was an instructor of theology at Peremyshl gymnasium, a relative of the famous bishop Kotsilovskii." See ibid., ark. 5.
25 SBU, f. 1, op. 1, spr. 1092, ark. 5–6. Compare with Dmitrii Vedeneiev, *Ateisty v mundirakh: Sovetskie spetssluzhby i religioznaia sfera Ukrainy* (Moscow: Algoritm, 2015).
26 SBU, f. 1, op. 1, spr. 858, ark. 1.
27 SBU, f. 1, op. 1, spr. 858, ark. 1–2. As KGB agents described this, "the school is located in the American military barracks on the outskirts of the city of Regensburg. A majority of American officers arrive to the school in their own cars. The teachers, excluding a Serbian Zaichich, who has his own car, use an American bus to get to the school in the morning, in midday, and in the evening." (ibid., ark. 1a). Compare with another description of this school, which used the Polish guards, in Wojciech Jerzy Muszyński, "The Polish Guards Companies of the U.S. Army After World War II," *The Polish Review*, Vol. 57, No. 4 (2012), pp. 75–86.
28 Ibid., 3–4.
29 Ibid., 167–168. "These teachers resided in the former hotel "Schilherchof" – Bonhofschtrasse 17. A commandant of this dormitory is a defector Andreichuk Petr Fedorovich, 55 years old, born in Western Ukraine (he lived a long time in the Ukrainian SSR). Together with him, his daughter, Galina Petrovna, 24 years old, lives, she teaches the music lessons, performs as a singer in the evenings (her

theatrical pseudonym is Galina Andre)." See a detailed description of the school and the school's guards from "the displaced people" (mostly from the Poles, who served earlier in the "Anders Army") in ibid., 167–171.

30 Ibid., 170.

31 Ibid., 171. The KGB agent *Vsevolod* added: "The students, recruited by the agents of American secret service, receive the political instructions and training for spying in the USSR and countries of people's democracy. The most active US agent, who recruited the students, is Thompson." See in ibid., 185.

32 Ibid., 182–183. According to the KGB agent's report, his name was "Avtorkhanov (pseudonym Kunta) Aleksandr Aleksandrovich, from Northern Caucasus, graduated from the institute of Red Professors in Leningrad, was a representative of TSKK on Northern Caucasus ... Very talented. He is a deputy director of the Institute for the studies of the USSR history and culture."

33 See the detailed KGB report about this school submitted to KGB supervisors in Kyiv on August 14, 1956, in SBU, f. 1, op. 1, spr. 858, ark. 195–200.

34 Ibid., 195-196. See also Jan-Hinnerk Antons, "Displaced Persons in Postwar Germany: Parallel Societies in a Hostile Environment," *Journal of Contemporary History*, January 2014, Vol. 49, No. 1, 92–114.

35 Ibid., ark. 2. The most famous Ukrainian patriots taught in this school. Some of them became the legends of the Ukrainian national movement such as "a head of school's staff – Petrishin Evgenii, OUN nickname 'Vernigora,' and teacher of the special subjects, simultaneously a head of UNG abroad – Borovets Taras Dmitrievich, nickname 'Taras Bulba'." See ibid., 194.

36 Ibid., 96–97.

37 Ibid., 98. According to the KGB report, "Together with Vasiliev, his wife Vasilieva Tatiana Konstantinovna (born in 1905) went abroad (she had a college music education, before the war she had taught music at Kiev House of Culture of workers of food industry. She is a capricious, pampered and 'spoilt' woman; she has bad relations with relatives of her husband and has strong influence on her husband. Under her pressure he fled from Kiev with Germans."

38 Ibid., 98–99.

39 Ibid., 100–101.

40 Ibid., 208–209.

41 Ibid., 191.

42 Ibid., 299, 191. According to the KGB, before the German occupation of Kyiv, Grechko worked as a teacher at the school No. 94 there.

43 See about this center in Michael Parrish, *The Lesser Terror: Soviet State Security, 1939-1953* (Westport, CT: Praeger Publishers, 1996), 157.

44 SBU, f. 1, op. 1, spr. 858, ark. 191–192, 199, 206–207, 299.

45 Ibid., 210, 301–302.

46 Ibid., 302–304.

47 Ibid., 305–306.

48 Ibid., 306, 391–393, 342–343, 344.

49 Ibid., 275–276.

50 Ibid., 277. Compare with my interview with Ivan Grigorovich K., a retired KGB officer, February 3, 2019, Kyiv.

51 Ibid., 277–279.

52 Ibid., 279. Compare with my interview with Ivan Grigorovich K., a retired KGB officer, February 3, 2019, Kyiv.

53 Interview with Ivan Grigorovich K., a retired KGB officer, February 3, 2019, Kyiv, Ukraine.

54 SBU, f.1, op. 1, spr. 858, ark. 184.

55 SBU, f. 1, op. 1, spr. 716, ark. 1–2; spr. 717, ark. 25–26.

56 See especially SBU, f. 1, op. 1, spr. 456, ark. 38. The KGB officer reported in January 1955: "It is known that in the American zone of occupation in Germany in the city of Regensburg, Bavaria, a *nevozvrashchenka*" (a former Soviet citizen, living abroad, who did not want to come back to the USSR - SZh.) Nina, who is 26-27 years old, a former resident of Odesa resides. Nina is married to a sergeant of the US C-I-C (Counter-Intelligence Corps) O'Smith or O'Shmidt. He works for the local US 'spy school' in Regensburg, and he is under her strong influence. It is known that she does not like Germans and she regrets now that previously she rejected her right to return to the USSR. We need to collect more information about this person, to study her connections with relatives, and, eventually, to recruit her as a KGB agent to use her for counter-intelligence purposes against Americans."

57 SBU, f. 1, op. 1, spr. 1678, ark. 3–4, 163–165.

2 The Legacy of the Early Cold War: Re-immigrants, the KGB Double Agents and "Zionist Jews"

The "Displaced Persons" and KGB Double Agents

The KGB special operations always targeted Russian/Ukrainian immigrant communities (especially among the displaced people [DP]) in Europe after WWII.[1] The typical criminal cases from the KGB office in Kyiv included those, which covered the stories of recruiting of the Russian and Ukrainian immigrants in France and Germany and re-hiring of American and British double agents after 1954 as the KGB spies. Using the nostalgic feelings of Russian and Ukrainian migrants, and playing on their patriotism, the KGB organized the most successful operations against the CIA, by re-recruiting the Ukrainians and Russians for the needs of the Soviet intelligence. One such an agent, Andrei I. Uvarov (born in 1919 in Zhdanov/Mariupol), was a member of the Russian noble family, who fled from the Russian Revolution of 1917 to France. By the efforts of CIA agents in the camps of displaced people in France, he was recruited for the intelligence work in the USSR. Being a son of a former "*beloemigrant*" (a person, who fought against the Red Army in the Russian Civil War, and then emigrated from Russia), Uvarov officially came back to the USSR in 1947. According to the KGB investigation, in 1937, as a French college student, he had already visited London and took classes of English there. During WWII, he lived in Erfurt in Germany, where he was employed as "a garage mechanic for a German state." After a capitulation of Germany, he returned to France, where he worked as an interpreter on the US airbase during November 1945–July 1946. Uvarov took the additional courses of Russian in December of 1946 with American instructors, left his mother in Paris, and moved to the USSR to live in his native city of Zhdanov. As the KGB investigators figured it out, Uvarov had already graduated from a special 6-month American intelligence school; and he was sent to the USSR with a special intelligence assignment by the CIA. At the same time, the KGB officers discovered that Uvarov was a "Russian nationalist," who hated "Jews and Ukrainian nationalists." As Uvarov revealed later himself, he especially could not stand those "Ukrainian nationalists," who were recruited by the same American spy instructors "for anti-Soviet activities inside Soviet Ukraine." Eventually,

DOI: 10.4324/9781003212522-3

the KGB used his "obvious Russian imperialist" chauvinism for re-recruiting him in 1954, and during 1954–1956, Uvarov turned in and denounced to the KGB the numerous CIA spies, who were predominantly the ethnic Ukrainians. It is noteworthy, that Uvarov and other double agents of Russian origin, during their interrogations, always blamed their Jewish instructors in France (such as a CIA instructor, a Jew, Yusef M. Krik), for a successful recruitment of "the Slavic emigrants" for the CIA service, using those emigrants' anti-Soviet intentions and nostalgic feelings.[2]

A typical case of different double agents – working for the Western intelligence – was presented in the KGB files by a story of a US spy *Vladimir*, whose real name was Dmitrii Shlykov, born in 1918 in Mariupol/Zhdanov, Stalino (Donetsk) Region. *Vladimir* had been trained as a special NKVD agent, and then he was sent to Zaporizhie region during WWII in 1942 "*v tyl vraga*" (behind the enemy front line) to organize the sabotage operations among the German troops there. Eventually, he was captured and arrested by Nazi, who re-recruited him as a German spy and used him against the Soviet army. After WWII, while he stayed at the DP camp in Germany, he was re-recruited by the US intelligence and used against the USSR. As it happened, *Vladimir* became the most effective CIA agent. The KGB failed to recruit him back again. *Vladimir* always resisted any KGB efforts to approach him, emphasizing in all personal conversations his "pro-American position" and "his dream to enjoy his life" in the USA after the ending of his "spy assignments." During one CIA "intelligence mission" in June 1953 in Western Ukraine, the KGB operatives were unable to capture him alive. *Vladimir* committed suicide, poisoning himself, and killing his "American dream."[3]

At the same time, after Stalin's death in 1953 and the official Communist party's criticism of Stalin "anti-spy campaigns," the KGB officers began revising and revaluating the criminal cases about the Western spies in Soviet Ukraine. The KGB supervisors realized that the number of the so-called American/British spies among the disposed persons (DPs), who returned to Soviet Ukraine from Europe, was obviously exaggerated by their colleagues in the late 1940s. As early as October 1952, the KGB administration in Kyiv recommended to their representatives in all the regions of Soviet Ukraine that there was a "necessity to figure out how repatriates from Europe ... were recruited by the American intelligence."[4] As it turned out, in some regions (like Stalino [Donetsk]), an overwhelming majority of the so-called spies among DPs had nothing to do with the US/British intelligence at all.[5] There were about the 41 recorded repatriates in Stalino region, who had previously claimed to be recruited by the US occupational forces in Germany for the anti-Soviet activities in the USSR. It turned out that an overwhelming majority of those people were uneducated women who had just invented their collaboration with Americans or had to admit this fact of collaboration under pressure from the interrogating KGB officers, trying to avoid a long detention and be released as soon as possible, etc. Double checking of these people demonstrated that they had nothing to do with American intelligence, or espionage; many of them just "slander themselves" (committing the acts of self-defamation). Some of them incriminated themselves being intimidated or confused after the arrest. The most typical example in the KGB documents was a story about a woman (Soviet repatriate), who initially rejected any accusation of her connection to the British or American intelligence, but being tired of the long interrogation, she admitted an act of collaboration with spies. In another case, a girl accepted this connection trying to be free, explaining to the KGB officer why she had lied: "I had an infant baby, who was waiting for me that time, therefore what I wanted was to finish the interrogation as soon as possible, and go to my baby and feed her ..." As a result of the KGB double-checking, 22 cases from 41 were closed (as untrue) cases of espionage and justified those DPs as normal repatriates to Soviet Ukraine.[6]

In February 1956, the KGB still had to figure out who were the "real spies" among hundreds of suspected DPs, who moved to Soviet Ukraine after WWII. Officially, according to "an Accounting-Recording Department of the KGB in a production in the [KGB] organs in Ukraine, there were 193 cases of the suspected foreign intelligence agents of the USA, 85 – English, and 5 – French intelligence service."[7] Even the KGB reports had to acknowledge that many of these "spy" cases had been invented by the KGB agents under the political pressure in the 1940s and the early 1950s.[8] According to the list of those DPs, who were searched by the KGB as possible US intelligence agents, and who were the Ukrainians by origin, but during WWII lived abroad, there were only indirect data about their connections to American of British intelligence officers, etc. (e.g., "some Ukrainian girl from DP camp slept with the US officer, and that was used by the KGB as the information about her possible connections to the US spies"). As the KGB administration in Kyiv concluded "that was the very strange circumstantial information: there was no direct proof about their recruitment by foreign intelligence."[9]

A similar situation existed in every region of Soviet Ukraine after WWII.[10] The most explicit case was provided by the KGB representatives in Dnipropetrovsk Region, Initially, according to their reports, for ten months of 1952 in this region there were 6 foreigners, 13 local residents earlier lived in the USA, 8 residents had recorded the connections with Americans on the Soviet soil, 11 residents went to the USA on scientific business trips, 1,500 residents still maintained the connections with Americans in the USA, 22,000 residents were repatriates from the American zone of occupation in Europe. Among them, the KGB found 493 trained agents of US/British intelligence service. But by the beginning of 1953, KGB records kept only so-called spy's cases for 143 professional agents from the initial amount of 493.[11] As it turned out, in Dnipropetrovsk Region, many those KGB criminal cases were mistakenly recorded as being "US spies' cases." As a result of double-checking in 1956, those KGB cases "were closed and sent to the archive as mistaken cases (*kak neobosnovano zavedionnye po okraske "amerikanskii shpionazh"*)." In March 10, 1956, from the initial hundred cases, there were remaining only 11 "questionable cases left of those, who were suspected to be the agents of the US intelligence."[12]

Yet, hundreds of criminal cases of the 1950s contained the unique information about the KGB "active measures" and special operations against the US intelligence in Soviet Ukraine, regarding the KGB double agents. Among numerous cases of such agents, the most remarkable, and to some extent, exemplary, was a story of Valentina Fedorovna Safianova (Сафьянова).[13] Her case demonstrates the major features and elements of the KGB strategy and tactics of recruiting and using the previously "disposed people" and their "questionable" past for needs of the KGB (Figure 2.1).

In May of 1953, the KGB investigators opened the criminal case of Safianova, based on the official and agents' materials, "which allowed to suspect Safianova of being an agent of the German (in the past, [during WWII]), and now of the American intelligence." According to the KGB information, Safianova was born in 1915 in the city of Kyiv into the family of the Russian-German dissent, had the Soviet high school diploma; "in her former life she was a ballerina, she was unmarried," lived in a city of Ismail, where she worked in an orchestra of a restaurant "Blue Danube."[14]

According to the reports of various KGB agents, during WWII, Safianova stayed in Kyiv, occupied by the Germans, and worked there in various theaters maintaining personal relations with numerous officers of Gestapo. As she testified ("not very convincingly"), one of those Gestapo officers proposed Safianova a business collaboration with German counter-intelligence, and she rejected this offer "because it was not paid well." But KGB agents found out that during WWII Safianova visited Vienna, Austria, numerous times "on the special German assignments." As one former agent of German counter-intelligence testified, Safianova became a member of the Russian "monarchical organization," which existed under German rule in a city of Kyiv, and through the entire period of Nazi occupation she maintained the very close relations with all the participants of that organization, reporting about them on regular basis to Gestapo. When German occupants retreated, she fled with them to Austria and then moved to Germany, where she re-established her connections with the White emigrant circles, staying in the American zone, and "she was pressured by Americans to migrate to the US." But, suddenly, she changed her mind, and instead of her moving to the USA, she arrived in the USSR in 1945 "in the order of repatriation," concealing from the Soviet administration "what she was doing in the American zone of occupation."[15]

After arrival from Germany, Safianova resided around five years in a town of Kozyatyn, the region of Vinnytsa, and taught music there in the local music school. The same year 1945, she was recruited by the Kozyatyn MVD station as a secret Soviet police agent "as a result of her obvious

Figure 2.1 Safianova – a double agent.

Soviet patriotic feelings," and during the entire period of this collaboration she "always presented herself among her KGB and MVD colleagues as an efficient, very-patriotic and anti-American." In 1950, Safianova, by her own decision, moved to reside in Kyiv, where, "on her own initiative, she immediately contacted directly an operative official of the 5th Department of MGB of the Ukrainian SSR." In a process of collaboration with the KGB officers, Safianova tried to use these connections for "her own personal interest," taking care of how much the KGB would pay for her information.

She even tried to trade with her KGB supervisors her own personal (sometime very intimate) information about her acquaintances, with whom she resided on the occupied territory and abroad during WWII. As a KGB agent, Safianova was sent to find out about the suspicious connections of some people had with the Western intelligence, but she failed to do this. She always "avoided the serious, deep investigation" of those people, limiting herself with providing her KGB supervisors of "the unworthy informational material." It became known later that she even revealed her "KGB status" to her stepmother, compromising herself. In December 1951, after being arrested for braking passport regime, she again "revealed her KGB status" to the policeman, who arrested her in Kyiv. As a result of such a behavior, in 1952, her supervisors from the 5th Directorate of KGB "excluded Safianova from KGB agent network."[16]

According to the KGB agents' reports, at the beginning of 1952, Safianova arrived to a city of Izmail, Odesa Region. She explained to her girlfriend (who happened to be a KGB agent *Novitskaia*) that she moved to Izmail to be closer to Vienna, where she could re-establish connections with the foreign intelligence with a help from the sailors who traveled abroad and the foreigners. She also confessed her intention to transfer abroad the intelligence information (important for her friends from the CIA), she could collect in Izmail. In particular, Safianova told another friend (who was also a KGB agent *Carmen*) that she came to Izmail with one goal: to establish her connections with "an Austrian citizen Ungard, a former Gestapo officer," she had had close relations with during the German occupation of Kyiv. The KGB discovered this contact of Safianova. It turned out that Heinrich Ungard did exist. He was an Austrian citizen, born in 1903, a former officer of the Nazi army during WWII. He lived in Vienna, was a successful businessman, with a workshop producing clothes and stuffed drapery, "in the capital city of Austria." Safianova intended to create "a practical connection to Ungard by sending him her letters" via the reliable persons who traveled to Vienna. As a KGB agent explained to his supervisors in Kyiv,

> With this purpose, she actively acquainted herself with sailors of Danube military fleet and Izmail shipping company, who traveled abroad, "checking carefully everybody by her personal investigation, or double checking using other people." Thus, she studied meticulously an inspector of Danube shipping company (who happened to be also a KGB agent *Antonov*) and tried to arrange a special meeting with him. In April of 1953 he was invited specially to a *kampania* of people, Safianova's friends. He was studied in advance by one of Safianova's close friends, a worker of the ship repair plant named Zhorzh. Zhorzh was a frequent visitor of the restaurant, where Safianova worked, who lived far beyond his means, and he met a KGB agent *Antonov* inviting him for a drink. During a special meeting, organized for checking *Antonov*, two musicians who worked together with Safianova, and a

brother of Zhorzh were present. This meeting was a pretext for a main conversation with Safianova. She cautiously expressed her interest in the conditions of working on the water transport, and she probed this agent from a point of view of his political steadiness. After this evening, expressing about her opinion on Antonov to another KGB agent *Carmen*, Safianova "confessed about her doubts for her future using him for establishing the connections abroad due to his political steadiness and his strict moral principles."[17]

In May 1953, the KGB "placed" another agent *Neizvestnyi* (*Unknown*), a "sailor of overseas travel," to offer the needed service to Safianova. She studied him, before allowing him to approach her. According to the KGB agent, she pretended in front of *Unknown* to be the real Soviet patriot, "painfully" reacted to his philistine anti-Soviet declarations, blaming him for being ideologically unstable. Simultaneously, she questioned him in detail about his parents, about their social past, acquaintances, way of life, the conditions of work in the water transport, in particular, abroad, about the ship security, about the checking of documents, and the personal belongings of the ship crew, and about who was in charge of all this; about Vienna, about a possibility to visit an American zone there, etc. Making sure, that she could trust this agent, Safianova confessed that she had also visited Vienna, although without explaining the details of her visit, at the same time she admitted that she knew this Austrian city very well, and she adored it. And she explained to the agent that she knew the German language perfectly well ("she was almost fluent in that language"), which gave her "an ability to feel herself free and comfortable in Vienna."[18]

As the KGB analyzed her behavior, Safianova built her conversation with the agent in such a way as to persuade *Unknown* that she needed to establish her personal connections with Vienna. She explained that she had many friends in Vienna, with whom she wanted to start correspondence if the agent would help her in this, to begin for the first time with transferring her letter to her acquaintance in Vienna. After probing this agent and making sure that he could be trusted, she questioned him in detail about a possibility of the illegal crossing of the border and, finally, asked *Unknown* to carry her two letters to Vienna. One letter an agent had to give to her good friend from the time of German occupation of Kiev, named Ungrad, an Austrian, Vienna's resident, and the second letter to an American commandant of the US zone. At the same time, she explained to *Unknown*, that due to the fact that her letters were composed in German, she, being very cautious, would translate them in Russian, so an agent would be sure that they did not look suspicious, and he would have no trouble with Soviet border guards. After some time, as a result of constant anti-Soviet criticism, expressed by the agent in their conversations, she gradually "began trusting him," they became close sexually and she eventually revealed her plans to him. Safianova explained to *Unknown* that she came from Kyiv following the special assignment of her "like-minded people" to contact the US intelligence service, to get the "needed guidance and begin their practical work." She confessed that she received the "special training in the intelligence skills" and graduated from the "special US spy school in Vienna." Until the present day she had still kept her German passport and special ID in a secure place, and she was sure that she would use these documents in the future. As the agent reported, without "concealing her hatred of the Soviet regime and expressing it in the sharp slanderous declarations," Safianova frequently explained to him a necessity of the "coordinated struggle" with the Soviet state, emphasizing a phrase that "we were not the only ones, we would be understood and supported by the entire Western civilized world."[19]

Safianova tried to persuade *Unknown* that he, using his official position of the Soviet sailor, could connect her through Ungrad with the US intelligence. At the same time, she explained that at the beginning he had to perform a role of the "simple message man," but if he performed this mission successfully, he could promote his career in the West and provide his future with funding, get education abroad, money and respect "through those American channels." She instructed *Unknown* that she would give him her letters immediately before the departure of his ship. According to the KGB officers, who monitored her, Safianova checked the ship's schedule and *Unknown*'s behavior being afraid of his cheating or provocation. In the morning of June 6, 1953, she gave *Unknown* her letter in German to deliver in Vienna for Ungrad, with an address in both the German and Russian language, and "her photo card from her old Vienna's visit as a parole for Ungrad."[20]

According to the KGB agent, on the surface, this letter had the innocent content, although it was a serious document, by which Safianova attempted to restore her connections with the US intelligence. She explained this to *Unknown*. The letter had such phrases, which she used to tell Ungrad face to face in their intimate situations, therefore their contents were only understood by him. In this letter she asked to find her friend Valentina, a former dancer from Kyiv Opera and her husband Vladimir Pommer. As the KGB realized using Ungrad and Pommer, Safianova intended to establish an immediate contact with the US intelligence. While *Unknown* would be traveling abroad, she had to connect with all her friends in Kyiv, that for the next trip abroad *Unknown* would be provided with precious secret materials, which he had to transfer to the US intelligence.[21]

The KGB agent reported that after her arrival in Izmail, Safianova "by her own initiative" contacted an officer of UMVD, "expressing her wish to continue collaboration with the organs of MVD, because she had an experience in this work and good characteristic by Ukrainian police officers." As it turned out, she tried to build her "own circle of trust" with MVD and KGB agents, using them for her own interests.[22] According to this report,

It was established fact now that in her collaboration with organs of MVD Safianova tried to use this [collaboration] for hostile purposes, in particular, avoiding suspicions about her contacts with the foreign (especially American) intelligence. She always presented her hidden hostile intentions, anti-Soviet views, her meetings with the important and necessary people, as a cover strategy in performing [the KGB] assignments, at the same time pursuing her own line of behavior in the "business interest" [of the KGB], which allowed her to tell [the KGB] which person would be an interesting personality for our operations, in this way manipulating our preferences. Being afraid that she could get in her contacts, surprisingly, a person who was our agent, Safianova in advance [just in case] tried to protect her own actions with distorted information for the organs of [the KGB].[23]

Suspecting *Unknown* as a possible KGB agent, Safianova told her KGB supervisor about *Unknown* and subsequent conversations with him in a distorted way, blaming *Unknown* in all anti-Soviet actions. She characterized to the KGB *Unknown* as a hostile man, who, after realizing that she had been in Vienna already, asked her to connect him to her old (from war times) acquaintances and then with the US intelligence. At the same time, criticizing him, Safianova tried to persuade her KGB supervisors that she could use him, manipulate him in the interest of the KGB. But her official supervisors had already realized that she "played her own game, using the KGB contacts for reaching the US intelligence officers in Vienna."[24] As the KGB officers discovered Safianova did have "the serious spy training and skills abroad" before coming to the USSR. They noted that she even had with her an ampoule with poison-potassium cyanide. At some point, during their regular meeting, the KGB supervisor demanded from her "in categorical form to give this poison to him, justifying his demand by some instruction, and [she] obeyed him."

As he reported later, "there are all grounds to consider that Safianova, certainly, [had] solid experience in the work as an agent of US intelligence and that [was] why she had been provided with poison. As an intelligence worker, she renounced her family life, and she prepared herself to an active future intelligence work ... According to her personal qualities, she [was] shrewd, quirky and insidious, and she tried to mask herself by any methods. Her purpose was to persuade the officers from the organs [of the MGB] to consider her to be a woman of easy virtue rather than a dangerous person pursuing hostile intelligence work ... It is obvious that all the time Safianova was directed by a special consultant-US spy, who monitored her intelligence work from abroad."[25]

The KGB administration developed a set of active measures in the special KGB "operation against Safianova." As the KGB supervisor of this operation explained, his "officers set a task to continue the measures which had begun already to setup and intercept the illegal channel of the connections between Safianova and the American intelligence in Vienna with having in mind of implantation of our agents in the intelligence agencies of the USA." "With this goal in mind," the KGB recommended to "prepare the agent *Unknown* to his trip to Vienna, Austria, to meet the Safianova's connections there."[26]

On June 15, 1953, a KGB agent *Unknown*, with Safianova's letter for Ungrad, sailed as a boatswain of a Soviet merchant ship *Neva* to Austria. But this KGB assignment became the entire failure for the KGB administration in Kyiv, which supervised this operation. For some reason, Ungrad avoided any contacts with *Unknown* in Vienna, trying to distance himself from a KGB agent. Eventually, an Austrian canceled all planned meetings with *Unknown*, who had to return to Izmail after this failed attempt to establish connections with the US intelligence in Vienna. Moreover, the entire KGB operation turned to be a complete disaster, when Safianova took an ampoule with poison and killed herself. Her girlfriends, who also were KGB agents, testified that before her suicide she had dreamed about the "wonderful America" and her possible life there. One KGB officer, who worked with a former Safianova's KGB supervisor during the 1970s, recalled, how the KGB administration realized that Safianova "felt a foul play" by her KGB colleagues and managed to inform her Austrian connections about the KGB operation before *Unknown*'s trip to Vienna in June 1953. The KGB tried to arrest her, and that is why she committed suicide. In this way, the KGB not only lost their double agent, but failed an opportunity to "infiltrate" the US intelligence service in Austria.[27]

Despite this scandal with Safianova, the KGB succeeded with other agents, recruited from former Ukrainian residents of DP camps in Western Europe. The best illustration of such a recruiting success was the case of a KGB agent *Natasha*, a student of the 3rd year of English at the Pedagogical Institute of Foreign Languages in a city of Odesa, who was recruited by the KGB "on 3rd March 1953 with a usage of compromising materials about her and her relatives."[28] Her real name was Raisa Fedorovna Pribyt. She was born in 1931 in a village of Zapolie, Kovel district, Volyn region (which belonged to Poland before 1939), where she resided with her parents. After a unification of Western Ukraine with Soviet Ukraine in 1939, her family moved to a town of Shepetovka, because her father, Fedor Yakovlevich Pribyt, who was a priest of the Ukrainian Orthodox Autocephalous Christian Church, fled from the persecution by Soviet administration, which considered this church to be the "illegal anti-Soviet Ukrainian nationalistic organization." Moreover, the KGB administration discovered that in 1923 he joined OUN and helped Ukrainian patriots the fight "the Polish (before 1939) and then Soviet (after 1939) occupants of Volyn." Pribyt moved with his family to Shepetovka (Shepetivka), the larger town to the east of Volyn, in Khmelnytskyi Region of Ukraine, trying to hide his identity and his "nationalistic connections" from the Soviet police.[29]

During the Nazi occupation of Ukraine, the Pribyt family lived in Shepetovka. Fedor Pribyt resumed his active functions as a priest of the Ukrainian Orthodox Autocephalous Church, supported by the Germans, who appointed him in 1941 a head of the local Orthodox Christian eparchy (*blagochinnyi okruga*). As the KGB investigators discovered, during this period of occupation, he "maintained very close relations with OUN and Germans, spread the Ukrainian nationalist and anti-Soviet propaganda, influencing the local Orthodox eparchy and all local population in the very anti-Soviet direction." In 1943 the Pribyt family and other priests of the Ukrainian Orthodox Autocephalous Church fled with the German troops to the West, trying to reach an Anglo-American zone. Before 1945, *Natasha* together with her parents lived in various DP camps "for fugitives" on the territory of Poland, Germany and Czechoslovakia. In 1945 her family arrived from Poland for re-settling in the USSR. To avoid the imminent arrest for his collaboration with OUN and Germans during WWII, *Natasha*'s father agreed to collaborate with the KGB in Soviet Ukraine. In 1949 he was recruited by the KGB as a KGB agent *Polevoi* "for the KGB actions abroad, but he did not fit KGB goals, maintaining secret connections with the Ukrainian nationalists and informing his nationalistic friends about all KGB operations against them in Germany." Therefore, he was arrested in 1950 by the KGB of Odesa Region "for a betrayal of the KGB secrets" and sent to "a labor camp" in Kizil, Molotov Region[30] (Figure 2.2).

The KGB recruiting officer used this "compromising family history," adding the fact that *Natasha*'s mother worked as an official of Odessa Theological Christian Seminary, to blackmail *Natasha*, threatening to show all this "compromising" information to the administration of *Natasha*'s institute and persuading her to work for the KGB office in Odesa. Eventually this officer was glad to recruit *Natasha*, positively characterized in his report,

> According to her personal qualities, *Natasha* is intelligent (*razvitaia*) and principled, but without any life experience. She has a wide circle of connections among the youth. She speaks Ukrainian very well, possesses knowledge of English and Polish. She slightly knows German language. She collaborates with MVD organs with desire. Right now, she is used for studying the people who present an interest to MVD from the institute of foreign languages. Agent *Natasha* will be used for a work with the American representatives for exploring their connections, who are suspected to be the agents of US intelligence service.[31]

Eventually, through the entire 1960s and 70s, *Natasha* became the most successful KGB agent in Soviet Ukraine, who compromised hundreds of "Ukrainian nationalists from US/Canadian anti-Soviet organizations" and "the US spies," who worked as American diplomats in the USSR (Figure 2.3).

Figure 2.2 KGB agent Natasha as an undergraduate student.

According to the KGB documentation, almost 85% of all displaced persons, who were former citizens of Soviet Ukraine, came back to the USSR after 1945 as the newly recruited KGB agents. And all of them had "compromising circumstances, such as collaboration with German or Romanian occupants during WWII, being the agents of Gestapo, etc." An overwhelming majority (more than 70%) of these displaced persons were the former "East Workers" (*Ostarbeiter*) from Ukraine, who were sent by the Nazi regime to Germany by force as the conscript labor during WWII. Some of them had been already recruited by the US intelligence in DP camps.[32] The typical case of such a double KGB agent was a spy career of Anna

Figure 2.3 KGB agent Natasha after recruitment.

Fedorovna Sosnovskaia. Sosnovskaia was born in 1925 in a village of Petrovka, Zaporizhian Region, and grew up in a Ukrainian wealthy peasant family, which was defined by the KGB as "the anti-Soviet kulak clan." She survived confiscations of her family's property and the arrests of her parents by the Soviet police. She even joined Komsomol and graduated from a teacher's college (*pedtekhnikum*). In April 1942, she was arrested by the new German village administration and sent as one of numerous Ukrainian *Ostarbeiters* to Germany, where she worked as a servant in the mansion of the soap producing businessman in Witten-Ruhr. According to the KGB information, after a defeat of Germany in May 1945, she stayed at the DP camp in the American zone of occupation, where she was recruited as a spy by American intelligence. In 1952 the KGB re-recruited her as a "double agent." In 1953 the KGB sent her into East Germany as a "wife" of a Soviet military officer, stationed there with Soviet troops. Eventually her KGB supervisors helped her "to desert to the American zone and renew her relations with her former American instructors from the US intelligence" to become a Soviet KGB agent inside the US secret service.[33]

Hundreds of former female "displaced persons" from the American zone of occupation were recruited as the KGB double agents, who used all their intelligence tools, including their personal sexual charms in their attempts to "infiltrate" the US intelligence in Europe. Numerous KGB reports provided this kind of stereotypical portrait of the successful female agent: "According to her personal qualities, she is well developed, cultured, resourceful, initiative-like, and very easy in establishing personal connections and attracting people (including the skills to use her female charms, attracting her male contacts sexually). As an agent, she is reasonably conspiratorial, very serious in performing her assignments; she urges them to perform accurately, enthusiastically wishes to work with the KGB organs."[34] At the same time, the KGB recruiters formulated the ideal description of the best model of the KGB double agent, who had to be "intellectually developed, resourceful, energetic, judicious, and had an ability to establish personal contacts, to be flexible and enterprising as well."[35] In January–February 1955, the KGB administration included this description of the KGB agent's "personal qualities" in its plan of the counter-intelligence work against the possible American agents. This plan of "the counter-intelligence work of the 2nd Department" of the Ukrainian KGB was sent out to all the regions of Soviet Ukraine, and the regional KGB offices used it through the entire 1950s.[36] This plan included: (1) "the collection of information and putting data on the special KGB records about the spying activities of the people, who could be suspected to be the American agents," using the KGB agents to study and "neutralize" those people; (2) "the establishing via KGB agents the existence of the suspicious connections" with American spies, using "various illegal channels and written correspondence" (from Ukraine) with persons, who resided abroad, especially in Austria and West Germany, who had links to the US intelligence or could be connected to the Americans there; (3) "a usage of the substitutes (the KGB undercover officers) for tricking" (provoking and compromising) the American intelligence agents from "the personnel of the US Embassy and the representatives of the US government," who visited Soviet Ukraine; (4) "a selection and professional training of the candidates of KGB agents sent abroad" and to be "infiltrated" into the American intelligence; (5) "finding those people, who were already living/ traveling abroad (on the business trips), and who fit "the model of the future KGB agent" for recruiting them; and (6) "studying the foreign sailors, who arrived in Soviet ports, with a goal to recruiting them as the new KGB agents."[37] Those measures were used by all KGB operatives in the 1960s and even in the 1970s.

For the KGB administration, its major threat derived from all anti-Soviet Ukrainian nationalistic actions inside Soviet Ukraine, which were "sponsored by the Ukrainian centers in America," and served (according to the KGB) as "a peculiar reserve of agents for the intelligence and subversive work in the USSR, using international tourism." These American Ukrainians were specially trained by the US intelligence and were sent as tourists for establishing contacts with the nationalistic elements inside Soviet Ukraine.[38]

As a result of those activities, the KGB noted a rise of anti-Soviet actions. Thus, in 1954–1964, the KGB discovered and liquidated 81 organizations of the "Ukrainian nationalists with 602 participants." A majority of them had the "certain connections with the Ukrainian diaspora from America." The participants of these groups had "such characteristics": 156 of them had already been indicted for the nationalistic activities, 56 were former members of OUN-UPA, 90 were relatives of the "Banderovites" and 300 had no previous records of nationalistic activities. Using their connections with the Ukrainian diaspora from America, these participants developed such arguments for their nationalistic activities: "(1) the limitations of the state sovereignty and democratic rights of Soviet Ukrainians; (2) the inequality of the economic situation of Ukraine comparing to other Soviet republics; with an abundance of natural resources, the Ukrainian people had a very low standard of living; (3) the forceful Russification and spiritual exploitation of the Ukrainian people; (4) the blaming of the politics of the communist party and Soviet government for the mistakes and misdemeanors of a few local politicians; (5) The dislike of the system of collective farms" in the Soviet Ukraine's agriculture.[39] Through the entire 1960s and the 1970s, the KGB leaders found the similar argumentation of all so-called anti-Soviet "nationalistic" groups in Soviet Ukraine. And, according to the KGB documents, the major "instigator" of this movement was the Ukrainian diaspora from the "capitalist America." In November 1975, the KGB administration tried to justify its operations against the patriotic Ukrainian intellectuals in Soviet Ukraine ("political dissidents") by presenting to Soviet Communist leadership in Kyiv their movement as "American/Canadian anti-Soviet operation." They called this phenomenon as a "case BLOC." The KGB submitted the detailed description of this criminal case about the connections between foreign, mostly American and Canadian, and "the local nationalists" in Soviet Ukraine among intellectuals with details of meetings of foreigners and Soviet Ukrainians with nicknames of all KGB agents, who testified about those connections, which were the result of the earlier KGB operations against the Ukrainian diaspora's links in Soviet Ukraine, such as *Kaskad, Bumerang, Pereval and Tsentr*.[40] Although all those operations were organized during the 1960s and 1970s, their major tactics still followed the models of KGB active measures of the late 1940s and the 1950s.

Another special target for the KGB in the 1950s, as a legacy of late Stalinism, was a behavior of the Soviet Jews and their relations with

Americans. The traditional Stalinist stereotype of Jewish-Zionist conspiracy and mythology of the Jewish Anti-Soviet connections with "American imperialism" survived in the KGB reports and still was evident in the official KGB discourse through the entire 1950s up to the 1980s.[41]

The KGB Operations against Soviet Jews and Anti-Semitism

In 1953, the KGB of Zhytomyr Region opened the first "anti-Jewish case" after Stalin, called a case of "Satellites" – about a group of the "Jewish nationalists, who pursued anti-Soviet activities." As it turned out, Aron M. Korol (who was born in 1882 in a town of Korostyshiv of Zhytomyr Region), a head of the local Jewish community in the same town, had established the connections with a committee of Jewish assistance in the USA (the American Jewish Joint Distribution Committee) as early as 1946. He composed a list of all Jews, who lived in Korostyshiv, and sent it to the US; he even organized "a special committee of American assistance to Jews of Korostyshiv, using his American connections." His friend Elia F. Tsypeniuk (who was born in 1900 in the same city), a director of a food shop in Korostyshiv, helped him to collect material for this list of Jews for the Americans. Srul' F. Vaisman and David Binder (all of them "were old enough to be arrested" by the KGB) also participated in the illegal "nationalistic Jewish meetings," organized by Korol. As the KGB operatives realized, all these old Jews from Korostyshiv were connected to "some American businessman Goodman, a Jewish activist who was born in Korostyshiv, then emigrated from Ukraine to the USA before WWII." As KGB investigators reported, a major goal of Korostyshiv Jews was "to unite all Jewish population in Soviet Ukraine and spread as far as possible the Soviet Jews' connections with the USA and Jewish organizations there; they worshiped a capitalist way of life in western countries, criticized Soviet laws, spread documents printed in Israel," etc. The KGB arrested all those Jewish activists, who were called "Zionists," but at the beginning of 1954 all those Korostyshiv activists were released and all members of their families immigrated to the US and Israel during the late 1950s.[42]

The second (chronologically) KGB "anti-Jewish" case was called "a case of Yankees," which involved seven so-called nationalistic Jews from Odesa Region, who "listened to the Voice of America and the Voice of Israel on the regular basis, disseminated anti-Soviet rumours, tried to organize anti-Soviet group and supported relations with Jews from Kharkiv, Dnipropetrovsk, Kyiv, Moscow and Leningrad." All those residents of Odesa "expressed their fascination, and even admiration for the American civilization and for the level of standard of living there, which was missing in the USSR." That is why the KGB officers called this group the "American Yankees." All members of this Odesa group were released from the arrest by the KGB, eventually, and by the beginning of the 1960s, all those Odesa "Yankees" immigrated to the US.[43]

At the same time, in 1954–1955, the KGB officials expressed an obvious alarm about the rise of massive and "aggressive every-day" anti-Semitism in Soviet Ukraine. They tried to stop a wave of the real anti-Semitic "pogroms" in various locations of Soviet Ukraine. After Stalin's death, the KGB operatives reported a "growth of Anti-Semitic expressions" and the numerous cases of physical attacks on Soviet Jews all over Ukraine; Jews were blamed in killing Stalin, they were physically attacked and beaten in Belgorod-Dnestrovskii, Odesa Region, in Ovruch, Zhytomyr Region, in Kyiv, Vinnytsia, and many other locations. Only by the beginning of 1955, the Soviet police managed to stop these acts of visible "aggressive" anti-Semitism.[44]

Another KGB strategy, which developed as a legacy of WWII, was an involvement of Jewish residents of Soviet Ukraine in the anti-American KGB operations. Since 1944–1945, the KGB had used Soviet "Jewish" connections with the Americans to recruit the Soviet Jews as their agents in the KGB counter-intelligence work against the US intelligence. Kyiv administration of the KGB continued this strategy after Stalin's death as well. In 1953, the first successful case of using the Soviet Jews connections with the United States for the KGB benefit in Soviet Ukraine involved a "young, intelligent and attractive" KGB agent *Maiskaia*.[45]

Her real name was Janet Iosifovna Bekker, and she was an undergraduate fourth year student at Odessa State Pedagogical Institute of the Foreign Languages in September 1953, when she was recruited by the KGB. Janet Bekker (*Maiskaia*) was born in 1925 in the city of New York, the USA, into a family of Jewish emigrants from tsarist Russia who fled anti-Jewish pogroms in 1914. In 1932, *Maiskaia*, together with her mother Faina Naftulovna Bekker, arrived to the USSR as tourists, and stayed in the city of Odesa. The same year, her mother applied for Soviet citizenship, which was immediately granted to her and her daughter. The KGB investigators discovered that *Maiskaia*'s father, Iosif Bekker, left his family and officially divorced Faina Bekker in 1930, back in the USA. So, after their return to the Soviet Union, he still lived in Los Angeles, California, where he died in 1940. In 1941, suddenly *Maiskaia* received an official letter from the US social security office about her right to get money "as her inheritance from the USA before her adulthood due to her father's death." For many years, *Maiskaia* and her mother had a long correspondence with *Iniurkollegiia* (Soviet office handling questions of the international law) in Moscow until 1951 about this question. In 1948, the US Embassy sent her a check for $56, but she rejected to receive this money (being afraid of "American provocation"). During 1950–1953, she followed the KGB recommendations, first, becoming a member of Odesa *Interclub* (a special KGB organization for the connections between Soviet and foreign citizens) in 1945, and then her participating in a meeting with an assistant to military-naval attaché of the USA and other foreigners, who visited Odesa. In August of 1952, on the Odesa beach she had a chance of meeting with a wife of military-naval attaché of the USA from Moscow office of the US Embassy. After all this experience, the KGB tested Janet Bekker's behavior, and her KGB supervisor praised how she handled her meetings with the Americans in Odesa. He especially noted that *Maiskaia*, being Jewish herself, distanced herself from "nationalistic Zionism," which, according to her, "was hostile to all Soviet patriotic Jews."[46] During her interrogation by Odesa KGB operatives, before recruiting, she confirmed all KGB data about her connections in the USA and provided the KGB "with the list of the people who came to Odessa for residence from abroad and had the real connections with foreigners and possible links to the foreign intelligence." As her KGB supervisor reported, *Maiskaia* "agreed for recruiting with a great desire and enthusiasm." Moreover, at the end of her interview with KGB operatives, *Maiskaia* told them that she was "sure that taking in consideration her biography, under certain conditions, she could be of great interest for the American intelligence." As her recruiter concluded his report on September 30, 1953, "her personal qualities would make her a mature, resourceful agent, and in addition she [is] fluent in English and very communicative." He finished his report about her recruitment as a new agent with a recommendation "to use *Maiskaia* as a substitute (*podstava*) [a KGB provocateur] for the officials of American Embassy" in Moscow.[47] As a result of this recommendation, *Maiskaia* was hired immediately, and eventually she built her successful KGB career working with the cases of the so-called nationalistic Zionism, which involved the American diplomats and tourists, who tried to help to emigrate Soviet Jews from Odesa and southern Ukraine to Israel or the USA in the 1960s through the 1970s. To some extent, *Maiskaia*'s involvement in these cases prevented the "massive Jewish exodus" from not only Odesa, but other Ukrainian cities with a significant Jewish population, such as Dnipropetrovsk.[48]

Numerous cases from the mid-50s also demonstrated how the KGB used a so-called Zionist factor in recruiting the Jewish participants of WWII as the new KGB agents in their operations against "American imperialism and Zionism." One of them was a case of an agent *Lector*.[49] His real name was Ivan Iosifovich Borovskii, a lieutenant colonel of the Soviet Army from the city of Odesa. He was born into a family of the Jewish merchant in 1917 in a village of Novopokrovka, Solonianka district of Katerynoslav/ Dnipropetrovsk Region. His family was killed in one of many anti-Jewish pogroms during the Civil War in Ukraine. Until 1925, *Lector* was brought up in the orphanage of the city of Dnipropetrovsk and got his new national identity – a Soviet "Ukrainian."[50] In 1931 he graduated from the seven-year school (*semiletka*) and then from *fabzauch* and *rabfak* (the special preparation classes for the entrance to the Soviet college) at the Transport Institute in Odesa. In 1934 *Lector* volunteered to join the Red Army, where he made a successful career from a private soldier to the military officer, becoming a commander of the military company and later "an assistant to a head of staff of the regiment." In 1942 he graduated from the higher special school of the Red Army and worked as "an assistant to head of the department of Main Intelligence of the Red Army" through the entire WWII. From September 1945 to June 1946 *Lector* lived on Philippines Islands and in Japan, where he worked as a senior assistant to "a head of the Information Department of the Allies Council from the USSR regarding Japan." Being in the city of Manila (Philippines), he established the "intimate relations with a white-emigrant Popova," who worked as an interpreter for the Japanese military intelligence.[51]

Before his departure for the USSR from Philippines, *Lector* met with an officer from the intelligence department of Douglas MacArthur headquarters, to whom he recommended Popova as a good teacher of Russian. This fact was concealed by *Lector* from his Soviet High Command in Japan. Besides his suspicious relations with Popova, he also maintained the personal connections with other US intelligence officers. The KGB investigators discovered that *Lector* also became acquainted in Tokyo with one American military officer with a rank of major, with whom he met in various hotels, supposedly for playing chess. *Lector* also had intimate relations with a Japanese woman named Sato, a waiter of the diner at the headquarters of MacArthur. During the same time, *Lector* became a good friend with an American Jew, Bella Dinaburg. According to the KGB information, she was an agent of the US counterintelligence, who worked as a secretary at the US Consulate in the city of Yokohama, Japan.[52] According to her official correspondence, Dinaburg supposedly had to come back to USA "for a study at the special intelligence school with a subsequent assignment for a work at one of the US diplomatic missions in the Soviet Union." According to the KGB agents, she tried to use *Lector* 's Jewish ethnic identity, explaining to him "the international solidarity of all Jews," but he rejected this idea, emphasizing the real "international solidarity of all workers around the world." But Dinaburg still wanted to influence his "Jewishness" for "the common Zionist cause."[53] So after the departure of *Lector* from Japan, Dinaburg even used her connections in the US Embassy in Moscow trying to find out his address in the USSR.

In June of 1946, *Lector* was sent to the military-diplomatic Academy of MVS (*ministerstvo vooruzhennykh sil SSSR* [the USSR Ministry of Military Forces, renamed in 1953 as the USSR Ministry of Defense]), where he worked until 1948 as a scientific associate at the department of arms of foreign states. According to the KGB reports, working at the academy, he "sometime expressed anti-Soviet views, demonstrated his dissatisfaction with his personal status and a situation in the country, praised the US army and the life in the USA, and showed his interest in the secret (classified) documents, which had no relation to his job." After his transfer in 1948 to a new job as a senior military censor of the district newspaper in the headquarters of Odesa military district, in the conversations and his reports, *Lector* always praised the US army and a life in the USA. He forbade publishing in the district newspaper the materials of the local journalists, who traveled abroad and "critically exposed the essence of American imperialism in their articles." As a result of such behavior "with his obvious sympathy for America," *Lector* was demoted, and on September 30, 1950, he was transferred to Odessa State University as a teacher in the military department, where he still worked in 1953, when he was recruited by the KGB.

The KGB used the fact of his "intimate relations with the foreign women" as a compromising factor for *Lector*'s recruitment. At the same time, the KGB decided to also use his old connections with the US intelligence officers and his obvious "Soviet patriotic" rejection of "international Zionism." According to the KGB supervisor's report,

> it was "considered to be appropriate to recruit him on the patriotic basis" [being aware of his distancing from Zionism], and "to demonstrate him 'a complete trust' for the future to 'substitute' (*podstavit'*), and [to use] him as our agent in operation [of compromising] one US official, who supposedly would arrive to Odesa. We assume that in this situation *Lector* would reveal himself [to this American visitor] about his old connections with the Americans in Philippines [and in Japan]. In this role *Lector* would be able to re-recruit this American [after our operation of discrediting and compromising this American official] as our own agent and would use him in our [active measures] against the US intelligence."[54]

This strategy worked and *Lector*, with his fluent English and Japanese, worked successfully against both US and Japanese intelligence in Odesa and Crimea for many years through the entire 1960s and the 1970s. *Lector* helped to discredit and compromise many American and Japanese officials, who visited Ukraine, and as a result, the KGB managed to blackmail them and obtain the precious information from those officials.[55]

The KGB especially was interested in using the American origin of those Soviet Jews, who became the candidates for recruitment. The typical story was a case of another Jewish agent with the nickname of *Aleksandrov*.[56] His real name was Maksim Semenovich Roberts, a senior research fellow at *Ukrgeologtrest* (a Soviet organization for the geological research), who worked also as a photojournalist in Kyiv. He was born into a family of Jewish emigrants from the Russian Empire in 1909 in a city of Denver, Colorado, in the US. In 1910 his mother returned with him to Russia. During the Soviet period, he moved to Soviet Ukraine, graduated from a college there, and worked for many years at the editorial board of some Ukrainian periodicals and as a freelance photo correspondent. During WWII *Aleksandrov* served in the Soviet Army and after demobilization he married a repatriate from the American zone of occupation in Europe, whose sister was a defector, living in the USA.[57] According to the KGB officers, who worked with his files, after his recruitment in 1956, *Aleksandrov* went to the USA and Israel on the numerous special KGB missions, "exposing various intelligence provocations of the international Zionism" against Soviet Jews of Kyiv and Dnipropetrovsk in the 1960s.[58]

Another group of "anti-Jewish" cases in the special KGB operations was related to the financial aspects of Jewish immigration abroad. The major goal of such cases was to get control over the "inheritance money" of the diseased Jewish immigrants in the USA, whose close relatives still lived in Soviet Ukraine and who became the legal heirs of the American property. During the 1950s and through the 1970s, these KGB special operations, targeting the American Jews with the Ukrainian roots, provided this organization with real hard currency from the West, creating a basis for the KGB financial capital. The first (chronologically) successful operation of "obtaining Jewish money from the US" was related to the Jacob Monich case of 1954.[59] In February 1954, in the county of Rockland, in the State of New York, a former "Russian" immigrant, a Jewish merchant Jacob Monich died, leaving an inheritance of around $40,000. His American lawyers announced that his eleven close relatives, who lived in the city of Dnipropetrovsk in Soviet Ukraine, had their legal right to inherit Monich's money. After studying the list of those relatives, at first, the KGB operatives selected one person from this list, who could represent all those relatives in the financial negotiations with Americans, and who agreed to collaborate with the KGB. It was a son of Jacob Monich's brother, Vladimir Arkhipovich Avramenko, who was born in 1919 in Dnipropetrovsk, a member of CPSU, a workshop foreman at the Dnipropetrovsk factory named after Voroshilov. But, eventually, the KGB supervisor changed this plan, because the KGB had already recruited another of Monich's relatives, a daughter of his sister, Anna Arkhipovna Avramenko. She was born in 1921 in Dnipropetrovsk and worked as a medical nurse at the 1st hospital for infectious diseases in the city of Dnipropetrovsk. The KGB recruited her on January 28, 1956, as their agent under pseudonym *Natasha*. During recruitment, *Natasha* told the KGB officer that her uncle moved to the USA in 1904, where he died in 1954. Before WWII, the relatives from Dnipropetrovsk maintained correspondence with him by regular mail. The US Embassy informed them about his death and "asked them to prepare the relevant documents for their right of a petition for inheritance." *Natasha* explained to the KGB officer that at the end of 1954 a representative of *Iniurkollegiia* (Soviet office handling questions of the international law) visited the Jacob Monich's relatives in Dnipropetrovsk and obtained some documents from them. The Monich's relatives kept petitioning the US Embassy in Moscow about their inheritance; but "their petition had not been answered positively yet."[60]

After recruiting *Natasha* as their agent, the KGB used her to continue those negotiations. The KGB organized a special meeting of *Natasha* with the Americans in Moscow. As a result of those negotiations, *Natasha* received Jacob Monich's inheritance and the KGB "appropriated" the American money for the "needs of Soviet government." In March 1956, the KGB again used *Natasha* in a similar case. Another Jewish emigrant died in 1955 in the US and bequeathed all his property to his Ukrainian relatives, who lived in the district of Novye Kaidaki, Dnipropetrovsk. When one

American Jew of the Russian origin offered Dnipropetrovsk relatives of that Jewish emigrant help to get their inheritance in the US, the KGB administration sent *Natasha* to interfere in those negotiations.[61] Eventually, because of *Natasha*'s actions, the "inheritance money" moved from the USA to the city of Dnipropetrovsk, and again the KGB established its total control of those funds. During the 1960s and the 1970s, such KGB operations with "Jewish money" became a lucrative business, adding cash in the form of foreign currency to the "coffers" of the KGB.[62]

The ambivalent attitudes toward Soviet Jews became a major feature of the KGB special operations. Despite official criticism of every-day anti-Semitism after Stalin, the KGB officials still treated Jewish nationalism as a creation of the American intelligence service, and Jews as potential traitors. On March 5, 1957, the Ukrainian KGB ordered to collect and present monthly "statistics about Jewish emigration and about submission of the requests for emigration of Jews for permanent residence abroad" to the political leadership of Soviet Ukraine. On December 21, 1957, they had a new order: to prepare and present these lists of Jewish emigration twice a year – by June 1 and by December 1. This routine had existed in the KGB service of Soviet Ukraine since 1957 until perestroika.[63] During the peak of Jewish emigration from Ukraine at the end of the 1960s through the 1970s, the KGB failed to stop this Jewish exodus, which especially effected the demographic situation in Zakrpathian, Lviv and Chernivtsi Regions, and the cities of Kyiv and Odesa.[64] What the KGB operatives introduced were the elements of blackmailing of the Ukrainian Jewish emigrants. According to Oleg Kalugin, a former KGB officer, during the 1970s, many Jews were allowed to immigrate to the USA and Israel after their agreement to collaborate with the KGB during their emigration. As a result, "huge numbers of Russian criminals and KGB spies … did inundate the United States."[65]

At the same time, during the emigration's process, the KGB recruited Soviet Jews as their active agents, and used this Jewish immigration in the USA for their own financial operations. All those KGB intelligence practices from the 1950s became "normalized" in the forms of the KGB active measures during the 1960s and the 1970s.[66] Since the 1970s, the KGB operatives began using their "assets" among the Soviet Jewish immigrants in the USA for various secret operations against the USA, which survived the collapse of the Soviet Union and now are under a control by the FSB – Russian successor of the KGB.[67]

Despite the official distancing from anti-Semitism, the KGB operations, especially during the 1970s, because of the official Soviet leadership position, took the very anti-Jewish approach. The KGB tried to prevent the immigration to the West of Jewish intellectuals with technical college education, who were involved in various "strategically important projects" (30–35% of all Soviet Ukrainian scientists in such projects were of the Jewish origin). The KGB operatives noted "a growth of the emigrational mood among the (Jewish) scientific-technical personnel" and reported about their "special measures" "to prevent leaking the secret information by the Soviet Jews" from Ukraine. The KGB analysts also worried that a majority of Jewish emigrants with college education from Soviet Ukraine, eventually, moved in 1973–1976 to the USA, a country of the "main adversary." Following the rule of "protection of the secret strategic information," the KGB administration tracked all the Soviet Jews with college education in Ukraine who planned to emigrate (17–18% in 1975–1976) and recommended to the Ukrainian Communist leadership the organization of series of the active measures to "stop them from emigration to Israel and the USA." These measures included "the implanting of the KGB agents in various Zionist organizations and groups in the USA, Israel and in Soviet Ukraine; fight against the Jewish extremism and nationalism inside [Soviet Ukraine]; compromising and discrediting the Jewish extremists" in Soviet Ukraine; "the dividing and complete destroying all Zionist groups inside the republic."[68] These measures took the obvious anti-Semitic overtones, when the KGB tried to stop playing "the Jewish popular and folk music (like *sem'-sorok* dance tune) in public places," such as restaurants and disco clubs of Soviet Ukraine during the 1970s. The KGB presented such music as "pro-Israel activities," which "had to be suppressed." According to their reports, those "songs and melodies of pro-Israel sense incited the nationalistic and emigrational trends among the persons of Jewish nationality" in Soviet Ukraine.[69]

As we see, even during the détente and improving of the relations with the USA of the 1970s, the KGB still were involved in various "anti-Jewish" operations, which eventually contributed to the deterioration of the Soviet-American relations and "killed" the spirit of détente.

All major elements of the KGB operations against both Ukrainian and Jewish nationalism in Soviet Ukraine were formed during the end of WWII and beginning of the early Cold War under Stalin. Since the 1950s until the end of the 1980s, these elements had been included in the new active measures and operations against the US and Canada. Unfortunately, this "Stalin's legacy" not only survived, but shaped the entire anti-American KGB operations during the Brezhnev period under a new KGB leadership of Yuri Andropov since May of 1967.

Notes

1 See about the Russian "displaced persons" in the CIA operations against the USSR in Benjamin Tromly, *Cold War Exiles and the CIA: Plotting to Free Russia* (New York: Oxford University Press, 2019). Compare with Francesco Alexander Cacciatore in Alexander Cacciatore, "Their Need Was Great": Émigrés and Anglo-American Intelligence Operations in the Early Cold War. Ph. D. dissertation, University of Westminster, March 2018.
2 SBU, f. 16, op. 1, spr. 882, ark. 37–46. When Yusef Krik was sent as an American spy to the USSR in 1945, he was detected by the KGB, arrested in 1947 and got the 25 years jail term. In this KGB operation, all other arrested US spies were the

former displaced persons from the "DP camps" in France, who were either Russian nationalists, like Uvarov, or Ukrainian nationalists, like Nikolai (Mykola) N. Nizevich. See ibid, ark. 38, 39, 40–41.

3 SBU, f. 1, op. 1, spr. 1680, ark. 320. See also my interview with Stepan Ivanovich T., a retired KGB officer, January 30, 2019, Kyiv, Ukraine. The similar case was related to another "displaced person" of the Ukrainian origin. According to the KGB report in August 1955, the Soviet agents learned about another agent of US intelligence who was sent to Ukraine in April 1955 in Ukraine. "He was Leshchenko Aleksandr A., born in 1922 in a village of Stepok in Zhitomir Region, who graduated from the Leningrad artillery high school in 1942. Then he was sent to the front, was captivated by Germans, than released and lived in his home village, where in January 1944 he was drafted again in the Soviet Army. After the war he fled to Western Germany, where he attended a British spy school in 1949-50, until 1954 he worked for Gehlen intelligence [The intelligence agency, established by the US occupational authorities in Western Germany in 1946]. In 1954 he was recruited by American intelligence OSS [the Office of Strategic Services] (*voenno-morskaia razvedka*)." The KGB established a special surveillance over Leshchenko's relatives in Ukraine and eventually he was arrested. See in SBU, f. 16, op. 1, spr. 912, ark. 117–118.

4 SBU, f.1, op. 1, spr. 754, ark. 17–18.

5 Ibid., 20–27.

6 Ibid., 21–22, 24, 25, 26. See also the numerous cases of the anti-American hysteria during 1948–1952. In 1952–53, the KGB tried to connect the detected groups of anti-Soviet college students to the American intelligence via the repatriates (former DPs), but they had to exaggerate the evidence without the real proofs. The typical case of such KGB approach (which was itself a reaction to the Stalinist ideological campaign against the "cosmopolitans") was a criminal case of "the Technicians'" (*tekhniki*) about a small group of the students from the mining tekhnikum in the city of Chistiakovo, Stalino (Donetsk) Region, which was started in December 1952. See f. 16, op. 1, spr. 881, ark. 251–256.

7 SBU, f. 1, op. 1, spr. 476, ark. 1.

8 Ibid., 4.

9 Ibid., 14–18.

10 Among all "repatriates from Europe (mainly from France) in villages and towns of Cherkasy Region, who had arrived in the region before 1955, only one attracted KGB attention, Sliva Vasilii D. from village of Moshny," whose wife complained about her suspicions that her husband was "recruited by Americans as their spy abroad." See in SBU, f. 1, op. 1, spr. 460, ark. 64–67.

11 SBU, f.1, op. 1, spr. 717, ark. 20–35, esp. 21.

12 Ibid., 34. See a list of "searching cases" of suspected agents belonging to US and English intelligence (altogether 16). All of them came from the DP camps in West Germany, all of them were identified by the testimonies of other arrested agents. Many of them collaborated with Germans during WWII and occupation of Dnipropetrovsk by Nazi troops, and then they fled to Germany. Ibid., 35–40.

13 See this case in SBU, f.1, op. 1, spr. 454, ark. 9–30.

14 Ibid., 10, 9.

15 Ibid., 10–11. As on KGB reported, "She was hiding her staying with Americans, in their apartments [in West Germany]."

16 Ibid., 11–12.

17 Ibid., 13–14.

18 Ibid., 14–15.

19 Ibid., 16.

20 Ibid., 17.

21 Ibid., 18.

22 Ibid., 18–19.

23 Ibid., 20–21.

24 Ibid., 21–22.

25 Ibid., 23–24. The KGB agents even found her secret notebook with "the notes of numerous addresses of people, living in different cities of Ukraine, with very serious compromising materials on some of them." See these notes in ibid., 25–28.

26 Ibid., 28–29.

27 See photos of Safianova in ibid., 31–32. I used also the information about this case from my interview with Ivan Grigorovich K., a retired KGB officer, February 3, 2019, Kyiv, Ukraine.

28 SBU, f. 1, op. 1, spr. 455, ark. 178.

29 Ibid., 178–179.

30 Ibid., 179.

31 Ibid., 180. See also photos of an "agent *Natasha*" on ark. 177a and 177b, spr. 455, f. 1., op.1.

32 SBU, f. 1, op. 1, spr. 731, ark. 46–47. "A majority of those [double] agents are from repatriates (disposed people who were in Germany and in the American zones of occupation)."

33 Ibid., 8–10.

34 SBU, f. 1, op. 1, spr. 455, ark. 184.

35 Ibid., 189.

36 See, e.g., such a plan in SBU, f. 1, op. 1, spr. 456, ark. 34–46.

37 Ibid., 34–35.

38 As the KGB operatives noted in their reports from America, the CIA operatives "selected in the reserve of their agents those Ukrainians, who were born in the USA, fluent in English, and who looked like the Americans; they had to know the Ukrainian language, the Soviet way of life, etc.; they could be include in the touristic groups, visiting the USSR, for collecting the intelligence information; they MUST be included in the touristic groups of the progressive (communist like) groups of the American Ukrainians." Quoted from SBU, f. 16, op. 1, spr. 949, ark. 422–423. Compare with the similar documents of 1984 in ibid., spr. 1215, ark. 35.

39 SBU, f. 16, op. 1, spr. 949, ark. 120–121.

40 SBU, f. 16, op. 1, spr. 1110, ark. 66–93.

41 SBU, f. 1, op. 1, spr. 456, 54–55, 56. In the official KGB of 1955 from Odesa, only local Jews had the illegal contacts with US diplomats, who visited the city of Odesa in March 1955: "On March 8, 1955, on Karl Marx street of Odesa [American diplomats] approached the diner and began to look at that diner's menu. Somebody approached them near this diner. It was a Jew who worked at a storage center in Odessa, Vitebskii Isaak. They went sightseeing in Odessa again, an hour before of their train departure, they visited a restaurant *Intourist* for a supper, and somebody tried to approach them again (he also was a Jew, a Soviet engineer) ... Except those two cases of contacts, the Americans behaved well and did not initiate any contacts with the Soviet citizens."

42 SBU, f. 16, op. 1, spr. 881, ark. 36–40.

43 Ibid. ark. 147–150.

44 Ibid., 121, 140–142. Some old retired KGB officers believed that many "outrageous cases of this kind" were removed from KGB/SBU files later. I refer to my interview with Ivan Grigorovich K., a retired KGB officer, February 3, 2019, Kyiv, Ukraine.

45 SBU, f. 1, op. 1, spr. 455, ark. 174–176.

46 Ibid., 175. Former KGB officer confirmed this in my interview with Ivan Grigorovich K., a retired KGB officer, February 3, 2019, Kyiv, Ukraine.

47 Ibid., 176. In the early 1960s,

48 The KGB officers from Dnipropetrovsk appreciated a role of this KGB agent in "creating the serious problems with emigration for the local Jewish residents." I refer to my old interview with Igor T.

49 SBU, f. 1, op. 1, spr. 454, ark. 375–379.

50 I got this explanation from a few KGB officers. One of them came from my interview with Ivan Grigorovich K., a retired KGB officer, February 3, 2019, Kyiv, Ukraine. Another came from Igor T. from Dnipro.

51 According to the KGB investigation, "Popova, a Russian, fled to Kharbin, then to Tokyo, worked for Japanese intelligence as a Russian interpreter. She has a daughter from a Japanese officer, she was sent to Philippines where she worked with her daughter for Japanese, trying to meet the members of Soviet military mission there." Ibid., 378.

52 As the KGB officers reported, "Dinaburg Bella, a Jew, a US citizen, a daughter of *"beloemigrant"* and agent of US counter-intelligence and Intelligence Service as well." Ibid., 379.

53 Interview with Ivan Grigorovich K.

54 Ibid., 379.

55 According to my interview with Ivan Grigorovich K., such agents played the role of "provocateurs" during various active measures, which targeted the "compromised" foreign visitors.

56 BSU, f. 1, op. 1, spr. 717, ark. 22–23.

57 Ibid., 23.

58 Interview with Igor T.

59 SBU, f. 1, op. 1, spr. 716, ark. 399–402.

60 Ibid., 401.

61 Ibid., 403–404.

62 Interview with Igor T. Compare with how the KGB and the FSB used the illegal businesses of Soviet Jewish emigrants in New York City, such as Semion Kislin and Semion Mogilevich, in Craig Unger, *American Kompromat: How the KGB Cultivated Donald Trump, and Related Tales of Sex, Greed, Power, and Treachery* (New York: Dutton, 2021), 28–36, 158–159.

63 SBU, f. 16, op. 1, spr. 919, ark. 142ff.

64 SBU, f. 16, op. 1, spr. 993, ark. 205–208.

65 Quoted from Craig Unger, *American Kompromat*, 31.

66 In the early 1960s, the KGB continued to monitor the families of the Ukrainian Jews, who used to live in the USA before WWII and later returned to the USSR as the Soviet citizens. After their experience with Soviet realities, some of those families tried to re-immigrate back to the US and contacted American officials from the US Embassy. The KGB arrested them and used "their Zionist-American" connections, as a pretext for their persecution. See the Rosenbergs family (father, son and daughter) case in the Kyiv KGB office in SBU, f. 16, op. 1, spr. 944, ark. 70–77.

67 Craig Unger, *American Kompromat*, 30–32.

68 See KGB reports about the "anti-Jewish" operations in SBU, f. 16, op. 1, spr. 1106, 51–53, 85–86, 119–126, 133–140; spr. 1151, ark. 277–281.

69 See about the KGB operations against Jewish music in SBU, f. 16, op. 1, spr. 1051, ark. 354–357.

3 Communists and the Political Left in Capitalist America: A Case of Peter Krawchuk and John Kolasky

In its struggle against the Ukrainian nationalists ("*banderovtsy*" in the official Soviet documents) in America, the Ukrainian KGB tried to also use the American Ukrainian Left Pro-Communist activists. Ukrainian Canadians, members of the Communist Party of Canada, became the "useful tools" of Soviet KGB meddling in the Ukrainian Diaspora affairs in America as early as the 1960s. One of those communists was Peter Krawchuk (Petro Kravchuk) (1911–1997), who had visited Soviet Ukraine, as a member of the Canadian Ukrainian Communist delegations, almost every year since 1947. From the early beginning he became connected to the KGB people among Soviet Ukrainian diplomats, such as Oleksii (Oleksa) Voina.[1] At the same time, the KGB administration tried to attack and discredit those Ukrainian Canadian Communists, such as John Kolasky (Ivan Koliaska) (1915–1997), who became frustrated with the realities of life in Soviet Ukraine in the 1960s, witnessing Russification, the official suppression of political opposition and a rise of authoritarianism there.[2]

Peter Krawchuk – "The Best Canadian Friend of Soviet Ukraine"

During the 1960s and through the 1980s, the entire reading audience in Soviet Ukraine knew the name of one Canadian Ukrainian, who became the "best American" friend of all Soviet Ukrainians.[3] His name was Petro Kravchuk (Peter Krawchuk in Canadian spelling). Almost every issue of *Vsesvit*, the Soviet Ukrainian magazine, which covered foreign literature and culture, published at least one article about this person or was written by Peter Krawchuk for Soviet Ukrainian audiences.[4] The Ukrainian state radio and television always broadcasted one or two interviews with him per year. For Soviet Americanists (the experts in American history, politics, economy and culture) Krawchuk became "the direct bridge" between Ukraine and "the attractive and forbidden capitalist America."[5] At the same time, for the KGB office in Kyiv, the people like Krawchuk, were the important "tools" for exploring and influencing not only the Ukrainian diaspora in North America (both in the US and Canada), but also the

DOI: 10.4324/9781003212522-4

political and cultural situation of the "main adversary" (the United States and Canada) (Figure 3.1).

Peter Krawchuk was born on July 6, 1911, in the village of Stoianiv, in the Radekhiv district of Lviv Region in Western Ukraine, into a peasant family. His grandfather Grigorii, originally from Eastern Ukraine ("Dnipro River region") in the Russian Empire, where he lived under the laws of serfdom, deserted from the Russian imperial army, and fled to the Austrian Empire. He settled there, married a local Ukrainian peasant girl and rented land from the local landlord to feed his growing family. His grandson Petro took classes in the local public school, called *gymnasia*, which was organized by the Ukrainian pedagogical society *Ridna shkola*. In 1926 the Polish administration closed this school, because of an involvement of the Ukrainian leftist pedagogues, who taught there. But eventually Petro was influenced by his Marxist teachers, and he continued his self-education in the public library of the Ukrainian *Prosvita* organization. After 1926 he became an active participant in the local Ukrainian farmers' cooperative movement and in the local Marxist youth groups. In 1929 Petro even joined the local

Figure 3.1 Peter Krawchuk.

Komsomol organization.[6] Trying to escape poverty and the persecution of Polish police, in March 1930, Petro Krawchuk immigrated to Canada, where his brothers Mykola (in 1911) and Ivan (in 1927) had already settled and became Canadian citizens.

Later on, one of his Canadian colleagues described this period of life in Krawchuk's official obituary as the following:

> Mr. Krawchuk arrived in Winnipeg in April 1930. He wasted no time in linking up with the pro-Communist Ukrainian Labor Farmer Temple Association (ULFTA). By 1931 he was a member of the Central Committee of the ULFTA's Youth Section. In 1936, he attended a ULFTA Higher Education Course, a six-month cadre training session. Upon graduation he was put to work at the ULFTA's flagship daily, *Ukrainski Robitnychi Visti* (Ukrainian Labor News). Mr. Krawchuk had found his home, and for the next 55 years he was to play a leading role in the Ukrainian Canadian pro-Communist press. He also broadened his other organizational activities, occupying executive positions and undertaking speaking tours. For the latter, Mr. Krawchuk was aided by a knack for storytelling, an affable manner and an exceptional memory. His growing stature within the organizational ranks was reflected by the fact that in 1940 he was among the ULFTA leaders interned (in his case until February 1942) after a number of left-wing organizations, including the ULFTA, were declared illegal by the Canadian government. Upon his release, he moved with his wife, Mary (née Sholdra, whom he married in 1936), to Toronto. In 1947 Mr. Krawchuk was part of a three-person mission to Ukraine that accompanied a large shipment of humanitarian aid for post-war reconstruction. He stayed on after the mission as a special correspondent for several pro-Communist Ukrainian newspapers in the West. After his return to Canada in 1949, Mr. Krawchuk spoke at public meetings about his generally favorable impressions of Ukraine. These gatherings aroused outrage among many recent Ukrainian arrivals to Canada, who tended to be strongly anti-Soviet in sentiment. Because of common outbreaks of violence, these meetings attracted the attention of the mainstream media. Mr. Krawchuk had been strident in his opposition to the admission of post-war refugees into Canada and participated vigorously in a smear campaign to portray them as fascist sympathizers.[7]

This official positive portrait dismissed the controversial character of the Krawchuk's relations with the KGB and political leadership of Soviet Ukraine, which Krawchuk himself in his memoirs mentioned many times, and which he tried to justify. Moreover, he acknowledged, as a majority of the Canadian leftists, that he took a side of Stalin's interpretation of the events in Soviet Ukraine after the Revolution of 1917, being in fact a very orthodox Stalinist in those days. As a result, Krawchuk took very negative and aggressive approaches against those Ukrainian emigrants who just recently, after WWII, arrived from Europe to Canada, whom he called "anti-Soviet pro-fascist nationalists."[8] After a release from Canadian prison in 1942, Krawchuk moved to Toronto where he joined the editorial staff of the newspaper *Ukrains'ke zhyttia* (The Ukrainian Life). Paradoxically, during this period of time, Krawchuk's political career symbolized the intellectual limitations of the Ukrainian Canadian Communist leadership, despite their "zeal and dedication" to the Leftist politics, when they worked for pro-communist organizations all their lives, without having time for improving their education and widening their intellectual erudition. As one of his former comrades described this, "with only a minimal formal education and a six-month higher educational course he emerged as one of the top Ukrainian communist leaders and journalists in Canada."[9]

During the summer of 1945 in Edmonton, Alberta, as a journalist of *Ukrains'ke zhyttia*, Krawchuk met with the members of the official delegation of the Ukrainian SSR, who were flying back to Ukraine from San-Francisco, where they took part in a session of the General Assembly of the United Nations and made a stopover in Canada. During the official dinner in Edmonton organized by the Ukrainian Canadians to honor the Ukrainian delegation, Krawchuk met with Dmytro Manuil'skyi, a minister of foreign affairs, an "academician" (member of the Ukrainian Academy of Sciences) Volodymyr Palladin, a writer Leonid Novichenko, and Oleksa Voina, a head of the special department of the Ukrainian SSR Ministry of Foreign Affairs. After this meeting, Krawchuk became a personal friend of Novichenko and Voina. His "special" friendship with Voina, who officially worked for the KGB, would shape Krawchuk's relations with Soviet Ukraine for many years to come. Moreover, Oleksa Voina, through his connections in Kyiv, will be the instrumental figure in the Soviet Ukrainian political hierarchy, providing support and funding for all Krawchuk's visits to Soviet Ukraine.[10]

On July 27–28, 1946, Canadian communists organized a Ukrainian festival in Edmonton, and they invited for this festival *Ukrains'ke tovarystvo kul'turnogo zv'iazku z zakordonom* (the Ukrainian Society of Cultural Relations with Abroad [USCRA]) from Kyiv, which sent a group of Soviet Ukrainian musicians, scholars and journalists.[11] Krawchuk not only became an active participant of this event as a journalist, he was also invited as a representative of TOUK (*Tovarystvo ob'iednanykh ukrainskykh kanadtsiv*) [AUUC (The Association of the United Ukrainian Canadians) in English] for all future meetings with the official Soviet Ukrainian delegations. In the fall of 1946 Krawchuk went to New York City for the official opening of the General Assembly of the United Nations as a special correspondent and as a representative of TOUK. Krawchuk participated in the meeting of the League of American Ukrainians with a delegation of Soviet Ukraine, including Manuil'skyi and Voina. This meeting with Voina strengthened his relations with the Ministry of Foreign Affairs and at the same time, (unknowingly for Krawchuk) with the KGB in Kyiv.[12]

Krawchuk's first trip to Soviet Ukraine started in December 1947. Canadian Ukrainians collected the money to help the children of Soviet Ukraine, especially those who lost their parents during WWII. Using these funds, Canadian pro-communist organizations purchased various gifts, food products for the Ukrainian orphans, and sent all of this by steamboat to Soviet Ukraine. Krawchuk was included in the official delegation, which supervised a reception of these gifts in Odesa sea port and their future distribution. As a journalist, representing various Communist periodicals form Canada, Krawchuk stayed in Soviet Ukraine longer and eventually spent almost two years there (without his family) from December 1947 until mid-1949. Although, he witnessed spreading Russification in Ukraine and talked to numerous Ukrainian intellectuals (like a poet Maksym Ryl'skyi), who complained to him about this, Krawchuk did not criticize Soviet authorities in public after his return to Canada.[13] Krawchuk "toured Canada in 1949 reporting on his recent trip" to the USSR. During one such presentation in Saskatchewan, on October 10, 1949, he addressed a crowd "which consisted of a few Displaced Persons" (DP), "recent arrivals from Europe and district residents" of the Ukrainian origin. According to witnesses, the "DPs heckled and challenged" his "praise of the Soviet Union, suggesting he 'was painting the wrong picture of the whole situation ... and that conditions are not as [Krawchuk described them].' The situation escalated and a fight broke out among audience members."[14] Among other acts of violence, another witness noted, "one woman slapped another man's face." The gathering broke up when "one Displaced Person [having] no handy weapon at his disposal, took off one of his shoes and threw it at [Krawchuk]." Shortly afterward, Krawchuk and his supporters retired to a nearby farm to finish the meeting. Krawchuk had met with similar opposition earlier that month at the Winnipeg Ukrainian Labour Temple. "The meeting was turned into a riot when some of the attending displaced persons raised objections to the manner Krawchuk answered their pertinent questions." The trend continued into December, when Krawchuk spoke at a gathering in Timmins, Ontario. *Ukrainske zhyttia* reported a "bloody clash ... resulting in the injuries of several persons ..."[15] As another Canadian contemporary of those events explained, "The relations between the Ukrainian pro-communists and the refugees were further aggravated by the communist glorification of Soviet power as the source of all virtue and righteousness. What irritated the newcomers most was the degrading language used in describing them."[16]

Krawchuk ... "after spending two years in Ukraine, also experienced the ire of the incensed refugees. Intimately acquainted with the situation in Ukraine, they fired a barrage of questions at him, which he could not answer ... The questioners, one hundred of the seven or eight hundred present, were interrupted, fighting ensued and the police were called to quell the riot." At the AUUC branch in Timmins in December 1949, the refugees "intended to challenge Krawchuk at the meeting. Denied admittance, they gathered in front of AUUC hall. Other citizens who were also hostile to the communists, joined them, forming a crowd about two hundred persons. Some began throwing bricks and stones, through the windows, others ripped off the railing along the stairs leading to the front entrance and battered down the door. Nine people were injured by missiles or personal assault."[17]

As a journalist of Canadian communist press, "Krawchuk specialized in denouncing the Ukrainian 'bourgeois nationalists.'"[18] But even his critics, such as John Kolasky, acknowledged that during the 1950s Krawchuk was "quite disturbed by the wide prevalence of the Russian language in Ukraine."[19] Yet, Krawchuk tried to be careful about openly criticizing the Soviet authorities in Canada. Meanwhile, he kept visiting Soviet Ukraine using the funding from the Soviet tourist agencies. Oleksa Voina helped Krawchuk publish his book in Soviet Ukraine in 1956 and to get good Soviet royalties for this publication. In 1962, the Soviet government helped him to enroll (free of charge) his daughter Larisa in the undergraduate program of Kyiv State University. During the 1950s and the 60s, Krawchuk supported all political decisions of the Soviet government. In 1955–1957, he took side of the CPSU and the KGB efforts to persuade expatriates to return to Soviet Ukraine from Latin America and Canada, and he blamed the "Ukrainian nationalists" for trying to stop and discredit this campaign.[20]

Krawchuk was always an active public critic of the so-called fascist Ukrainian nationalism, which tried to break relations between Ukrainian Canadians and Soviet Ukraine. The KGB provided him (via the Soviet Embassy) with the information about the Ukrainian nationalists' collaborating with the Nazis during the German occupation of Soviet Ukraine. Krawchuk used this KGB material for his numerous publications under the pseudonym of Marko Terlytsia.[21] In February of 1962, the Ukrainian KGB organized assistance in collecting the documentary materials in the Soviet Ukrainian state archives about the collaboration of one Canadian Ukrainian Yulian Tarnovych with Nazis during WWII. After the war Tarnovych fled with Germans, and eventually, he settled in Canada. Krawchuk, who was an editor of the Ukrainian Canadian Left periodical *Zhyttia i Slovo*, in his publications criticized Ukrainian nationalists in Canada, such as Tarnovych, for their collaboration with Germans in Nazi's occupied Ukraine during the war. Tarnovych sued Krawchuk for his public criticism, which was published in the numerous issues of Krawchuk's periodical. Meanwhile, the KGB decided to help and provide Krawchuk with "*kompromat*" of documents about the crimes committed by Tarnovych during WWII for the ongoing session of the Canadian court in December 1962. Thus, the KGB proved that Tarnovych was an editor-in-chief of and a major author for the newspaper *Ridna zemlia*, which openly supported the Nazi occupational regime in Lviv. They provided Krawchuk also with the materials of Tarnovych publications in a SS Galychyna division's newspaper *Do peremogy* during the war. Moreover, the KGB agents gave Krawchuk and

Figure 3.2 John Kolasky.

other Canadian Communists the documentary materials about OUN-Nazi collaboration to discredit the leaders of Ukrainian nationalists in America, such as Yaroslav Stetsko, Lev Dobrianskii and Peter Stark, who played a prominent role in the Ukrainian Congress Committee of America.[22]

Paradoxically, the KGB used Krawchuk not only against "Ukrainian nationalists," but also against those Canadian Ukrainian communists who openly criticized Russification of Soviet Ukraine. The most scandalous case of such a cooperation with Soviet authorities against "deviation of Canadian comrades" was a story of a Canadian communist John Kolasky. This story revealed not only a danger of such cooperation, but also demonstrated a precarious nature of the relations between American/ Canadian communists and the Communist Party of the Soviet Union (Figure 3.2).

Russification of Soviet Ukraine, John Kolasky and the KGB

In 1968, Peter Krawchuk and other Canadian Communists became directly involved in the special ideological campaign, organized by the KGB to discredit John Kolasky (Ivan Koliaska). In 1963–1965 Kolasky was a student of the Higher Party School of the Central Committee of the Communist Party of Ukraine in Kyiv, and then in 1968, after his return to Canada, he managed to publish an "anti-Soviet book" about the state system of education in Soviet Ukraine, exposing the official policy of Russification there.[23] According to his official obituary,

John Kolasky was born on October 5, 1915, in Cobalt, a mining town in northern Ontario. Like many other young men searching for work,

John Kolasky rode freight trains during the Great Depression. Like many of his generation, this experience radicalized him: he became a Marxist and joined the Communist Party of Canada. In the post-war period, Mr. Kolasky studied at the universities of Saskatchewan and Manitoba, as well as at the University of Toronto, where he received an M.A. in history in 1950. He subsequently taught high school in Manitoba and Ontario. In 1963, the pro-Communist Association of United Ukrainian Canadians sent him to Ukraine to attend the Higher School of the Central Committee of the Communist Party of Ukraine. Here, Mr. Kolasky's illusions about the Soviet Union were shattered. He soon realized that it was not a workers' state, and also recognized the harmful effects of Russification on the Ukrainian language and culture. It is not common for a middle-aged man to break with strongly held convictions, as well as to have the courage and honesty to state openly and unequivocally that he was mistaken. Yet that is exactly what Mr. Kolasky did. While still in Ukraine, he became aware of the growing movement of dissent against Soviet policies, and soon befriended activists of the young Ukrainian intelligentsia (Shestydesiatnyky). He also began to gather information on Russification policies and practices in Ukraine. When it was discovered by the authorities that he was sending this information abroad, Mr. Kolasky was arrested, imprisoned, interrogated for several weeks and then expelled from Ukraine in 1965.[24]

Meanwhile, the KGB documents allow us to explore the "Kolasky case" (*Koliaska* in the official Soviet spelling) in detail. As early as January 14, 1965, the KGB officers reported about the "nationalistic views" of Kolasky, who expressed them publicly, and about his meetings with the Ukrainian "nationalistic intellectuals" during 1964 in Kyiv. According to their first report, in September 1963, "Ivan Vasilievich Kolasky, a Canadian teacher from the secondary school in Toronto, who was highly recommended by the Association of the United Ukrainian Canadians (AUUC), the progressive organization which fights the Ukrainian nationalists in America," arrived in Kyiv to start his studies. Kolasky already had a good reputation of a loyal Canadian Communist, who had visited the Soviet Union in 1962 as a leader of the tourist group sent by AUUC. As the KGB agents noted, during all his official meetings and conversations with Soviet people, Kolasky declared that after his graduation from the Kyiv communist party's school and his return to Canada, his main goal would be the constant struggle against the enemies of the Soviet Union. He always emphasized that he was "a communist on the frontline of the fight with the enemies of the USSR and had already contributed a lot to a progressive movement in Canada."[25] At the same time, the KGB agent noticed in Kolasky's communications with Soviet people the certain ideological evaluations, which contradicted the traditional image of Soviet Marxist-Leninist. During one conversation with his acquaintance in Chernivtsy in August 1964, Kolasky showed that he was well aware of the activities of the Canadian Trotskyites, and called them "brave, decisive guys", who were "the supporters of peace and democracy," and who, according to his opinion, played "a positive role in the political life of Canada."[26] Moreover, Kolasky doubted that AUUC and other active progressive organizations of the Ukrainian immigrants were capable to pursue any positive work in America uniting American Ukrainians. According to him, the most influential among Canadian Ukrainians was the *Ukrainske national'ne ob'edinennia* (UNO), which as he noted, "recently took a loyal positive approach towards the USSR." The KGB agents in Canada informed their supervisors in Kyiv that Kolasky visited the meetings of this organization on the regular basis and he was well acquainted with its members. Telling about the drifting UNO to the political left, Kolasky confessed to his friends about his plans to create a new "democratic emigrant organization" in Canada: a combination of AUUC and UNO and to become its leader. That was why Kolasky tried to use his visits to Ukraine to establish good relations with and get support from the Soviet Ukrainian authorities. Yet, the KGB agents complained that Kolasky's actions "contradicted the AUUC goals and weakened it from inside [by connecting it to *Banderovtsy*]," while AUUC was "a progressive pro-Soviet organization" of the Ukrainian diaspora "fighting Ukrainian nationalists in America."[27]

The special KGB report noted that Kolasky observed the various sides of life in Soviet Ukraine "only from the nationalist positions," praised in public the conditions of life in capitalist countries, initiated discussions with Soviet Ukrainians ["whenever he had an opportunity"] about the national question in Ukraine. He established very close connections with a writer Borys D. Antonenko-Davydovych (1899–1984), who was released from the Soviet jail and exile, and returned to Kyiv in 1957.[28] Kolasky collected the "anti-Soviet information [about the police persecution of Ukrainian intellectuals]" from Antonenko and, "using a special secret code of writing," put it in his notebooks, "emphasizing [in a conversation with Antonenko] that he had to know such precious facts." As the KGB agents discovered, Kolasky offered Antonenko his assistance in publishing abroad Antonenko's written works and poetry, which were not allowed to be published in the USSR. Moreover, he helped Antonenko to get the forbidden anti-Soviet publications from Canada, bringing the clippings from these publications to Kyiv. Those officers noted that Kolasky in his conversations with the Soviet officials from the Society of Cultural Connections with Ukrainians Abroad (SCCUA) tried to "prove an inappropriateness of the exposure and compromising of the Ukrainian nationalists, including the war criminals" by *Visti z Ukrainy* (a Soviet periodical released by the SCCUA for the Ukrainians living abroad), stating that the SCCUA "had to search for re-convincing that category of emigrants with the goal of attracting them to the Soviet side." As the KGB operatives reported, Kolasky even publicly characterized "as moderate and loyal to the USSR such nationalists, like a former editor of *Banderovite* newspaper *Gomin Ukrainy* Rakhmannyi-Oliinyk, a leader of

Ukrainskoi golovnoj vyzvol'noi rady Marunchak, an editor of the newspaper *Vil'ne slovo* Stepan Rossokha and Canadian senator Pavlo Yuzyk." The KGB officers were afraid that Kolasky could use his studies from the communist party school in Kyiv for "collecting the tendentious anti-Soviet information," and after his return to Canada "for undermining and weakening a position of the AUUC and other progressive" pro-Soviet organizations in America. Therefore, the KGB leaders recommended to the communist party school's administration to "pay the special attention to Kolasky's ideological education."[29]

Meanwhile, on January 13, 1965, the KGB prepared the special "Memorandum about Criticism of Russification in Soviet Ukraine by Koliaska, Canadian Communist, a teacher from Toronto" for the communist party leadership in Kyiv.[30] The KGB officers informed their supervisors that Kolasky collected the information about Russification and "raised this issue all the time talking with the local Ukrainians." In his conversations with the Soviet administration, Kolasky "insisted on changing Soviet attitudes toward the Ukrainian nationalists in America, trying to attract them on Soviet side and criticized orthodox leadership of TOUK like Krawchuk, who blindly believe and follow official Soviet propaganda," at the same time he "praised American Trotskyites as brave and decisive fellows, who played a very progressive role in political life of Canada and the United States, because, according to him, they were proponents of peace and democracy."[31]

As the final KGB report about Kolasky, which was submitted on January 6, 1968, noted, "In the Ukrainian SSR, according to Kolasky, there was uprooting (*iskorenenie*) of Ukrainian language and culture; in all schools of Soviet Ukraine, Russian language as a language of instruction was domineering, because Soviet political leadership ignored Lenin's national policy [and replaced it with Stalin's politics of Russification]."[32] Being "tendentiously inclined toward national politics of CPSU, he illegally spread the slanderous materials in Ukraine, including the [openly] nationalistic anti-Soviet documents, with a criticism of the national policy in the USSR, about so-called Russification of the Ukrainian nation during socialism." The documents "he collected, Kolasky illegally sent in Canada."[33]

Eventually, Kolasky was arrested by the KGB for doing this and all his materials in Kyiv were confiscated by the KGB officers. During the KGB interrogations, Kolasky "accepted his guilt and repented, promising to avoid such actions in the future." Under a pressure from the KGB, Kolasky's studies in Kyiv were interrupted and he had to return to Canada. In August 1965, Kolasky was sent back to Canada (without a publication in Soviet press about his actions). But he started his criticism of Russification of Soviet Ukraine again, addressing "the nationalistic meeting" in New York City in 1966, and then preparing his book, which would be published in 1968. The KGB recommended the CPSU leadership to inform Canadian Communists about the anti-Soviet activities of Koliaska. Moreover, in 1968, the KGB recommended immediately using the loyal American and Canadian Communists, like Peter Krawchuk, to organize an ideological campaign to discredit John Kolasky (Ivan Koliaska).[34]

Meanwhile, after his return to Canada, Kolasky shared his Soviet experience with Canadian media, which presented his story about a publication of that book as following:

> Disillusioned with Soviet reality and incensed by Russification, he (Kolasky) had collected materials which revealed the nature of the Soviet national policy and had surreptitiously channeled them to Canada. The book was based on a mass of Soviet documents, statistical and other data and unpublished materials not available in the West. It was a comprehensive study which revealed a planned drive by the central authorities in Moscow to impose arbitrarily the Russian language and culture on non-Russians ... Coming out of time when the question of Russification had aroused considerable interest, the book became an instant sensation. A Toronto daily in a frontpage review described it as "a time bomb ... designed to explode the myth of Soviet impartiality and equality in policies towards minority nationalities in the USSR."[35]

According to Kolasky, "it was no longer possible to deny the existence of planned and arbitrary Russification." Kolasky's book "caused considerable confusion among the members of the Ukrainian pro-communist organizations and consternation among their leaders." While the Ukrainian nationalist and other press discussed at great length the evidence presented in the book, the Ukrainian left media remained silent. In 1969 a pro-communist paper reprinted an attack on the book from a Soviet journal "for the information of our readers" but deleted the phrase "at the expense of imperialist moneybags" which is "probably regarded as libelous and which referred to the supposed source of funds for the book's publication."[36]

> As Kolasky noted, more evidence of Russification were published and indicated that Russification in Ukraine was being intensified. "To pacify the activists," Communist leaders had a special closed (AUUC) meeting on March 3, 1968, to discuss this issue. "The report, delivered by Krawchuk, alternated between praise for and criticism of Soviet policies. He enumerated the achievements in Ukraine and declared that "only Soviet power brought national freedom for Ukrainians."[37]

At the same time, even Krawchuk and his pro-Soviet comrades tried to raise the question of Russification with Soviet officials in Ukraine after their first trips to the USSR, and they were very critical of the dominance of the Russian language in Soviet Ukraine.[38] When in March of 1966, this issue of Russification was raised at the 12th Convention of the AUUC in Winnipeg,

"Krawchuk attempted to reassure the delegates. He replied that mistakes had been committed in relation to the national question, especially the Ukrainian language," that the Canadian communist leadership "had taken a stand on the matter several years ago and that the latest pronouncements of Soviet leaders indicated that the problem was under consideration."[39] In late March 1967, a special delegation of six Canadian Communists, including Krawchuk as an editor of *Zhyttia i Slovo*, were sent to Soviet Ukraine. As Kolasky explained, their purpose was to visit Ukraine "on a mission of inquiry and discussion concerning the policy and the experience of the Communist Party and the Government of Ukraine in dealing with the national question."[40] It was Kolasky's reference to the attempt by the Communist Party of Canada (CPC) to investigate a situation with the Russification in Ukraine. As a reaction to Kolasky's scandal of 1965, the group of six Canadian Communists, including Krawchuk, did, indeed, visit for a three weeks Soviet Ukraine, and submitted a final report which was very critical of Soviet nationalities policy. As Krawchuk's younger colleague described this later,

> It was, in fact, a bombshell that ignited a major controversy. Moscow applied strong pressure on the CPC to withdraw the report. Mr. Krawchuk and the other Ukrainian delegates of the mission fought against this, but to no avail. In October 1969 the report was withdrawn as an official CPC document, although it was acknowledged as having been received for information purposes. Mr. Krawchuk was personally criticized in the course of this controversy and, ironically, accused of aiding the "bourgeois nationalists."[41]

Soviet administration organized a pressure on Canadian communists to remove a report about Russification in Ukraine. The AUUC followed Moscow's orders (sent through the Soviet Embassy in Ottawa) and in April expelled Kolasky from the CPC and on May 21, 1968, the AUUC publicly indicted Kolasky for his anti-Soviet position. As Kolasky described this himself: "The charges were never presented to [him] in writing but were read to him. He was charged with conduct in Ukraine that was incompatible with membership in the AUUC, conduct that included the covert collection and transmission to Canada of materials on the national policy which Soviet authorities wished to suppress." With Krawchuk acting as prosecutor and the other members as judges, Kolasky was expelled from the AUUC. "Thus an organization which prided itself on being democratic and boasted a Canadian charter, expelled one of its veterans for participating in acts designed to expose Russification against which its leaders had only recently protested in report."[42]

After the recent scandal with Kolasky, suddenly, the KGB discovered a new wave of criticism from their own traditionally loyal supporters in Canada, like a group of Peter Krawchuk, who at the end of 1966 submitted a very detailed critical report to the Communist Party of Canada, blaming

Soviet leadership in Russification of Soviet Ukraine. During 1968, the KGB realized that Krawchuk took a critical position against Russification, "organizing his group among Canadian communists, who protested against negative developments in Soviet Ukraine." Now the KGB organized a special campaign to discredit Krawchuk and his followers in Canada as well.[43]

The first sign of the alarm about such a "dangerous Ukrainian nationalistic trend" among the loyal pro-Soviet Canadian communists came to the KGB office and the Ukrainian Communist Party leadership in Kyiv on February 19, 1968, from V. I. Yusko, an official of a consular office at the Soviet embassy in Canada. He reported that he invited to his office and had the long conversations with the activists of the AUUC, Roman (Ray) Dowhopoluk, Yurii (George) Krenz and Anton (Anthony) Bilecki. Eventually, Yusko summarized his conversations with them in the notes of his personal diary, which he submitted to the Soviet authorities in Kyiv. The KGB officers used these notes for their own investigation of this "dangerous trend."[44]

As Yusko noted, Dowhopoluk, Krenz and Bilecki told him about the appearance of "a new group among progressive Canadians, who blamed the Soviet leadership for serious mistakes in the national politics and for the limitations of the democratic rights of the citizens" of Soviet Ukraine, which "prevented the spreading of the progressive [communist] movement among Ukrainian Canadians." As they explained to him, a special delegation of the Canadian Communist Party raised these issues before the Soviet Communist leadership during its visit to the USSR in November 1966. After those negotiations with the Soviet leadership, Canadian communists composed their memorandum, approved by the Central Committee of CPC in Toronto.

According to Dowhopoluk's explanation, there were three groups among Canadian Communists, which differed in their approaches to these issues. One, represented by Krawchuk, "who was struggling to become a leader of the AUUC," tried to push the Soviet leadership in a direction of "the correcting the errors" in the issues of national question and democratization of political life in Soviet Ukraine. Peter Krawchuk initiated a serious discussion of all those questions with the communist leaders of Ukraine as early as 1966. The second group in CPC accepted Krawchuk's criticism of those mistakes made by the Soviet leaders, but it tried to avoid the "public criticism of and their interference in the internal affairs of the CPSU."[45] The third group of the Canadian communists "categorically rejected their right to judge the decisions of their comrades, Soviet communists." Dowhopoluk belonged to the last group.[46] According to Yusko, Krenz shared Dowhopoluk's position. He was "very frustrated with the new trends in progressive movement" among Canadian communists of the Ukrainian origin, who "now followed the Ukrainian nationalists and criticized Soviet nationality policy." Krenz blamed Krawchuk's group of Canadian communists in this politics. According to Krenz, Krawchuk "paid too much attention to the arguments of the Ukrainian nationalists about

Russification, collaborating with them, even supporting their idea of a creation of the separate pavilion of Soviet Ukraine for EKSPO-67 in Montreal.[47]

Only one Canadian guest of the Soviet embassy in 1968, Bilecki, entirely supported Krawchuk in these conversations with the Soviet official. He criticized the Soviet leaders for putting the limitations for the visits by the Ukrainian Canadians of their relatives in Soviet Ukraine. As Bilecki explained this to Yusko, the Soviet officials put various limits to these visits and called the Canadian guests "the rebels" (*smutiany*). In contrast to his comrades, guests of the Soviet embassy, who tried to be loyal to the Soviet authorities, Bilecki defended "the right of any Communist party in the world to criticize CPSU," protecting in this way "the democratic principles of internationalist Marxist politics."[48]

After this attempt to influence the position of Ukrainian Canadian communists, using the officials of the Soviet embassy, the KGB continued to monitor a development of these dangerous "nationalist trends" among the Canadian Left. The KGB analysts studied the numerous publications in Canadian press and radio broadcasting in both Canada and the USA "about criticism of Russification of Soviet Ukraine." According to their report, in early 1968 the Canadian Communist bulletin *Viewpoint* and a Communist newspaper *Zhyttia i slovo* not only openly criticized Communist leaders of Soviet Ukraine about "a betrayal of the national interests of the Ukrainian nation," but also "predicted the division among Canadian communists, caused by Russification and a lack of democracy in Soviet Ukraine."[49]

At the same time, in February and March of 1968, in their reports, the KGB analysts raised an alarm about the numerous discussions in the "emigrant nationalistic press" and in the Voice of America broadcasting in the USA and Canada about the "divisions between Canadian and Soviet communists," blaming Soviet leadership in Russification of Ukraine, and using John Kolasky's book about "the education in Soviet Ukraine" for their "anti-Soviet criticism."[50] The KGB analysts noted in their analysis "the alarming thing that this anti-Soviet book was written by a Communist with 30-years membership [Kolasky], who had an access to the confidential information and secret sources in Kyiv;" and they predicted that this would lead to "the serious divisions inside the Party of Canadian Communists, among whom 50% are Ukrainians."[51]

In September 1968, these analysts reported the first signs of such divisions during a meeting of Vsevolod Holub-Holubnychyi, the head of the Discussion Club Roundtable in New York, with the leadership of the AUUC in Toronto, Canada, and they noted the negative role of Peter Krawchuk during this meeting, who tried to create a new theoretical journal, which would unite the entire Ukrainian emigration "betraying the interests of [the communist movement by attracting the nationalists on his side]." Moreover, the KGB agents, who attended this meeting, noted the open criticism by the majority of the AUUC members of the "corrupt Krawchuk," who "was tempted by the Soviet resorts (*соблазнился на советские курорты*) and privileges [offered him by the Soviet authorities]."[52] But the most serious concern for the KGB was Krawchuk's constant and public criticism of Russification of Soviet Ukraine, especially after 1968. At the end of this year, Krawchuk's periodical published a poem "To My Brother," written by a Ukrainian Canadian AUUC member Mykhailo Sribniak. This poem criticized Russification and the imperial attitudes of Russians toward Ukrainians. In it, the author wrote of "that which has for years weighed upon our hearts" and asked, "Where is that equality … that has been set down on paper?" He replied that there was none. Instead, there prevailed "coarse brutality." Sribniak concluded his poem with the question: "How long will you continue to keep us, your younger brothers, in subjection?" Since the Russians regarded themselves as the elder brothers of the Ukrainians, the reference in the poem was obvious. This publication was another sign that Krawchuk "moved out of the control of the Soviet authorities."[53]

As KGB agents reported, Peter Krawchuk always complained about the increasing of everyday Russification of the Ukrainian society in his confidential conversations with the Ukrainian intellectuals in Soviet Ukraine. Even after his distancing from Kolasky's critical position about this issue, in October 1969 he told his Ukrainian acquaintances that he raised the issue of Russification after his visit to Soviet Ukraine in 1966 in his report and supported his criticism during discussion with Tim Buck and other Canadian communists in the Plenum of CPC. According to the KGB officer, [in October 1969] "Kravchuk considered that material level of life of Soviet people increased dramatically comparing to the previous years, although he worried that 'CPSU did not fulfill the Leninist principles of national politics in Ukraine.' Kravchuk also reported that visiting TsK KPU (the Central Committee of the Communist Party of Ukraine), he intended to continue a conversation about the arrests of the Ukrainian writers (*literatorov*) and about the alleged ousting the Ukrainian language with the Russian one (*вытеснение украинского языка русским*)."[54]

As the KGB reported, an official delegation of the AUUC, including Krawchuk and Bilecki, was invited by the Society of Cultural Connections with Ukrainians living Abroad [SCCUA] to visit Soviet Ukraine in October 1969. During October 16–25, 1969, the Canadian guests visited Western Ukraine and participated in the thirty-year anniversary of the unification of Western Ukraine with Soviet Ukraine. After their arrival to Kyiv on October 26, they met the Soviet officials at the Central Committee of KPU and the Ukrainian Council of Ministers and tried to discuss the issue "about the arrests of representatives of creative intellectuals in Ukraine, which, according to their words, would negatively affect the activities of progressive pro-Soviet organizations [of the Ukrainian Diaspora] in the United States and Canada."[55]

The KGB agent, who was present during Krawchuk's conversation with the Soviet officials in Kyiv on October 27, 1969, described in detail its major themes. First, Krawchuk tried to justify his difficult "problematic position of a person who was a Ukrainian patriot" [criticizing Russification and ousting Ukrainian language from the life of Soviet Ukrainians] and "at the same time, who was a Canadian communist [trying to follow the party line]. Krawchuk explained that he was criticized from both sides ("was under the double fire"): from the Ukrainian nationalists abroad [for being inconsistent in his criticism of Russification], and from the Ukrainian patriotic intellectuals in Soviet Ukraine [for being silent during repressions of those intellectuals by the Soviet police]. Then he criticized the KPU officials, who could not understand the major principles of political democracy, which existed in "capitalist Canada." Krawchuk explained that in the recent situation of "democratic dialogue" the Canadian pro-communist organizations such as the AUUC "had to develop the new approaches for work with the Ukrainian emigrants, rather than just literally follow the recommendations of *Radians'ka Ukraina* [the official Soviet periodical from Kyiv]." He complained that the officials of the Soviet Embassy in Canada called him to visit them on the regular basis, and usually shouted their orders "how to behave" and demanded that he re-publish Soviet newspaper essays in his Canadian periodical, ["treating him as a servant"]. Krawchuk criticized the Soviet government official visitors to Canada, who publicly tried to interfere in the AUUC politics, after spending just two or three days in Canada, without understanding the situation in this ["foreign to them"] country and imposed their ["sometime very stupid and unprofessional"] opinion on Canadians.[56]

Moreover, the KGB reports demonstrated that Krawchuk gradually took the position of John Kolasky, another Canadian communist, who "deviated from Soviet interpretations of Leninist nationality policy." In 1969, the KGB agents noted how Krawchuk established his personal contacts with the Ukrainian "dissidents," the former close friends of Kolasky in 1963–1965. Krawchuk openly maintained his personal contacts with Oles Honchar, whose novel *Sobor* was officially criticized by the Soviet administration as a "nationalistic book," and the Ukrainian "dissident" writers, such as Borys Antonenko-Davydovych and Zinoviia Franko.[57] That is why even in the 1980s, the KGB continued its close surveillance over Krawchuk's actions in both Canada and Soviet Ukraine, trying to stop his "anti-Soviet criticism of the Russification of Soviet Ukraine." But at the same time, the KGB created other, more personal, means of control over the Canadian Ukrainian communists, such as Peter Krawchuk.[58]

The KGB administration in Kyiv also was afraid of establishing of the new connections between the Canadian Ukrainians, especially their Left Pro-Communist groups, such as Peter Krawchuk's group, and the Chinese Communist leadership. According to the KGB agents in Canada, the Ukrainian diaspora in their criticism of the Russification of Soviet Ukraine and their demands for more democracy and autonomy for Ukraine found "overwhelming support in Maoist China." Thus, in 1972 the KGB agents reported to the Ukrainian Communist leadership about the creation of the Canadian travel agency *Travel Unlimited* in 1971, which "became the direct connection between the Ukrainian Canadians and Chinese Maoists," including "their tight connections" to Chinese communist regime. One of those Canadians, Mokryi Roman, who was a friend of both Peter Krawchuk and John Kolasky, "took classes in the Higher Party School in Kyiv in Soviet Ukraine in 1963-66, using recommendation of AUUC."[59] The KGB agents noted that in November 1979, a group of Chinese Communists visited Harvard University, where "they met Omelyan Prytsak at Harvard Ukrainian Research Institute, and they expressed their obvious interest in a situation with political dissidents in Ukraine."[60] Since 1972 until the 1980s, the KGB reported on regular basis about these growing contacts between the Ukrainian Canadian Left and the "Maoist" Chinese leadership. As the participants of these events noted, this moment of the Chinese connections, besides the "Fascist nature of Canadian Ukrainians" was used by the KGB leadership to discredit the role of Ukrainian diaspora in America in their criticism of the "ideological unreliability" of even pro-Communist Ukrainians, who lived in America.[61]

Peter Krawchuk as a Link between the "Seductive" America and the "Corrupt Soviet System," and the Problems of Soviet Material Support

Despite all their criticism of Russification, persecution of the Ukrainian intellectuals in Soviet Ukraine and their public attempts to distance from the anti-democratic and anti-Ukrainian politics of the Soviet authorities, the Canadian Ukrainian pro-communist activists, such as Peter Krawchuk, were unable to completely cut their relations with the Soviet administration of Ukraine. Their material well-being, even their Canadian businesses depended on those relations. As Leonid Leshchenko, a Soviet Ukrainian Americanist scholar, who knew Krawchuk personally very well, noted,

> [F]or all of us, Soviet Ukrainian scholars, who dreamed to visit the capitalist America, Peter Krawchuk became the important personal connection, allowing to fulfill our dream to go there by receiving his official invitation to do this. To some extent, he was a crucial link between the dream world of the "seductive" America, uniting both the US and Canada in one imaginative entity, and the Soviet Ukrainian intellectuals (scholars, writers, artists, musicians), who represented through the KGB, or through various Soviet professional organizations (still connected to the KGB), the corrupt Soviet system of power. At the same time, this Soviet system established its material control over Krawchuk, using not only the Soviet officials in bribing him and monitoring his behavior, but using also us, the Ukrainian intellectuals, who visited Canada as the Soviet contacts of Krawchuk, bringing him

the more personal, but still initiated by the same system, messages-reminders of control and dependence. These connections exacerbated the tragedy of personal drama for the pro-communist Ukrainian Canadians, like Krawchuk, who loved Ukraine, but who became controlled and manipulated by the same political system, which had already Russified and corrupted their Motherland. Moreover, the Soviet system funded financially all Krawchuk's trips abroad and even his capitalist enterprises in Canada as well.[62]

This was a tragic paradox of the life of Canadian communists of the Ukrainian origin, such as Krawchuk. On the one side, he supported the major ideological and political campaigns, initiated by the Soviet communist leadership, and publicly promoted and supported the Soviet international initiatives. On the other side, Peter Krawchuk understood the "dangerous" influences of the KGB in "corrupting" both Soviet Ukrainian politicians and intellectuals and American/Canadian communists. In his conversations, recorded by the KGB agents, in his published memoirs he always was critical of these KGB connections and those Soviet Ukrainians, connected to the KGB, who contacted him during his lifetime.[63] Krawchuk had his own serious personal conflicts with the leading figures in the political establishment of Soviet Ukraine, blaming them in "a betrayal of the national interests" of Soviet Ukrainians. He could not stand Professor Yuri Kondufor, a director of the Institute of History of Ukraine in 1978–1993, who "blindly followed the orders of Moscow and the KGB." Krawchuk also distanced himself from another "servant of Kremlin," Heorhii Shevel, who was head of propaganda and agitation of the Central Committee of KPU in 1961–1970 and the Minister of Foreign Affairs of Soviet Ukraine in 1970–1980.[64] In his memoirs, Krawchuk left a very negative portrayal of Shevel as a typical Soviet bureaucrat: "[Shevel] appeared to be even worse, than Kondufor, he looked pompous, bombastic, rude and uncultured. He was so impudent. During the official meetings, when somebody in his official presentation said something, which Shevel did not like, he would interrupt this presenter with his critical caustic phrases to confuse [this presenter] completely. I could never understand how this [rude and uncultured] person could serve for ten years as a minister of foreign affairs of the Ukrainian SSR. Probably, Moscow needed only such 'Ukrainian ministers' [like Shevel]."[65] In his personal memoirs, Krawchuk left hundreds of these negative portraits of Soviet officials, like Kondufor and Shevel. Still, Krawchuk's career (with the Soviet support he served as president of the AUUC from 1979 to 1991) and even his wealth depended on his good personal relations with those Soviet bureaucrats.

Peter Krawchuk, as many of his comrades, Canadian communists, profited from the material support of Soviet authorities. Their children were enrolled in various educational institutions in Kyiv. As John Kolasky noted, "special arrangements were made in hospitals, sanatoria and resorts to accommodate those members who required medical treatment or rest." Their articles and books were published in the Soviet Union. "The honoraria and royalties were deposited in the author's savings accounts. The roubles could not be converted into hard currency and taken abroad but the recipients could use them on their succeeding visits to purchase Soviet paintings, expensive Persian lamb coats for their wives and other rare and expensive items."[66]

Officially, Canadian Ukrainian communists established their commercial relations with the Soviet Union as early as 1955. During that year, using Soviet financial support, they founded the first Ukrainian communist corporation in Canada *Ukraynska Knyha* as a local business enterprise operating under a Metropolitan Toronto license. The board of directors of this corporation included Peter Krawchuk among many other prominent Ukrainian Canadian communists. They were given a monopoly on the export of parcels to the USSR, and in return were obliged to collect import duties for the Soviet government on the parcels they forwarded. "Thus, although they were Canadian citizens, domiciled in Canada and operating a business on Canadian soil, the directors became agents of the Soviet government, collecting Soviet custom duties. Ukrainians in Canada, both pro-communists and nationalists, were anxious to assist their relations in Ukraine. Parcels moved in a steady stream and *Knyha* prospered. Sub-agencies were established in a number of localities, among them Montreal, Hamilton, Sudbury and the Lakehead." By the 1970s, various branches of this corporation had authorized capital from $20,000 to $50,000.[67]

In 1959, using the Soviet financial support, Canadian Ukrainian communist leaders, such as Krawchuk, founded their own capitalist enterprise, new international tourist company, Globe Tours, to provide travel facilities for those wishing to visit the Soviet Union. The Soviet government granted to this company the legal rights to be the only official representative of the Soviet travel agency, *Inturist*, in Canada, and guaranteed it an exclusive monopoly on group travel to Soviet Ukraine. According to Canadian law, the Globe Tours company was incorporated in a province of Manitoba in November 1959 as a private company under the name of Globe Trade Limited. The name of the company was changed in 1963 to Globe Trade and Travel.[68]

As John Kolasky described this "communist business,"

> Travel between Canada and the USSR was expanded in 1966. By agreement between the two countries, Air Canada obtained landing rights in Moscow and *Aeroflot* in Montreal. The Soviet ocean liner, *Pushkin*, established a regular route between Leningrad and Montreal. Simultaneously, Globe Tours expanded. It opened an office in Edmonton in 1966 under the name, East-West Travel, as a branch of Globe Tours in Winnipeg. The same year Globe Tours obtained a license to operate in Ontario. Two years later the company moved its headquarters to 962 Boor Street West in Toronto. The board of directors was enlarged to include Anthony Bilecki as president, Ray

Dowhopoluk as vice-president and manager, Stanley Ziniuk as secretary, Peter Krawchuk as treasurer and Michael Seychuk, Michael Mokry, Peter Prokop, John Chitrenky and George Solomon as directors. The most localities *Knyha* and Globe Tours conducted their operations from buildings purchased by the Ukrainian communist leaders for that purpose. In Toronto they formed a syndicate, Taras Investments, on October 31, 1957 "to invest in real estate mortgages and other securities." The charter was issued to Stanley Ziniuk, Peter Krawchuk, Mary Prokop, Mary Skrypnyk and John Boychuk who became the directors. Boychuk also held the position of manager. The authorized capital of the private company was $300,000.[69]

During the 1970s and 1980s, Peter Krawchuk visited Soviet Ukraine almost every year. He also was very busy with receiving Soviet official guests in Canada almost every month during the same time. Krawchuk and other "left" Canadian Ukrainians became actively engaged in the KGB counter-propaganda campaigns against those representatives of the Ukrainian diaspora, who collaborated with the Nazis during WWII.

During the 1970s, the KGB not only provided American and Canadian "left" media with the archival documents, but also with video materials, and contributed to three editions of the book about the Nazis' crimes in Soviet Ukraine, entitled *Lest We Forget* (*Chtoby my ne zabyli*).[70] For this book, the KGB provided with the copies of the archival documents Michael Hanusiak, American-Ukrainian Communist, an editor-in-chief of pro-Soviet newspaper *News from Ukraine*. Hanusiak together with Samuel Pevzner from the Jewish Cultural Clubs and Societies, another Leftist organization, prepared a publication of *Lest We Forget* book in 1973 with the full list of the Ukrainian nationalists, members of OUN [Organization of the Ukrainian Nationalists], who committed crimes against Jews, collaborating with Nazis.[71] In December of 1976, the KGB initiated the publication of the 3rd edition this book in the USA and Canada, simultaneously trying to trigger the investigations of the Ukrainian nationalists' war crimes. All these publications and video materials were used to compromise and discredit the American Ukrainians not only like "bourgeois nationalists," but also like the "fascist collaborators."[72] Moreover, the KGB promoted various publications, from such influential newspapers like *The New York Times* to the local periodical from Indiana like *Elkhart Truth*, and broadcasting in American and Canadian television "with the shocking information about the crimes committed by the Ukrainian activists of OUN against the Jewish population" of Soviet Ukraine during WWII. In the KGB interpretation, which they promoted in the USA and Canada during the 1970s, the Ukrainian nationalists "initiated genocide against the Jews," and now the same "Ukrainian nationalistic criminals" found "shelter in peace" in America, participating in various "anti-Soviet provocations." The major goal of the KGB was not only to "compromise and decompose from inside the OUN abroad," but also to "strengthen the discord between the Ukrainian nationalists and Jewish Zionists," "undermining and weakening" each of those "anti-Soviet groups."[73] The major operation of the KGB against the Ukrainian Diaspora in America had a code name "Retribution," trying not only to discredit "the Ukrainian nationalists" in both the USA and Canada, but also to prevent the anti-Soviet alliance "between the Ukrainian and Jewish nationalists" in America.[74]

In 1981, the KGB administration in Kyiv especially worried that the leaders of the Ukrainian and Jewish diaspora in America established "the good and friendly relations," using the meetings of the heads of the Ukrainian Catholic Church of the USA, the Society of Jewish-Ukrainian Relations from Israel and the American Jewish Committee on April 2 and May 4 of 1981 to "perpetuate a memory of a former leader of the Ukrainian Uniate Church Sheptytskyi," who saved the Jews in Ukraine during WWII. The KGB agents reported from the USA that this was another attempt to use the "anti-Soviet interpretations of this war history" to initiate the "mutual actions of collaboration between the Ukrainian nationalists (ounovtsy) and Zionists to protect the civil rights of the Jews and Ukrainians who reside in the Soviet Union." The major goal of the KGB operations in America was to continue "a campaign of compromising and discrediting of the Ukrainian nationalists, together with their 'spiritual father' Sheptytskyi, as the Nazi's allies in the Fascists' crimes against Soviet Jews."[75] In this campaign, the KGB anticipated the active position of the pro-Communist American Ukrainians, such as Krawchuk, and his personal friend of Michael Hanusiak, who were actively used for pro-Soviet propaganda. To some extent, "despite their timid attempts to criticize publicly in Canada Russification politics of the Soviet government in Soviet Ukraine," Krawchuk and his "Leftist" colleagues in the USA and Canada "became the useful tools in all those KGB operations, which overall discredited and presented in the negative light all the Ukrainian diaspora in America."[76]

Peter Krawchuk was also engaged in various research projects to study the Ukrainian farmers and workers in immigration together with the Academy of Sciences of the Ukrainian SSR. All these Canadian-Ukrainian projects were not only funded by the Soviet state, but also controlled by the KGB through various Soviet scholars and officials, like Arnold Shlepakov. Shlepakov became one of those "KGB people," who infiltrated the American Studies in the Soviet Union, especially during the beginning of the Soviet-American exchange program in the late of 1950s.[77]

Notes

1 Petro Kravchuk, *Bez nedomovok: Spogady* (Kyiv: Literaturna Ukraina, 1995), 44, 45–46. Compare with my analysis in Sergei I. Zhuk, *Soviet Americana: The Cultural History of Russian and Ukrainian Americanists* (London and New York: I.B. Tauris, 2018), 80–81, 107–108.

2 See his memoirs: John Kolasky, *Two Years in Soviet Ukraine: A Canadian's Personal Account of Russian Oppression and the Growing Opposition* (Toronto: Peter Martin Associates Books, 1970), idem, *The Shattered Illusion: The History of Ukrainian Pro-Communist Organizations in Canada* (Toronto: Peter Martin Associates Books, 1979), esp. chapter IX: "Differences with the USSR," 155–176. See also Rhonda L. Hinther, "Generation Gap: Canada's Postwar Ukrainian Left," in *Re-Imagining Ukrainian Canadians: History, Politics, and Identity*, Ed. by Rhonda L. Hinther and Jim Mochoruk (Toronto: University of Toronto Press, 2011), 23–53, and Jaroslav Petryshyn, "The 'Ethnic Question' Personified: Ukrainian Canadians and Canadian-Soviet Relations 1917–1991," *Re-Imagining Ukrainian Canadians*, 223–256, and Jennifer Anderson, "Polishing the Soviet Image: The Canadian-Soviet Friendship Society and the 'Progressive Ethnic Groups,' 1949–1957," *Re-Imagining Ukrainian Canadians*, 279–328.

3 See Ivan Drach, "Nash kanads'kyi drug," in Petro Kravchuk, *Ukraintsi v Kanadi: Statti, narysy, pamflety* (Kyiv: Dnipro, 1981), 5–8.

4 See numerous Krawchuk's publications in this Ukrainian periodical, with the editor's praising him as "the best Canadian/ American friend" of Soviet Ukraine: Petro Kravchuk, "Vinnipegovi – 100 rokiv," *Vsesvit*, 1974, no. 12, 207–220; Ol'ga Kabkova, a review of Petro Kravchuk, "Ukraintsi v Kanadi", Kyiv, "Dnipro", 1981, in *Vsesvit*, 1982, no. 4, 152; Les' Taniuk (Moscow) a review of "Nasha Stsena" Toronto, 1981, Uporiadkuvav Petro Kravchuk, in *Vsesvit*, 1982, no. 4, 152–154. See especially his biography, written by Arnol'd Shlepakov, "Storinky zhyttia i borot'by" in *Vsesvit*, 1981, no. 9, 201–202, where Krawchuk was presented as "the best," "the most reliable," "honest, and devoted American friend" of Soviet Ukraine.

5 See especially Krawchuk's personal connections with two Soviet Ukrainian historians of the USA and Canada from Kyiv, such as Arnold Shlepakov and Leonid Leshchenko, in Sergei I. Zhuk, *Soviet Americana*, 81–82, 84, 110–111, 220–222, 225, 240.

6 Petro Kravchuk, *Bez nedomovok*, 5, 7, 12–13, 18, 22. See also an obituary, written by Andrij Makuch, *The Ukrainian Weekly*, April 13, 1997, No. 15, Vol. LXV, p. 4.

7 Andrij Makuch, Op. cit.

8 Petro Kravchuk, *Bez nedomovok*, 32–33, 62–63.

9 John Kolasky, *The Shattered Illusion*, 205.

10 Ibid., 44. Krawchuk acknowledged this important role of Voina especially during his first visit to Ukraine in 1947-49.

11 See about a history of the Ukrainian Society of Cultural Relations with Abroad (later re-named as the Ukrainian Association of Friendship and Cultural Relations with Foreign Countries) in V. M. Danylenko, *Ukraina v mizhnarodnykh naukovo-tekhnichnykh zv'iazkakh (70–80-i rr.)* (Kyiv: Instytut istorii Ukrainy. Instytut ukrais'koi arkheografii, 1993), *Na skryzhaliakh istorii: Z istorii vzaiemozv'iazkiv uriadovykh struktur i hromads'kykh kil Ukrainy z ukrains'ko-kanads'koiu hromadoiu v drugii polovyni 1940–1980-ti roky*, Ed. by P. Tron'ko a. o. (Kyiv: Instytut istorii Ukrainy NANU, Fundatsiia ukrains'koi spadshchyny Al'berty, 2003), Stanislav Yu. Lazebnyk, Olha B. Havura, *Rozdumy na mostu z dvobichnym rukhom* (Kyiv: Etnos, 2004); Stanislav Lazebnyk, *Zakordonne ukrainstvo: vytoky ta siogodennia* (Kyiv: Istyna, 2007), and Sergei I. Zhuk, *Soviet Americana*, 81, 223–224, 304.

12 Ibid., 46–47. Krawchuk's Soviet colleagues explained his close connections to Voina in this way. See in my interview with Leonid Leshchenko, April 12, 2012, Kyiv, Ukraine. See also description of all those events in John Kolasky, *The Shattered Illusion*, 53–54.

13 Krawchuk, Op. cit., 47–50, 57–61, 61–62.

14 Quoted from Rhonda L. Hinther, "Generation Gap," 36. She mistakenly put year 1948 in her narrative.

15 Ibid., 36–37. See also John Kolasky, *The Shattered Illusion*, 59.

16 John Kolasky, *The Shattered Illusion*, 103.

17 John Kolasky, *The Shattered Illusion*, 104.

18 Ibid., 131.

19 Ibid., 152.

20 See about the role of his Canadian periodical in this campaign in Serge Cipko, "Monitoring the 'Return to the Homeland' Campaign: Canadian Reports on Resettlement in the USSR from South America, 1955–1957," in *Re-Imagining Ukrainian Canadians*, 257–278, citation on pp. 268–269.

21 John Kolasky, *The Shattered Illusion*, 86, 103.

22 SBU, f. 16, op. 1, spr. 968, ark. 44–56, esp. 46–47.

23 SBU, f. 16, op. 1, spr. 969, ark. 33–43; John Kolasky, *Education in Soviet Ukraine: A Study in Discrimination and Russification* (Toronto: Peter Martin Associates, 1968). See also Bohdan Klid, "Obituary: John Kolasky, former communist and writer," *The Ukrainian Weekly*, November 23, 1997, No.47, Vol. LXV.

24 Bohdan Klid, Op.cit.

25 SBU, f. 16, op. 1, spr. 949, ark. 64.

26 Ibid., 65.

27 Ibid., 66.

28 See in detail about Borys Antonenko-Davydovych and his role in the Soviet dissident movement in: G. P. Kalantaevska, N. N. Prokopenko, S. V. Voropai, "Literary Environment and Literary Situation in Ukraine in 60 – 70's of XX Century in the Context of the Correspondence of B. Antonenko-Davydovych," *Philologichni traktaty*, 2018, Vol. 10, No. 4, 94–104.

29 SBU, f. 16, op. 1, spr. 949, ark. 66–67.

30 Ibid., 68–79.

31 Ibid., 79.

32 SBU, f. 16, op. 1, spr. 969, ark. 39–40. The KGB also sent a special telegram to the Communist party administration in Kyiv about their decision: "From September 1963 to July 1965, Ivan Vasilievich Koliaska, a Ukrainian, a member of the Communist Party of Canada, with a college degree, a teacher from Toronto, took classes at the Higher Party School in Kyiv. He was recommended for this school by TOUK (the Association of the United Ukrainians of Canada [AUUC]) ["progressive organization of Ukrainian emigrants, led by Communists.] But he took a very aggressive nationalistic anti-Soviet position." Ibid., 40–41. See a complete text of this telegram on ark. 40–43.

33 Ibid., 40–41.

34 SBU, f. 16, op. 1, spr. 969, ark. 41–43: "Before his removal from Kyiv in 1965, he promised in public that he 'would never use the anti-Soviet materials to damage an international reputation of Soviet Ukraine.' He did not follow his promises: in June of 1966 in New York at the meeting of the Ukrainian nationalists he spoke spreading the slanderous information about the situation in Soviet Ukraine." The KGB tried to prevent publications about "the anti-Soviet actions of Canadian Communist" in Soviet Ukraine by the Soviet media. Their report of 1968 mentioned his book: John Kolasky, *Education in Soviet Ukraine*.

35 *Telegram*, February 17, 1968; John Kolasky, *The Shattered Illusion*, 168. See how the KGB tried to discredit Kolasky in America: SBU, f. 16, op. 1, spr. 970, ark. 148–150.

36 *Zhyttia i slovo*, February 10, 1969, and John Kolasky, *The Shattered Illusion*, 168–169.

37 John Kolasky, *The Shattered Illusion*, 169. He dismissed the recent arrests of dissidents with the statement that: "We cannot be judges of whether they have the right to arrest in Ukraine," but criticized the refusal by Soviet authorities to grant visas and permission to visit native villages." Krawchuk complained about the Soviet officials' decision not to allow Canadian Ukrainians to visit their villages. As one contemporary noted, "the problem of obtaining tourist visas to the USSR and permission to visit native villages was an even greater irritant, especially to the rank and file members and sympathizers, than Russification. ... By 1968 the problem has become so acute that it could no longer be ignored. Krawchuk condemned Soviet authorities for such refusals in his report to the closed membership meeting of the AUUC on March 3, 1968, declaring that: "Everyone has a right to go to his native village ... It should not be necessary to beg on one's knees to go to Ukraine." At the thirteenth convention of the AUUC on April 12–15, 1968, Krawchuk, in his report again raised the question of tourist visas to villages. He underlined the gravity of the problem when he declared that it was "the subject of everyday conversation and discussion ... in every locality across Canada where Ukrainians live." John Kolasky, *The Shattered Illusion*, 172.

38 Ibid. 160.

39 Ibid. 163.

40 Ibid., 164. See how Krawchuk described this in his memoirs in Kravchuk, Op. cit., 94–95, 102–105, 118–121.

41 Andrij Makuch, Op. cit. As one Canadian historian explained, Ukrainian Canadian Communists, including Krawchuk, had to reject or challenge the Communist Party of Canada (CPC) policy and perspectives where issues of Ukrainian culture and language were concerned. The most serious conflict between TOUK (AUUC) leaders and the CPC came in 1967 over the issue of Russification in Soviet Ukraine. "After the war, charges made by DPs, concerns brought back by tourists (many of whom had associations with the AUUC) who had visited Soviet Ukraine, and accusations made by former CPC and AUUC member John Kolasky brought to surface the Russification controversy." In 1967 CPC sent a delegation to investigate. After a three-week tour of Soviet Ukraine, the delegation returned and "submitted an explosive report. There were many problems with Russian being the official language in Ukraine, they asserted. They felt that while there had been some improvements over the previous years, there was still much work to do to ensure the presence and use of Ukrainian in Ukraine. Implying that the Ukrainian language had been marginalized, they insisted that 'the Ukrainian language has to be encouraged, promoted, and developed in all areas of life in Ukraine. It is not to be forced upon the people, whether of Ukrainian, Russian, or other origins, but the climate has to be created for its freest flourishing and interdevelopment with other languages and cultures.'" "Despite strong arm-twisting" by both the CPC and the CPSU, both of which were "extremely displeased with the report," the Ukrainian Canadian Communists "refused to back down or retract their findings." Quoted from Rhonda L. Hinther, "Generation Gap," 39.

42 John Kolasky, *The Shattered Illusion*, 170.

43 SBU, f. 16, op. 1, spr. 970, ark. 68–73, 99–102.

44 SBU, f. 16, op. 1, spr. 970, ark. 68–73.

45 Ibid., 68–69.

46 Ibid., 70. "Dowhopoluk told about a closure of a newspaper of the AUUC *the Ukrainian Canadian* and a replacement of this paper with a new journal and about a struggle for leadership among the Canadian Left. The main goal of this

decision was to remove the old leaders and replace them with the aggressive critics of Russification of Soviet Ukraine."

47 This was the 1967 International and Universal Exposition, the World's Fair held in Montreal, Quebec, Canada, from April 27 to October 29, 1967. The USSR had its own separate pavilion at this exhibition, but the Soviet national republics were not represented by their separate "shows" in it. This lack of "national representation" in the Soviet pavilion led to another criticism by Canadian Ukrainians. See about this in Kravchuk, Op. cit., 110–111. Compare with SBU, f. 16, op. 1, spr. 970, ark. 71–72. "According to Krenz, a leader of CPC Tim Buck was against the position of Krawchuk and his followers."

48 SBU, f. 16, op. 1, spr. 970, ark. 73.

49 Ibid., 99–102.

50 Ibid., 103–106, 158–195.

51 Cited from ibid., 159.

52 SBU, f. 16, op. 1, spr. 977, ark. 353–356. Quotation is from ark. 354. As an agent reported, "the youth does not follow him and his followers, the older members are retiring, and the entire activity of [the AUUC] members is declining" ("Молодежь за ними не идет, старики отходят от дел, и общая активность падает" in the original).

53 John Kolasky, *The Shattered Illusion*, 182. I quote my interview with Arnold Shlepakov, August 29, 1991, Kyiv. See also Petro Kravchuk, *Bez nedomovok*, 133–134.

54 SBU, f. 16, op. 1, spr. 989, ark. 121.

55 Ibid., 138–139.

56 Ibid., 218–219. See also Kravchuk, Op. cit., 150–151.

57 Kravchuk, Op. cit., 150–151. See also about a scandal around Honchar's novel in Sergei Zhuk, *Rock and Roll in the Rocket City: The West, Identity, and Ideology in Soviet Dniepropetrovsk, 1960–1985* (Baltimore, MD: Johns Hopkins University Press & Washington, D.C.: Woodrow Wilson Center Press, 2010), 53–64.

58 See about his visit to Ukraine in December 1980 in: Kravchuk, Op. cit., 209–210, and see a note in the KGB documents on September 5, 1980, about a necessity to prepare in advance the KGB operatives for Krawchuk's visit to Kyiv to continue "to study the politics of Russification" in Soviet Ukraine in: SBU, f. 16, op. 1, spr. 1172, ark. 56–57.

59 SBU, f. 16, op. 1, spr. 1045, ark. 252–253.

60 SBU, f. 16, op. 1, spr. 1164, ark. 23–24.

61 Interview with Leonid K., retired KGB officer, Kyiv, February 9, 2019.

62 Interview with Leonid Leshchenko, July 23, 2012, Kyiv.

63 Although, we should be careful, using his personal memoirs and historical studies. According to Canadian scholars, despite "the fascinating" Krawchuk's analysis in his studies (and memoirs) about the Canadian Left, his research "was problematic on several levels: first, it was marked by an element of self-exoneration that was worrisome; second, Krawchuk at the time of publication had not released control of the documents on which he based his strongest claims concerning the fight between Ukrainian leftists and the Anglo-Celtic leaders of CPC; and finally, he tended to misidentify certain documents as to time and place, which rendered suspect his chronology as well as parts of his analysis." Quoted from Jim Mochoruk, "'Pop & Co' versus Buck and the 'Lenin School Boys': Ukrainian Canadians and the Communist Party of Canada, 1921–1931," in *Re-Imagining Ukrainian Canadians*, 331–375, citation from p. 334.

64 I quote my interview with Leonid Leshchenko, July 23, 2012, Kyiv. See also Olga Bertelsen, "Political Affinities and Maneuvering of Soviet Political Elites: Heorhii Shevel and Ukraine's Ministry of Strange Affairs in the 1970s," *Nationalities*

Papers: The Journal of Nationalism and Ethnicity, Vol. 47, No. 3 (2019), pp. 394–411.

65 Kravchuk, Op. cit., 101–102.

66 John Kolasky, *The Shattered Illusion*, 207.

67 John Kolasky, *The Shattered Illusion*, 212. This information was proven by my interview with Leonid Leshchenko, July 23, 2012, Kyiv.

68 John Kolasky, *The Shattered Illusion*, 213. "[Anthony] Bilecki became its president and [Michael] Seychuk, its secretary. In 1963, [Ray] Dowhopoluk replaced Seychuk as secretary."

69 John Kolasky, *The Shattered Illusion*, 214. "On October 7, 1966, Boychuk retired as manager and on December 29, 1967, as director. He was replaced by [William] Harasym who also became vice-president."

70 Michael Hanusiak and Sam Pevzner, *Lest We Forget*, (New York: The Ukrainian American League, 1973).

71 See about the first edition of the book in 1973 in SBU, f. 16, op. 1, spr. 1108, ark. 69–70.

72 SBU, f. 16, op. 1, spr. 1112, ark. 137–139. According to the KGB investigation, after the publication of *Lest We Forget* book, "the Americans began persecutions against Ukrainian nationalist S. Koval'chuk." See SBU, f. 16, op. 1, spr. 1127, ar. 59–61, 95.

73 SBU, f. 16, op. 1, spr. 1111, ark. 185–187. Citation is from page 187.

74 See how the KGB head Stepan Mukha from Kyiv described this operation "Retribution" in his report to the Communist leadership of Soviet Ukraine in October 1985: SBU f. 16, op. 1, spr. 1230, ark. 169 and 170. I use a paraphrased translation of this report by Olga Bertelsen in her article, "The KGB Operation 'Retribution' and John Demjaniuk," in *Russian Active Measures: Yesterday, Today and Tomorrow*, Edited by Olga Bertelsen (New York: ibidem Press and Columbia University Press, 2021), 119 and 120. According to this report, the KGB administration in Kyiv used their special tactics for this operation, which included "1) gathering intelligence about OUN members who had functioned in the Soviet Union and Soviet territories occupied by the Nazis and who managed to escape from the Soviet 'sword' to the West; 2) identifying OUN members who became active in the anti-communist human rights movement in the West and channeling evidence of their collaboration with the Nazis to Western government; 3) publishing and distributing in the United States and Canada two editions of the book by the American Communist of Ukrainian origin Michael Hanusiak entitled *Lest We Forget* (*Chtoby my ne zabyli*); 4) creating three counterpropaganda films and sharing them with 17 anti-fascist organizations in the West; 5) publishing articles in American mass media about mass demonstrations in Ukraine demanding to extradite Nazi collaborators to the USSR where they would be brought to justice; 6) publishing articles in pro-Soviet Western Ukrainian newspapers, such as *News from Ukraine*, in which Ukrainian emigrants would be portrayed as Nazi collaborators; 6) sending petitions of the same content written by Soviet citizens and addressed to the American government." The KGB agents helped Canadian newspaper *Toronto Star* to publish articles about the crimes of SS-Halychyna, and distributed a book in Canada *We Accuse (My obviniaiem)* about the Nazis' using the Ukrainian collaborators. The same KGB agents sent archival materials about 59 Ukrainian collaborators and their war crimes to the Canadian government, which established a special commission in February 1985 to gather information about war criminals and Nazi collaborators, who lived in Canada. See in SBU, f. 16, op. 1, spr. 1230, ark. 170.

75 SBU, f. 16, op. 1, spr. 1184, ark. 64–65.

76 I paraphrased from my interview with Leonid Leshchenko.

77 The retired KGB officers called people like Shlepakov "our people." See my interview with Stepan Ivanovich T., a retired KGB officer, January 30, 2019, Kyiv, Ukraine. Compare with Sergei I. Zhuk, "The 'KGB People,' Soviet Americanists and Soviet-American Academic Exchanges, 1958–1985," *The Soviet and Post-Soviet Review*, 2017, vol. 44, No. 2, 133–167.

4 Arnold Shlepakov, Ukrainian Diaspora in America and Academic Exchanges

Arnold Shlepakov as a KGB Connection to the American/Canadian Left

As it turned out, Arnold Shlepakov (1930–1996), a founding father of the Ukrainian American Studies, served as the major connection between Peter Krawchuk and other American/Canadian Left Ukrainians to the official academic hierarchy in Soviet Ukraine through the entire period of the late socialism, after Stalin. At the Institute of History in Kyiv, during his graduate studies in the 1950s, Arnold Shlepakov's mentor was the famous Soviet diplomat and scholar of diplomatic history, directly connected to the KGB, Dr. Oleksii (Oleksa) D. Voina, who suggested that for his dissertation Shlepakov use various official letters of those Canadian Ukrainians, who supported the reunification of all Ukrainian lands into one Soviet Ukrainian state following World War II. In 1953, Voina sent his student to the archival collection of the Ukrainian SSR Ministry of Foreign Affairs. Eventually this visit to the Ministry of Foreign Affairs required the young Shlepakov's "clearance" by the KGB. As some of his colleagues assumed, this research activity in the ministry's documentary collections in 1953–1955 led not only to the establishment of Shlepakov's strong personal connections with the KGB, but also to his rising interest in the history of Ukrainian emigration to the US and Canada. After the KGB's official approval of Shlepakov as an "ideologically reliable student of Soviet foreign policy," Oleksii Voina recommended Shlepakov to work with those Canadian Ukrainians who visited Soviet Ukraine. (According to the official requirements, to meet a foreigner, Shlepakov had to be officially approved by the KGB)[1] (Figure 4.1).

In 1956, Peter (Petro) Krawchuk visited Kyiv and brought to Voina his new book manuscript about the history of Ukrainian emigration in Canada.[2] Voina read the manuscript and recommended it for publication. Moreover, Voina introduced Krawchuk to two young talented historians from the Institute of History: Fedir Shevchenko and Arnold Shlepakov, who agreed to edit Krawchuk's text for publication in the Ukrainian language by the Soviet Ukrainian Publishing House. The Soviet administration

DOI: 10.4324/9781003212522-5

Figure 4.1 Arnold Shlepakov in 1987.

assigned two official Soviet editors of this manuscript who were the old professors from the same institute in Kyiv: Fedir Los' and Luka Kyzia. But the actual editing was done primarily by Shevchenko and Shlepakov. This was the beginning of important contacts with foreigners for the young Shlepakov. Beginning in 1956, he had established strong personal connections with the Canadian citizen Peter Krawchuk, and began corresponding regularly not only with Krawchuk, but also with other Ukrainian Canadians.[3] Shlepakov was actively engaged in the activities of the Ukrainian Society for Cultural Relations with Abroad (*Ukrains'ke tovarystvo kul'turnogo zv'iazku z zakordonom*). As a representative of the Ukrainian Academy of Sciences this young scholar participated in all of the meetings, which included American and Canadian guests.[4]

Moreover, Shlepakov became Krawchuk's very close friend, exchanging books with him, helping this Canadian guest every time he visited Ukraine. Very often, Shlepakov tapped Krawchuk as a precious source of information about Canada and the history of the working-class movement in North America. Between 1956 and 1972, Shlepakov sent Krawchuk at least five letters annually. As a member of the editorial boards of major Ukrainian periodicals such as *Ukrains'kyi istorychnyi zhurnal* and *Vsesvit*, Shlepakov also invited Krawchuk to publish his materials about Ukrainian Canadians in these Soviet Ukrainian magazines.[5] In 1961, Shlepakov played an important role in assisting Krawchuk to make arrangements during his family's visit to Ukraine regarding the enrollment of Krawchuk's daughter Larisa in Kyiv State University as an undergraduate student. In fact, Mykola (Nikolai in Russian) Pidhornyi, the first secretary of the Central Committee of the Communist Party of Ukraine, assisted Larisa Krawchuk in becoming a KDU student. But Shlepakov attempted to demonstrate to Krawchuk his usefulness as well.[6]

As a result of all these communicational efforts, by 1961, – thanks to Krawchuk's contacts and the books sent from Canada by Krawchuk, – Shlepakov had accumulated a significant amount of material for his new research topic on the Ukrainian farmers' and workers' immigration to the US and Canada. Eventually, Shlepakov published this material in the form of a book, based mostly on secondary published sources from the US and Canada, provided to him by his Canadian colleagues such as Krawchuk. It is noteworthy that Shlepakov's first monograph on the first Ukrainian emigrants to Canada was written in good Ukrainian; he later presented a copy of his book as a gift to the Ukrainian Canadian Krawchuk, the latter being a representative of the very "Ukrainian labor migration" described in Shlepakov's monograph.[7]

After 1966, Shlepakov became somewhat of an "academic" celebrity due to his sky-rocketing career in traditional academic scholarship and Soviet diplomacy as well. He was appointed an official adviser to both the Ukrainian SSR Ministry of Foreign Affairs and the International Department of the Ukrainian SSR Academy of Sciences. The KGB began requesting his recommendations for the list of candidates whose future travel plans would include the USA and Canada. As early as the spring of 1965, responding to the request of KGB officials from the first (international) department of the Institute of History, Shlepakov provided a positive recommendation and approval for the vice president of the KDU (*prorektor z naukovii roboty*) Dr. A.Z. Zhmudskii, and the chair of the KDU Department of Geography, Professor A. M. Marinich to visit the University of Alberta in Edmonton, Canada, from April 28 to May 12, 1966.[8]

From November 1966 until May 1967 Shlepakov traveled throughout France and Switzerland as an official representative of Soviet Ukraine under UNESCO funding. As part of his travels to attend a UNESCO conference in Paris, Shlepakov actively participated in the international discussion regarding necessary reforms in the system of science and college education in developing nations. Beginning in September 1970, for three years in a row, Shlepakov was a member of the official Soviet Ukrainian delegation to the sessions of the General Assembly of the United Nations in New York City. He became the "real star" of the Soviet Ukrainian "academic diplomacy."[9]

Shlepakov always denied about his connections to the KGB. Although in some of his trips to the US, Shlepakov collected "the strategic information from the available American publications in social science," and he reported this information to the first (KGB) department of his institute during the late 1960s and early 1970s.[10] One of such his reports about "four studies of the American scholars on the theory of the planning management and the perspective forecasting of the scientific-technical progress, which were related to the US military-industrial complex and to the state strategic doctrine, regarding the scientific and technological future of the USA" was even incorporated in the official KGB letter to the Ukrainian Communist leadership on May 18, 1972.[11] Still, Shlepakov publicly tried to distance himself from the KGB and "its people."[12]

However, some of his close friends noticed strange changes in Shlepakov's personality during this period of time. He became more secretive and moodier. During the 1960s, in private conversations with his close friends, Shlepakov used to boast about the new "forbidden" pamphlets of the Soviet dissidents or the "forbidden" books from the West, which he would receive by means of his Canadian or American colleagues. After 1970, Shlepakov ceased boasting about such literature and began avoiding "dangerous conversations involving criticism of Soviet politics and communist ideology." Leonid Leshchenko connected these changes in Shlepakov's behavior to certain scandals in his private life, which were used by the KGB for manipulating and influencing Shlepakov. On the one hand, "during the 1970s, Shlepakov became more active in organizing various conferences and collective publications, involving all of his long-time friends and colleagues in these projects but on the other hand with the sky-rocketing ascent of his public academic career gradually he turned into a typical Soviet academic bureaucrat, distancing himself from these same long-term friends."[13]

As early as 1969, Shlepakov was elected Chair of the Department of Modern and Contemporary History of Foreign Countries at the Institute of History and as a corresponding member of the Academy of Sciences of the Ukrainian SSR that same year. In 1970, he became a full professor of world history. In essence, Shlepakov not only supervised the studies of the history of foreign countries at the Institute (until 1978), but also played an important role in its administration, fulfilling the role of deputy director of the Institute of History during 1971–1974.[14]

By the 1980s, Shlepakov stopped producing anything original in American Studies. Similar to many Soviet "official" Americanists (including G. Arbatov and G. Sevostianov in Moscow), he became mainly an "official academic" organizer of various forms of "institutionalization" of American Studies in Kyiv. Shlepakov continued to publish, but mostly as an editor of various collective monographs, occasionally contributing one or two chapters to such publications.[15] He served as an editor of every major academic and popular publication in Soviet Ukraine, focusing on the history and culture of the "capitalist Western countries." More specifically, Shlepakov would lend his editorial expertise to a broad spectrum of publications and topics ranging from various purely academic editions about the international solidarity of the working class in the struggle against fascism, to themes of national relations in the US and Canada, in such Ukrainian magazines as *Ukrainskyi istorychnyi zhurnal, Vsesvit* and *Visnyk* of the Ukrainian Academy of Sciences. Shlepakov was also a major organizer of all official receptions for the delegations of foreign scholars and scientists in the Ukrainian Academy of Sciences in Kyiv.[16]

Eventually, Shlepakov's "organizing genius" contributed to the creation of a new research institute, devoted to the special study of foreign (mainly capitalist) countries of the world. As Shlepakov recalled he "always dreamed of creating something similar to Inozemtsev's IMEMO but in Kyiv, in Ukraine."[17] That is how he proposed to transform the "overgrown department of modern and contemporary history at the Institute of History" into a new separate academic institution, which officially began functioning under Shlepakov's leadership in October 1978. It was located in downtown Kyiv, and the Soviet administration approved its official title, proposed by Shlepakov, – the Institute of Social and Economic Problems of Foreign Countries (ISEPZK – in Ukrainian abbreviation). Shlepakov also initiated the publication of his institute's periodical *The World Abroad: Social-Political and Economic Problems*, in which he published materials devoted to American Studies, sometimes including the participation of scholars from the US as well.[18]

During the existence of "Shlepakov's Institute" (as ISEPZK was known in Kyiv and Moscow), its director assembled talented Ukrainian scholars committed toward researching important issues on international politics, diplomacy and American Studies. Eventually, by the end of the 1980s (in addition to the traditional ideological anti-Western themes) the Institute's personnel concentrated on such research topics as "the international divisions of labor and structures of the world's economic relations; national problems in Western Europe and the Americas; migrational processes and the status of immigrants; economic and scientific-technological aspects of the protection of nature and other ecological issues; the West's relations with the developing countries of the Middle East."[19] However, the most important and unique research topic which Shlepakov proposed to his colleagues at ISEPZK was the study of the Ukrainian diaspora throughout the entire world, and especially in North America. As Shlepakov used to joke,

> Our Institute in Kyiv was a true pioneer in Soviet academia regarding the study of various aspects of the Ukrainian immigration to Canada and the US; we found our unique academic niche in the Soviet study of America because we knew our Ukrainian language and culture and we could communicate with American and Canadian Ukrainians in our own native language. None of the Russian Americanists in Moscow or Leningrad could speak our language; therefore they lost the academic competition of establishing the important contacts with Americans or Canadians of Ukrainian origin. And we, the Ukrainian Americanists in Kyiv, won this competition against Muscovites.[20]

As his close friends later underscored, through his institute, Shlepakov consolidated the most talented Ukrainian scholars with different research interests in one group of genuine experts in immigration and national processes in the industrial Western countries, especially in North America. As his close friend and colleague Leonid Leshchenko noted, "Shlepakov created, from all of us, the first (and the most respected) school of Ukrainian Americanists in the Soviet Union." During the 1980s, Leonid Leshchenko and his younger colleagues, such as Volodymyr B. Yevtukh, began their original research on the US and Canada, under the inspiration and support of Shlepakov.[21] Until 1991, "Shlepakov's Institute" functioned as the leading Soviet center for the study of American/Canadian Ukrainians, which was a new and flourishing field in American Studies in the USSR. At the same time, in October 1985, Shlepakov and his Institute supported Peter Krawchuk's initiative to organize the Canadian Society for Ukrainian Labor Research in Toronto. Shlepakov not only delivered a special address to the first meeting of this Society, but also brought a promise of the official Soviet funding for the international research about "the Ukrainian working immigration" in Canada.[22]

Despite all of Shlepakov's activities in the promotion of American Studies in Soviet Ukraine and Ukrainian Studies in Canada, many contemporaries, including his Kyiv and Moscow colleagues, noticed "how cautious and conservative" he had become in his analysis of American politics, ideology and culture after 1979. As a famous Soviet Americanist Nikolai Bolkhovitinov observed, "after accepting the position of director of his new institute" Shlepakov changed for the worse, "openly demonstrating anti-Americanism even in very intimate conversations with his colleagues." To some extent, Shlepakov's many years of collaboration with the KGB and his connections with the Soviet academic leadership shaped his identity and worldview.[23] Another Soviet Americanist Sergei Burin noted, "in the 1980s, Shlepakov suddenly had a different personality – that of an ideological reactionary; I could not recognize him anymore." Even the more ideologically cautious and conformist Moscow Americanists, such as Robert Ivanov and Igor Dementiev, complained about "the overly aggressive anti-Americanism" that was expressed in public by Shlepakov.[24]

Shlepakov also took a very cautious and conservative ideological position regarding perestroika, when Mikhail Gorbachev began his reforms in 1986. As director of a very important "Cold War institution" in Soviet Ukraine, Shlepakov was afraid that the "improvement of Soviet-American relations" would lead to the "dismantling of ISEPZK in Kyiv and ISKAN (Institute of the USA and Canada) in Moscow" and to "ideological confusion in Soviet society and, eventually, to economic and political chaos." In August 1991, he believed that Gorbachev and Yeltsin "were shitting through (*prosyraiut* in Russian) the great country of the Soviet Union." To some extent, he also criticized the Moscow Americanists, and Gorbachev's consultants, including such experts as Arbatov, whose "consulting misled and disoriented the

Soviet leadership, and eventually, contributed to the failure of Soviet diplomacy in its competition with the United States." I still recall his last phrase from our last conversation in Kyiv: "Arbatov and Gorbachev surrendered our motherland – the Soviet Union – to the Americans!"[25]

Manipulating Shlepakov's "dependence on the directive organs" and his ideological conservatism, the KGB used him for various international ideological campaigns "against the bourgeois falsifiers of history" in the West. The most shameful among such campaigns at the beginning of perestroika was devoted to the official Soviet denial of materials about the *Holodomor*, – the artificial famine in Soviet Ukraine during the period of collectivization in 1929–1933, – as presented in Robert Conquest's book of 1986, and interpreted by Soviet ideologists as "a complete falsification."[26] The KGB began tracing the plans about a publication of this book as early as June 1981. The KGB administration initiated a series of propagandist actions, which would include the public declarations about this book by famous historians of Soviet Ukraine, such as Shlepakov.[27] According to his close friends, "under strong pressure from the KGB, Shlepakov, who had never read Conquest's book and had never been an expert on the history of Stalin's collectivization, agreed to sign a special Soviet letter of recommendation in the form of petition to the Communist Party of Canada criticizing Conquest's study while at the same time approving the publication in Canada of a book, which would reject a plausibility of all the facts about the *Holodomor*, as presented in Conquest's study."[28] Eventually, such a "pro-Stalin" book, supported by Shlepakov, was published in Canada in 1987.[29]

A Canadian friend of Shlepakov's, Peter Krawchuk, recalled in his memoirs how he was shocked to see in Toronto a photocopy of the "Soviet recommendation letter" regarding the publication of an anti-Conquest book personally signed by Shlepakov.[30] One year before his death, in 1996, Krawchuk recalled this story:

> As recently as 1987, after *glasnost* and *perestroika* were introduced by Mikhail Gorbachev, when the Communist Party of Canada asked for a truthful explanation of the 1932–1933 famine, it received denials from Moscow. Then the Communist Party of Canada insisted that the Kobzar Publishing Company [in Canada] publish the book 'Fraud, Famine and Fascism,' by Douglas Tuttle, which denies that the 1932–1933 famine in Ukraine was artificially organized by the Stalin regime. The book was recommended for publication by Yuriy Kondufor, director of the Institute of History in the Academy of Sciences of Ukraine, by Academician Arnold Shlepakov, director of the Institute of Social and Economic Problems of Foreign Countries, and by Vasyl Yurchuk, director of the Institute of Party History. The book eventually was published but not by the Kobzar Publishing Company, even though it was pressured very hard to do so.[31]

Shlepakov never accepted criticism addressed at him about his participation in such campaigns. Until June 1991, he served as director of his institute. During perestroika, Shlepakov was still an active official of the Presidium of the Ukrainian Academy of Sciences, teaching various courses on diplomacy and American history at Kyiv State University, and editing a number of collective monographs of his colleagues. However, after 1991, Shlepakov ceased producing original research work. His close friends recalled that during the last years of his life Shlepakov never demonstrated publicly his frustration about the collapse of the Soviet Union and the end of his leadership in ISEPZK, which by the end of 1991 was restructured and renamed the Institute of World Economy and International Relations of the National Academy of Sciences of Ukraine. But Leonid Leshchenko noticed that Shlepakov began drinking heavily again, and in confidential conversations he used to repeat only one phrase: "after 1991 Soviet American Studies died completely." Leshchenko thought that the end of Shlepakov's Institute in its original format in June 1991 contributed not only to his emotional shock, but also to Shlepakov's gradual mental demise and his unexpected death in 1996.[32]

According to Leonid Leshchenko, after 1964, the year of his first visit to the capitalist America, until perestroika in the 1980s, Arnold Shlepakov played the major instrumental role in the "unofficial channel of connections" between Peter Krawchuk and the KGB headquarter in Kyiv, Soviet Ukraine. All Ukrainian colleagues knew about "the special personal relations" between Krawchuk and Shlepakov, who became a "frequent guest" of Krawchuk's house in Toronto.[33] Paradoxically, Krawchuk mentioned Shlepakov's name only a few times in his memoirs. At the same time, his family archive in Toronto contains many of Shlepakov's personal letters to Krawchuk, starting with their correspondence in 1957.[34] Moreover, in 1991, Arnold Shlepakov in his conversation with the author of this text boasted about Krawchuk's dependence on the financial support from both the Soviet government and the KGB, which Shlepakov provided through his personal connections in Kyiv.[35]

Soviet Cultural Diplomacy, Ukrainian Studies and Ukrainian Diaspora in America

A story of the relations between the Ukrainian Canadian Communist Peter Krawchuk and Soviet Ukrainian scholars, such as Arnold Shlepakov, revealed to be just another KGB effort to control and manipulate the Ukrainian Diaspora in Northern America, using not only Canadian communists but also their connections to the intellectuals in Soviet Ukraine. The major goal of the special operations, or active measures of the KGB in Northern America was to discredit and "weaken" the "Ukrainian nationalists" there. Peter Krawchuk and other American/Canadian Ukrainian communists became the useful tools for those KGB operations.

The KGB also used the officials (many of them KGB officers) of the Soviet embassies in the US and Canada to influence the American/Canadian Left in "the desired direction."[36] After 1968, every year the Soviet representatives had the special meetings at the Soviet embassy in Canada to give the instructions to the Ukrainian Canadian Communists on how to behave in the Canadian public life and how to understand and interpret the realities of life in Soviet Ukraine for the Canadian public. The KGB used the Soviet embassies in both Canada and the US for such "special meetings" with the American "progressives" and "sympathizers" of the USSR and Soviet communism for not only collecting the important information about a situation in both countries, but also for instructing and influencing ("advising") pro-Soviet Americans "in a direction of organizing and promoting of the massive American support for the Soviet domestic and international policy."[37]

As the KGB agents reported, the demographic composition of the recent, after WWII, Ukrainian diaspora in America could be used also for influencing those "American Ukrainians in pro-Soviet direction." Many of them were "former displaced persons, who collaborated with the German Fascist occupants and fled to America from retribution." But at the same time, a "considerable number of people" among those Ukrainian emigrants were "the former members of Soviet military troops, held in captivity during the war; and Soviet citizens, brought by force by Germans to work in Germany, and being under influence of hostile propaganda, were afraid to return to their Motherland." The absolute majority of them were "loyal to the USSR, many of them and their children had not accepted the US citizenship yet, and they wanted to return to the Motherland which they missed and recalled with warmth." But they were afraid of persecution by the Soviet administration. "More educated wanted the Soviet authority to define their status and their rights as deported people, and they should have legal guarantee for their return." Therefore, the KGB administration recommended the Soviet diplomats in the USA and Canada "to target such American Ukrainians" in their "diplomatic actions on the American soil, trying to attract them on the Soviet side."[38]

The KGB administration also recommended using popular Soviet Ukrainian writers, such as "a young and talented Vitaly Korotich," for cultural diplomacy of the Soviet Ukrainian government in "capitalist America" "for a creation of the positive humane image" of Soviet Ukraine. Korotich, who became the famous figure in the West as a symbol of perestroika when he was appointed as an editor-in-chief of magazine *Ogonyok* in Moscow in 1986, had made a career of the Ukrainian poet and writer after his graduation of the medical school in Kyiv in 1959. In 1966–1967, Korotich was appointed an editor-in-chief of the Ukrainian popular magazine *Ranok*. In February of 1965, Korotich visited Canada as "a UNESCO *stipendiat* (grant holder)" and immediately attracted attention of the local Ukrainian community in Toronto as a representative of the progressively minded Soviet Ukrainian young intellectuals, known as *shestydesiatnyky*. Peter Krawchuk met Korotich in Toronto and became "his good friend." As Krawchuk recalled, Korotich "told that in Ukraine there was a lot of negative going on, but he expressed his belief in the [moral] strength of [Ukrainian] people: consciousness was growing, especially among the brave youth, which was afraid of nothing."[39] Korotich's reputation of the "opened minded and democratically oriented" person made him popular not only among the politically Left American Ukrainians, but also among the politically moderate representatives of the Ukrainian diaspora.[40]

After these contacts with the Left Canadian Ukrainians, such as Krawchuk, the KGB began supporting Korotich as their "useful asset" in promoting Soviet cultural diplomacy in North America. As early as July 1968, the KGB recommended the Soviet leadership in Kyiv supporting a diplomatic career of Korotich:

> During his visit to Canada and the USA as UNESCO stipend receiver a writer Korotich Vitaly Alekseievich established the wide contacts among progressive and so-called neutral part of Ukrainian emigration, had numerous meetings with participants of different Ukrainian nationalist organizations and publications, which he used for propaganda of achievements of Soviet Ukraine in sphere of culture and organizing of the profitable ideological influence (*okazaniia na nikh vygodnogo ideologicheskogo vliianiia*) in them …For an activation of work of [the Permanent Mission of Soviet Ukraine at the United Nations Organization (UNO)] among local population [especially among the American Ukrainians] and foreign representatives (*prestavitel'stv*) it is useful to send Korotich in Permanent Mission of Ukraine at UNO … This would give an opportunity to the [Soviet] Government to more actively establish the necessary contacts among journalists, diplomats and public figures (*obshchestvennykh deiatelei*) of the USA, to set a regular publication of press-releases and other propagandist documents, which could be prepared by the Ministry of Foreign Affairs of the Ukrainian SSR, RATAU and other interested institutions and organizations, and in this way to strengthen abroad the achievements of the Soviet Union and Ukrainian SSR … Working in the Government, Korotich V. A. could be also very useful in exploring widely the Ukrainian emigration and giving practical assistance to the Ukrainian progressive newspapers and journals in the USA and Canada.[41]

Unfortunately for Korotich's diplomatic career, his "too close" relations with American Ukrainians (even on the political Left, like Krawchuk) were considered to be suspicious by the KGB. Eventually, the KGB administration in Kyiv collected the information, which discredited Korotich as "a greedy, corrupt and westernized person," who frequently changed his opinion, joining the Ukrainian nationalists, "demonstrating his ideological unreliability." As a result, the communist leadership of Soviet Ukraine, under pressure from the KGB headquarters, which provided the compromising material on Korotich, not only stopped his diplomatic career, but removed his name from the list of the possible editors-in-chief of *Vsesvit* journal in 1971.[42]

As one KGB officer, a contemporary of these events, joked, "even the most talented Soviet Ukrainian intellectuals, the useful assets of the KGB, such as Vitaly Korotich, lost their careers in Soviet cultural diplomacy among Ukrainian Americans and were eventually discredited and compromised by their too friendly relations with Canadian Left and such Ukrainian Canadian Communists, like Krawchuk. Even Canadian Ukrainian Communists were too nationalistic for the KGB administration in Kyiv. So everybody in Soviet Ukraine, like Korotich, who contacted them too often, became suspected as well."[43]

At the same time, besides the meddling into the internal affairs of the American and Canadian Left, the KGB officials noted and tried to monitor the rise of various centers of Ukrainian studies abroad. A special attention was directed to the founding in January 1968 of Harvard Ukrainian Research Institute, and to its first director Omelyan Prytsak (1919–2006), who, according to the KGB information, had collaborated with Nazis during WWII, and had connections with US intelligence as well. The KGB noted about the organization of the similar center at Columbia University; the American Ukrainians collected more than $300,000 for those centers at Harvard and Columbia. Through the entire 1970s and the 1980s, the KGB tried to discredit Ukrainian scholars of all those centers, presenting them as Nazi collaborators and American spies.[44]

The KGB tried to discredit any attempt of serious research in the Ukrainian Studies by American and Canadian scholars, especially by those who had a Ukrainian ethnic background. They organized the special series of the "active measures" against those American/Canadian scholars who visited Soviet Ukraine according to the academic exchange program to do their research work in the Ukrainian archives and libraries. The first official complaint from the KGB about "the spying activities" of the young American exchange scholars ("*stazhor*" in Russian) was filed on April 2, 1976. It was about "a *stazhor* associated with Kyiv State University (KDU)," "an American of the Ukrainian origin John Himka, suspected in involvement with the USA intelligence," who tried to get an access to "the archives and libraries of the Ukrainian Academy of Sciences, of the Institutes of Literature, and History, and of KDU." The "second American *stazhor* Nachtell, an economist-sociologist" tried to get an access to the documents on planning and organization of the public transport routes in the big cities of the USSR, using the special archival materials" from the government offices in Kyiv.[45] In April of 1978, the KGB reported that "during the last two years," the CIA and Canadian intelligence service used channels of the academic exchange, such as IREX, for sending to Soviet Ukraine "the special intelligence agents for the collection of the special information and organization of the actions of the ideological diversions." According to this KGB report, "two heads of IREX, Kassof A[llen] and Matushevski D., who are suspected being connected to the CIA, and four scholars (*stazhory*) of the Ukrainian origin (Himka J., Pleshchinski V., husband and wife Tsishkevich Igor and Miroslava), and a researcher from the Russian research center at Harvard University Grimsted Patricia, (all of them with connections to American intelligence)," visited Soviet Ukraine, using IREX funding.[46]

The KGB noted that the very themes of their research (about social-democratic movement in Galicia by Himka, Volhynia and Lublin Unia by Pleshchinski, about the Ukrainian theatrical-decorative art in the 1920s by Miroslava Tsishkevich) "gave them opportunity to work with the ideologically harmful material of the nationalistic character," which would result in the publications, used by "foreign nationalistic centers for the anti-Soviet purposes." All these guests had the constant consultations with American intelligence agents on the premises of the US consulate in Kyiv, and "developed and supported their connections with the Ukrainian nationalistic" intellectuals, "justifying and inspiring their anti-Soviet actions" in Soviet Ukraine. As the KGB agents interpreted, John "Himka, who had the links to the CIA officers, not only looked for establishing connections" with anti-Soviet dissidents, but also requested an access to "the special archival and librarian funds" of Kyiv University and the Institute of History of the Academy of Sciences of the Ukrainian SSR (which was denied by the KGB).[47] In 1976, the KGB agents, following Himka's research about the left, communist groups in Galicia, decided that this "emphasis" on the "Ukrainian nationalistic" social-democrats was directly related to the CIA efforts to undermine the international nature of socialism in Soviet Ukraine. Paradoxically, the KGB agents spied on and limited the research activities of John-Paul Himka, a young Canadian scholar, who openly associated himself with the political Left in Canada and expressed in public his sympathy for the communist movement in Northern America.[48]

But "the most ideologically dangerous," according to the KGB evaluations, were activities of a couple of Tsishkevich, who were famous for their "militant" Ukrainian "nationalist actions in America" and whose parents collaborated with the Nazis in Ukraine during WWII. To discredit such American academic visitors, the KGB used those Soviet scholars who worked for this organization, such as Arnold Shlepakov. Eventually they closed an access to the archival resources for those foreign guests. As a result of such KGB actions, various talented American and Canadian scholars of the Ukrainian dissent, were discredited as "the Ukrainian nationalists" and denied the entry to Soviet Ukraine or rejected access to the library and archival collections there.[49] Moreover, in 1977 the KGB submitted the official proposal to the Ukrainian Ministry of Higher and Special Education about "the limitation of the number of American exchange students and scholars of the Ukrainian dissent, invited for their research in Soviet Ukraine"[50]

Even the official international organizations of Soviet Ukraine, such as the Society of the Cultural Connections with Ukrainians Abroad (SCCUA) participated in the KGB campaigns against "Ukrainian nationalists" in America. All these KGB campaigns pushed the Soviet administration in a direction of changing and making more effective the SCCUA, created in 1960, transforming it in "an efficient Soviet instrument for influencing domestic politics in America (in both the US and Canada) in the positive pro-Soviet direction."[51] These KGB practices had existed until the collapse of the Soviet Union, and they affected both academic and cultural exchange with Canada and the US through the entire 1970s and the 1980s.

During this period of time, the special KGB instructions always reminded about a threat from the US intelligence, targeting the Soviet Ukrainian tourists, visiting the USA and Canada. They emphasized that "the [American] adversary continued to direct his efforts on the individual study, ideological indoctrination, creation of the compromising situations, regarding the Soviet citizens as target for recruiting some of them by the [US] intelligence, to an inclination to non-return in the USSR, getting the intelligence information from them by various means."[52] The US and Canadian intelligence used the "specially trained and prepared representatives of the Ukrainian emigration for the ideological indoctrination and hostile influence on the Soviet citizens from Ukraine."[53] That is why, to fight these "counter-intelligence efforts" and protect "the ideological security" of Soviet Ukrainians traveling in North America, the KGB cultivated the group of the so-called Soviet sympathizers such Peter Krawchuk among American Ukrainians and stimulated the intensive contacts with them through "the KGB people" among Soviet Ukrainian intellectuals, such as Arnold Shlepakov.[54] Eventually, during the 1970s, this connection between American/Canadian Ukrainians, such as Krawchuk, and the "KGB people" among Soviet Ukrainian intellectuals, such as Shlepakov, made a model for all KGB operations, targeting not only the Ukrainian Diaspora in America, but also the academic and cultural exchange programs between Soviet Ukraine and the "capitalist America."

Notes

1 Arkhiv Akademii nauk Ukrainy, Institut istorii (hereafter – ANANU), Opys 1-L, Otdel kadrov, spr. 1277, ark. 55. During this time Shlepakov wrote and published the typical (for Soviet historian) anti-American and anti-capitalist propaganda materials. See, e.g., A. N. Shlepakov, *Ukraina v planakh mizhnarodnoi reaktsii naperedodni drugoi svitovoi viiny* (Kyiv: Derzhavne vydav-vo polytychnoi literatury URSR, 1959), idem, *V roky zrostannia voennoi nebezpeky* (Kyiv: Derzhavne vydav-vo polytychnoi literatury URSR, 1963). The CIA operatives also suspected

the KGB connections of the relatively young scholar such as Shlepakov. See 'declassified and released the Central Intelligence Agency's material' from 1964 about Shlepakov traveling abroad with his wife. See a link: http://www.foia.cia. gov/sites/default/files/document_conversions/1705143/AERODYNA-MIC%20%20%20VOL.%2030%20%20(OPERATIONS)_0003.pdf

2 See his autobiography: Petro Kravchuk, *Bez nedomovok: Spogady* (Kyiv: Literaturna Ukraina, 1995). See about the Soviet financial (and other) support of the Leftist Canadian Ukrainians, such as Krawchuk, in: John Kolasky, *The Shattered Illusion: The History of Ukrainian Pro-Communist Organizations in Canada* (Toronto: PMA Books, 1979), especially pp. 205, 206–208. See more details about those connections of the Leftist Canadians (like Krawchuk) and the Soviet administration in M. H. Marunchak, *The Ukrainian Canadians: A History* (Winnipeg/Ottawa: Ukrainian Free Academy of Sciences, 1976), 494–495; Andrij Makuch, 'Ukrainian Pro-Communists: Revolutionaries into Businessmen,' *Student*, December 1979, p. 9, 11, and other publications of Andrij Makuch about Peter Krawchuk in *The Ukrainian Weekly*, 13 April 1997, No. 15, p. 4; *Journal of Ukrainian Studies*, Vol. 23, No. 1 (Summer 1998), pp. 148–150. See about the overall issues regarding the Soviet perception of Canada in Joseph Laurence Black, *Canada in the Soviet Mirror: Ideology and Perception in Soviet Foreign Affairs, 1917-1991* (Ottawa: Carleton University Press, 1998).

3 Eventually Krawchuk's book, edited and proof-read by Shlepakov, was published in 1963 in Soviet Ukraine: Petro Krawchuk, *Na kanads'kii zemli* (Lviv: Knyzhkovo-zhurnal'ne vydavnytstvo, 1963). See about this in his book of memoirs: idem, *Bez nedomovok: Spogady* (Kyiv: Literaturna Ukraina, 1995), 67.

4 *Ukrains'ke tovarystvo kul'turnogo sv'iazku z zakordonom* existed during 1926–1959, from January 1959 it was renamed as *Ukrains'ke tovarystvo druzhby i kul'turnogo sv'iazku z zarubiwnymy krainamy* (1959–1985). See about a history of such Soviet organizations, created by the USSR for "cultural diplomacy" in Michael David-Fox, *Showcasing the Great Experiment: Cultural Diplomacy and Western Visitors to the Soviet Union, 1921-1941* (New York: Oxford University Press, 2012), V. M. Danylenko, *Ukraina v mizhnarodnykh, Na skryzhaliakh istorii*, and Stanislav Yu. Lazebnyk, Olha B. Havura, *Rozdumy na mostu z dvobichnym rukhom* (Kyiv: Etnos, 2004). During the late 1950s and the early 1960s, young Shlepakov was used by the 'directive organs' for various contacts with the official guests from the United States and Canada. See documents in Tsentral'nyi Derzhavnyi Arkhiv Vyshchykh Organiv Derzhavnoi Vlady i Organiv Derzhavnogo Upravlinnia Ukrainy (hereafter – TsDAVOVUU), fond 5110, op. 1, tom 2, d. 1192, l. 1-3, ll. 1193, 1-5. See also in detail about the relations between Ukrainian Canadians and Soviet Ukraine in Jaroslav Petryshyn, 'The 'Ethnic Question' Personified: Ukrainian Canadians and Canadian-Soviet Relations 1917-1991,' *Re-Imagining Ukrainian Canadians: History, Politics, and Identity*, Edited by Rhonda L. Hinther and Jim Mochoruk (Toronto: University of Toronto Press, 2011), 223–256; Jennifer Anderson, 'Polishing the Soviet Image: The Canadian-Soviet Friendship Society and the 'Progressive Ethnic Groups,' 1949-1957,' *Re-Imagining Ukrainian Canadians*, 279–328.

5 I also use the Private Archive of Larissa Stavroff (Krawchuk) [hereafter – Stavroff archive] in Toronto, Canada, which I visited in March 2012. Stavroff archive, file 64: Shlepakov Arnold, letter from 10 April 1957 about an invitation for submission to 'the new Ukrainian periodical *Ukrains'kyi istorychnyi zhurnal.*' See also their publications after Shlepakov's joining the editorial board of *Vsesvit*: Petro Kravchuk, 'Kanadtsi ukrains'kogo pokhodzhennia vchora i siogodni,' *Vsesvit*, 1981, No. 9, 192–199, and Arnol'd Shlepakov, 'Storinky zhyttia i borot'by,' ibid., 200–201.

6 See in Petro Kravchuk, *Bez nedomovok*, 73–75, and my interview with Leonid Leshchenko, 31 July 2012, Kyiv.

7 A. M. Shlepakov, *Ukrains'ka trudova immigratsiia v SShA i Kanadi (kinets' XIX – poch. XX st.)* (Kyiv: Naukova dumka, 1960). See especially Stavroff archive, file 64: Shlepakov Arnold, personal letters from 7 August 1956 to 17 December 1972.

8 TsDAVOVUU, fond 4621, op. 13, spr. 217, ark. 2–37.

9 ANANU, Opys 1-L, Otdel kadrov, spr. 1277, ark. 55-64; *Visnyk NAN Ukrainy*, 2010, No. 5, 45.

10 Interview with Leonid Leshchenko, Kyiv, 25 June 2013.

11 SBU, f. 16, op. 1, spr. 1043, ark. 312–313. Shlepakov boasted about this in his conversation with me in 1991. See in my interview with Arnold Shlepakov, Kyiv, 29 August 1991.

12 Interview with Arnold Shlepakov, Kyiv, 29 August 1991.

13 Interview with Leonid Leshchenko, 25 June 2013, Kyiv. Leshchenko suggested in his conversation with me that in his youth, Shlepakov had homosexual relations and was caught by the police in a kind of 'illegal sexual act.' The KGB used this incident for blackmailing and manipulating him. Shlepakov began drinking alcohol as a result of this situation. Other colleagues also mentioned that despite his marriage to E. N. Roslavets, deputy director of the Kyiv Museum of Western and Eastern Art, Shlepakov never demonstrated his romantic feelings to women, or expressed his interest in women in any other form, etc. See also ANANU, Opys 1-L, Otdel kadrov, spr. 1277, l. 56.

14 Of course, occasionally, Shlepakov reproduced his old original material on Slavic immigration to the United States and US immigrational politics and published them in the prestigious collective monographs in Moscow. See, e.g., his contributions to the book, published by the Institute of Ethnography at the USSR Academy of Sciences: A. N. Shlepakov, 'Slavianskie gruppy v SShA,' *Natsional'nye protsessy v SShA*, Edited by S. A. Gonionskiy, A. V. Efimov, and Sh. A. Bogina (Moscow: Nauka, 1973), 278–298; and idem, 'Rasovo-natsional'nye osnovy immigratsionnoi politiki SShA v 20–60-kh godakh XX v.,' *Natsional'nye protsessy v SShA*, 312–327.

15 I use the phrase by Sergei Burin regarding 'Arbatov and Sevostianov as the officially appointed *nachal'niki sovetskoi amerikanistiki*' (the bosses and official representatives of American studies in the USSR). See A. N. Shlepakov, *Biografiia statui Svobody: Istoricheskii ocherk* (Moscow: Mysl, 1969); idem, *SShA: Sotsial'naia struktura obshchestva i ego natsional'nyi sostav* (Kiev: Naukova dumka, 1976); V. A. Gorbik and A. N. Shlepakov, *Gosudarstvennaia politika i obostrenie natsional'nykh otnoshenii v stranakh kapitala* (Kiev: Naukova dumka, 1979); I. S. Khmil, A. N. Shlepakov, *Sotsial'naia struktura i sotsial'naia politika SShA, Velikobritanii, FRG, Frantsii i Kanady* (Kiev: Naukova dumka, 1980); A. N. Shlepakov and L. A. Smirnova, *SShA: 'Pokhishchenie umov' v proshlom i nastiashchem* (Moscow: Mysl, 1983). He also edited numerous collective monographs. Altogether Shlepakov (as an author and an editor) published more than 200 books. See his various editorial projects: *Ukraina i zarubizhnyi svit*, Ed. by O. A. Makarenko, A. N. Shlepakov a.o. (Kyiv: Vyd-vo politychnoi literatury, 1970); *Mizhnarodna solidarnist' u borot'bi proty fashyzmu*, Ed. by A. N. Shlepakov, V. N. Gulevych, B. M. Zabarko a.o. (Kyiv: Naukova dumka, 1970); *Dvizhenie mezhdunarodnoi solidarnosti trudiashchikhsia, 1924-1932*, Ed. by A. N. Shlepakov and L. G. Babichenko (Kiev: Naukova dumka, 1980); *Sotsial'no-ekonomicheskaia i politicheskaia diskriminatsiia trudiashchikhsia v kapitalisticheskom mire, 60-70-e gg. XX v.*, Ed by A. N. Shlepakov (Kiev: Naukova dumka, 1980).

16 E-mail correspondence with Volodymyr Yakimets, 10–12 March 2012.

17 The phrase belongs to Volodymyr Yakimets.

18 *Zarubezhnyi mir, sotsial'no-politicheskie i ekonomicheskie problemy* (Kiev: Naukova dumka, 1981–1991). See especially volume 19 for the year of 1990, pp. 103–109, 109–115. See also about how the Ukrainian Communist Party's leadership supported Shelpakov's Insitute in the memoirs of Vladymyr Shcherbytsky's personal secretary: Vitaliy K. Vrublevskiy, *Vladimir Shcherbitskiy: zapiski pomoshchnika: slukhi, legendy, dokumenty* (Kyiv: Dovira, 1993), 180–181. Note the very condescending attitude of Moscow leadership towards the Ukrainian efforts to create the first research center for American Studies in Kyiv. See the documents in ANANU, Opys 1-L, Otdel kadrov, spr. 1277, l. 77 (about Shlepakov), spr. 1198, l. 48 (about Yevtukh joining Shlepakov).

19 *Visnyk NAN Ukrainy*, 2010, No. 5, 43.

20 Interview with Arnold Shlepakov, Kyiv, 29 August 1991.

21 Among the numerous publications, initiated by Shlepakov, see, especially V. B. Yevtukh, *Istoriografiia natsional'nykh otnoshenii v SShA i Kanade (60-70-e gody)* (Kiev: Naukova dumka, 1982); *Rabochii klass i natsional'nyi vopros v stranakh Zapadnoi Evropy i Severnoi Ameriki, 60-80-e gg.*, Ed by A. N. Shlepakov, V. B. Yevtukh a.o. (Kiev: Naukova dumka, 1985); A. M. Shlepakov, *Ukrains'ki kanadtsi v istorychnykh zv'iazkakh iz zemleiu bat'kiv* (Kyiv: Naukova dumka, 1990). However, the best study by Yevtukh in 1991 was edited by his Moscow colleague, Valery Tishkov, rather than by his mentor Shlepakov. See V. B. Yevtukh, *Kontsepsii etnosotsial'nogo razvitiia SShAi Kanady: tipologiia, traditsii, evoliutsiia* (Kiev: Naukova dumka, 1991).

22 Interview with Arnold Shlepakov, Kiev, 29 August 1991; Petro Kravchuk, *Bez nedomovok: Spogady*, 240–241; Peter Krawchuk, *Our History: The Ukrainian Labour-Farmer Movement in Canada, 1907-1991*, Translated from Ukrainian by Mary Skrypnyk, edited by John Boyd (Toronto: Lugus, 1996), 474–475.

23 Interview with Stepan Ivanovich T., a retired KGB officer, January 30, 2019, Kyiv, Ukraine.

24 Interview with Robert F. Ivanov, Moscow, September 6, 1998.

25 Interview with Arnold Shlepakov, August 29, 1991, Kiev. This conversation was in Russian, and it had more criticism of Muscovites, Arbatov and Gorbachev than in my previous interview. He always denied his connections to the KGB, when I raised this question.

26 Robert Conquest, *The Harvest of Sorrow: Soviet Collectivization and the Terror-Famine* (New York: Oxford University Press, 1986).

27 SBU, f. 16, op. 1, spr. 1185, ark. 87.

28 Interview with Leonid Leshchenko, 25 June 2013, Kyiv.

29 Douglas Tuttle, *Fraud, Famine and Fascism: The Ukrainian Genocide Myth from Hitler to Harvard* (Toronto: Progress Books, 1987).

30 Petro Kravchuk, *Bez nedomovok: Spogady*, 244.

31 Peter Krawchuk, *Our History*, 250. See also about this story in: Roman Serbyn, 'Echoes of the Holocaust in Jewish-Ukrainian Relations: The Canadian Experience,' *Ukrainian Quarterly*, vol. 60, no. 12 (2004), 223, and Frank Sysyn, 'Thirty Years of Research on the Holodomor: A Balance Sheet,' *East/West: Journal of Ukrainian Studies*, vol. II, no. 1 (2015), 7.

32 Interview with Leonid Leshchenko, 25 June 2013, Kyiv. In Ukrainian, the Shlepakov's phrase about the demise of American Studies sounded like this in Ukrainian "*Radians'ka amerikanistika pomerla povnistiu.*"

33 Interview with Leonid Leshchenko, 25 June 2013, Kyiv.

34 See the Private Archive of Larissa Stavroff (Krawchuk) in Toronto, Canada, which I visited in March 2012. Stavroff archive, file 64: Arnold Shlepakov.

35 Interview with Arnold Shlepakov, August 29, 1991, Kiev.

36 The most famous case of Soviet pressure on the American Left was to persuade them that Soviet suppression of Prague Spring was justifiable. As John Kolasky described this: "Sergei Molochkov, formerly in charge of relations with the CPC in the apparatus of the CC of the CPSU and the liaison between the Soviet party and the CPC and the ethnic mass organizations, had been in Canada as an employee of the Soviet embassy in Ottawa since 1967. He made a trip across Canada to persuade the Ukrainian leaders to alter their stand in the hope of finding support for the Soviet position [about an invasion of Czechoslovakia]." See in John Kolasky, *The Shattered Illusion*, 175. See about this also in Petro Kravchuk, *Bez nedomovok: Spogady*, 121–126.

37 SBU, f. 16, op. 1, spr. 970, ark. 68–73.

38 Ibid., spr. 1006, ark. 163–164.

39 Krawchuk, Op. cit., 83.

40 SBU, f. 16, op. 1, spr. 1006, ark. 173–174. During the special meetings of the Ukrainian Canadian Congress and the Association of the United Ukrainian Canadians, the representatives of Ukrainian Canadians always voted for Korotich, as their "the most favorable guest" from Soviet Ukraine.

41 SBU, op. 1, f. 16, spr. 974, ark. 321–322. The KGB administration ended this report to the Ukrainian communist leadership with a phrase: "We report this for your consideration."

42 Ibid., spr. 1009, ark. 338–341; spr. 1011, ark. 102–103.

43 Interview with Leonid K., retired KGB officer, Kyiv, February 9, 2019.

44 See SBU, f. 16, op. 1, spr. 970, ark. 50, 62–63, 147ff. Among many cases of KGB disinformation in Canada see how the KGB in Soviet Ukraine used a journalist Sydney Gordon from the newspaper of the Communist Party of Canada, *The Canadian Tribune,* to promote publications of materials against Ukrainian nationalists. See SBU, f. 16, op. 1, spr. 1119, ark. 234–235.

45 SBU, f. 16, op. 1, spr. 1116, ark. 210–212. I was unable to identify a real name of the second American scholar.

46 SBU, f. 16, op. 1, spr. 1144, ark. 175.

47 Ibid., 176.

48 SBU, f. 16, op.1, spr. 1116, ar. 210–212. Compare with an interview by Stepan Ivanovich, a retired KGB officer in Kyiv. The result of Himka's research in Soviet Ukraine was his future book: John-Paul Himka, *Socialism in Galicia: The Emergence of Polish Social Democracy and Ukrainian Radicalism, 1860–1890* (Harvard University Press: Cambridge, Mass., 1983).

49 Ibid., spr. 1144, ark. 176–178. Frank Sysyn told me about various cases (including his own) of such KGB treatment of American and Canadian scholars of the Ukrainian origin. See also my article about the IREX exchange and the denial by the Soviet side of Soviet visa for the academic research in Soviet Ukraine according to the exchange agreements to those American scholars like Frank Sysyn, whose research was "too ideologically dangerous – with nationalistic or religious bias." Sergei Zhuk, "'Academic Détente': IREX Files, Academic Reports, and 'American' Adventures of Soviet Americanists during the Brezhnev Era," *Cahiers du monde russe*, Janvier –juin 2013, Vol. 54, No. 1–2, 297–328.

50 SBU, f. 16, op. 1, spr. 1144, ark. 178.

51 SBU, f. 16, op. 1, spr. 970, ark. 225–227.

52 Ibid., spr. 1024, ark. 87.

53 Ibid., ark. 89-90. The KGB documents provided a plenty of proofs of such "provocations" against the tourists from Soviet Ukraine during 1970–71. The "Ukrainian nationalists" organized the anti-Soviet debates in New York City with representatives of SCCUA in September 1970. The similar scandal

happened during the radio show with a participation of Soviet Ukrainians in Montreal, Canada. The students from Georgetown University, who specialized in the Ukrainian Studies, met Soviet tourists from Ukraine with anti-Soviet demonstrations.

54 I paraphrased my interview with Igor T., a former KGB officer in Dnipropetrovsk.

Part II

The KGB vs. Politicians and Tourists from "Capitalist America"

From the early opening of Soviet Ukraine to the visits of foreign guests after 1953, the KGB developed various tactics of surveillance over foreign visitors, reporting about them and their contacts with Soviet Ukrainians. Again, the most important objects of KGB operations inside Ukraine were Americans and Canadians of the Ukrainian origin, who visited the Ukrainian SSR. They were tourists, diplomats, students, scholars and workers at various 16 American exhibitions, organized in Kyiv and other cities of Soviet Ukraine throughout late socialism, starting in 1961 with an exhibit "Plastic USA" and finishing in 1989–1991 with an exhibition "Design USA."[1] For the KGB, all those visitors were potential American and Canadian spies, employed by the CIA. At the same time, numerous American exhibits became an object of industrial espionage by the Soviet KGB agents, who, beginning with a 1961 exhibition, collected not only the important technological and financial information from Americans, but also learned how to use various economic, financial and technological practices of their American guests, demonstrated at their exhibitions.[2]

During the beginning of the Cold War, the major problem for the Ukrainian KGB officers (like for all their colleagues from other Soviet re-publics) was to "fight the American spies on the Soviet soil." As early as 1946–1947, the KGB issued the special instructions how to identify an American spy, how to expose and unmask this spy, how to prevent his/her spying actions inside the Soviet Union and how to organize an arrest of this spy. Even, after Stalin's death in 1953, the major purpose of the Ukrainian KGB special operations still remained "an exposure and neutralization of the foreign spies" in Soviet Ukraine.[3] According to the KGB analysts, all American visitors to Soviet Ukraine were suspected to be directly connected to the American intelligence. The first category of those "potential American spies" included the American diplomats and other officials from the US Embassy in the Soviet Union. In 1947, the first time after WWII, the KGB composed a list of those American diplomats, who visited Kyiv, with a description of their "spying" activities, and reported them to the Soviet Ukrainian authorities. Since 1947 the KGB in Soviet Ukraine had organized a series of the active measures and the special operations to monitor the

DOI: 10.4324/9781003212522-6

American diplomats' "movements" in the republic, using the specially trained KGB agents.[4] Until the collapse of the Soviet Union in 1991, these active measures became the regular practices of the KGB officers in Soviet Ukraine, regarding the American and Canadian guests.

5 "*Shpionomania*," or the American Spies Hysteria in Soviet Ukraine

The KGB Active Measures against US Diplomats

After Stalin death, the KGB tried to use fewer active measures against the US officials, who were visiting the Soviet Union. Still, in 1953 the KGB officers continued their surveillance over all US official visitors in Soviet Ukraine. The first (chronologically) KGB operation against a US diplomat, who visited Kyiv, was recorded as early as October 1953. This operation of surveillance was focused on the official visit by Marshall McDuffie, a former chief of UNRRA's mission to Ukraine, who arrived to Kyiv from Minsk on October 25, 1953.[5] The KGB provided "a model report" for this visit. They informed the communist party leadership of Ukraine that McDuffie was born in 1909 in the New York City in the family of Christian Protestants. He graduated from Yale University, which was famous "for preparation of the American diplomats." McDuffie worked in the lend-lease office and oversaw the problems of economic warfare during WWII. After the war, he led the section of the US Department of State responsible for UNRRA. From March to July 1946, he was a chief of the UNRRA's mission to Soviet Ukraine; and during his stay in Ukraine, the KGB "characterized him to be a progressive American."[6] McDuffie announced to the Soviet officials in Kyiv that for his trip to Ukraine in 1953 he had already had the official Khrushchev's permission. He explained that he personally knew Khrushchev, met him, and on his way back to Moscow would continue his meetings with Khrushchev and would share with him his impressions from this visit to Kyiv.[7]

McDuffie explained that he would like to visit two collective farms, two-three industrial factories, a school, Kyiv State University (KDU), the farmers markets, food stores and house construction sites in Soviet Ukraine. He asked for a permission to make photos, and the Soviet administration allowed him to make pictures of everything, except the photos of bridges. Besides Kyiv, McDuffie wanted to visit Zaporizhie or Poltava, where he planned to see the graves of the American soldiers who died during the WWII and who were buried in Poltava.[8]

During his first day of visit to Kyiv, he attended the religious service at St Vladimir cathedral, and was surprised that he saw only very old people

DOI: 10.4324/9781003212522-7

there. The KGB agents reported that McDuffie liked the new public advertisements in downtown Kyiv, which used the colored electric lights and modern images. He was especially impressed with the movie theater *Kiev*, where he noticed a symphonic orchestra playing in the foyer and the visitors attending the movie theater's library with a wide variety of available books and periodicals for reading by the visitors. McDuffie said that American movie theaters had none of this. He asked about the US films shown in this theater. At the end of his excursion in this theater, McDuffie watched the second part of the Soviet movie *Korabli shturmuiut bastiony* and the beginning of the Austrian film *Moi malen'kii drug*.[9]

At the end of his surveillance assignment, the KGB agent submitted his detailed final report about McDuffie's behavior during his visit to Soviet Ukraine. As it turned out, this KGB officer could not find any signs of the "spying activities by this American diplomat." What he discovered in "this American's behavior" was the signs of real curiosity and interest about how the ordinary Soviet people lived. For this American, his visit to Ukraine resulted in a series of the "shocking revelations." After his visiting various food stores in downtown Kyiv, McDuffie was sincerely surprised by the long lines of people, waiting for butter and milk near those stores. He could not understand the printed advertisements in the same stores about the limits "for five eggs only for one customer," and he saw how local customers after buying their ratio of five eggs took the line of people again to get their "another five eggs."[10] The KGB agent was surprised by the fact that McDuffie was constantly making the written notes of prices in Kyiv shops, making photos of the lines of people at various food stores and shops. At the same time, the same KGB officer devoted a half of his official report to the information, which McDuffie shared with him about his previous job of an attorney in New York City, about his former salary, the apartment rent in New York, the conditions of living in the American cities and about the standards of life of the American workers, which were obviously much better than in the USSR, if "they [the US industrial workers] could afford to get their personal automobiles, using their salaries."[11]

In early November of 1953, McDuffie traveled to Zaporizhie and Kharkiv, where he rejected help of an expert interpreter (and the KGB agent), who knew languages, explaining, "I do not need the spies to escort me." In all Ukrainian cities he visited, McDuffie made photos of the "long lines of people at the local shops, the badly dressed people, and the old, dilapidated buildings." In Kharkiv, he was even arrested by the local police for trying to photo the lines of people near the shops. He was released from arrest, before he went from Kharkiv to Moscow to see the military parade on the Red Square on November 7.[12] After his return from Moscow to Ukraine on November 10, 1953, McDuffie resumed his visits to the Ukrainian collective farms, industrial factories, his meetings with Soviet officials, where "he publicly defended the US policy against the Soviet expansion in the world, trying to persuade the

Ukrainians that the ordinary American workers lived much better than their Soviet counterparts."[13]

The KGB supervisors, who monitored McDuffie's actions, were frustrated with his "lack of the apparent spying activities." They found only one complaint about McDuffie's "misbehavior" in October–November 1953: but it was not related to the US intelligence, it was McDuffie's "interest in the Ukrainian women." From the early beginning of his visit, McDuffie told the KGB agent that the residents of Ukraine were dressed and looked better than the people from other parts of the Soviet Union. He especially liked the Ukrainian women. In Kharkiv hotel *Inturist*, the local official reported that McDuffie "behaved cheekily and tactlessly with the women, the officials of *Inturist*." On November 2, "he tried to convince a female visitor of the restaurant to come with him to his room (she rejected his offer)." On November 3, he tried to convince a female official from the radio station of *Inturist* to come to his room, "he offered her 100 rubles to give to a hotel maid as a bribe to conceal from the hotel administration a fact of that female official's visit to his room." Following advice of the KGB officer, she returned money to McDuffie, explaining that Soviet women could not be bought by the money. According to her testimony, McDuffie "behaved like a sadist, trying to seduce," and, eventually, he raped her.[14] All KGB reports in November 1953 contained the detailed description of McDuffie's sexual adventures and numerous other cases of his hitting on women, the *Inturist* officials. Eventually, the KGB acknowledged that American diplomat had nothing to do with the American intelligence service and they dropped their criminal investigation of McDuffie, "complaining that Moscow administration allowed those American perverts to go to Ukraine and seduce our women with impunity, because of those perverts' diplomatic immunity."[15]

Khrushchev's liberalization of the foreigners' travels inside Soviet Ukraine affected the KGB operations as well. The KGB tried to protect the strategically important objects such as a port of Odesa in southern Ukraine from the visits of foreign diplomats. Especially, the KGB operatives worried about the visits of the US officials from the US Embassy to Odesa. According to the KGB reports in March 1955, 63 US officials had visited Odesa since 1950.[16] Despite any attempts to find some criminal activities, the KGB agents did not discover any serious misdemeanors or crimes committed by those US diplomats. In March 1955, following the group of the US officials from the US Embassy in Odesa, the KGB noticed only 11 cases of the attempted contacts by the Odesa Jews with American diplomats. All these cases were initiated by the Soviet citizens of Jewish origin in Odesa. Eventually, the KGB concentrated only on the obvious connections of US diplomats to the open anti-Soviet actions or the collection of the intelligence information in the city of Odesa. Through the entire 1950s, the KGB failed to find any poofs of "spying activities" of the US diplomats in the southern Ukrainian ports such as Odesa.[17]

Eventually, the KGB found a few attempts of American diplomats to spy on the ship-building factories in the southern Ukrainian cities, such as Kherson and Nikolaev. In March of 1957, the KGB operatives reported that during their visit to Kherson, two assistants of military-maritime attaché of the US Embassy tried to visit the territory of the secret shipbuilding plant #873 there, and twice tried to visit Nikolaev, the city which was closed to foreigners. Eventually they reported that the officials of the US, British and French embassies, while visiting Kyiv, Odesa, and other cities of Ukraine, tried to buy the books and various publications by local publishers about shipbuilding. But after this alarm in 1957, the KGB prevented any attempt of the foreigners' spying in the locations of Soviet ship-building centers in southern Ukraine, banning their trips. Through the entire history of late socialism, until the end of the 1980s, the KGB operatives could not find any connections of the US diplomats to this particular kind of spying.[18]

Another model case of the KGB active measures against American spies was related to the visits to Soviet Ukraine in 1957–1958 by Harry George Barnes Jr. (1926–2012), the second secretary of the US Embassy, who was treated by the Ukrainian KGB as a professional CIA agent. The KGB even gave him a KGB nickname *a Baron* for their files. Harry G. Barnes Jr. graduated from Amherst College and Columbia University and served in the U.S. Army in 1944–1946. He entered the U.S. Foreign Service as a consular officer in Bombay, India, in 1951, and served as a head of the consular section of the US Embassy in Prague in 1953–1955. Barnes worked as a publications-procurement officer at the US Embassy in Moscow in 1957–1959. After this diplomatic service, during 1959–1962, he was a political officer in the Office of the Soviet Affairs in the US Department of State[19] (Figure 5.1).

As KGB agents reported to their supervisors, Barnes "arrived in the USSR in October 1956." Using local trains from Kyiv, he visited Kharkiv in May 1957, Dnipropetrovsk in September 1957 and Lviv and Uzhgorod in April–May 1958.[20] In May 1958, he went to Kyiv, following the US Ambassador Llewellyn Thompson (1904–1972), who introduced Philadelphia symphony orchestra to the Soviet audiences, and stayed all the time with an ambassador and musicians during their visit to Ukraine, while American orchestra performed music for numerous Ukrainian classic music fans. As it turned out, Barnes had already visited Kyiv five times, and again the KGB officers were surprised that "he was not interested in sightseeing, nor in visiting the historical monuments or museums (of the city)." Barnes "paid a special attention only to ten [Kyiv] bookstores, visiting them often; and his most popular book shop was *Akademkniga* on Lenin Street 42 (where he spent all his free time, while visiting Kyiv)." As another KGB agent followed him and reported about an American's movements in Kyiv, Barnes also visited the Ministry of Foreign Affairs of the Ukrainian SSR, the Statistical Office of Soviet Ukraine, Polish and Czech Consulates, and Kyiv City Council: "Besides visiting Kyiv, he traveled once to Kharkiv, Dnipropetrovsk,

Figure 5.1 Young Barnes.

Simferopol, Yalta, Lviv and Uzhgorod. Everywhere he was interested only in buying the literature, published by the local publishing houses: in Crimea – the books about Sevastopol, in Kharkiv – the books about economy of Kyiv, Kharkiv, Lviv and Stalino, written by the local authors [of Soviet Ukraine]."[21]

Meanwhile, the KGB agents organized a series of the special active measures, targeting Barnes. On May 4, 1957, Barnes and two attachés from the US Embassy arrived in their car from Moscow to Kharkiv. The KGB agents "tried to prevent [the Americans'] spying actions, not allowing them to visit the regime objects, and revealing any possible contacts of them with Soviet citizens." One of the agents was especially busy, trying to prevent the Americans' deviation from their allowed (by the KGB) route and itinerary. He was shocked to find out that the Americans' major goal during their trip was "just to buy the Soviet books," printed by the local Ukrainian publishers. The same agent reported that in Kharkiv Barnes also bought *Thematic Plan of Publications* by Kharkiv Regional Publishing House. One US official, Barnes' colleague, in the some "kolkhoz field of Kharkiv region came out from the car and attentively observed the growing plants and state of soil." The next day, near a town of Chuguev, the Americans watched the military training tank drills on the special *tankodrom* [tank training ground] (Soviet administration allowed them to observe these drills):

> After this, in Kharkiv, when Barnes' colleagues returned to Moscow, he went to a bookstore, where a local seller Bystritskaia suggested Barnes to go to a Kharkiv University publishing office, and she took him there. The same day in Kharkiv Barnes visited *Knizhnaia palata UkrSSR*, where he communicated with officials in Russian without an interpreter. With his wife, Barnes went sightseeing [followed by the KGB agent], and in the evening, they traveled by train to Kyiv. In this train the KGB agent Khalin was put in their railway car compartment. During this trip, Barnes realized that Khalin was a Jew, that was why he told Khalin about his service in the army during the WWII together with his friends, American Jews, and Barnes also told how the American state funded his college education after the war, praised Israel to Khalin, told that the American Jews tried to help all Jews all over the world to move to Israel. As Khalin explained, he was surprised to know [from Barnes] about a possibility of US college education free of charge and a respect for the people of the Jewish origin in the USA.[22]

Eventually, Barnes visited all Ukrainian cities he wanted to visit, except Dnipropetrovsk, which the KGB closed to foreigners by the end of 1957.[23] In his conversations with the KGB agents, he explained that he was buying the Ukrainian books for the Library of Congress and the libraries of various American universities and colleges. When the KGB agents checked the lists of books ordered by Barnes from various Ukrainian book shops, they could not find any proof of the special intelligence operation conducted by the American diplomats. The list of those books, ordered by Barnes, included a wide range of titles – from the purely scientific subjects on agriculture or civil machine building to the historical studies of Soviet Ukraine and a biography of the Ukrainian poet Ivan Franko (1856–1916).

At the end of the KGB meticulous surveyance operation, the overwhelming majority of the KGB agents' reports, after their long conversations (sometimes involving a dinner and wine tasting) in the railway car compartments with Barnes and his wife during their Ukrainian travels, contained the more interesting details of the everyday life in the USA, about the US-Soviet relations and international affairs, than about the Americans' supposed spying activities. Sometimes, the agents' reports looked like the ethnographic studies of the foreign mentality and culture, reporting about "the obligatory finger prints for foreigners to visit the USA," about the American feature films and Soviet audience, about the reading tastes of Barnes, who could read in the train Turgenev's *Zapiski okhotnika* in Russian and a historical study *Three Who Made a Revolution* about Lenin, Trotskii and Stalin in English, which looked like anti-Soviet propaganda,[24] about Barnes' delight after his watching the ballet *Raimonda* in Kyiv Opera and Ballet Theater, about his curiosity, asking about meanings of some Russian words, like *chopornyi* (prim, smug). The KGB supervisors could not find any description of the professional intelligence work in those reports. Only twice they suspected some "foul game" in Barnes' behavior. One time, a "blonde girl" approached Barnes in downtown Kyiv and tried to speak to him in fluent English. It turned out to be a false alarm: it was one Ukrainian enthusiastic college student of foreign languages, who just wanted to practice her English conversational skills with a real American diplomat (Figure 5.2).

Another story was more complicated. The KGB officers from Kyiv sounded alarm and reported this as a serious problem, when on October 21, 1958, "an official from the US Embassy, a US citizen and a professional intelligence officer Barnes had a suspicious and long telephone conversation from Moscow to Kyiv with a man, a Soviet citizen." For the KGB, this telephone call was a breaching of the diplomatic protocol, raising a fear of spying and secret recruiting of the Soviet citizens for the needs of American intelligence. After a special KGB investigation, it turned out that a man on a phone was Viktor Petrovich Gontar, who was born in 1905 in a town of Radzivilov of Rivne Region, now a director of Kyiv Theater of Opera and Ballet named after Shevchenko.[25] According to the KGB report, "from 28

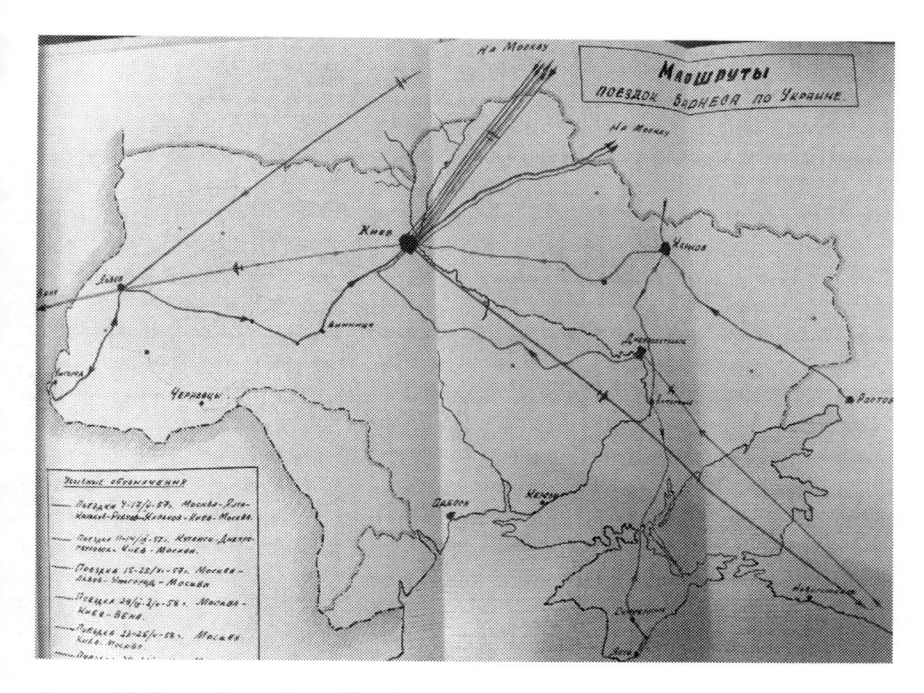

Figure 5.2 Barnes' travels in Ukraine.

to 31 October 1958, with a group of the American artists, the second secretary of US Embassy, Harry George Barnes, Jr. was visiting Kyiv. During his visit, Barnes met Gontar three times in Kyiv. On October 29, he had a private conversation in the theater with Gontar without witnesses in Gontar's theater office. Next day he had the similar secret meeting in the same office. At the same time, Barnes organized the special meetings [without the KGB permission] of Gontar with the American artists whom he brought to the capital of Soviet Ukraine."[26] Initially, the KGB representatives, who followed Barnes from Moscow, even planned a special operation ("active measures") against Barnes and Gontar. But after a thorough investigation, they could not find any proofs of Barnes' spying and Gontar's collaborating with the US intelligence. Moreover, eventually, they realized that Gontar had been married to Yulia Khrushcheva (1916–1981), a daughter of the Soviet leader, Nikita S. Khrushchev.[27] Once the KGB officers from Kyiv office even tried to arrest Gontar and Barnes, but their actions were stopped by their Moscow supervisors, who prevented this action, which would create the international scandal. The Ukrainian KGB dropped the criminal case against Barnes by the end of 1959.[28] To some extent, the "Barnes' case" became a model for the KGB treatment of the American (and Canadian) diplomats in Soviet Ukraine. Between 1956 and 1990 almost every month the KGB administration from Kyiv office submitted the official reports about "the suspicious actions" of American/ Canadian diplomats in Ukraine. Only a few of them had something to do directly with espionage (Figure 5.3).

The "Spy Mania" and the Public Trials of "American Spies" in Soviet Ukraine

More successful for the KGB were the "espionage cases," involving the foreign tourists who happened to work for the US intelligence, and they were caught in Ukraine while performing their intelligence assignments. In the early 1960s, the KGB even organized a series of the show public trials for these "American spies." To some extent, it was a KGB reaction to the American U-2 spy scandal, when in May 1960 the Soviets shot down the American spy plane U-2 and captured its pilot, Francis Gary Powers.[29] Another KGB reaction was connected to the series of public revelations by American media in May 1960 about the Soviet spying activities inside of the USA of 12 Soviet secret agents of the KGB (including the recently arrested in New York KGB colonel Rudolf Abel).[30]

The KGB office in Kyiv was especially worried about a case of the Vadim Kiriliuk, who represented the official Ukrainian delegation at the General Assembly of the United Nations in New York City. Vadim Aleksandrovich Kiriliuk was born in 1928 in the Ukrainian city of Vinnytsia. After his graduation from the law department of Kyiv State University, he joined the KGB and moved to Moscow. Before September 1955, Kiriliuk was working

Figure 5.3 Barnes and Gontar.

as a KGB junior security officer. In 1955–1957 he studied at the special KGB school in Moscow. After his graduation from this KGB school, Kiriliuk worked at the First Main Directorate of the KGB, which was in charge of the foreign operations and intelligence activities abroad. According to this Directorate's order, in 1958 Kiriliuk was included in the official delegation of Soviet Ukraine, which participated in the work of the General Assembly of the United Nations Organization (UNO) in New York City. While living in the US, Kiriliuk was hired by the Ministry of Foreign Affairs of Soviet Ukraine to represent it in the Secretariat of the UNO, where he had worked until January 1960. According to the KGB report, "in April 1959, Iosif Zatirka, a US citizen of the Ukrainian origin, visited the Soviet Embassy in Mexico and offered the secret written information about the USA and agreed to help [the KGB with the classified information] in the USA. Due to the fact that Zatirka gave the precious information, which presented the [strategic] interest [to the USSR], the KGB residents in the USA decided that Kiriliuk would continue to work with him inside the US under a nickname of George."[31] As it turned out, after the first meetings with Kiriliuk/George, Zatirka "encountered some problems performing the KGB assignments," he "got scared, and then later denounced" Kiriliuk ("as a KGB spy") to the American police. As a result, following Zatirka's denunciation of Kiriliuk, the American government sent a special note of complaint to the General Secretary of the UNO about the spying activities of Kiriliuk. Using his family emergency as a pretext to retire from an official position at the UNO, Kiriliuk managed to escape safely from New York City to the USSR in January 1960.

But his behavior created a scandal, compromising a membership of Soviet Ukraine and its official delegation at the United Nations in the USA. Former KGB officers, who still remember the situation of the 1960s, noted that this "Kiriliuk's case" inspired a series of the active measures against "the CIA agents" inside Soviet Ukraine. According to those officers, the wave of "spy scare" ("*shpionomania*") of the 1960s in the USSR, and especially in Soviet Ukraine, was the KGB "peculiar" response to the "public exposure of the Soviet spies" inside the USA, such as a "Kiriliuk's case."[32]

The first response of the KGB, which took place in Soviet Ukraine during July–December 1961, was a special KGB operation against and a public trial of two "American" spies, who happened to be the Dutch tourists Ewert Reidon and Lou de Yaher. They were arrested in Yalta, Crimea, on August 22, 1961. As the KGB officers reported, "these auto tourists behaved suspiciously: in Yalta they tried to get into the forbidden location of the secret military objects, they even stole the city of Yalta phone number book; on August 19, during their crossing of the state borders [of the USSR], the Soviet officials organized the search of those [tourists'] belongings and found 14 pieces of papers with the written notes about the Soviet strategic [secret] objects, then on 48 block notes' pages – a list of their photos they made, and found 12 camera films with the pictures of the Soviet radar equipment and other strategic and military objects. They were arrested; and they immediately confessed that they had been working for the NATO and the US intelligence, being hired by the American intelligence officer."[33] (Figure 5.4)

Eventually, after the long-lasting interrogations by the KGB officers, these Dutch "tourist spies" wrote their detailed confessions about their recruitment by the American intelligence officers and their intelligence assignments, they were supposed to complete during their travels to the USSR. According to the KGB records of those tourists' interrogations, one of them, Ewert Reidon, was born in 1931 in Hamburg, Germany; his mother was German, his father was Danish. In 1939, his family moved to Holland and settled there. In 1950 Reidon entered as an engineer student into a special technical school of ship mechanics in Middelburg, Netherlands; in 1955 he got married and began sailing to earn some money for his new family. According to his official explanation, in 1957 Reidon had to leave a

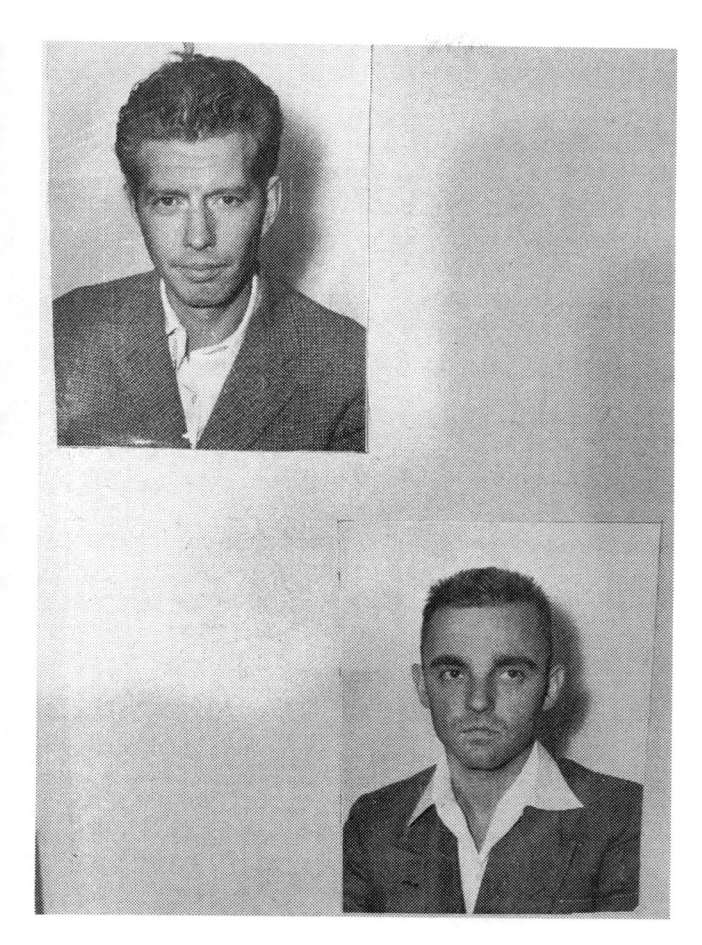

Figure 5.4 Dutch spies Reidon and De Yaher.

ship because of his "financial mistakes" during his buying of the special technical equipment for the ship. As the KGB figured out, Reidon just stole the ship crew's money to pay his family debts. To avoid an oncoming arrest, a desperate Reidon was looking for any source of funding. That was how a man of 45-years old with a name Nadort from Rotterdam, offered him a possibility to make money by making photos from the Dutch ships sailing to Klaipeda, Soviet Lithuania, and Ventspils, Soviet Latvia. Nadort gave him a special instruction about the Soviet ships, submarines and radars. After 1957, Reidon got a diploma of a ship engineer in Holland and received the first professional intelligence assignment. Nadort asked Reidon to make pictures of the Soviet ships in Arkhangelsk, following his special instructions; but he did not like his photos, and did not pay Reidon money, he had promised. In 1958 Reidon was approached by someone with a name Otto who introduced Reidon to an American intelligence officer who instructed him what to do – to make photos of radars and the plants producing liquid oxygen in the Soviet Union. But this time such photos should be made from a car. As it turned out, Otto and his friend Van Maurik worked for the CIA. Later on, they connected Reidon to another Dutchman, who needed badly the American money. This Dutchman was De Yaher, a driver of an automobile Renault 4. The American agents instructed Reidon and Yaher, what to shoot and how to make photos, using the pipelines and industrial objects in Holland as "the exercise models" for the Dutchmen's future assignment in the USSR[34] (Figure 5.5).

Later in the investigation, the KGB officials reported to the Ukrainian party and state administration that both Reidon and De Yaher were recruited and prepared "by the special US intelligence instructors in Holland to be the NATO intelligence agents." Reidon had already had his first spying experience, while visiting the Soviet ports, such as Klaipeda, Mezen', Ventspils, Arkhangel'sk and Polish port Gdansk; De Yaher had such an experience in China, visiting a port of Shanghai. They were collecting the intelligence information during their trip in Soviet Ukraine using the car Renault 4, which belonged to De Yaher. Lou De Yaher, who was born in 1936, worked as a supplier of the ships from Amsterdam, and he was an

Figure 5.5 Reidon after arrest.

experienced driver, whose driving skills were used by the American and British recruiters for the future intelligence service during Reidon's and Yaher's touristic trip by a car in the Soviet Union.[35]

After his arrest, Reidon told to the KGB officers about the various details of his intelligence assignment and confessed that he was afraid of this arrest, because he had realized that the KGB agents followed them all the time after their crossing the Soviet state border. Reidon told a KGB investigator that in May 1961, Otto, an American intelligence officer, who had already offered him the intelligence job for money, explained him that the specific intelligence instructions would be given to Reidon by a special American agent in one café in Amsterdam during the same evening:

> [That American recruiting agent] took out from his briefcase a Soviet *"Inturist* map" with the tourist itineraries inside the USSR and pointed to one particular itinerary Uzhgorod-Lvov-Kiev-Kharkov-Zaporozhie-Yalta-Odessa-Kiev-Lvov-Uzhgorod, proposing him to arrange a tourist trip via a Dutch tourist bureau for this itinerary. As he explained [to Reidon], the Americans were mainly interested in the information about the rocket technology of the Soviet Union, the railroad cisterns with liquid oxygen, which is a rocket fuel, and also about the road branches from the central highways with their exact locations on a map. Besides, this American recruiter emphasized that the Americans were especially interested in engaging [Reidon and Yaher] in a collection of the intelligence information about the locations and characteristics of the rocket and radar installations; aerodromes and airplanes on them; locations of the storage places for keeping the liquid fuel for the rockets; location of the tank drilling fields and tanks themselves. This American agent outlined that [Reidon and Yaher] (if possible) had to make photos of the strategic objects, and to make the detailed drawings of them.[36]

In 1957, the same American recruiter had promised that Reidon's wife would be materially supported by the US intelligence service, and he promised to pay her 120 guldens weekly.[37] The KGB investigators also realized that the British intelligence officers were actively involved in this process of recruitment. The most active among them was Ernst Henry Van Maurik, an English intelligence agent, who participated in recruiting both Reidon and his co-agent Lou de Yaher. The KGB found out that Van Maurik was a resident at the Moscow British Embassy from September 1948 to August 1950, and he had already served as a British Secret Intelligence Service agent in West Berlin in 1954–1956[38] (Figure 5.6).

After a thorough KGB interrogation, both Dutchmen became the objects for punishment by the Soviet judicial system. The KGB insisted that they should be indicted as the criminals at the open public trial, with a presence of the foreign journalists (including the Dutch ones), and with the subsequent publications of the trial's proceedings in media on October 2–5,

Figure 5.6 De Yaher after arrest.

1961. The KGB also recommended that a term of imprisonment for those Dutch agents should be 10–12 years in jail.[39] The open public trial started on October 4, 1961, with a presence of 50 representatives of various Soviet organizations, and 30 Soviet and foreign journalists. After the official reading of an indictment on October 5, both Dutchmen publicly confessed in committing their crime – "being the American spies, recruited by the NATO intelligence," Reidon – in 1957, and De Yaher – in 1959 – to collect the intelligence information in the USSR. Despite their sincere confession, each of these Dutch tourists was sentenced to 13 years of imprisonment[40] (Figures 5.7 and 5.8).

The second case for the open public trial of the "American spies" in the capital city of Soviet Ukraine was generated by an arrest of and by the consequent investigation related to two West German tourists: Adolf Werner and his wife Hermine Werner (August–December 1961).[41] Their arrest was the direct result of the numerous "denunciation reports" by Soviet vigilantes to the police about "two [strange] foreigners who were making pictures of the military objects in Sevastopol harbor, which is prohibited ..." But they "still kept making photos of Soviet military ships and submarines, despite the [Soviet people] trying to stop their illegal actions" on August 23, 1961[42] (Figures 5.9 and 5.10).

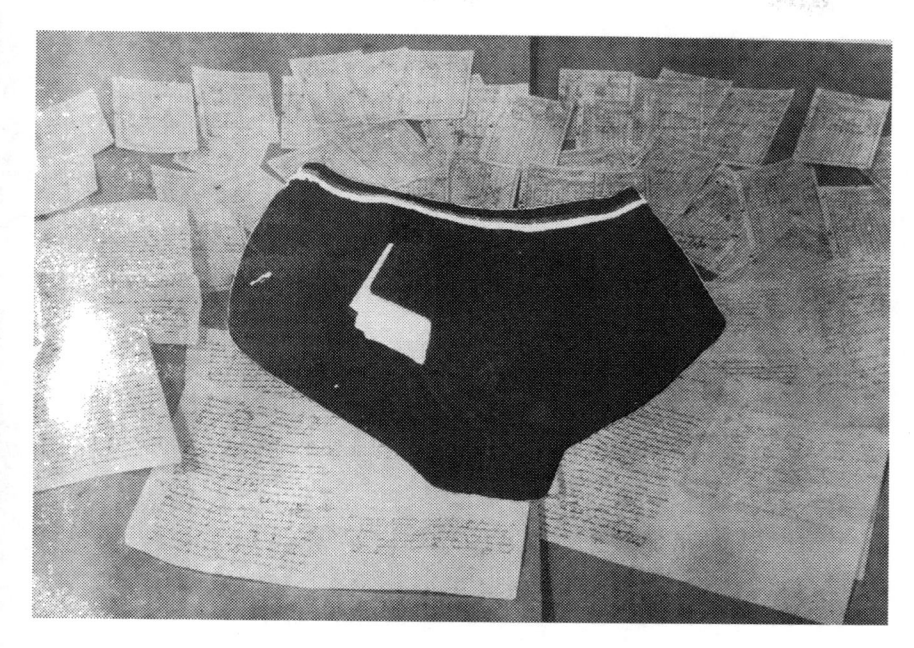

Figure 5.7 Dutch spies' papers.

Figure 5.8 Dutch spies' equipment.

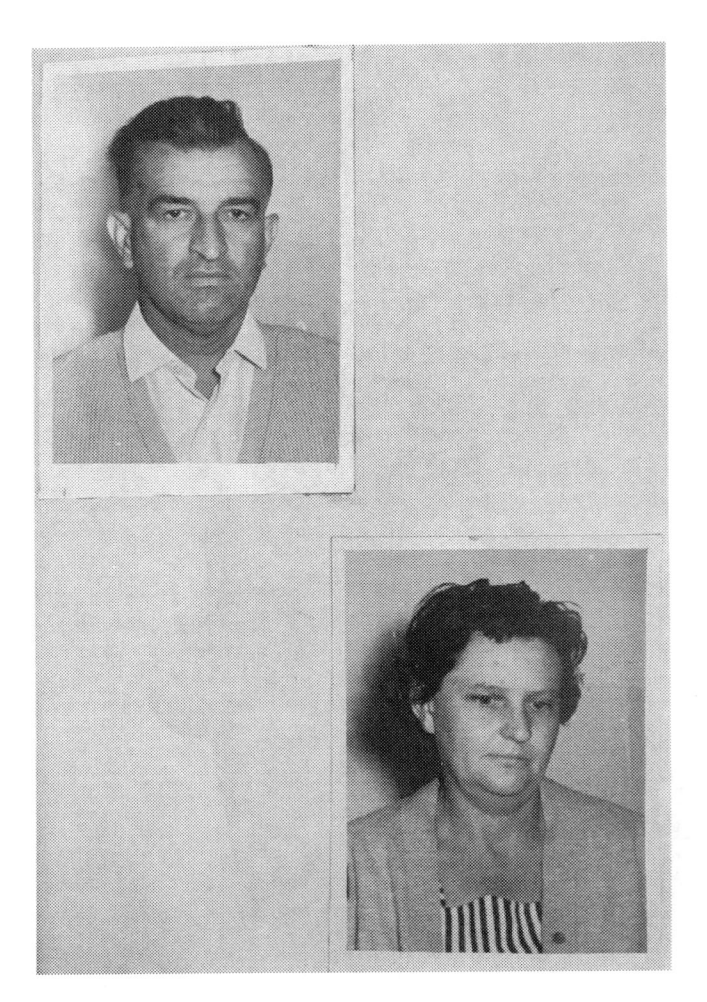

Figure 5.9 The Werners couple.

This pair of the West German tourists traveled to Crimea from August 20 to 30, 1961, by transit via Odessa on a steamboat *Litva* as the auto-tourists from West Germany together with their car Volkswagen KAEA 332. According to the KGB reports, Adolf Werner "was born in 1910 in [a town of] Kanitz [now Czech town of Dolni Koinice]" and his wife Hermine "was born in 1916 as Hermine Fischer in a town of Franzensbad [now Polish town of Františkovy Lázně]." Their itinerary included Yalta-Simferopol-Zaporizhie-Kharkiv-Kyiv-Chernivtsy. When they made a stop at Yalta camping, they had already been followed by two KGB agents from Zaporizhie, Sokolov and Yurezanskii, who stayed in a tent nearby. Adolf

Figure 5.10 Werner's car.

initiated his contacts with them, when he realized they were residents of the big industrial Soviet city. In a friendly conversation, these agents learnt from Adolf that the Werners lived in a German city of Karlsruhe, where Adolf was in charge of a big shoes store, that he had already participated in WWII as an officer in "Hitler's Army in a SS division," which occupied Kharkiv, Kursk, Kryvyi Rig and Nikopol. Adolf explained them that he wanted to visit the "locations of his former military adventures." As it turned out, he understood very well the special military questions, at least those regarding Soviet tanks and artillery during WWII.[43] Adolf told the KGB agents that at the end of the war he was kept as a prisoner of war by the Americans. After his release from an American prison, he returned to in Germany, where he restored his pre-war business and soon he began to travel abroad. In 1958 he even took part in "the international scientific-archeological expedition" on the mountain of Ararat in Armenia. Eventually the agents learnt that Adolf had a younger son in the German army, the older one was in the publishing business, and Adolf's daughter worked as an accountant in Germany. As the KGB agents realized, the Werners were the typical middle-class German couple, which worked together, and Hermine helped Adolf in his footwear store from its beginning. Adolf had two sisters living in the USA. At the end of a conversation with the KGB agents, Werner confessed that he did not like the Soviet realities, but he was afraid to openly demonstrate his dislike of the Soviet regime.[44]

The Werners visited the USSR as a part of Czech tourists' group who went to Sevastopol, where Adolf made photos of the haven, Black Sea bay and military objects, etc. Eventually, the Werners complained to the KGB agents that the "vigilant Soviet citizens immediately reported about the suspicious activities" of German tourists to Crimean police, which "stopped [the German couple] from making photos." After their meeting at a camping site, Adolf invited one of the agents, Yurezanskii, to join Germans in their car for a ride to a town of Bakhchisaray in central Crimea and to Ai-Petri, a peak in the Crimean Mountains, where he still "kept making pictures of military and strategically important objects."[45] As it turned out, Werner planned to go to Sevastopol, using Yurezanskii "to avoid a curiosity of the Soviets," but he changed his mind. Eventually, when the Werners went to another Crimean city of Feodosia, changing their official itinerary, they were stopped by the Soviet policeman (an officer of GAI [Soviet Road police]), which intimidated them very much, because they were afraid of the policemen, who noticed that Werner's wife was making the strange ("looked like secret") notes on the special paper. While staying at Kharkiv's camping site, Adolf attracted an attention of the local residents by asking them "how the Soviet administration treated those Soviet women who gave birth to children from German soldiers" during WWII. The Soviet police noticed that the Werners drove around Kharkiv and Kyiv, near the special military objects, and, finally, on September 1, 1961, they were stopped by the military policemen, for making pictures of the Soviet tanks near a city of Boryspil not far from Kyiv. The Werners were immediately arrested by the Soviet military officers for doing this. Following this arrest, the spouses were separated and sent to the different locations for an interrogation by the KGB. In the Werners' bags, the KGB officers found the films and the notes in German and English about the Soviet military objects and the so-called spy reports made by invisible ink ("composed from a special liquid purging substance") about the Werners' trip. After the KGB found the pens with invisible ink (liquid "purgen"), which could be shown only after a special treatment by liquid ammonia, and the secret hand-written notes, Adolf Werner confessed that he arrived in Ukraine with "the spying goals on the assignments of the US intelligence." He confessed that he had been recruited by an American Johnson/Bauer, who introduced himself as a representative of one newspaper agency of the USA in Germany in March 1961. Eventually, Werner had eight conspiratorial meetings with Johnson/Bauer, during which he received the special instructions how to collect the strategically important information about the military and industrial objects, located in Ukraine, especially in the port cities of Sevastopol and Odesa. During the last two meetings, there was present an official of US intelligence with a name of "Daan," who gave Werner the tools of invisible writing and explained how to use them, while making the intelligence notes. Werner's wife knew about this and actively assisted him in collecting the information. On September 2, 1961, this testimony was officially reported as "the Werners' confession" about "their committing the crime against the Soviet state; and they testified about their spying acts on behalf of the American intelligence."[46] (Figure 5.11)

The KGB agents, who followed the Werners, reported that Adolf Werner openly expressed the obvious pro-fascist views and anti-Semitism in public, praised the living conditions in West Germany, "cautiously tried to push the KGB agents in a direction of the betrayal of Motherland," telling them that in the West they would be much better off, than in the USSR. In conversation with Yurezanskii, he proposed him to go to GDR (East Germany) as a tourist, and then to escape to West Germany and ask for the political asylum there.[47]

Searching Werner's personal belongings, the KGB officers found 12 films, 10 of which contained the photo pictures of the port structures in Crimea, with the military ships and radar objects and the lines of radio-relay connections on background. In the Adolf Werner's hand-written notes, the KGB officers discovered also the detailed information about a dislocation of military ships, submarines, defense structures in Crimea, airports, etc.[48] Later, in his written confession, Adolf explained that he had attracted the attention of an American journalist Johnson, who represented the US

Figure 5.11 Werner spying in Crimea.

newspaper in Germany, by Werner's publications about his automobile travels abroad, which he described in his numerous articles, which were published in various magazines in Germany, and by his widely publicized plans to visit the USSR. After reading these materials, Johnson approached Werner and promised to cover all Werner's travel expenses and asked him to consult any German tourist firm about a cost of the possible trip to Ukraine so they could calculate those travel expenses. Johnson, who revealed his real name later as Bauer, explained to Werner how and what to collect as the important information about Soviet military objects, especially in the port of Sevastopol in Crimea; how to understand the differences in the Soviet military uniforms, etc. Werner confessed that he wanted only to collect the information "driven by his curiosity about the USSR as an unknown interesting foreign country," that he was "naïve enough to be recruited by an American for doing espionage."[49] As the KGB investigation found out, Werner had been recruited by an American intelligence officer Johnson/Bauer, who lived in Stuttgart under a cover of the journalist for the US newspaper "Zarubezhnaia khronika" [*New York Times*], "with one purpose – to collect the information of espionage character in the USSR." As Werner confessed, "Johnson told me that if during my travel I would see the military objects, aerodromes, locations of military troops, radio stations, radar installations, movement of military officials, and also bridges and other strategic constructions, I should make notes and record their exact location, describing under which circumstances I saw them." Johnson promised Werner financial compensation for this information. For the mailing connections, Werner had to use an address in Switzerland, to where he needed to send a postcard, signed "Adi" twice a week (Figures 5.12–5.14).

Figure 5.12 Werner's spying equipment.

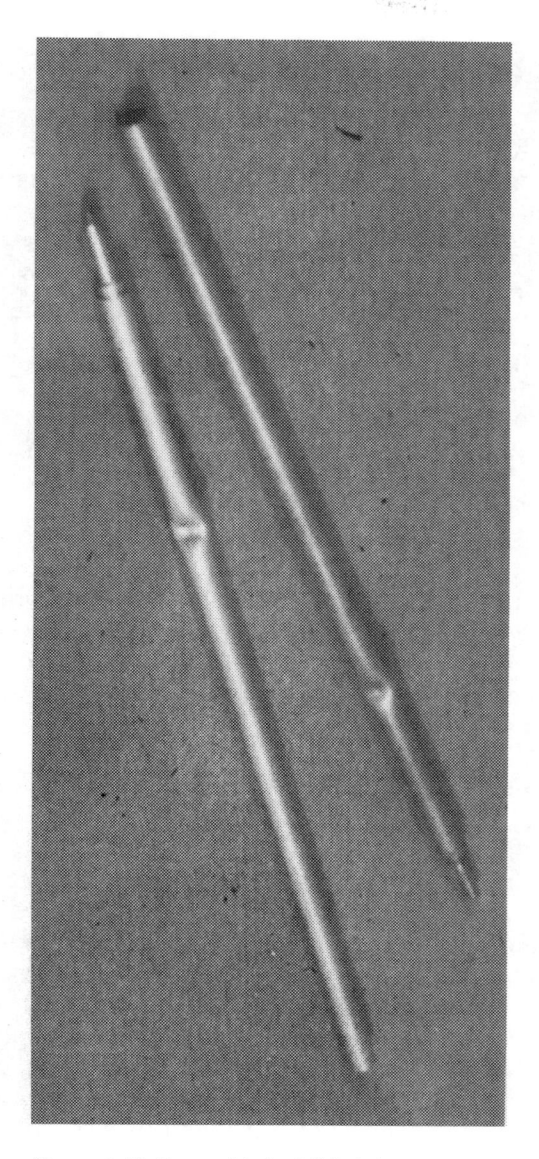

Figure 5.13 Pens with invisible ink.

Werner continued, "I collected all data of my espionage by way of photographing and by personal observation over military objects and the various constructions of defense importance. During my travel, I noted everything, related to the military objects, i.e., locations of military troops, barracks, aerodromes, radar installations, concentrations and

Figure 5.14 Spy (Werners') money.

> movements of combat technology and troops, an existence of large industrial objects, the bridges with length more than 40 meters, an existence of military ships in the seaports, where I visited, and other data I recorded in a journal with road notes by my secretive handwriting, using invisible ink."[50]

At the end of the KGB interrogation, Adolf Werner appealed to Soviet court to reduce his sentence, arguing that he "was old enough (51 years old) and he confessed in all his crimes and collaborated with investigators, that he did not receive money or any compensation from the Americans and he did not finish all the American intelligence assignments." His wife Hermine in her appeal "blamed her husband who explained her everything too late only during their travels in the USSR." Soviets declined their appeal.[51] The KGB administration did everything possible to finish its investigation as soon as possible and send this case to the Military Tribunal of Kiev Military District, which made its decision on October 19–20, 1961. At the same time, the KGB recommended to the Ukrainian Communist leadership to organize a public trial of the Werners on October 27–28, 1961, with a presence of 250–300 representatives of public and mass media, including 10–15 foreign correspondents ("the journalists from the USA and FRG were **especially** invited"). During this public trial, Soviet court announced that Adolf Werner received 15 years, and his wife Hermine – 7 years of imprisonment. Eventually, in February 1962, the Werners were officially indicted according to the KGB scenario and were sent to the Soviet prison as "the **American spies**."[52]

The KGB's Preparations for the Counter-Intelligence Measures against American Spies

Since 1953, after Stalin's death, the KGB administration had tried to adjust its strategy and tactics to the new requirements of Nikita Khrushchev's leadership. Eventually, this affected the KGB special operations, targeting the Americans and Canadians as well. The KGB administration in Soviet Ukraine followed the instructions of the KGB headquarters in Moscow, which had sent the new rules of counter-intelligence actions against the capitalist countries' intelligence activities on March 3, 1958. In response to these All-Union requirements, the Ukrainian KGB officials developed their own detailed program of counter-intelligence actions, which was approved on March 26, 1959. The major goal of the new KGB measures was to "use effectively the international touristic travels, composition of the touristic groups, especially those, which traveled in the capitalist countries, such as the USA and Canada, infiltration of the KGB agents into those groups, and exposure of the agents of foreign intelligence ..."[53]

According to these new instructions, each group of the Soviet tourists traveling abroad had to have (at least) one disguised KGB agent (*operativnyi rabotnik organov KGB*), who "did the special assignments of fighting" the foreign (especially US) "intelligence operations." These assignments included: "protection of [the Soviet] tourists from the provocations and other hostile actions of foreign intelligence and anti-Soviet organizations; prevention of the facts of dishonorable behavior of tourists; prevention of the betrayal of Motherland by some tourists; prevention of the leaking of the secret information about the USSR; detection of the various forms and methods of the work of foreign intelligence and the anti-Soviet organizations against the Soviet tourists; performance of the special operative tasks; collection of the intelligence information; for performing of these tasks, [the persons responsible for selecting a tourist group] needed to use only those agents, who were the members of the group; the residents of Soviet intelligence would be informed in advance about an arrival [of the agent in the tourist group] and the contacts [for this agent] would be according to a special password; after [the agent's] return from fulfilling the assignment, this agent had to submit a report about the assignment's performance in 5 days [after return to the USSR] with all attached information about facts and names of foreigners, tourists, etc."[54]

On June 27, 1959, the KGB administration submitted the special recommendations to the regional branches of the KGB about "initiating the search for the candidates for a replacement of a position of an adviser for science and technology" at the Soviet embassies in the US, England, Federal Republic of Germany and Switzerland. The major requirement of those recommendations was that the possible candidates "should know foreign languages (especially English) and be the experts in one of the fields such as chemistry, oil industry, automatics, radio electronics, analytical instrumentation, electric industry, and had a practical experience serving as a director of an industrial plant or as a chief constructor of the constructing department at such a plant, and had at least a Ph.D. (*kandidatskaia stepen'*) in science, and, finally, had a wide erudition and a broad technological and cultural knowledge."[55] At the same time, on July 20, 1959, for their own officers, traveling abroad, the KGB administration sent a short description of the "signs of American spy, who acted as a tourist," the major "feature" of which was "an intense interest in the Soviet strategic secrets."[56] Inside Ukraine, the KGB recommended for those operatives, who were selected for an intelligence work inside the USA, to make contacts with "the possible old spies-agents who used to work in capitalist countries and now settled in Ukraine," and try to develop various forms of "their own active measures" and "to investigate" those spies' possible contacts in the West. At the same time, the KGB administration complained about "the foreign language illiteracy" of the freshly recruited young KGB officers for the work in the USA and emphasized on a necessity of recruiting the real experts in foreign languages, such as English, German, French, Spanish, Arabic as the future KGB agents, "especially for sending them in the international organizations in New York City, Geneva and Vienna."[57]

As a result of these efforts, the KGB administrations started the recruiting campaigns among the faculty and graduate students at the Ukrainian colleges to send them abroad to the USA as a part of the exchange program group in 1960 and formed a group of 48 candidates for this operation. Moreover, the KGB tried to enforce their counter-intelligence measures against the possible American Anti-Soviet actions. According to the KGB information, received in April 1960, the US, West German and other foreign intelligence services tried to recruit Soviet citizens abroad and persuade them to stay in the West. To resist these actions, the KGB administration ordered to send the specially trained agents from the faculty and students at Soviet Ukrainian colleges in the groups of the recommended and selected people (with an obligatory knowledge of at least two foreign languages) for the intelligence work in the capitalist countries. As a result, in Kyiv, a special school was organized for the training of the recruited agents from the faculty and students to prepare them for intelligence and counter-intelligence work, especially in the USA. During the first official program of exchange with the US in 1960, seven specially trained Ukrainian agents were recommended for the travel to the USA: three graduate students and four faculty members. This became a long tradition of the Kyiv office of the KGB: only the recruited KGB agents participated in all academic exchange programs of Soviet Ukraine with the US. The KGB engaged the official Ukrainian venues, responsible for cultural and academic exchanges with the Ukrainian diaspora, such as the Society for Cultural Relations with Ukrainians Abroad and its newspaper *Visti z Ukrainy* and its radio station, in their spying activities against American and Canadian visitors of Ukrainian origin. Such practices existed in Soviet Ukraine until the beginning of the 1990s.[58] The peak of infiltration of the KGB agents in the touristic groups composed by the Society for Cultural Relations with Ukrainians Abroad for its official visits in the USA and Canada was during the détente of the 1970s. Almost every year, the KGB reported to the Ukrainian communist party leadership about "their adding of one or two KGB officers to such tourist trips" to America. Usually a high-ranked officer, like in May of 1974, – a colonel of the KGB Aleksandr A. Diachenko (under a name of Demidenko) – was included in such a group as a supervisor and "controller" of the Soviet tourists' contacts with the Ukrainian diaspora in America.[59] Even in 1983, among 288 official members of delegations from Soviet Ukraine, visiting the US and Canada, there were 35 agents of the KGB and 10 KGB operatives. During August – September 1983, during the concert tour in Canada of the vocal-instrumental ensemble *Chervona Ruta*, the KGB used four participants of this group as their agents *Ivanov, Vissarion, Krisitinov* and *Kas'ianovskii* for "protecting the Soviet musicians from the provocative actions of the adversary."[60]

Khrushchev's "opening" of Soviet society to a dialogue with capitalist countries and a new international diplomacy of peaceful co-existence created the new channels for the KGB operations abroad. The first possible venue for such operations was an organization of various Soviet exhibitions in foreign countries. As early as December 1961, the KGB recommended to their operatives "to explore possibilities and recruit as KGB agents those Soviet experts, who go to the international exhibits and fairs; about recruiting the Soviet citizens (the experts in various fields of interest, who often went abroad and who were fluent in foreign languages, especially in English) as the KGB agents; and about possibilities of recruiting the foreign citizens during communications with Soviet experts at various Soviet exhibits in foreign countries."[61] During 1962, the Ukrainian KGB actively participated in organizing 19 Soviet exhibits and fairs abroad, including one in the USA, from January 14 to April 14, 1962, which was entitled as the "Ukrainian children's artistic and technical creativity" (*Vystavka detskogo khudozhestvennogo i tekhnicheskogo tvorchestva*).[62]

Another channel for the KGB operations was connected to a participation of Soviet Ukraine in various international organizations. On February 23, 1962, the KGB administration in Kyiv discussed the opportunity how to use international organizations, especially in the USA, where Soviet Ukraine was a member, as a venue for intelligence work and spying for the benefit of the KGB.[63] As KGB analysts reported, "there were 37 such organizations, among which the most important for intelligence work and KGB operations were the United Nations Organization (hereafter – UNO) in New York City, UNESCO in Paris, France, European Section of the UNO, the Economic Commission of UNO for Europe, and the World Organization of Labor in Geneva, Switzerland and the International Atomic Energy Agency (MAGATE in Russian abbreviation – SZh.) in Vienna, Austria. The new expanding quotas of a representation for those organizations from Soviet Ukraine gave [the KGB] opportunity to infiltrate these organizations with the KGB agents, representing Ukraine."[64] The KGB operatives, who worked in New York City, provided the detailed analysis of a history and structure of the UNO, paying "a special attention to the office of chancellery (*kantseliariia*) of UNO General Secretary and its office of human resources (*upravlenie kadrov*)." According to their reports, "in the last department there was a unique concentration of the personal files of various UNO officials from other nations and the UNO personnel, which would allow [under the certain circumstances] to a KGB candidate to study the possibility of using those files' information" for the future KGB special operations.[65]

The KGB supervisors submitted the detailed instructions to their agents how various departments of the organizations such as UNESCO and the European Section of the UNO "allowed numerous possibilities for espionage through various contacts, etc."[66] According to the KGB analysis, the Economic Commission of UNO for Europe "offered [to the KGB agents] a unique opportunity of establishing the contacts with the representatives of governments and the business circles of the main adversary, and for an acquaintance with economy of those nations."[67] Another useful venue for the KGB espionage was the World Organization of Labor, which "gave [to the KGB agents] a plenty of opportunities to use it for establishing the personal connections with the state, business and trade union circles of our main adversary; [and the KGB agents] had to try to promote themselves to the leading positions and the offices of this organization as the official representatives of Soviet Ukraine."[68] The KGB administration also provided their operatives with the detailed instructions how to work and build their careers inside those organizations.[69] As these instructions specified, "the major task of all assignments for the KGB agents in all those organizations [was] a study (*izuchenie*) of representatives of the states of our main adversary [the US, Canada, UK etc.]."[70] And they recommended to use various parties with drinking and the receptions in these organizations to establish the personal connections with important people, etc. "In Geneva," this document emphasized, "there [was] a unique relaxing atmosphere for the citizens of the USA and UK, without a control from their states, so they [the official representatives of those nations] could be more open for the contacts with the Soviet citizens."[71] The KGB administration especially suggested using Christmas holidays (in December) and Easter holidays (in April) "for establishing more intimate contacts" with the representatives of "the main adversary."[72]

The KGB also tried to change the entire strategy of preparation of the special operations against the US in 1959–1962. The KGB administration in Kyiv recommended to the regional KGB offices "to improve work for preparing and training the best candidates in various spheres: journalism, humanities and science – to serve as the secret agents of the KGB against the main adversary."[73] Another part of such strategy was "a tight and smart control" over the mail sent abroad. On March 9, 1962, a special KGB order emphasized "a necessity to improve checking and controlling a regular mail sent by foreigners from Soviet Ukraine." This document reminded to the KGB operatives,

> that our practice showed how the American spies tried to send their intelligence information, using the channels of the Soviet regular mail service. In August 1961, an American spy [Adolf] Werner used Soviet post office to send a secret message by telegram to Switzerland. In September 1961, the American spies in Crimea Sonntag and Naumann sent 11 postcards abroad, using "cipher text" messages. These cards had a return address, which turned out to be a safe house of the US intelligence [in Europe].[74]

Since the early 1960s, the KGB office in Soviet Ukraine identified the most important radio transmitters abroad used by the US intelligence against Soviet Ukraine. Every year the KGB recommended its officers to include this information in their analysis of the CIA activities. On the regular basis, the KGB administration informed about "a special schedule and forms of radio broadcasting of the spy centers from the USA, located in Frankfurt-am-Main (Germany) and Athens (Greece) and the spy centers from England, located in London and on an island Cyprus, for their agents in Ukraine;" about "the techniques of reception and deciphering of radio-broadcasting for agents by foreign intelligence;" about "a schedule of radiobroadcasting of American intelligence for their agents in Soviet Ukraine;" how "to use the preventive measures against foreigners, who visited Ukraine, to limit their possibility of recruiting the Soviet citizens," and about "the measures of control over the foreigners who visited Ukraine to prevent their espionage or subversive actions against Soviet state."[75]

According to the annual KGB reports, still the most important goal of the KGB administration was to prepare the well-trained agents for the intelligence work abroad. Only during one year of 1969, the Ukrainian KGB sent its 23 agents in various international organizations, located in the USA; 200 KGB agents traveled in the USA as research specialists, collecting the intelligence information there; 40 KGB operatives worked abroad for hiring the foreigners as the future KGB agents; 3 KGB agents had been already "implemented in the US intelligence"; 2 were "implemented in the Zionist and clerical groups" in the USA and Israel: 292 KGB agents were engaged in the counter-intelligence operations against the Ukrainian nationalist centers in the USA and Canada.[76] The similar numbers were reported the almost every year in the 1970s as well.

The most important target of the KGB operations against foreign visitors was the groups of American and Canadian tourists. Majority of those tourists were people of the Ukrainian origin. The number of such American Ukrainian visitors grew through the 1960s, reaching a peak of 3,500 tourists in 1972.

During the détente the Ukrainians from the USA and Canada dominated the tourist groups visiting Soviet Ukraine: in 1973–4873, in 1974–5734 and in 1975–6626 were tourists of the Ukrainian origin.[77]

After 1957 the number of KGB operations against foreign visitors had grown from 10 to 12 in the late 1950s to a more than a hundred annually by the beginning of the 1980s. Thus, in August of 1969, the Ukrainian KGB organized a special operation against 73 faculty members and students of Indiana University who visited Soviet Ukraine in the summer of 1969, and who tried to collect "the classified information" in Ukraine.[78] The KGB operatives presented a visit of the tourist group from Indiana University as a part of American intelligence operation. According to their report, this group was specially trained during four-week course in Bloomington, Indiana, where its participants studied Russian language, history, geography, literature and the fine arts of the USSR. Before their trip to Ukraine, they were instructed by the people directly connected to the CIA, such as Mr. Gribble, and by the special representatives of the US Department of State. Special KGB agents worked with members of this group from Indiana, portraying the "Anti-Soviet" character of all lecture courses and seminars taken by the participants of this touristic group, emphasizing the topics for discussions such as "the advantages of the American liberties over the Soviet ones" or the "significance of Solzhenitsyn's work for the development of the Soviet literature." All KGB agents, who worked with this group, noticed the "counter-intelligence character" of the special CIA instructions for those tourists, which prepared the Americans to the inevitable encounters with the KGB and gave them an advice how to avoid the "compromising situation" during the travels in the Soviet Union. The KGB agents quoted the special CIA instructions about a collection of the intelligence information during this travel, focusing on such questions like the following: "(1) In which cities you had more opportunities to find Soviet friends, to have useful conversations with them and why?; (2) In which locations you had better conditions to get contacts with the Soviet citizens and why?; and (3) What were major results of your trip, what was your first acquaintance with the life of Soviet people; how did this travel influence your views, plans and convictions?"[79]

At the end of August of 1969, the KGB operatives retrieved from the American tourists what they considered to be "the CIA questionnaire." Among those "CIA questions for collecting the information," in their reports the KGB analysts emphasized as the most important 22 items for the inquiry, including the questions about the average Soviet salary, about the Soviet citizens' attitudes toward the Americans, about "how did the Soviet prisons look like and how did the Soviet police arrest the criminals," "what were the positive and the negative sides of communism," etc. The similar "CIA questions" were found in the papers of American and Canadian tourists almost every month, especially during the 1970s.[80] Close reading of some of those documents generated some time the serious doubts among the

KGB administration in Kyiv about the links of every American tourist, who visited Soviet Ukraine, to the American intelligence. But the directives from "the Center," from Moscow, pushed the local KGB operatives from Ukraine in the direction of looking for any proof of the criminal intentions of any American guest. So, as a result, the Ukrainian KGB officers, following the orders from Moscow, treated all tourists from the "capitalist West," and especially from the US and Canada, as potential spies. The kind of treatment dominated all KGB active measures, targeting American tourists, until the end of perestroika in Soviet Ukraine. As the retired KGB officers from Kyiv joked, "to promote their careers and get material bonuses from their supervisors, the local [KGB] operatives had to be very innovative and imaginative to incriminate those American tourists who visited Soviet Ukraine as the CIA spies; if those accusations were not enough, charges in Ukrainian nationalism, Zionism or in spreading of the religious ideas and American propaganda became very helpful in the organization of the special operations against the American guests."[81]

Notes

1 SBU, f. 1, op. 1, spr. 1566–1574, 9 volumes.
2 SBU, f. 1, op. 1, spr. 1567, vol. 2, ark. 86–95ff.
3 SBU, f.1, op. 1, spr. 708, entitled as "The American spies, who visited Ukraine (*Amerikanskie razvedchiki posetivshie Ukrainu*) (March 3, 1947 – August 28, 1950)," ark. 1–289, citations are on ark. 12, 35. These documents are about the visits of the US officials from the US embassy to various cities of Ukraine with the detailed analysis of the questions they asked during their travels, and how the KGB tried to limit their contacts with Soviet citizens, replacing them with KGB agents all the time.
4 See the KGB case of 1947 of surveillance over US diplomats in Kyiv, using various KGB agents, who followed every movement of the American diplomats in Ukraine, in SBU, f. 16, op. 1, spr. 931, ark. 8–15.
5 See a KGB report (October 27, 1953) in SBU, f. 16, op. 1, spr. 931, ark. 98–103. The United Nations Relief and Rehabilitation Administration (UNRRA) was an international relief agency, largely dominated by the United States but representing 44 nations. Founded in 1943, it became part of the United Nations Organization in 1945, and it largely shut down its operations in 1947. Its purpose was to "plan, co-ordinate, administer or arrange for the administration of measures for the relief of victims of war in any area under the control of any of the United Nations through the provision of food, fuel, clothing, shelter and other basic necessities, medical and other essential services." See in *The Department of State Bulletin*, September 7, 1945, Vol. 13, Issue 1, p. 382. McDuffie was a director of the European branch of the Foreign Economic Administration. In 1947 McDuffie met Nikita Khrushchev in Kyiv. See about this meeting in William Taubman, *Khrushchev: The Man and His Era* (New York: W. W. Norton, 2003), 191.
6 SBU, f. 16, op. 1, spr. 931, ark. 98–99. The report became known as "a model" one to the KGB operatives because it laid a pattern how the KGB operatives had to deal with the American diplomats in the new political situation after Stalin's death.
7 See also about McDuffie's contacts with Khrushchev in Simo Mikkonen, "Soviet-American Art Exchanges during the Thaw: From Bold Openings to

Hasty Retreats," in *Art and Political Reality*, ed. by M. Kurisoo. Proceedings in the Art Museum of Estonia, Vol. 8 (Tallinn: Art Museum of Estonia – Kumu Art Museum, 2013), 57–76.

8 SBU, f. 16, op. 1, spr. 931, ark. 99. See also the recent study based on the KGB archival documents about the American pilots, technical personnel and soldiers, who were posted in Poltava region during WWII: Serhii Plokhy, *Forgotten Bastards of the Eastern Front: American Airmen behind the Soviet Lines and the Collapse of the Grand Alliance* (New York: Oxford University Press, 2019).

9 SBU, f. 16, op. 1, spr. 931, ark. 100. Film *Korabli shturmuiut bastiony* (*Ships Attack the Bastions*) was a 1953 historic drama directed by Mikhail Romm about the Russian naval commander and admiral of the 18th century, Fedor Ushakov. Another film of 1951 was a melodrama made in the Soviet zone of occupation of Austria under the title *Das Herz einer Frau* (*The Woman's Heart*) by a German director Georg Jacoby.

10 SBU, f. 16, op. 1, spr. 931, ark. 101.

11 Ibid., 101–104.

12 Ibid., 104–107.

13 Ibid., 108–116.

14 Ibid., 117–118. In her report she denied the fact of the sexual intercourse with McDuffie.

15 The KGB officers, who had known about those complaints, joked about those sexual adventures of an American diplomat for many years later. I quote my interview with Bohdan Josypovych K., a retired KGB/SBU officer, February 9, 2019, Kyiv, Ukraine.

16 SBU, f. 1, op. 1, spr. 456, ark. 51.

17 The typical KGB agents' report about the US officials' visit in March 1955 looked like this: "[American diplomats] went sightseeing in Odessa, and in the evening, they visited a movie cinema where they watched a film "*Miatezhnyi korabl'*" (a 1935 US film *Mutiny on the Bounty*, directed by Frank Lloyd and starring Clark Gable). After the film they approached a line of the people near a food store, who waited for sugar, and asked how much people could get sugar after waiting in such a long line. After receiving an answer that they could get only a half of kilogram of sugar, they left this line. On March 8, the Americans visited almost all shops on the central streets of the city. In a bookstore, they bought books "Soviet Ukraine," "Kiev," and "Architecture of the Buildings in the USSR." After this, they visited the October Market, where they expressed their interest in the food prices, made photos of auto-races, bought a few pieces of carrot, and they returned to their hotel using a taxi. After their dinner, the Americans also went to downtown. On Karl Marx Street they approached the diner and began to look at that diner's menu. Somebody approached them near this diner. It was a Jew who worked at a special storage in Odesa, Vitebskii Isaak. They went sightseeing in Odessa again, an hour before of their train's departure, they visited a restaurant *Inturist* for a supper, somebody tried to approach them again (he also was a Jew, a Soviet engineer). Ibid., 54–55. Only in June 1955, the Odesa KGB received information from Boston, from Anna Timson of the Ukrainian origin, a sister of the KGB agent "Jack," "(she lives in Roxbury, Mass.) who reported that a US journalist from a newspaper Boston Evening Traveler going to Odesa to collect the anti-Soviet information for publication in the US, so the KGB operatives were ready to receive this journalist and organize their counter-propaganda." Ibid., 73–74.

18 SBU, f. 16, op. 1, spr. 919, ark. 33–35.

19 Douglas Martin, "Harry Barnes, Jr., a Top U.S. Diplomat, Is Dead at 86," *The New York Times*, August 17, 2012. See also an extensive interview of Barnes: The

Association for Diplomatic Studies and Training Foreign Affairs Oral History Project AMBASSADOR HARRY G. BARNES, JR. Interviewed by Charles Stuart Kennedy, Initial Interview Date: April 25, 2001.

20 SBU, f. 1, op. 1, spr. 1406, ark. 1–3. Before this, they noted, he had worked in Czechoslovakia at the US Embassy, "ideologically influencing, and indoctrinating the Czech citizens. He [wa]s proficient in Russian language, … Barnes served as a professional intelligence officer – a (so-called) spy agent-tourist … [We noted his very strange activities during all his trips to Ukraine, collecting all available printed information]. He was [always] engaged in buying the large numbers of various Soviet books and sending them to the USA by regular mail."

21 Ibid., 6–8. *Akademkniga* was a Soviet chain of special bookstores, which distributed scientific and scholarly literature, published by a variety of the special academic publishing houses of the USSR.

22 Ibid., 18–23.

23 See about the closing of Dnipropetrovsk in Sergei I. Zhuk, *Rock and Roll in the Rocket City: The West, Identity, and Ideology in Soviet Dniepropetrovsk, 1960–1985* (Baltimore, MD: Johns Hopkins University Press & Washington, D.C.: Woodrow Wilson Center Press, 2010), 18–23.

24 It was a book by a former American Communist Bertram Wolfe, published in 1948 in the USA.

25 SBU, f. 16, op. 1, spr. 944, ark. 36.

26 Ibid., 37–38.

27 See about Gontar (as a director of Dumka State Choir from Kyiv during WWII) in Khrushchev's son memoirs: Sergei N. Khrushchev, *Nikita Khrushchev and the Creation of a Superpower* (University Park, PA: The Pennsylvania State University Press, 2000), 24.

28 SBU, f. 16, op. 1, spr. 944, ark., 39, 40, 46, 49, 51, 52–67, 68 (including photos of Barnes' meetings with Gontar in Kyiv).

29 Christopher Andrew and Vasili Mitrokhin, *The Sword and the Shield: The Mitrokhin Archive and the Secret History of the KGB* (New York: Basic Books, 1999), 174.

30 See about Rudolf Abel (Vilyam Willie Fisher) in Christopher Andrew and Vasili Mitrokhin, *The Sword and the Shield*, 146–148, 156–157ff. Compare with a scandal of a GRU Colonel Oleg Pentkovsky, who worked for M16 and CIA in Op. cit., 182, 183.

31 SBU, f. 16, op. 1, spr. 944, ark. 98–101. Citation from ark. 100.

32 See my interviews with the KGB retired officers, Stepan Ivanovich in Kyiv and Igor T. in Dnipropetrovsk.

33 SBU, f. 1, op. 1, spr. 1440, ark. 72.

34 Ibid., 6–11. They provided the KGB officers with a detailed story how they went to car trip on 15 July, and on 21 August reached Uzhgorod; and how they tried to make pictures of Soviet radars and other military objects during their tourist travels in Soviet Ukraine. They even tried to use special electronic equipment, given by Nadort. Ibid., 12–18.

35 SBU, f. 1, op. 1, spr. 1441, ark. 331–333.

36 Ibid. 340–341.

37 Ibid., 341–342.

38 Ibid., 342.

39 Ibid., 331–332. See a detailed information about their interrogation in 1961 in Kyiv on ark. 335–347 and the text of an official indictment in espionage on 23.09.1961 on ark. 344–347. Compare with the publication on October 10, 1961 of the indictment from 28.09.1961.

40 Ibid., 353–354, 370, 373. See also how foreign journalists reacted to this decision and how they contacted Dutchmen on October 4 and 5, 1961, on ark. 376–378, and an analysis of foreign journalists' coverage of this trial on ark. 379–382. This case was covered by Soviet and foreign press, invited by the KGB, including such publications as *Newsweek*. See about this in two paragraphs, cited from the American periodical *Newsweek* in Curtis Peebles, *Twilight Warriors: Covert Air Operations against the USSR* (Naval Institute Press, 2005) in a chapter "Spy Scare," p. 156–157.

41 SBU, f. 1, op. 1, spr. 1442, ark. 1–273.

42 Ibid., 37–38.

43 Ibid., 89–90.

44 Ibid., 90.

45 Ibid., 91.

46 Ibid., 92–96, 125–126.

47 Ibid., 116.

48 Ibid., 108–110.

49 Ibid., 127–128.

50 Ibid., 238–240.

51 Ibid., 246.

52 Ibid., 193–195, 197. See also a text of the official indictment on February 28, 1962, on ark. 211–215, and various photos of their equipment, money and bottles of secret invisible ink, - on ark. 140–144.

53 SBU, f. 16, op. 1, spr. 927, ark. 48–49.

54 Ibid., 62–65. Number of Soviet tourists, traveling to "capitalist America," was rapidly growing in 1959. According to the list of soviet tourists (from various regions of Ukraine), going abroad to the USA and Canada (May-December 1959): from Dnipropetrovsk – to Canada 2, to the US 5; from Kyiv – to Canada 10, to the US 38; from Lviv – to the US 8; from Odesa – to the US 9; from Stalino – to the US 10; from Kharkiv – to the US 14. See in ibid., 50–61.

55 Ibid., 126–127.

56 Ibid., 139.

57 Ibid., 167, 168.

58 SBU, f. 16, op. 1, spr. 932, ark. 147–152. See about the Ukrainian official venues, used by the KGB in ibid., spr. 937, ark. 242–243. Among the first recruits of the KGB for exchange programs with the USA and Canada were such scholars as "Pavel Arsentievich Lavrov, born in 1903, a chair of history of the Ukrainian SSR, Kyiv State University" and Arnold Shlepakov a historian-Americanist from the Institute of History, the Ukrainian SSR Academy of Sciences. See ibid., spr. 932, ark. 149. All former KGB officers, whom I interviewed about this, confirmed an existence of this old practice.

59 SBU, f. 16, op. 1, spr. 1089, ark. 251–256.

60 SBU, f. 16, op. 1, spr.1217, ar. 160, 161.

61 SBU, f. 16, op. 1, spr. 937, ark. 244–247.

62 Ibid., 248–249.

63 SBU, f. 16, op. 1, spr. 938, ark. 92–109.

64 Ibid., 92–93.

65 Ibid., 94–95. In the Russian original it sounded like this: *"eto dalo by nashemu agentu vozmozhnost' navedeniia navodok na ob'ektov i ikh pervichnogo izucheniia."*

66 Ibid. 95–97, 97–98.

67 Ibid. 99–100.

68 Ibid., 100–102.

69 Ibid., 102–104.

70 Ibid., 105.

71 Ibid., 106.
72 Ibid., 107.
73 Ibid., 108.
74 Ibid., 136–139. In the original text the KGB wrote how *"obratnyj adres na tele-grame sluzhil kak konspirativnaia kvartira amerikanskoi razvedki."* Ibid. 139.
75 SBU, f. 16, op. 1, spr. 939 (March 1963), ark. 31–32, 34–38, 40–46, 48, 49–50.
76 SBU, f. 16, op. 1, spr. 993, ark. 115–117.
77 SBU, f. 16, op. 1, spr. 1077, ark. 343; spr. 1118, ark. 35.
78 SBU, f. 16, op. 1, spr. 988, ark. 84–88, 95–96. This list of guest from Indiana included also an American auto-tourist Lawrence Gobroski (born in 1916), a high school teacher of geography and history, who tried to collect secret information as well.
79 SBU, f. 16, op. 1, spr. 988, ark. 84–86.
80 Ibid., 95–96.
81 Interview with Stepan Ivanovich T., a retired KGB officer, January 30, 2019, Kyiv, Ukraine. Other retired officers also expressed the similar reaction. See my interview with Igor T. in Dnipropetrovsk.

6 The US Exhibitions and Technological/Industrial Espionage

The KGB Operations against American Exhibitions in Soviet Ukraine

Traditionally, all public events, involving foreign guests, such as an organization of the foreign exhibitions, became the objects of the special KGB operations. The exhibitions from the US, the main adversary of the Soviet Union, took the priority position in all KGB active measures, which developed the special counterintelligence and counter-propagandist operations against such "American efforts of public and cultural diplomacy" in the Cold War.[1]

The first recorded description of the KGB actions, regarding American exhibitions, was related to the official opening of a US exhibit "Plastics USA" in Kyiv, which functioned from May 10 to June 14, 1961. As the KGB administration reported to the Ukrainian political leadership, "we expect 35 US citizens [responsible for the opening], some of them could be spies. We need to intensify work with our agents to find our connections with US espionage infrastructure in Ukraine and prevent American attempts to recruit Soviet citizens, especially on the premises of the American exhibit [in Kyiv]."[2] At the same time, the KGB tried to prevent the actions of the American tourists of Ukrainian origin, who could use the public international events, like US exhibit in Kyiv for the "anti-Soviet nationalistic actions." According to the KGB officers, they expected an arrival of "a group 117 Ukrainian Americans from the League of American Ukrainians, who plan to visit [a US exhibit] and then at the end of May to visit the locations of their origin and meet their relatives [in Ukraine]." The KGB administration ordered "to check the strategic secrets of those locations, if they permitted such visits; and to prevent the anti-Soviet influences from these Ukrainian nationalists from the US."[3]

Through the entire history of post-Stalin socialism, the KGB supervised and controlled all official actions of Soviet administration and Soviet visitors, regarding various functions of 16 American exhibitions, organized in Soviet Ukraine. Among numerous KGB records about these exhibits from the US, the most extensive and detailed files of the KGB are devoted to the

DOI: 10.4324/9781003212522-8

events of 1964 – the US exhibition "Communications USA." Sixty-five U.S. companies in the communications field provided electronics hardware for this exhibition that covered print and electronic media in the U.S. All major patterns of the KGB active measures, regarding the public events, organized by Americans in Soviet Ukraine after 1956, with the special tactical models of counter-intelligence work, which would be used through the entire history of post-Stalin Soviet socialism, were presented in these KGB files of 1964 about the KGB operations against the officials of the American exhibition "Communications USA."[4] (Figure 6.1)

According to the KGB plan of counter-intelligence work, KGB operatives were ready for the official US exhibit functioning "from 27 September to 1 November 1964 on the territory of the Exhibition of Achievements of the Economy of the Ukrainian SSR (VDNKh – in Russian)" in Kyiv, with an installation of exhibit "beginning on 18 September, its dismantling on 1–6 November 1964." As early as September 3, 1964, the KGB administration in Kyiv explained to the Ukrainian party leadership the strategy and tactics of

Figure 6.1 US officials at the opening of the US exhibit "Communications USA".

counter-intelligence measures: 1. Some of the American officials, who were linked to the US intelligence, would use this exhibition for collecting the intelligence information, for establishing the contacts with Soviet citizens to study and provoke some of them and use them in "pursuing the ideological sabotage." 2. "It was not excluded, that [the American hosts of the exhibit] would try to establish the connections with the possible [or potential] agents of the main adversary [the USA] among Soviet citizens." 3. The counter-intelligence measures against US intelligence would include the special operations "not only to prevent the attempts of spying, but also to stop American propaganda." 4. As part of this plan, the KGB administration "guaranteed" that all serving Soviet personnel for this exhibit was represented by the KGB officers. At the same time, the KGB organized meticulous selection of the special agents "from the highly qualified experts of the Ministry of Communication, physics, radio and television, etc., and their inclusion in the serving exhibit personnel." As the KGB administration became aware, "the Americans had required the teachers of Russian were sent for their assistance" by the Kyiv city administration; and again, it should be used as a pretext to engage more well-trained KGB agents during the exhibit's existence. 5. The Ukrainian KGB also studied "the previous Leningrad experience," when during July – August 1964 the Americans used the same exhibit in Leningrad for "the intense American propaganda." Therefore, it was important to organize counter propaganda, using the groups of Soviet propagandists, various media, including local Kyiv newspapers, radio and television. 6. The KGB also noted that "it was necessary to prevent the contacts [of the Americans] with the people of bad behavior (*fartsovshchiki*, speculators, *stiliagi*, the women of light behavior)." 7. The KGB recommended an operation of "circular cleaning," which included the establishing of the KGB control over all mailing service around the US exhibition on VDNKh, and around hotel *Moskva*, where the Americans were staying as guests during the exhibition; and it was the necessary for the KGB exploring the American safes and the American locations of keeping their secret documents in the hotel rooms. 8. The final measure included the obligatory control over all taxi drivers, who provided service for the locations in Kyiv, visited by the Americans.[5]

Overall, according to the numerous KGB reports, at the end, the KGB failed in a majority of those items of its counter-intelligence plan. As it turned out, the human curiosity of the Soviet guests and of the KGB agents not only about American communications and modern technology, but also about the details of everyday American life, effected various KGB operations against the Americans, distracting the attention of those agents from the intelligence work to the attractive realities of the life "behind the iron curtain in capitalist America."[6]

First of all, the KGB operatives had to analyze the previous experience of their colleagues from Leningrad during the opening of the same exhibition during July-August of 1964.[7] The first installation of this exhibit in

Leningrad, which acted from July 27 to August 12, 1964, was visited on average by 12,000 Soviet guests daily; all together, approximately 280,000 people visited it. Many visitors came from Moscow and other regions of Russia and the Baltic states near Leningrad.[8] Leningrad KGB reports noted the American attempts to collect intelligence data and to organize various propagandist actions "to promote the American way of life and various products of American popular culture among Soviet visitors (especially audio tapes with jazz [and rock] music)."[9] Despite various efforts of Leningrad KGB officers and party ideologists to develop the counter-propagandist measures of the Soviet media against Americans, including the special Leningrad television show about American exhibition "The Contacts with a Strategy" (written and directed by K. Golovakov), Soviet guests "demonstrated massive enthusiasm about American civilization" and became involved in the "apparent anti-Soviet propagandist actions, which were triumphantly described in a broadcast of the Russian Service of the Voice of America [radio show]."[10] Therefore, the KGB administration from Leningrad provided their Ukrainian colleagues with the important information about the members of the US exhibit team and the practical recommendations, regarding counterintelligence and counter-propagandist measures. As a result, Kyiv KGB administration followed their Leningrad colleagues' recommendations in developing their own anti-American operations.

The KGB operatives began with an analysis of the official lists and biographies of the American participants. According to the KGB data, among 52 official American members of the exhibit crew, 16 of them had either the obvious or the hidden connections to the CIA and other forms of US intelligence. Moreover, for the Ukrainian KGB at least three of them presented a model of the traditional threat for the Ukrainian citizens: one – Roksana Smishkevich – was an American Ukrainian, who tried "to establish connections with Ukrainian nationalists, and was caught doing this during her first visit to the USSR in 1963," and three other – a married couple of Finegold Leo and Joan and Sandra Helms, – were the American Jews, who "were famous for visiting Jewish synagogues [in Kyiv], supporting Soviet Jews in their desire to flee to Israel from the USSR."[11]

From September 28 to October 20, – 140,000 Soviet visitors, and to October 31, 1964, – overall, more than 192,000 people – visited the US exhibit.[12] But, paradoxically, for 25 KGB special agents, who controlled a participation of the Soviet visitors in this exhibition, major concern was not connected to espionage, or Ukrainian or Jewish nationalism.[13] From the very opening of this exhibit, the problems of cultural consumption and youth culture took much more time and attention from the KGB operatives. On October 8, 1964, the police arrested a large group of Soviet high school and college students, who visited the US exhibit, with a bag full of music records; as it turned out all those records belonged to an American official from the same exhibition, Ronald Walter, who was with this group. On October 10 and 11, Walter (although his exhibit stand was not working at that time) collected a group of the young people (mainly Kyiv college students) and "organized American propaganda" among them. On October 12, he "spread American propaganda among Soviet college students," exhibition visitors, telling them that "all American students had been provided with stipends, which was a lie, revealed by Soviet students themselves, and he accepted this." His colleague, Space Eleonora spread the music records among Soviet youth and helped them to record the "jazz [rock] music" on music tapes (bobiny), "and in this way she corrupted (depraved) the Soviet youth, especially the high school students of 8–10 grades." Soviet administration of the exhibition informed the American administration about this kind of behavior.[14]

The KGB noted also a special meeting of Adams, an exhibition official, with Vaintraub, a Soviet *fartsovshchik*, in a Kyiv restaurant, where Vaintraub boasted about his deals, his travels to Sochi, praised American way of life, and asked the Americans to sell him an American transistor radio. On October 22, another US official Michael Myers was "caught again in publicly and loudly broadcasting the Voice of America radio shows" despite the constant complaint about this practice by the senior retired KGB officers, who pretended to be the regular visitors of this exhibition. Moreover, Myers continued to record "the jazz music" on the tapes, which Soviet visitors brought for him. On October 27, in front of the crowd of guests, Myers "explained loudly" to one Soviet visitor, who asked about a help with taping American music for him that his tape with this music would be immediately confiscated by the Soviet police; but if the police "would allow him to have his music tape, it meant that this visitor was definitely a police agent."[15]

As all KGB agents acknowledged in their reports, other US officials also participated in spreading "rock and roll music products" among young Soviet visitors. According to one KGB agent, one American exhibit official Francis Derham "helped the Soviet youth to record jazz/beat music in their magnetic tapes." The representatives of Soviet administration complained about these music recordings and asked Americans to stop recording on the tapes the "jazz music of decadent character" for the Soviet high school and college students. Despite these warnings, Derham kept giving the music records ("both the original vinyl records and magnetic tapes") to Soviet adolescent visitors, who "requested them in advance, creating a long line waiting for their turn."[16] In their numerous reports, the KGB agents complained about the unusual positive enthusiasm of the local Ukrainian visitors of the American exhibit in Kyiv, comparing this to their previous Leningrad experience, when Russian visitors were always critical and vigilant. Kyiv residents had never submitted the serious complaint about Americans. The KGB officers even suggested that they needed some kind of pretext to start a pressure on the American administration.[17]

As the KGB agents realized, Soviet visitors, especially young ones, demonstrated the obvious curiosity about "how the ordinary Americans lived." Even the regular technical report of the KGB expert about the technical equipment (about antennas, television sets, etc.) used at the US exhibit, which was submitted daily to the KGB supervisor, emphasized this kind of "unhealthy interest and curiosity": "According to my impressions, a majority of visitors, especially the youth, asked the American guides [about every-day life in the USA] and started the conversations with them not about the technical questions, but rather the questions about the standard of living of the population, about the cost of living, prices for consumer goods, about domestic and foreign policy of the United States ..."[18] All KGB technical experts also noted this interest in "the style of living in the USA," which Soviet students showed during their visits. According to the KGB agents' summary, the American guides from the exhibit "were not very good technical experts, but rather good communicators and propagandists."[19] Both Communist ideologists and the KGB supervisors engaged various Soviet mass media in the counter-propagandist efforts against American guides. The KGB administration even analyzed various measures regarding this exhibit, from the radio and television broadcasting to a publication of an article at a newspaper *Vechernii Kiev* as an example of counter-propagandist measures against this exhibit's influence on the Soviet visitors, especially on the local youth.[20]

The American exhibit became a peculiar social and cultural laboratory for the KGB officers "to study the changes in the behavioral patterns of the Americans on the Soviet soil." The KGB analysts, who expected 230 American official guests for opening this event in Kyiv,[21] even prepared the special report about the new behavioral developments, demonstrated by the American officials in the 1960s. It is noteworthy that these notes about "the characteristic moments in US officials' behavior" from the special KGB report on December 17, 1964, looked like a shocking discovery for the KGB operatives about the "inner freedom" of the Americans whose behavior in Kyiv during the dates of US exhibit did not fit to the patterns of the Soviet behavioral stereotypes. Eventually, this report became a guide to the KGB agents in Ukraine about "what to expect from the American guests today":

... 1. In contrast from the last years, all the exhibit officials confidently oriented themselves in the city conditions, behaved themselves quietly, freely contacted the Soviet citizens inside the exhibition and while traveling around the city as well ... 2. 90% of all contacts, established by Americans, happened inside the exhibit, 10% of their meetings with Soviet contacts took place in the city and various public places. 3. The officials, collectively or individually, which was more common, attended public places, outskirts of the city, apartments of their acquaintances, dormitories, staying there until late time and consuming too much alcoholic beverages there. 4. The Americans frequently invited their acquaintances in their own hotel rooms, participated in gift giving and exchange of the books and other items inside the exhibit, in the foyer of the hotel, and on the city streets, without any precautions and checking out the situation.[22]

The KGB analysts studied a behavior of each American official, who worked for the exhibition. Among them, they found a variety of behavioral models that fitted the KGB's image of the American spies. The typical KGB study of the possible spy's behavior was a case of Robert Francis Drouin. According to this KGB study, Drouin presented himself as an engineer of television, but a special KGB agent checked his expertise and discovered that Drouin was not an expert in the field of television engineering and had a very sketchy ("*poverkhnostnoe znanie*") knowledge of television, but "at the same time he expressed an unusual interest in Kiev Institute of Foreign Languages and demonstrated a good knowledge of Russian language and culture." After a serious study of Drouin's behavior, the KGB analysts suspected him "to be a professional US spy and intelligence agent." As a proof, the KGB found out about existence of two his connections with Soviet persons, who were "famous for their anti-Soviet behavior."[23] Besides of the leaders of the exhibition, who were the employees of the US Department of State, i.e., CIA agents, in KGB taxonomy, the other US officials who demonstrated the unusual technical skills were also included in the list of the "suspected CIA agents." An exhibit technician, Bruno Bartangoli, was part of this list as an expert for finding Soviet eavesdropping equipment (*liternaia tekhnika*); "he was always invited [by the US administration] to trace the suspicious devices," planted by the KGB on the premises of the US exhibition.[24]

Special part of the "active measures" against the Americans included also a "sexual scenario" of seducing, provoking and publicly discrediting of the certain US officials. The major target of the special KGB operation inside of the US exhibit, involving such a "sexual scenario," was the youngest, 23-years old (she was born in 1942), "attractive" female exhibition employee, Evangeline (Evangelina – in Russian spelling) Vassiliades, who worked at the US exhibition's department of telephone connections, the department controlled by two "well-known" US intelligence officers.[25] The main strategy of such an operation "sexual scenario" of seducing included "establishing the operative contacts with her by the KGB agents to discredit and compromise her, and subsequently to persuade her to cooperate with the organs [of the KGB]."[26]

According to the KGB investigation, Evangeline Vassiliades was born and raised in Washington, DC. As a KGB agent reported, "She grew up in a family of three. Her father was an owner of a small automobile renting firm *Vassiliades End* with an annual profit of $9000. [He] also had a business of the radio sets re-sale." Evangeline Vassiliades graduated from Vassar College (in New York State), "her major was a teacher of history" but she also took the additional classes of foreign languages and music. She "studied

Russian for 4 years, but she does not speak Russian fluently." After graduating from the college, she wrote 300-page dissertation to earn her Ph.D. in Musicology from New York University. As the KGB officer commented, "Her specialty was a history of music (*istorik-muzykoved*); for many years, she studied at the graduate school of the university in New York City. She explained [to the KGB agent] that she got her job position at this exhibition 'using her personal connections in the US.'"[27]

Senior Lieutenant of the KGB Skorikov composed her detailed intimate portrait – the "recommendations" for the KGB agents how to use Vassiliades for their special operations, targeting her. According to this document,

> [Vassiliades] loves music, plays an oboe, she plans to write a special study about a history of music. She feels unwell, does not drink nor smoke. She has a fiancé in America. Her schedule is flexible, she is often late, leaves her place during working time. She is hostile to Soviet reality, actively propagandizes the living conditions in the USA, allows anti-Soviet declarations in public. She has no certain place at the exhibit, usually attracts a lot of young visitors, very communicative, can arrange meeting with any one at any place.[28]

As it turned out, Vassiliades had a fiancé in Washington, DC, "who missed her very much." At the same time, the KGB discovered that despite an existence of her American boyfriend, Vassiliades had the intimate connections with the Soviet men, while being with US exhibition in Leningrad. The KGB office in Leningrad provided their Kyiv colleagues with a document testifying that Vassiliades had "the very close intimate relations with some Arkadii Aleksandrovich Tereshchenko" in Leningrad. Moreover, in Kyiv, the KGB agents noticed "her flirting with young male visitors all the time." After a couple of personal meetings with Vassiliades, a KGB agent "G" wrote in his reports that he "was sure that, at the end, Vassiliades would be ready to establish the steady intimate relations with" him.[29]

Given the fact that Vassiliades had connections with the important US officials, directly related to the US intelligence, she "presented an operative interest" for the KGB. Therefore, the KGB administration in Kyiv decided to compromise her and "to establish an operative contact with her." They offered three versions of her compromising and discrediting ("creating a *kompromat* on her (*kompromat na neio*)"):

1 To use Arkadii Tereshchenko (who was connected to the KGB), a Leningrad boyfriend of Vassiliades, for having sexual relations with her ("to sleep with her" in Russian original) in the *Inturist* Hotel in Kyiv, to make photo of their sexual relations, and then to blackmail her later, using those pictures.

2 To use KGB agent "G," who could bring his friend (another KGB agent), and that friend would try to seduce her after having a dinner and

alcohol drinks in the same *Inturist* Hotel, while an agent "G" would try to make the pictures of that sexual intercourse and blackmail her afterward.

3   If all previous versions would fail to seduce Vassiliades and to involve her into the intimate sexual connections with the KGB agents, the next best option would be to "use a loud public scandal in a room of the same *Inturist* Hotel," which would attract an attention of the group of the public witnesses ("*obshchestvennost*" [the operative group of the special KGB agents]), who would interrupt "the scandal" and would find "compromising sexual scene, involving Vassiliades," and who would "publicly testify and record" for the police "the bad behavior of her as a misdemeanor and the braking of the norms, etc., and then to blackmail her." To begin this special operation, the KGB officers would establish a special surveillance over her, "to study her behavior and her personal connections in Kyiv until the initiating of the operative contact with her."[30]

Initially, the KGB tried to use the audio tapes with recording of the popular music as a device to attract the female American officials from the exhibition, like Evangeline Vassiliades, who were ready to help Soviet visitors to record rock music. One of the first plans of the KGB operations against Vassiliades started with the establishing of the friendly relations with the female members of the American personnel of the exhibition, using the recordings of jazz and rock music on the tapes as a pretext for these relations. After these first contacts, "using music tapes as a channel [for acquaintance]," the KGB agents planned to build the important connections with these female members of the American personnel, inviting them, including Evangeline Vassiliades, to visit a restaurant for a dinner there. Eventually, these plans failed. Despite the fact that all American female officials, like Evangelina Vassiliades, became very drunk and "merry enough" during the planned "seduction dinner," the KGB agents failed in their process of seduction and could not use this meeting for establishing the intimate relations with these American girls.[31]

The official reports of the KGB agent *Leshchenko*, who was in charge of the "new stage of seduction of American girls," allow us to reconstruct in details a development of the special operation, targeting Evangeline Vassiliades after the failure of "sexual scenario." This new agent, *Leshchenko*, was assigned to this operation as a replacement of other agents who failed during the "old stage of seduction."[32] *Leshchenko* established his connections with Vassiliades at the exhibition through his interest in and obvious enthusiasm for American "beat" (rock) music. After a few casual meetings at the exhibition, he followed her from the exhibition's exit and arranged a new surprising meeting with her outside of the exhibit territory at Kyiv *Glavpochtampt* (the main city post office on Khreshchatyk Street) on October 16 at 20:30 and strolled together with Vassiliades in downtown

Kyiv until 23:00. At the beginning of their conversation, when she asked him about a firing of Aleksei Adzhubei, Khrushchev's son-in-law, from his office of the editor-in-chief of *Izvestia* newspaper, *Leshchenko* could not discuss it "because [he] had had no clue why it happened, ... ([he] had no information about this event, although an American knew this in details already)." After *Leshchenko*'s awkward pause and his attempt to avoid "the dangerous political discussions," Vassiliades changed a subject of their conversation, and told him that "she loved symphonic music, and in Kyiv she continued taking classes of oboe classic music provided by Svetlana, a local music teacher, who was recommended to her by the music conservatory people; she explained that her goal was to improve her spoken Russian here in Kyiv [that was why she agreed to work at the US exhibit in 1964]." She also explained *Leshchenko* that only one guide (at the laser exhibit's stand) among all American personnel of the exhibition – Ronald Walter – had the most fluent Russian: he lived one year with a Russian family in the USA. She told *Leshchenko* that another US official from the exhibit, Michael Myers, recently visited a university dorm in Kyiv and listened to the local students playing (the completely new and unknown to him kind of) jazz music, which he had not recorded at the exhibition, so he felt proud of those Soviet students who knew the new modern music from the West. Evangeline rejected drinking alcohol in the restaurant with *Leshchenko*, she "was very shy and drank only coffee and ate only ice cream." Eventually, at the end of their conversation in the restaurant, she realized that *Leshchenko* "needed a funnier and more relaxed girl than herself as his companion, and she promised to bring her girlfriend (another female member of the US personnel of the exhibition) for him the next time."[33] Trying to build confidence among Evangeline's American friends, *Leshchenko* presented himself as a "beat (rock) music fan," asking the Americans about the available sources for obtaining his favorite "beat" music recordings. But when this KGB agent approached other American guides who helped him earlier with the recording of music on his tapes, all these American officials declared him that he was allowed to record only one music record per an audio tape, according to the official requirements of the Soviet administration.[34]

Eventually, all the efforts of the Kiev KGB team to provoke Evangeline according to their "sexual scenario" failed. All KGB agents, including those who tried to build intimate relations with Vassiliades, the "young and attractive American woman," complained that "they had no necessary conditions for establishing the intimate relations with Evangeline." Moreover, after a long conversation with her, they realized that the entire story about her love affair in Leningrad was "exaggerated" by the KGB operatives who initiated their operation against Vassiliades. As one contemporary joked, "the American girl from the exhibit challenged all the KGB sexual plans of seduction, challenging them with her modesty, decency and sincerity, destroying the false Soviet stereotypes about the decadent and erotic bourgeois American civilization."[35]

The similar "sexual" scenario of seduction was used toward another US female official, an American of the Russian dissent, Aleksandra Evgenievna Shiriaeva. According to this scenario, a handsome KGB agent, a former Soviet Navy officer, used his charms to seduce and then influence her in "the anti-American pro-Russian direction." This US official, Shiriaeva, "was born in 1898 in St. Petersburg," Russia. After the revolution of 1917 "she worked at the Soviet secondary school and *likbez*."[36] In 1926 she went "for two years for a business trip abroad, met there one American, married him and stayed with him in the USA." She "had a college pedagogical education from St. Petersburg, and later she graduated from the library school in the US." She came to the Soviet Union with a US exhibition because "she developed the strong nostalgic feelings for Russia." The KGB agents used her nostalgic feelings and her interest in Russian poetry (she even translated two volumes of work by the Soviet writer Konstantin Paustovsky in English). In her conversation with a KGB agent, who became her "admirer," she confessed that she "always was skeptical of those Russian emigrants who were hostile to Russia." Eventually, all KGB plans to seduce and recruit Shiriaeva failed. As a KGB agent reported, after a few months of her living in Soviet Russia and Ukraine, working for the US exhibition, Shiriaeva became so frustrated and disappointed with the Soviet realities of everyday life, "especially with the economic problems, ideological hypocrisy and bureaucratization (of Soviet society)," that she began distancing herself from all Soviet visitors, including her KGB admirer. By the end of her staying with US exhibit in Kyiv, Shiriaeva broke all her contacts with the Soviet citizens.[37]

A series of the KGB operations against the US officials of the American exhibition revealed other few transgressions of the American guests, which the KGB administration tried to use for "discrediting, blackmailing to get the strategic secret information from them [the Americans]." The KGB officers found three letters in the hidden place in the bag of the new official of the exhibit Patricia Ruth Freeburg (born 1934 in the state of Minnesota), who arrived to Boryspil airport, Kyiv, from Vienna, Austria, on October 21, 1964. These letters were in Russian in the Soviet mailing envelopes and were addressed to Michurina Antonina Nikolaevna from Leningrad. KGB agents took these letters, promising to send them, but they copied them and sent to their Leningrad KGB colleagues.[38]

In another case related to the same American exhibition, the KGB even tried to recruit as their agent another American official Bill Konigsford, who was leaving the exhibit for the US in October 1964. He worked with the most interesting item at this exhibit – a computer machine IBM-1440, which attracted the KGB attention. The special agent who "led" Konigsford reported that "Bill Konigsford impressed us as a serious conscientious engineer. He devoted the significant part of his personal time to his self-education. He expressed his desire to make acquaintance with the people who knew the special technical terminology. He was considerate regarding the Soviet administration and sometime even was friendly toward [the Soviet political system]." The KGB agents began following him since the American exhibition in Moscow and used him to get all necessary information; he was helpful for the KGB, by "providing the very serious information about the US computer program [which had been already implemented (stolen from him by the KGB-SZh.) in the Soviet computer science research in Kyiv]."[39]

The KGB also tried to exploit the youth and inexperience of some US officials to compromise and discredit them. One of those young officials was a 23-years-old Eleonora Space ("born in 1941"). She worked in Kyiv at the US exhibition as a guide at the department of stereo radio and sound recording equipment. She was fluent in Russian, unmarried, and according to the KGB agent, "as a woman, she was very attractive, and sociable, with the excellent communicative skills." As this agent confessed to his KGB supervisors, he failed to recruit and use her in the interests of the Soviet intelligence, despite "her respect for the Soviet people and Russian culture." As he reported,

> [Eleonora Space] was working as a guide, she was always relaxed, produced an impression of the serious girl, she actively participated in the conversations with the US exhibition's visitors; she did not allow anti-Soviet declarations in public. But as a guide she was unprepared technically. For visitors who were young people, Space systematically tape-recorded American jazz music of the decadent character, like "twist" etc. After Soviet administration protested against those actions, American administration forbid her and her other colleagues to tape recording of the American pop music. With her friends, she also broke the rules for foreigners, going without the official permission to Crimea, where they visited the forbidden zone near Sevastopol. But as it turned out, she was not a CIA agent; she was a graduate student from the University of California, a linguist. After finishing her job and graduating from her school, she planned to teach the languages (including Russian) at the American colleges. Still, after a special operation, Eleonora Space provided us [the KGB] with precious technical information about the stereo sound recording [which our Soviet scientists in Kyiv would incorporate in their own research] ...[40]

The KGB reports were missing facts about the details of technical information provided by Eleonora Space. But the technological espionage at the US exhibition was part of the special KGB operations. Almost each KGB report from this exhibition contained the material, related directly or indirectly to the industrial espionage. Many cases of the so-called sexual scenarios, including the blackmail of a homosexual couple of the US officials, or the attempts of seduction of the female members of the US personnel, pursued the goal of getting more technical, engineering information

Figure 6.2 US exhibit official 1.

about the American innovations in the field of communications. More than a half of the KGB agents, assigned to the US exhibition, were the experts in physics, engineering, and communications, who helped to evaluate the American technological information presented at the exhibition[41] (Figures 6.2–6.7).

This model of KGB special operations was implemented each time when the US exhibits were opened in Soviet Ukraine. It worked successfully in September 1969 during the US exhibit "Education USA," when the Ukrainian KGB agents prevented the "massive propagandist actions about the American way of life" of the American guides, targeting almost 13,100 Soviet visitors, at the same time stealing the innovative computer technologies, presented by the American guests in their exhibit stands.[42] Using the model of 1964 KGB operations, in October 1972, in Donetsk, the local KGB office organized its counter-propagandist and counter-intelligence measures against the US officials who worked for the US exhibition "Research and Development USA." They were fighting against "the propagandist efforts of the Americans to demonstrate the tangible benefits of private enterprise. The exhibition was planned around 26 'blue chip' corporations with strong R&D (Research and Development) programs, many of which were tied to space programs. The exhibition displayed a range of products and artifacts, from

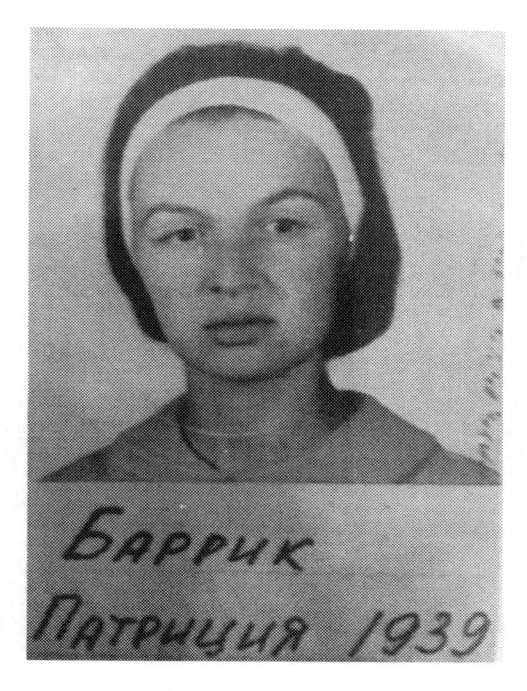

Figure 6.3 US exhibit official 2.

the 'Apollo-10' command module to kitchen appliances." During this exhibition, Donetsk KGB officers organized the special massive campaign of discreditation of one US official of the Ukrainian origin, Andrei (Andrii) Chernodolskii, who criticized "in public the technical backwardness of the USSR," using "the American technical achievements as a proof of this Soviet lagging behind [the civilized West]." Eventually, the KGB operatives tried to expel him from Ukraine in October 1972, spreading the rumors about Chernodolskii to be "a secret CIA agent."[43]

Another US exhibition "Outdoor Recreation USA" took place in the city of Odesa from April 5 to May 12, 1974. The US Ambassador Walter J. Stoessel and members of the US Embassy personally participated in the public opening of this exhibition, including the official reception with a participation of the Soviet and Communist administration of the city. Thirty-six US officials of the exhibition included two officers of the US intelligence and five members of the US personnel, "who were suspected to have the CIA connections." Using experience of the special KGB operations against the US exhibition of 1964, the Odesa KGB officers added the new scenario to the traditional KGB models – the one of a "neutralization" of the people of Jewish origin, who were denied immigration to Israel by the Soviet administration, and the so-called civil rights activists, who tried to

Figure 6.4 US exhibit official 3.

submit their petitions to the American personnel of the exhibit for presenting their cases to the US government.[44] The KGB discovered that Odesa exhibit became a center of the Ukrainian nationalist activities, triggered by "the suspected CIA agent," who previously had problems with the KGB in 1972 in Donetsk – Andrii Chernodolskii. This time, Chernodolskii attracted those Soviet dissidents, who were considered to be "the Ukrainian nationalists." These "nationalists" arrived in Odesa from the different cities of Soviet Ukraine to meet Chernodolskii and establish contacts with the Ukrainian diaspora in America. Eventually, the KGB cut all his attempts to establish the close contacts with "the local Ukrainian nationalists" and arrested all his Ukrainian guests.[45] In May of 1974, the KGB agents noted that Chernodolskii traveled to Kyiv, meeting various "Ukrainian nationalists, including a writer Berdnik, promising them the material support from the USA and Canada, including the special copy making equipment," recommending his Ukrainian followers to "create the anti-government opposition instead the futile efforts of struggle for independent Ukraine." After Chernodolskii's departure from Kyiv to Moscow and then to the US on May 22, 1974, the KGB established the constant control over "the movements of all [Chernodolskii's] correspondents in Soviet Ukraine, eventually blocking all their anti-Soviet actions."[46]

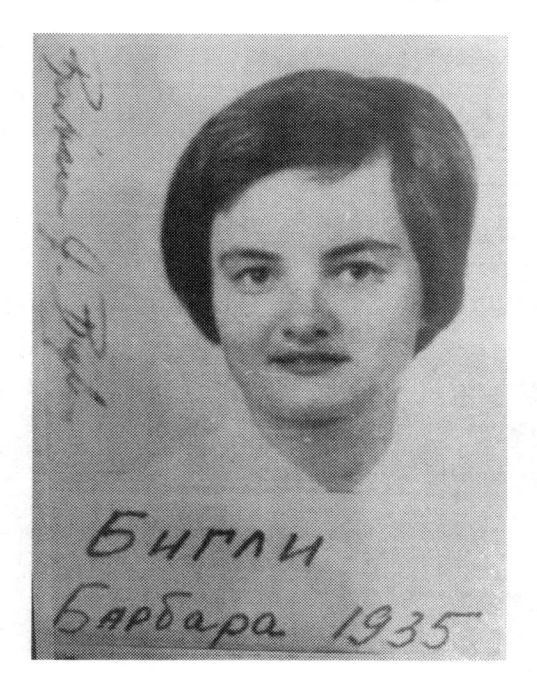

Figure 6.5 US exhibit official 4.

From July 15, 1976, in Kyiv, the KGB planned its operations against another US exhibition – "Photography USA." This time the counter-intelligence measures against 38 members of the American personnel of this exhibit included: "the discovery and prevention of intelligence activities and the acts of ideological sabotage by the adversary, prevention of the attempts by the Soviet citizen to establish the criminal contacts with the foreigners, a creation of the conditions for the promotion/infiltration of the agents (op-erative sources) of the KGB into the intelligence service of the adversary and into the foreign anti-Soviet centers."[47]

The KGB agents organized a series of "the prevention acts" against the American guides, who tried to collect the strategic information from the Soviet visitors of this US exhibit. This information included the facts "about a pollution of Soviet rivers and seas, about the special cities closed to for-eigners, about various cases of anti-Semitism, about the uprisings of Soviet people, provoked by the lack of food products ..." The KGB officers also detected a special radio transmitting device, used by the Americans for espionage on the premises of the exhibition. They stopped various propa-gandist actions of the American guides, who "praised in public the ad-vantages of the American economic and political system comparing to the Soviet one, explaining in detail the achievements of the American democracy

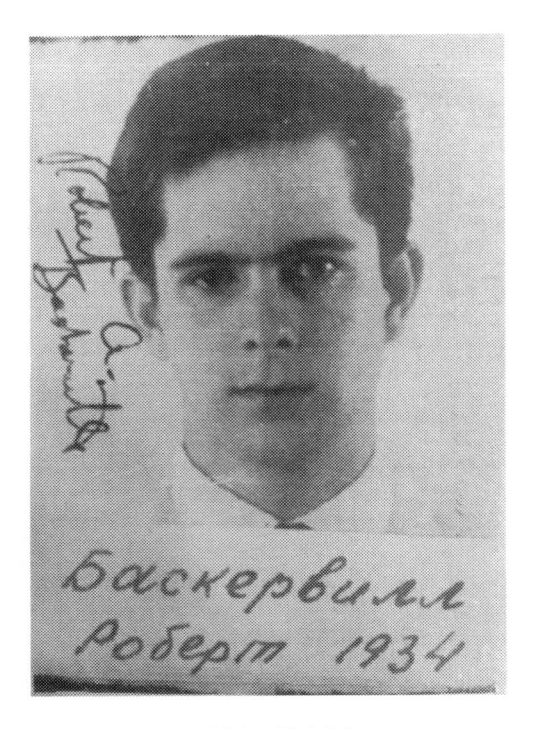

Figure 6.6 US exhibit official 5.

to the Soviet visitors."[48] The KGB administration organized the special groups of Soviet workers (the specially trained KGB agents), who resisted American propaganda in public, "criticizing the lies and hypocrisy of American capitalism," and were writing (on the regular basis) "their critical complaints about American propaganda in the special review book of the US exhibition (*kniga otzyvov*)."[49]

The final KGB report to the Communist party leadership of Ukraine described in detail the counter-intelligence actions, regarding this US exhibition of 1976. "Photography USA" exhibition worked in Kyiv from July 15 to August 15, 1976, and it was organized by the USIA (the United States Information Agency). Thirty eight Americans, including eight agents of the US intelligence, were employed by this exhibition. The USIA spent for organization of this exhibition $2,175,000. Approximately 300,000 guests visited this exhibition. The KGB confessed about its failure to prevent the numerous crowds of Soviet visitors during the first days of the exhibition from the influence of American propaganda: "the crowd gathered at the entrance to listen the American guides about the advantages of American civilization and technology, including the art of photography, and about the democratic character of the American trade unions and political parties,

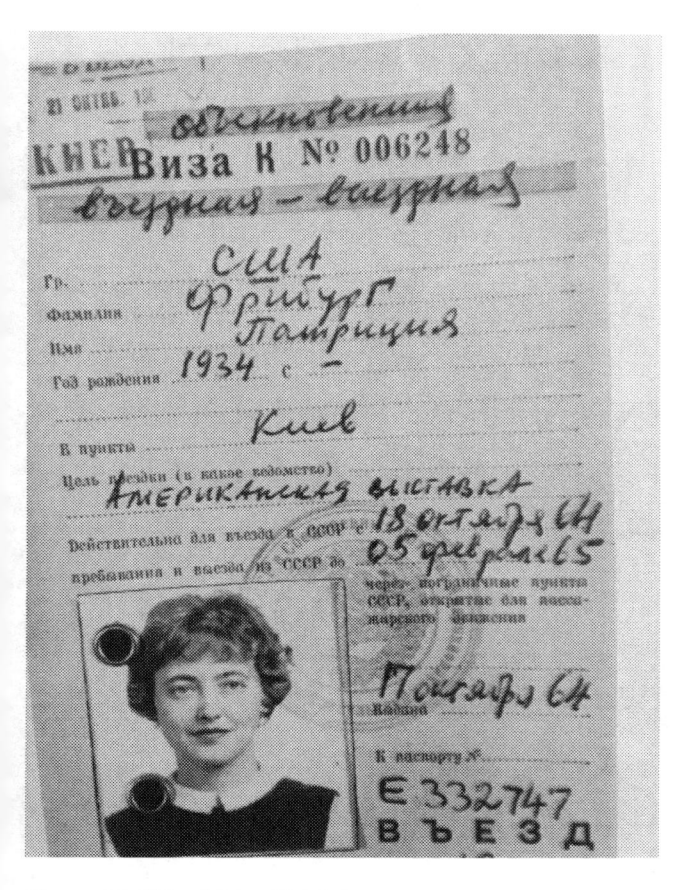

Figure 6.7 US exhibit official 6.

etc." As the KGB reported, the US exhibition was used "for collection of the political information in Kyiv and actions of the ideological diversion. Its main task was propaganda of the American way of life."[50] American guides were "very well prepared for their propaganda campaign among Soviet people of the different social groups (they had special training, studying various tastes and preferences of the Soviet audience)." 44% of all visitors were young people from 16 to 24 years old; for them, the US guides told stories about "the entertainment and leisure of the American youth, about sex and love."[51] The KGB agents discovered the special card collection composed by the US officials with the detailed personal data of 71 people, who represented various levels of the Soviet administration in Kyiv, important for the American organizers of this exhibition. At the same time, Americans made photos of all Soviet visitors, and the KGB agents found at least 900 photo portraits of them.[52]

Eventually, the KGB officers succeeded in isolating US officials from the contacts with Soviet citizens: a majority of those Soviet visitors, who contacted US personnel during the work of the exhibition, were the KGB agents. As one contemporary joked, during the détente in 1976, "Kyiv KGB was more restricting and anti-American then Moscow and Leningrad KGB in their operations against Americans," comparing to their practices of 1964 at the end of Khrushchev's era.[53] Moreover, the KGB operations included the acts of the apparent technological espionage, when the KGB operatives were stealing the American technical reports, including the official reports of the director of this exhibition. This feature of the KGB active measures, regarding the US exhibitions in Soviet Ukraine – industrial/technological espionage – became more important than other goals and operations during the 1970s.[54]

This became obvious during the functioning of another US exhibition – "Agriculture USA," – which worked in Kyiv from April 21 to May 23, 1978. As an official US booklet presented, "this exhibit [with 50 members of the working personnel] demonstrated the richness of the American agricultural scene, from high-tech agribusiness to life on the family farm; with 26 American manufacturers who lent their products, and agricultural experts from US business and American government who attended showings of the exhibition." The KGB formulated the special tasks for its "active measures" targeting this exhibition: "preventing the collection of secret information by the Americans; preventing the contacts of the Americans with the nationalist, Zionist and other anti-Soviet elements among Soviet population; limiting the propagandist influences of the exhibition on the Soviet citizens."[55] In the case of this exhibition, the KGB analysts figured out that the major goal of the Americans was "the propaganda of the American way of life. [They brought 250 printed advertising booklets, and 2,000 copies of the magazine *America*]." They noted a "dangerous ideological role" of two members of the exhibition's personnel: the director of this exhibition, Craig Thomas, who was a former CIA official, and V. Lupan, a former journalist of the Voice of America, who had a Ukrainian background, and whose parents collaborated with the Nazis in Ukraine during WWII.[56]

The public opening of the US exhibition on April 21, 1978, attracted numerous US officials, including the representatives of the US Embassy in Moscow, and leaders of the International Communication Agency (ICA)/ former USIA, such as its director John Reinhardt. For the KGB officials, who obviously demonstrated Soviet "non-official" racism, it was a real shock to discover that a head of this organization was an Afro-American (*negr po proiskhozhdeniu*).[57] The KGB discovered that all major guides at the exhibition had "a special training about their propagandist anti-Soviet, pro-American goals, reading the special literature (of tendentious, anti-Soviet character)." The KGB analysts informed the Ukrainian Communist leadership that "the nationalist activists" of the Ukrainian diaspora in America submitted to the US President Carter the official protest for using only the Russian language in the US exhibition organized in Kyiv, a capital city of

Ukraine.[58] Meanwhile, using the new eve-dropping technologies, the KGB agents obtained the audio tapes of the conversations of the US officials from the exhibition, who emphasized the propagandist character of their efforts, planning their "propagandist pro-American actions" for more than 300,000 Soviet "potential" visitors, "trying to influence them and change the country [the USSR] in a positive pro-American friendly direction."[59]

The KGB officers acknowledged a success of this US exhibition, eventually: "during the first two days only 17,000 Soviet guests visited this event; during one Sunday, almost 13,000 people attended, with the long lines of people (150 meters long) waiting for permission to enter, creating chaos and serious problems for the traffic, when the crowds were blocking all roads and lanes nearby ... (this exhibition became the most attractive public event in the city of Kyiv for the last years)."[60] Every day, the KGB sent the special groups of 30 people, (KGB agents), who tried to impose their own (usually provocative anti-American) topics for discussion, involving the American guides. These groups also included 10 Soviet experts in agriculture, who had to defend "the collectivist basis and advantages of Soviet economy" during the regular lectures performed by American guides.[61] When some Soviet teachers from Kyiv secondary schools tried to organize the special tours to the US exhibition for their students, the KGB administration interfered and did not allow them to do this. Moreover, later, those teachers, who organized those "excursions," were punished for these "unsanctioned actions."[62]

At the same time, the KGB officers tried to isolate and discredit those US officials who were the most active in their anti-Soviet propagandist acts. Special KGB operations targeted two US officials – V. Lupan, a former journalist from the Ukrainian department of the Voice of America, and a guide E. Mashchokki, who had connections with the American intelligence. The KGB investigation demonstrated that Lupan was sent in Kyiv by "American Ukrainian nationalistic centers," to provoke "nationalistic discussions" on the premises of the US exhibition, and "establish relations with the Ukrainian intellectuals, who were nationalistically inclined." The KGB operations against Lupan and Mashchokki involved the acts of blackmailing, using drugs and women of *legkogo povedeniia* (prostitutes). When all those "active measures" failed, the KGB administration submitted the official protest to the US officials with a request to expel Lupan and Maschokki from the Soviet Ukraine for "their numerous acts of the anti-Soviet propaganda." The KGB also organized a series of publications in Soviet press, and the special radio and television shows during May of 1978, trying to discredit "the American unfriendly anti-Soviet provocative behavior during the functioning of the US exhibition."[63]

Industrial and Technological Espionage Home and Abroad

Besides the traditional counter-propagandist actions, the industrial/technological espionage became major part of the KGB "active measures" targeting Americans at home and abroad. As we see the KGB officers actively collected the technical information from the US exhibitions all the time. This practice especially characterized the KGB operations abroad.[64] As the KGB reported this to the party and state leadership, "the special scientific-technical information was obtained by the operative way and implemented in the interested organizations." Such information was reported annually on regular basis. The most detailed report about such kind of espionage was submitted on July 11, 1968, describing the items collected by the KGB agents from Ukraine in the foreign countries during the first half of that year.[65]

The first category of the items was related to the requests for technological espionage from the military-industrial commission of the USSR Council of Ministers. It included "two models (multiplier unit and photoelement) of the American electronic computer the IBM System/360, which were implemented in the Center [in Moscow]"; and "the information of the Japanese firm Mitsubishi about the photoelectric marking material in the shipbuilding, which was also implemented in the Center [in Moscow]." All those items were obtained by the KGB officers from Soviet Ukraine in the USA.[66]

A special attention was devoted to the problems of computing technology, radio electronics and communications. The KGB agents provided the Ukrainian research institutes with the technical materials of the firm General Electric (USA), Siemens (West Germany) and Olivetti (Italy) related to the software and computer programming systems (all of them stolen in the USA); the technical materials of computer IBM system 360/60; the technical materials of computer systems of General Electric with a time division; materials in digital, analog and hybrid computing, algorithmic languages, programs and computer elements, on microelectronics, integrated circuits and semiconductor devices (all this information was implemented at the Institute of Cybernetics of the Academy of Sciences of the Ukrainian SSR); the information on self-adjusting systems, on the regulation of the position of earth satellites, control of spaceships (all this implemented at the scientific research institute of Kiev Higher Military Aviation Engineering School of the Soviet Air Force).[67]

Another priority of the KGB industrial espionage in the USA was focused on the problems of astronomy and space research. This part included the materials of Harvard University on the study of solar radiation on artificial earth satellites (implemented in the USSR Academy of Sciences); the information on the American space project Saturn-Apollo (implemented in the USSR Ministry of General Engineering); the "classified works" of the Atomic Energy Commission of England on scientific results on solar research and other matters (implemented in the Crimean observatory); the photographs of near-equatorial zone of the Moon, captured by the American station Surveyor VI (directed to the [KGB] Center).[68]

Other problems of science and technology also attracted attention of the KGB in Kyiv. Among them, the most important included sixty works of the

American scientific centers on plasma research (implemented in the USSR Ministry of Medium Machine Building); the information for testing geometrically similar tanker models (implemented in the USSR Ministry of ship-building industry); the set of information on new types of synthetic rubbers, coatings, adhesives and samples of certain types of these products; the information on problematic issues of physics of low temperatures, materials science, metallurgy and welding.[69] As V. Nikitchenko, a chair of the Ukrainian KGB, summarized, for the first half of 1968, his colleagues from the Ukrainian branch of this organization obtained via technological espionage in the USA and implemented in the special research centers of Soviet Ukraine more than 200 samples of scientific-technological information and models of the new technologies.[70]

The Ukrainian scientists, who worked for the KGB, used the opportunity of academic exchange for stealing at least 23 items of "the scientific-technological information of radio-electronics and computer technology from the USA" during the fall of 1971, which were immediately implemented in the All-Union ministries related to the Soviet defense. At the same time, in October of 1971, at least 38 items of "the scientific-technological information about the applied problems of radio-electronics," stolen by the "the KGB of Ukraine" from the USA, were implemented in Kiev scientific-research institute of radio-electronics.[71] Even on the eve of the official visit of the US President Richard Nixon to Kyiv in May 1972, the Ukrainian scientists and scholars, who visited the US as the participants of the academic exchange program, provided the KGB with the stolen precious technological information. These stolen technological items included "the special programming software from the American firm IBM"; "the technological details of American production of the cars with electric transmission"; "four studies of the American scholars on the theory of the planning management and the perspective forecasting of the scientific-technical progress, which were related to the US military-industrial complex and to the state strategic doctrine, regarding the scientific and technological future of the USA"; "thirteen informational items regarding the American mining firm the American Magnesium Corporation about the questions of electrolytic production of aluminum and magnesium"; and many others. Moreover, on May 18, 1972, during the beginning of the détente, the KGB administration boasted to the Petro Shelest, the First Secretary of the Communist Party of Ukraine, about the successes of such industrial and technological espionage, organized by members of the Ukrainian Academy of Science and prominent Soviet scientists from Soviet Ukraine, who participated in exchange programs with American scholars and managed to retrieve "the wealth of scientific-technological information," which "satisfied the request of the USSR military-industrial commission, of various USSR defense industries, the State Committee on Science and Technology at the USSR Council of Ministers, and were implemented in various central departments of the USSR."[72]

Every year, the KGB provided the results of this kind of industrial/technological espionage to the Ukrainian communist leadership. The most typical report about such "active measures" in the USA, involving the acts of direct espionage, was submitted by the leaders of the Ukrainian KGB on April 25, 1978, about the KGB actions in 1977. The same goal was pursued – "to obtain the important documentation and the samples of technology in the USA," important "for the defense industry and the entire economy of the USSR."[74]

The most important 20 documents obtained by the KGB operations in the USA in 1977 provided the information about "the new type of the bacteriological weapon, biological impact of the electromagnetic fields, the trends of the development of electronics in the USA, materials science, rocket building, creation of the new types of steel for the military industry, the directions in constructions of gyroscopes; samples of cumulative projectiles, samples of the American buoys for detecting the submarines, the results of the research about the heat pipes for spaceships, etc."[75] All this information was implemented in the special departments of the "defense industries," and the research institutes of the USSR Academy of Sciences. In Soviet Ukraine, the KGB provided the implementation of "the stolen innovations from the USA" in the factories of a constructor O. Antonov in Kyiv, in an abrasive plant in Zaporizhie, and in other factories and research centers (including the defense industry plants, such as *Yuzhmash* in Dnipropetrovsk).[76] Almost every year during the 1980s (including the period of perestroika), the Soviet "technological spies" kept stealing "American technological secrets" in the USA and bringing them to Soviet Ukraine, where the local scientists and engineers implemented the American innovations for the needs of Soviet "defense industries."[77]

Despite the official emphasis of the KGB operations on the counter-propagandist efforts and on the prevention of establishing the connections of Americans with the anti-Soviet elements among Soviet citizens, such as "Ukrainian nationalists and Jewish Zionists," the main result of the KGB's "actual measures" against the US exhibitions and "its operations on the American soil" was a typical industrial and technological espionage. The KGB provided with precious technological and industrial information the Soviet military factories and research centers. As the KGB officers, who supervised these operations in Kyiv, revealed,

[Between] 1965 and 1987, almost 90% of all technological innovations in all research institutes and the factories of the "military-industrial complex" of Soviet Ukraine were based on the stolen information from the capitalist countries by the specially trained KGB agents. And at least 80% of all those "secret samples" of important technological "inventions" came directly from the United States of America. Paradoxically, a majority of these technological secrets were stolen from the American laboratories and colleges by the Soviet engineers and scientists, who participated in the international academic exchanges programs and who executed the KGB orders, performing the functions of the Soviet spies on the American soil.[78]

****

At the same time, the KGB administration was aware of the similar practices of American intelligence, which targeted especially those Soviet scientists, who traveled abroad, and who had access to "the secret, strategically important for the defense, information." According to the KGB estimates, a majority (60%) of the Soviet scientists, who travelled abroad, had a direct access to the "secret research and documentation," and possessed a "classified information, which was interesting for the adversary."[79] Starting with 1970–1971, according to the KGB reports, the US intelligence had "aspired to bring the chosen Soviet scientist (with an access to the secret technological information) abroad, using for this various international scientific conferences, with covering all travel expenses, creating the appropriate conditions for the deep study of this scientist." The US intelligence used also the open manner of the so-called panel discussions during the conferences for obtaining the precious technological information especially about nuclear physics and computer sciences from the Soviet participants. Using "the CIA secret reports from America," the KGB officers informed the Soviet leadership in Kyiv that the American intelligence officers obtained more secret information about the usage of nuclear energy in Soviet Ukraine from one conference alone, which took place in Vienna, Austria, in 1967, than from the regular traditional technological espionage during ten previous years.[80] So the main purpose of the KGB special preparation for the Soviet participants in academic exchange with Americans was to re-direct "the Soviet scientists from the scientific discussions in the conferences in America" to the more practical issues of "stealing the important technological information" from Americans.[81]

The KGB reports blamed the American scientists in spying on their Soviet colleagues abroad. They noted that Americans always tried to "steal the secret information about the rocket construction [especially, the rocket fuel oxidizer] and space exploration during the international conferences" in 1975 and 1976.[73]

During the 1970s, more than 60% of all KGB reports to the Ukrainian Communist leadership included the detailed description of the spying activities of various American scholars sent to Soviet Union on the academic exchange program. These scholars (*stazhors* in the official reports) collected not only the technical, but also political information in Soviet Ukraine about "the reaction of Soviet population to the political decisions of the Soviet government," etc. Some of these scholars used their Soviet colleagues to help to collect such political information in exchange for various gifts and money. Among the numerous cases of such "spying acts" of American exchange scholars, "connected to the CIA," the most typical was a story of

Georgii N. Shevchenko (born in 1938), a teacher of English at the Odesa Pedagogical Institute. During the graduate studies in 1971–1974 at Moscow State University, Shevchenko established friendly relations with two American exchange scholars, G. Brown and Ronald Vroon, who by giving Shevchenko American cigarettes and coffee and other products from the special shop at the US Embassy, asked him for some personal favors. These favors included "sending the letters to various Soviet citizens and indicating (to the Americans) the KGB agents among students, who assisted American visitors." Eventually, in 1977 after return of Shevchenko to Odesa, Brown and Vroon kept visiting him illegally in Ukraine, asking him to collect the information "about deterioration in food supply in the cities of Odesa and Nikolaev, about the Russification of Ukraine, and the negative reaction of the population of Soviet Ukraine to the decision of Soviet government." At the end of this story, in September of 1979, the KGB office in Odesa "invited Shevchenko for the prophylactic conversation." This special conversation resulted in hiring a former teacher of English Shevchenko as a new KGB agent for "preventing the spying activities of the American exchange scholars."[82]

The international academic exchanges between Soviet and American scholars and scientists, especially during the détente, became a useful channel for not only the direct industrial and technological espionage by the Soviet participants in the US, but also for improving the American-Soviet relations, involving the Soviet "academics" and journalists, connected to the KGB.[83]

Unfortunately, this process created the un-expected problems in co-operation between two superpowers, which sometime looked like the meddling in the domestic politics. As Anatoly Dobrynin, the Soviet Ambassador, described this situation in his memoirs,

> Basically, two kinds of people were involved. First there was the normal run of scientists, academics, journalists, and others who came to America, contacted different people, and expressed their own views on the Soviet-American relations, sometime critical. After they returned home they shared their impressions and information with their official sponsors in Moscow or the Foreign Ministry. Lacking real experience in diplomacy and knowing no details of our negotiations, they often improvised in their conversations with Americans, - just to leave an impression of their own importance. This was often the case with academicians and professors specializing in foreign relations. Their dilettantish activities in diplomacy were not always helpful ... But others were directly used by Soviet intelligence, such as the journalist Victor Louis, who was of dubious character and had been specially named by Kissinger. When Louis visited Washington he did not contact our embassy, and I never saw him in the United States or at home. In their own search for political information in the West, Louis and people like him presented themselves as more knowledgeable than Soviet

diplomats about the inner secrets of the Kremlin and more suitable for finding "compromises" in our relations. They were trying to establish contacts outside of official channels with some influential people in the administration as well as those in opposition. But they were doing more harm than good by their free and incompetent performance in Washington.[84]

Therefore, Dobrynin complained about this situation to the Soviet leadership, asking the KGB not to interfere in the American diplomacy and domestic politics. According to his memoirs, "the practice of sending the most objectionable people to the United States was discontinued, and Soviet citizens were advised to steer clear of domestic disputes or outright criticism of foreign governments, above all when they visited the United States."[85]

But in reality, the KGB continued both collaboration with their American colleagues and the meddling in US politics, which took the different forms before, during and after the détente. The next chapter will focus on these KGB controversial practices of using and influencing the American and Canadian politicians in an advantageous direction for Soviet diplomacy and politics abroad.

Notes

1 Interview with Stepan Ivanovich T., a retired KGB officer, January 30, 2019, Kyiv, Ukraine.
2 SBU, f. 16, op. 1, spr. 937, ark. 92.
3 Ibid., spr. 937, ark. 112–113.
4 SBU, f. 1, op. 1, spr. 1566, Tom 1, see especially a plan of counter-intelligence work on ark. 1a-10.
5 Ibid., 1–9.
6 All the retired KGB officers confirmed this in their conversation with me.
7 Ibid., 72–91. "In Leningrad 135,000 people visited this exhibit for 33 days." Ibid., 145.
8 See "U.S. Communications Show Is Opened in Leningrad," in *The New York Times*, July 25, 1964.
9 Ibid., 85–87.
10 Ibid., 98–118, 124–125.
11 Ibid., 57, 66.
12 Ibid., 169, 215.
13 Ibid., 235.
14 Ibid., 195–196. It turned out that the KGB operatives always referred to the tapes of rock music as "jazz music."
15 Ibid., 205, 206. The KGB agent, who reported this story, assumed that Americans "understood very well that majority of Soviet visitors, who approached them were in fact" the KGB agents.
16 SBU, f. 1, op. 1, spr. 1567, ark. 151–152.
17 SBU, f. 1, op. 1, spr. 1570, ark. 38–39.
18 SBU, f. 1, op. 1, spr. 1566, ark. 270.
19 Ibid., 273, 274a.
20 Ibid., 223–223a.

21 Ibid., 144.
22 Ibid., 214.
23 SBU, f. 1, op. 1, spr. 1567, ark. 88–94. The KGB suspected that Drouin's wife – "Betty Drouin (b. 1938) was involved in her husband secret operations." As one KGB agent reported, "nothing suspicious was noted, but she kept turning on her radio set loudly, while talking to her husband to avoid [the KGB eavesdropping]." Ibid., 95–97. Quotation is from ark. 97.
24 SBU, f. 1, op. 1, spr. 1568, ark. 56–57.
25 Special plan of active measures was approved on October 14, 1964, targeting this young woman. The name of the plan was *Plan agenturno-operativnykh meropriiatii po kompromentatsii sotrudnitsy amerikanskoi vystavki "Sredstva sviazi SShA – Vassiliades E.* See in SBU, f. 1, op. 1, spr. 1568 (Volume 3), ark. 218–224.
26 Ibid., 218.
27 Ibid., 218–219, 301. See also her obituary: JARDINE--Evangeline Vassiliades, in *The New York Times*, April 19, 2013, and *The Frederick News-Post*, April 12, 2013.
28 Ibid., 301.
29 Ibid., 219–220.
30 Ibid., 221–224.
31 Ibid., 225–228, 229.
32 The KGB officers still remember these terms for such operations. See in my interview with Stepan Ivanovich K., the retired KGB officer in Kyiv.
33 Ibid. 229. This report demonstrates an obvious lack of political information about changes in the political elites in Moscow among the KGB operatives in Kyiv.
34 Ibid. 230.
35 Ibid., 231–232. See also my interview with Stepan Ivanovich K., the retired KGB officer in Kyiv.
36 *Likbez* was a campaign of eradication of illiteracy in Soviet Russia and Soviet Union in the 1920s and 1930s. The term was also used for various schools and courses established during the campaign.
37 SBU, f. 1, op. 1, spr. 1570, ark. 199–219, 220–225. See also how the KGB tried to use another Russian American in "Spravka on the official of US Exhibit Gorohoff Kenneth:" "(born in 1934), whose parents were Russians who met each other in Manchuria, China; he was an expert on a history of Far East (studied at George Washington University at the Institute on Soviet-Chinese relations), he loves to talk and boasts all the time (this feature could be used by organs [the KGB])." SBU, f. 1, op. 1, spr. 1567, ark. 1–5.
38 SBU, f.1, op.1, spr. 1569, ark. 1-1a, 2–5.
39 Ibid., 12–14. KGB agents, including *Leshchenko*, tried to use another exhibit official, William Svenning, (born 1936), from the firm "Boing," an expert in the iron measure tools, a Stanford University graduate; he loved to drink alcohol. The KGB agents tried to use his love to drink and sauna/bath, but they failed to exploit him. All other documents contain the detailed description of various attempts to use him and his American girl friend in various anti-American provocations. Ibid., 160, 169–171.
40 SBU, f. 1, op. 1, spr. 1570, ark. 1–2.
41 At the beginning, the KGB operatives tried to be very skeptical about the technical information of the US exhibition. See in SBU, f. 1, op. 1, spr. 1566, ark. 275, 276, 282. a special group of the KGB agents was sent to the exhibit on 9 October 1964 to explore a possibility of usage of the special intelligence equipment from the USA and camouflaged under disguise of other devices. The KGB experts noted that "all devices and technological specimen presented at this

exhibition were outdated and did not present something new and advanced ..."
Reported on 23 October 1964: The similar note about "it is not interesting,
nothing is new exhibited, etc." Using an amateur radio station at the exhibition,
the American intelligence was able: 1. to advertise an exhibition in the USSR and
attract visitors to it; 2. to practically explore the running of radio waves from the
USA, West Germany and UK ...; 3. Popularize the massive amateur radio stations in the USA; 4. To get the necessary information about spreading amateur
radio service in the USSR (31 December 1964)." See also SBU, f. 1, op. 1, spr.
1573 (Vol. 8), ark. 1–78, 113–116, 127–130.

42 SBU, f. 16, op. 1, spr. 988, ark. 272–273, 295.
43 SBU, f. 16, op. 1, spr. 1056, ark. 13.
44 Ibid., spr. 1089, ark. 351–352, 366–368.
45 Ibid., 366–368.
46 SBU, f. 16, op. 1, spr. 1092, ark. 112–114.
47 SBU, f. 16, op. 1, spr. 1122, ark. 52–53.
48 Ibid., ark. 53.
49 Ibid., 54–56.
50 Ibid., 201. Compare also spr. 1119, ark. 261–262.
51 Ibid. 202.
52 Ibid., 203
53 Ibid., 204; interview with Stepan Ivanovich T., a retired KGB officer, January 30,
    2019, Kyiv, Ukraine. He referred to the US exhibition of 1964.
54 SBU, f. 16, op. 1, spr. 1119, ark. 337, 338–355.
55 SBU, f. 16, op. 1, spr. 1144, ark. 87.
56 Ibid., 88.
57 Ibid., 112.
58 Ibid., 113, 114.
59 Ibid., 114–115.
60 Ibid., 117. Overall, more than 45,000 Soviet citizens attended this US exhibition.
61 Ibid., 224.
62 Ibid., 258.
63 Ibid. 170–173, 223–226, 279–281, 296–298, 388–391.
64 See how the KGB targeted various scientific research centers in the USA, stealing
    the technological innovations of the American scientists and engineers, during the
    regular academic research exchanges in 1964-65 in SBU, f. 16, op. 1, spr. 949, ark.
    424–426, 427–429.
65 SBU, f. 16, op. 1, spr. 974, ark. 42–45.
66 Ibid., 42.
67 Ibid., 43.
68 Ibid., 44.
69 Ibid., 44–45.
70 Ibid., 45.
71 SBU, f. 16, op. 1, spr. 1026, ark. 174–175, and ark. 235–236.
72 SBU, f. 16, op. 1, spr. 1043, ark. 312–315.
73 SBU, f. 16, op. 1, spr. 1127, ark. 80–81.
74 SBU, f. 16, op. 1, spr. 1144, ark. 137.
75 Ibid., 138.
76 Ibid., 138–139. See about this "rocket factory" in Sergei I. Zhuk, *Rock and Roll in
    the Rocket City: The West, Identity, and Ideology in Soviet Dniepropetrovsk,
    1960–1985* (Baltimore, MD: Johns Hopkins University Press & Washington,
    D.C.: Woodrow Wilson Center Press, 2010), 5, 18–28, 86–87, 221–228.
77 See the most detailed information about such scientific-technical intelligence
    work on December 29, 1980 in SBU, f. 16, op. 1, spr. 1175, ark. 260–262.

78 Interview with Stepan Ivanovich K. in Kyiv, and Igor T., former KGB officers from Kyiv and Dnipropetrovsk, Ukraine.
79 SBU, f. 16, op. 1, spr. 1024, ark. 90.
80 Ibid., ark. 92
81 Interview with Igor T. in Dnipropetrovsk.
82 SBU, f. 16, op. 1, spr. 1162, ark. 138–141.
83 See my article: Sergei Zhuk, "The KGB People" Sergei I. Zhuk, "The 'KGB People,' Soviet Americanists and Soviet-American Academic Exchanges, 1958–1985," *The Soviet and Post-Soviet Review*, 2017, vol. 44, No. 2, 133–167.
84 Anatoly Dobrynin, *In Confidence: Moscow's Ambassador to America's Six Cold War Presidents (1962–1986)* (New York: Times Books, 1995), 353–354.
85 Ibid., 354.

7 "Using the American Officials": From the KGB-CIA Collaboration to the Meddling in the US Politics

The KGB as an organ of state security participated not only in the protection of the Soviet state leaders, but also of those high American guests who were invited to visit the Soviet Union, including the city of Kyiv in Soviet Ukraine. In this case, the KGB operatives had to collaborate with the American organs of state security, first of all, with the CIA, to protect the US Presidents and other American politicians, preparing and protecting their visits to the USSR. As a Soviet ambassador Anatoly Dobrynin noted, this practice had always been existing in the American-Soviet relations:

> Secret services of both our countries cooperated quietly but very expertly in protecting leaders and officials when they visited the United States or the Soviet Union. Fortunately this protection never failed. More than that, they occasionally exchanged intelligence information about possible attempts on some high officials traveling in third countries. I have personal knowledge of at least two warnings I passed on from Moscow in total confidence, one report about preparations for an attempt on the life of the Director of the CIA, and another on the life of Henry Kissinger during the Paris peace talks on Vietnam.[1]

But the first real attempt of such KGB-CIA collaboration started with a historical Khrushchev's visit to the USA in 1959, and especially during the preparation for a Paris summit conference of 1960 and a following Dwight Eisenhower's visit to the USSR in June of 1960.

Failed Collaboration in 1960 and 1972

The first case of the actual cooperation between two security service teams took place during the planning of the US president visit to the USSR in 1960.[2] Instead of spying on the Americans, the KGB administration initiated the special measures of the "working together with the Americans [the American secret service] to provide the security of the official visit" for the US President, Dwight D. Eisenhower.[3] As early as April 15, 1960, the KGB office in Kyiv received the official documents about the preparations

DOI: 10.4324/9781003212522-9

for the US president's official visit to the USSR from June 10 to 19, 1960, with a special stopover in Kyiv, Ukraine, during June 14 and 15. KGB officers had the special order to arrange the "professional" security service in a collaboration with US President secret service people, on the one hand, and simultaneously, on the other hand, "isolating/protecting the American president from the connections and personal communications with various anti-Soviet elements, such as the Ukrainian nationalists, the Jewish Zionists and Christian sectarians [on the Soviet soil]."[4]

In early April of 1960, the KGB officers, who were responsible for "the security details" of Eisenhower's visit, began reading the Russian translation of various American documents about "providing the security service for the American politicians." Some of them anticipated the special negotiations during May 1960 with the officers from the US secret service and the CIA about the details of the security for both Eisenhower and Khrushchev. The Soviet and American administrations planned a US president's arrival at Boryspil airport (near Kyiv) at 11:30 in the morning of Tuesday, June 14, 1960, and spending all that day in Kyiv and nearby countryside. The most serious problem for both American and Soviet security experts was providing a reliable security for Eisenhower and his colleagues from 14:45 to 18:30, when US President had to go sightseeing in Kyiv, and then visiting various collective farms near Kyiv. The KGB experts especially were afraid of the attempts by some anti-Soviet Ukrainian nationalists to use Eisenhower's visit to Ukrainian villages "for anti-Soviet propaganda and for asking about the official American support for Ukrainian language and culture in the USSR." At the same time, the KGB officers tried to prevent "any anti-Soviet provocations by Zionists and other enemies of Soviet state" during a planned Eisenhower's visit to Kyiv's radio and television stations from 19:10 to 20:15 in the evening. Both the KGB and CIA officers were supposed "to collaborate openly, assisting each other" during the final stage of US president visit – the final dinner at Mariyinsky Palace (downtown Kyiv), and the official concert there in honor of Eisenhower from 20:30 to 23:00 on June 14, 1960.[5]

At the same time, the KGB office in Kyiv developed its own plan of the active measures, targeting various groups of American journalists, who were following the US president and covering his visit and the future negotiations with a Soviet leader. In his note from April 15, 1960, an Eisenhower's press secretary, James C. Hagerty, explained to the Soviet KGB representatives, that many of those journalists would arrive early, before the beginning of Eisenhower's visit. The KGB officers reacted to this note with planning the special operations against American journalists (who were suspected in being the CIA secret agents). According to Hagerty's information, the first group of American journalists would include approximately 100 correspondents of various American media, who would arrive in Moscow and Kyiv earlier and would follow Eisenhower's travels from Moscow to Kyiv, to Irkutsk and Khabarovsk, until his final destination in Tokyo, Japan. The second group of 40–50 American journalists would stay only in Moscow and Kyiv and cover the negotiations between the American and Soviet leaders during their summit meeting in Paris; and they would not follow Eisenhower in Japan, they would stay later in Europe covering the Europeans' reactions to this visit. Hagerty also informed the Soviet administration about an arrival of the third group of 50–75 American journalists, who were specially assigned to follow the US President during his travels in the European part of the USSR, covering his visit to Kyiv. As early as April 23, the KGB administration in Kyiv began its planning of the operations against American journalists, who would come with Eisenhower. The KGB officers just waited for the lists with the names of those journalists from James Hagerty. He promised to provide those lists to Soviet administration by April 30, 1960. But the KGB administration had never received those lists.[6]

Meanwhile, the security's scenario about a collaboration between the KGB and the CIA security experts had to be discussed and elaborated by the end of May by both Americans and Soviets. But all these preparations were stopped because of U-2 spy scandal, which happened on May 1, 1960. Eisenhower's visit to Moscow and Kyiv and his meetings with Khrushchev, including a summit conference in Paris, were canceled. All the KGB efforts for collaboration with CIA security experts were canceled as well. So the first historical attempt to provide this collaboration on the Soviet soil failed in 1960. As one contemporary of those events noted, "of course, the Soviet KGB security specialists had already collaborated with American state security experts during the historical Khrushchev's visit to America in 1959; but it happened on the American soil and was controlled mainly by American security service; and the unique attempt to establish the professional relations between the KGB and the CIA people in Moscow and Kyiv in 1960 failed, adding more misunderstanding during the Cuban Missile Crisis a few years later."[7]

As a participant of those events, Soviet ambassador Anatoly Dobrynin explained later,

> After the collapse of the summit conference of 1960, Soviet-American relations deteriorated considerably. They were confined to partial fulfillment of a program of scientific, technical, and cultural exchange. Eisenhower's presidential trip to the Soviet Union never took place. A hunting lodge, specially built for his visit on the beautiful shore of Lake Baikal, was locally known as "Eisenhower's Cottage," but he never saw it.[8]

According to Cold War historians, a cancelation of Eisenhower's visit was a real diplomatic failure,

> On May 5, 1960, the eve of the summit conference, Khrushchev suddenly announced that the Soviets had shot down a U-2 American

reconnaissance plane which had been violating Russian territorial sovereignty. The United States first denied that the aircraft had been on a spying mission but then became trapped when Khrushchev produced the pilot who had parachuted for safety. After some hesitation Eisenhower accepted full responsibility for the incident. He also finally announced that there would be no future overflights. The damage, however, had been done. The Paris Summit [and Eisenhower's visit to Russia and Ukraine – SZh.] was aborted.[9]

Only many years later, under another Soviet leader, Leonid Brezhnev, during a peak of détente (a relaxation of US-Soviet tensions), Richard Nixon's visit to the USSR in 1972 provided the KGB officers with a new possibility for Soviet-American collaboration, including a cooperation regarding the state security issues.

In twelve years, a new Republican president of the USA, Richard Nixon would visit not only Moscow, but also Kyiv, a capital city of Soviet Ukraine.[10] And the KGB administration began its preparations for this visit as early as 1971. At the same time, the KGB administration in Kyiv was cautious about the mutual actions with those American officials from the US Embassy in Moscow, who in November 1971, were noticed as "openly spying" in the city of Odesa. The KGB experts also tried to prevent the American guests from using various issues of Ukrainian or Jewish nationalism to interfere in the domestic problems of Soviet Ukraine.[11] At the same time, the KGB operatives in Kyiv began collecting the information about the "possible contacts with the American side in the future," using the official visit of the US governors to Kyiv on October 10–12, 1971, organizing a series of the public survey of various social groups – from the local residents of the capital city of Soviet Ukraine to its foreign visitors – about a reaction to the possible future visit of US President to Soviet Ukraine.[12]

The first goal of the KGB operations in the preparation for this visit was to prevent the "spying and ideological-political provocations [from the American side]." At the very early stage of preparation for a Nixon's visit, the KGB analysts realized that Richard Nixon as early as 1970 had already had the meetings with the representatives of Ukrainian diaspora in America, such as Vladimir Starosolsky, to discuss the problems of Soviet Ukraine, which of course, was considered by the KGB as an obvious "ideological-political provocation."[13] Moreover, various American *"banderovtsy"* (the Ukrainian nationalists, who collaborated with the Nazi troops during WWII, according to the language of the KGB documents) approached Nixon before his planned visit to the USSR demanding to "defend the national and cultural interests of the Ukrainians, protecting them from the forceful Russification." Later on, the KGB officers, responsible for the contacts with the American secret service, were surprised with the historical erudition of Nixon, who mentioned in public the names of major figures of the Ukrainian national history, such as Bohdan Khmelnytskyi, Taras Shevchenko, Pavlo Skoropadskyi and Ivan Mazepa.[14] As the KGB agents reported from the USA, in his conversation with the American Ukrainians, Nixon even said once that the civilized "world would win in many respects from a victory of the Swedish king Charles XII over (Russian tsar) Peter I [in 1709]."[15] Some of those contemporaries of the events, former KGB officers from Kyiv, joked that Nixon had much better the historical erudition than Brezhnev or Shcherbytskyi.[16]

A special group of the KGB operatives was selected to monitor the US President's visit to Soviet Ukraine. They were ready to receive the American official delegation and a group of 26 American journalists, who would come to cover a Nixon's visit. According to the KGB analysts' study, "two of those journalists (Pete and Paine) had an established reputation of being the CIA spies," and 24 of them were "suspected to have connections to the US intelligence." Five of them were "famous for the obvious anti-Soviet pro-Zionist views," which could be used during a Nixon's visit.[17] On May 25, 1972, the KGB agents in the US informed their supervisors about the attempts of the Ukrainian nationalists to use Nixon's visit for the "rising a question of the Ukrainian autonomy." They also described the KGB efforts to divide "ideologically" those American Ukrainian nationalists, who visited Nixon, and at the same time to "strengthen a more moderate and pro-Soviet part of the Ukrainian emigration in America."[18] As the KGB administration reported to the Ukrainian Communist Party leadership, before Nixon's visit to Moscow and Kyiv, the representatives of numerous Ukrainian American organizations met with Nixon almost daily and organized their "loud anti-Soviet demonstrations" in Washington, D.C., protesting against a Nixon's visit to Ukraine.

> The KGB agents noticed especially the actions of the Coordinate Committee of the Ukrainian Women Organization of Metropolitan New York, "led by Protsiuk Elena, Karpinskaia Sophia (*mel'nikovtsy*) and Stepaniak Daria (Organization of the Ukrainian Liberated Front), who actively approached many US politicians with demands to criticize the USSR for the human rights violations: they achieved some of their anti-Soviet goals; their protest [anti-Soviet in the support of the Ukrainian autonomy] petition was signed by 200 Ukrainians in the USA. They also tried to persuade Nixon to support their anti-Soviet position, and to convince him [during his meetings with Brezhnev] to raise an issue of the illegal arrests of Ukrainian nationalistic intellectuals by the Soviet authorities."[19]

Meanwhile, the KGB operatives informed their American colleagues from CIA about the hostile (anti-Nixon) intentions of some groups of the people living in Ukraine, including not only the Ukrainian Jews and Ukrainian nationalists, but also foreign students, who "could use a Nixon's visit" for "some aggressive actions, such as the clashes with the police [*militsiia*]," during his visit to Kyiv. They were afraid of the reaction of foreign students in the colleges of Kyiv "to Nixon's visit; Arabs and Vietnamese were against it, and they were ready for even the terrorist actions against the Americans."[20] The KGB administration also tried to prevent the "hostile and anti-Soviet public actions of the American tourists, who could use the official Nixon's visit for the expression of their anti-Soviet feelings." Thus, the KGB officers reported about "an arrest of the US tourists in Odesa (26 students from the University of San-Antonio from Texas, who visited Kyiv on May 23–24, 1972), who made photo of themselves using a Soviet flag as a background for their washed underwear in their hotel's room," which was considered by the Soviet police as "the hooligan criminal acts."[21]

The KGB also informed their American colleagues from "the US security service" about the hostile intentions of Vietnamese and Arab students in Kyiv. Simultaneously, the KGB started its own operations "to prevent various terrorist acts against the Americans and protect the life of the US President." As the KGB agents noted, one of the Vietnamese students, who studied at Kyiv State University, publicly declared that "all Vietnamese students at KDU disliked very much a fact that during the Nixon's visit to Kyiv they would be evacuated from the city... Hopefully, – he said, – some of them will stay in Kyiv to organize the anti-Nixon demonstration and throw the rotten eggs at Nixon and in such a way to demonstrate their protest against the American politics [of aggression] in Vietnam."[22]

The KGB agents collected the information about the plans of Vietnamese and Arab student communities (*zemliachestva*) in Ukraine to organize the anti-American and the anti-Nixon public demonstrations with the posters and the "aggressive actions" against the American official delegation. Following the KGB recommendation, the Soviet city administration even took the foreign passports of all Vietnamese students in Kyiv and sent them by the official order "to rest in countryside [under the police control]" to prevent their acts against Nixon.[23] The South American students from Kyiv State University planned to throw the rotten eggs in Nixon and the burning of the US flag in front of the US President in downtown Kyiv. To remove those foreign students from Kyiv, the KGB administration together with the administration of Kyiv colleges and the Kyiv University arranged the special touristic trip for those students to the town of Kaniv (in Cherkasy Region) and to other historical places, far from Kyiv, during May 29–30, 1972.[24]

At the same time, the KGB administration together with the Ukrainian Soviet leadership developed the special operation of the "imitating the overwhelming support and welcome of the US President Richard Nixon's visit in Kyiv by all residents of Soviet Ukraine." The KGB operatives in Kyiv "arranged sending of more than 100 letters by Soviet citizens to the US President wishing him a successful ending of his visit and the productive negotiations [with the Soviet leadership]." The KGB even formed a special "group of Soviet Ukrainian volunteers [mainly the KGB agents]," who would be ready to greet the official US delegation in downtown Kyiv "to demonstrate the massive support by the Kyiv's residents of the American President."[25]

Meanwhile, the KGB organized a series of the special "preventive measures" during Nixon's visit to Kyiv. The KGB officers warned personally hundreds of the so-called Zionist extremists and Jewish activists, who had planned "the scandalous anti-Soviet actions, petitioning Nixon for help and support of the Soviet Jews, especially those who resided in Ukraine." The KGB representatives visited each household of those activists in Kyiv and tried to collect "the signed letters with a special warning about future incarceration (*podpiska o neuchastii*)" from them about not moving from their apartments during Nixon's visit and not approaching the American delegation during this visit." Three of those Jewish activists rejected to sign these KGB letters and were arrested.[26] The KGB administration planned the similar actions against "the Ukrainian nationalistic intellectuals" in Kyiv, requesting to sign the letters about "forbidding their attempts to petition the Americans with the anti-Soviet nationalistic demands."[27] Meanwhile, the KGB agents active inside the USA warned about the Ukrainian nationalists, attempts to influence Nixon in the "anti-Soviet direction." Plus, the local operatives in Kyiv got the important information from Ivan Koropetskii, the American Professor of the Ukrainian origin from Temple University in Philadelphia, who visited Soviet Ukraine. He informed the KGB agents that before Nixon's trip to the USSR, Lev Dobriansky, Professor of Economics from Georgetown University, personally visited the White House and had a long conversation with Richard Nixon about the situation in Soviet Ukraine.[28] Dobriansky was a prominent Ukrainian nationalist, and the chairman of National Captive Nations Committee. Dobriansky wrote the Captive Nations Week Resolution, which was adopted by the US Congress and was signed into law by President Dwight D. Eisenhower in July 1959. Dobriansky was also a president of the Ukrainian Congress Committee of America. He met Nixon and tried to persuade him to visit Kyiv and stress a necessity of the autonomy for Ukraine in the Soviet Union during his talks with Brezhnev. According to the KGB information, Henry Kissinger invited Dobriansky for this conversation in the White House with President Richard Nixon "as a reminder about an inclusion of the so-called Ukrainian question and the facts of the numerous arrests of the Ukrainian intellectuals by the KGB in the future discussions with the Soviet leader" during Nixon's visit to Kyiv.[29]

According to the KGB agents, the representatives of the Ukrainian diaspora sent a special letter to Nixon with the request from all Ukrainians living abroad "to achieve a release of all the arrested [Soviet] Ukrainian intellectuals, whose only crime was an expression of their love for Ukraine, its culture and the Ukrainian people."[30] So the KGB operatives in May of 1972 were ready to deal with the attempts of the local "Ukrainian nationalists" to use the American support of "the Ukrainian autonomy" and to stage the anti-Soviet actions of protest during Nixon's visit with "the demands of liberation of the arrested Ukrainian patriots."[31]

After digesting and analyzing all this information, the representatives of the KGB office in Kyiv had to concentrate on the more practical and urgent assignments related to the meeting of Nixon and Brezhnev: the security and protection of both leaders and the practical every-day collaboration between the Soviet and American secret service and the state security agents. In early May of 1972, the agents of the US secret service of president protection contacted the Kyiv KGB office and exchanged the information about the possible threats from various groups to Nixon and Brezhnev in Kyiv. Thus they gave to the representatives of the Ninth Chief Directorate of the KGB of Soviet Ukraine, responsible for providing bodyguard services, the important information about the Zionist and Ukrainian nationalist groups in the USA, including two special telegrams about the anti-Soviet demonstrations of the Ukrainian nationalists in the USA, organized by the Ukrainian Congress Committee of America. They also gave the detailed information about the anti-Soviet actions of the Jewish Defense League. At the same time the representatives of the US secret service declared that they "had no proofs that any of those groups were planning to send their representatives in the USSR to threaten" the visit of Nixon and Brezhnev to Kyiv.[32] But through the confidential channels of communication with the Soviet administration the American officials noted about the possible "provocations" organized by various Zionist groups during the Nixon's visit. As the KGB administration reported, "an assistant of the deputy of senior special agent of US secret service Harry Jennings" in conversation with a representative of the government protection of the KGB at the Council of Ministers of the Ukrainian SSR expressed "his personal interest in stopping (by any available means) of any [Soviet] Zionist elements' attempts to prevent or interrupt the Nixon's visit to Kyiv" in 1972.[33]

On May 27, 1972, Jacob D. Beam, the US Ambassador, arrived with his colleagues from the US Embassy in Moscow to Kyiv to arrange the details of the US President's visit. The US secret service contacted the representatives of the Ninth Chief Directorate of the KGB of Soviet Ukraine about the arrival of the special American airplane with the special "communication" car for controlling the security operations in Kyiv and protecting the US President. The KGB personnel and the US security service officers agreed about "the special actions" of the Americans in the airport of Boryspil and in a Kyiv hotel *Lybid*, where the members of the American delegation would stay, and in a hotel *Dnipro* checking the security for the press-conference on May 29, and preparing a restaurant *Vitriak* for the official reception with a dinner on May 26 for 40 guests, including 20 Soviet citizens.[34] The US security service agents complained to the Ukrainian KGB colleagues about the lack of protection efforts during the Moscow visit of Nixon, and about misunderstanding and non-professional behavior of Moscow KGB officials, responsible for the state security. Both the KGB and the US security officers agreed to collaborate in protecting "privacy and security of both leaders" in Kyiv, especially controlling the behavior of the intrusive and importunate journalists, containing "the most aggressive" of them. American and Soviet security officers checked the list of 150–200 correspondents of various media, who were invited to cover the official visit. Overall, 311 foreign journalists, camera men and technicians from various radio and TV stations were expected to arrive in Kyiv for this occasion.[35]

The US officials and CIA representatives requested from the KGB and the Ministry of Foreign Affairs of Soviet Ukraine to give them the detailed information about all US tourists who will be staying in Kyiv during May 29–30. During these unusual friendly contacts, "the American and Soviet security officers" not only exchanged the information about the tourists, but also talked to each other and "learned more about each other." During one such a conversation in the restaurant of the hotel *Dnipro*, while checking the radio and amplifiers equipment, one KGB operative told his American colleagues about the everyday life of ordinary Soviet people, about the system of education in Soviet Ukraine, how to enter the Soviet college, about the student stipends, etc. A Major John Barnett, a head of the American communication group, explained to his Soviet colleagues the "roots of the anti-Soviet attitudes," which existed in the American system of education. He told that his nine-old son sincerely believed that his father "would not return alive from Russia." According to Barnett, it was a direct result of the system of upbringing in American schools, the main goal of which was to install in the children the disgust and fear of the USSR. As he commented to his Soviet listeners, "our [American] people receive the distorted information about your country, and when I arrived here I realized how we were deceived … If our people would know the truth about you [Soviet people], they will not want to fight you any more … I was shocked that Soviet people turned out to be peaceful without any hostile feeling about Americans … Our and your leaders could agree about peace. There are all necessary conditions for that … I would not want that our children were fighting each other. The war is terrible, nobody needs the war …"[36] After this conversation, John Barnett told his Soviet colleagues, "thanks a lot, it seems to me, that today I learnt more about you and you became closer to me." The American officers even organized the special farewell dinner for their Soviet colleagues, including all technicians and interpreters, on May 31, 1972.[37] As one participant of those events, who performed the role of the official interpreter during this meeting, recalled, "All the representatives of the Soviet side of those negotiations in Kyiv were sincerely and pleasantly surprised with simplicity and democratic behavior of our American colleagues: they were open to listen to our personal stories and drink to our health, expressing their sympathy to the people of Soviet Ukraine and the delight of our beautiful city of Kyiv!"[38]

Of course, the KGB operatives still continued their spying operations on their American colleagues and foreign journalists. Thus they submitted the special report about the "suspicious contacts" between the US science attaché from the US Embassy and the US exchange scientist Oleh Tretiak on May 25, 1972, at the restaurant of the hotel *Lybid*. The KGB officers were afraid of the Ukrainian "nationalistic" origin of Tretiak, who was affiliated during his research trip with the Institute of Cybernetics of the Ukrainian SSR Academy of Sciences. They suspected Tretiak in various Ukrainian nationalistic provocations; but it turned out that they were wrong; the American scientist had nothing to do with the "nationalistic" anti-Soviet activities in Kyiv.[39]

Numerous KGB operations were directed against the American attempts to use the multiple systems of radio transformers and other systems of the communications during the Nixon's visit. The KGB tried to prevent the acts of the direct espionage by the American intelligence, using Soviet telephone lines to detect and collect the classified information about the Soviet secret military factories, such as the rocket-producing plant *Yuzhmash* in Dnipropetrovsk.[40] But overall, the good professional and friendly relations were established between the KGB and the CIA officers during May of 1972. Even the numerous official KGB reports to the Ukrainian Communist leadership described the "warm personal human relationships" and growth of sympathy between the Soviet and the US officials and KGB agents; so, when the technical problems emerged either with a US President's airplane or the American cars during Nixon's visit, Soviet KGB operatives "were ready to help and protect" the American guests.[41]

Yet, the Soviet side of the state security of this visit had to deal with the domestic "terrorist threats," both the real and imaginative ones. As early as April 23, 1972, the KGB office in Kyiv received a signal about the preparations of the terrorist acts against the Soviet leaders during the Nixon's visit in Kyiv.[42] Two friends, former graduate students from the Polytechnic Institute in Lviv, Vladimir Borodatyi and Evgenii Prutskov, wrote the letters to each other suggesting "the possible killing of Nixon during his visit in Kyiv." Another signal, which reached the KGB office, was about the Ukrainian Zionists' attempt to assassinate Nixon, blaming a famous Jewish activist Semion Gluzman in organization of this "terrorist acts." Eventually this activist was arrested by the KGB. (As it turned out, it was a false alarm, triggered by some vigilante, who was a Gluzman's neighbor). Overall, the KGB investigated five "signals," involving the criminal cases of such attempts of the killing of either Nixon or Brezhnev. As the results of thorough KGB investigation demonstrated, four of these cases were either bad jokes or the product of the "sick imagination" of the mentally sick people. Only one case, which involved Grigorii Kotovskii, a researcher from the Institute of Zoology of the Academy of Sciences of the Ukrainian SSR in Kyiv, was serious enough. Kotovskii (born in 1951) was expelled from Kyiv State University in 1970 for "his aggressive behavior." He planned to buy the guns to kill the US President. In early May of 1972, the police arrested him and confiscated from his possession 2 air rifles and sets of the rifle bullets, 2 knives, and 50 cartridges for the military rifle as well. Eventually, the KGB operatives realized that Kotovskii was "mentally sick person" as well and he was sent to the mental asylum.[43]

After preventing these acts of the domestic terrorism, the administration of Kyiv KGB focused on the American guests during the Nixon's visit to Kyiv. The major goal of all KGB operations during May 21–22, 1972, regarding the American guests, "was to produce the positive good impressions on the Americans from their visit" to Kyiv. Few day before, on May 19, during the special reception and dinner at restaurant *Natalka* with the workers from the factory *Vulkan* the American visitors "became friendly and participated in free discussions and in an exchange of their opinions in relaxed atmosphere" of "friendship and mutual understanding."[44] Later on, the KGB administration reported, that the Ukrainian officers of the KGB "prepared and performed the special measures to impress the Americans in a positive way and to create beneficial influence on their guests," for them to remember the residents of Kyiv as the "friendly and hospitable people."[45] Many American officials confessed to the Ukrainian hosts, that they were surprised by "the very different picture of Soviet life they saw in Ukraine, comparing to the negative anti-Soviet images of American official propaganda about the hard conditions of life of the Soviet ordinary people, who lived much better and happier life in reality." Few of the US President bodyguards expressed their admiration of the ordinary Ukrainians and by the warm reception organized by the Soviet hosts in Kyiv. All KGB agents noted "a very friendly approach by John Barnett, who was interested in what radio shows of the Voice of America or Free Europe the Soviet people listened to; he asked about an opinion of the Soviet people about Nixon's visit, about social composition of Soviet guests at the restaurant, etc." Paradoxically, despite all positive description of the American officials in their official reports, the KGB still planned a special operation to use those friendly Americans, such as Major John Barnett, as "the KGB useful assets."[46]

Meanwhile, following the orders from Moscow, the KGB officers from Soviet Ukraine were collecting the details of information about preparation, organization and the security efforts by their American colleagues through the entire April and May of 1972, until Nixon's leave of the Soviet Union for Iran. The KGB agents in Kyiv retrieved the major secret communications of the American intelligence about the Nixon's visit from the hotel *Lybid*, the official residence of the members of American delegation. According to the KGB analysts who worked with this American "secret communications," to prepare Nixon's visit to Ukraine, the US security service used the information provided by the Canadians about the official visit of Pierre Trudeau, a Prime Minister of Canada, to Kyiv in May 1971. One of the major Canadians' recommendations, which was used by the CIA agents, was "to collect the personal information about all Soviet guests for the official receptions in Kyiv" and "to make photos of various objects in Kyiv, including those academic institutions, which worked for the Soviet defense." As a result of these findings, in a response to the "American spying activities," the KGB office in Kyiv organized their "active measures" to prevent the spying actions of the "CIA people" during the official visit of the US President, which was secretly called *The Cold Banner* in the US intelligence papers. The major effort of the KGB administration was also to "track down and expose the CIA agents" at the Soviet-American symposium "Building the Organizational Structures in Management" on May 29–June 1, 1972 at the Institute of Cybernetics in Kyiv. According to the KGB investigation, the CIA used the Nixon's visit to Kyiv as a pretext for their spying operation against Soviet scientists during this international symposium.[47]

Numerous KGB official reports of 1972 and the testimony of the retired KGB officers, the Soviet participants of the events, noted this ambiguous nature of the American-Soviet/CIA-KGB collaboration during the détente's beginning: "On the one hand, there were friendly receptions and state security coordination for both Soviet and American agents, on the other hand, the spying on each other continued, with checking radio connections, protecting 'state interests' and trying ideologically to influence their opponents."[48]

Moreover, on the wake of the Nixon's visit, the Ukrainian administration of the KGB organized two special operations: one – against the CIA spying via the inter-city long-distance telephone calls, and another – against "the American influences" on the Soviet youth during the concerts of Western popular music. As the KGB specialists noticed, the Nixon's visit led to increase of the US intelligence radio spying and eavesdropping through major inter-city telephone lines. As a result, the important secret information from the strategically important factories of Soviet Ukraine, such as *Yuzhmash* in Dnipropetrovsk, the airplane engine-building plant in Zaporizhie, the factory of automatics named after Petrovskyi in Kyiv, *Kommunar* factory in Kharkiv, the factory of heavy machine-building in Zhdanov, was compromised and stolen by the Americans in May 1972. As the KGB administration reported on May 30, 1972, the activities of the US intelligence in Soviet Ukraine reached a peak by the end of May 1972, when "through the special radio control of the long-distance calls, radio-communication and the schedule of rented airplanes of the Southern machine-building factory (*Yuzhmash*) [in Dnipropetrovsk], the [American] adversary managed to retrieve some data about the types and number of the rockets produced by this factory."[49] The KGB supervisors from various "closed/secret factories" of Soviet Ukraine were afraid that the influx of the US intelligence specialists, following the visit of the US President in 1972 in Kyiv, could lead to a breach of secrecy for many plants of Soviet Ukraine, which worked for Soviet defense.

The KGB analysts also were afraid that Nixon's visit could be the "bad inspiration" for the young residents of Kyiv, who were "emboldened" to demonstrate their "pro-American signs in public" and behave "provocatively" during the concerts of foreign musicians in Kyiv. Suddenly, "the children of Soviet Ukraine found a political justification for their behavior of complete Americanization in the US president's official visit to Ukraine."[50]

During May 21–25, 1972, the West German James (Hans) Last Orchestra performed at the Palace of Sport in downtown Kyiv for the Soviet (overwhelmingly young) audience. Each concert these Western musicians (17 from West Germany, 11 from England, 3 from Sweden, Belgium and Switzerland) began with the slow numbers, but finished with such music that "gradually could turn on the audience." They usually ended their performance with a composition "in style of the Beatles music," which "causes unhealthy hype among part of the youth, bringing them to ecstasy." According to the KGB reports, those young people, "reckoning themselves as hippies, having losing control over their behavior, imitated everything, which" Western musicians demonstrated on stage, "including the signs 'V', which are symbolic for the 'right hippies,' and which are used by the Neo-Nazis in West Germany."[51] Later on, the KGB analysts acknowledged their mistake with interpretations of the signs V (standing for "victory"), which was used by the progressive youth in the West as a symbol of the struggle for peace, and which had nothing to do with fascism. As former KGB officers, who witnessed the "unhealthy enthusiasm" of young residents of Kyiv during the James Last Orchestra's concert, explained that major concern of the KGB administration about the opening the Soviet society during the détente was "a danger of massive imitation of pro-American behavior" among the Soviet youth. The spread of the official Soviet information about the US President's visit in 1972, and the official promotion of the acts of Western popular culture such as the James Last Orchestra's concert "stimulated among the Soviet youth the negative reactions to the Soviet reality," producing "the anti-Soviet social groups, such as *fartsovshchiks* (black marketers), *bitlomans* (rock music fans) and hippies."[52]

But according to the testimony of the former KGB officers, who still remembered the situation of the 1970s, overall, the major goal of the KGB actions regarding the US Presidents' visits "was not a fight with the US spying/intelligence activities, nor a protection of the Soviet youth from the US cultural influences, but rather influencing the American politicians, by creating their positive and attractive images of the Soviet realities; by using those politicians as 'the useful assets,' the KGB promoted the Soviet political interests in the American society, in fact, by the meddling in the US politics through those (sometimes very gullible and impressive) politicians, who happened to be visiting the Soviet Union."[53]

"Influencing American Politicians" and Meddling in American Politics, Education and Religious Affairs

The KGB operatives tried to achieve this goal in the major KGB operations targeting the official American guests. The first famous story of such KGB meddling in the US politics was a case of Hubert Humphrey (1911–1978), a US Vice-President to Lyndon Johnson. In the spring of 1968 during the presidential elections in the USA, the Soviet leadership tried to help to win

Hubert Humphrey. As Anatoly Dobrynin, the Soviet Ambassador in Washington, D.C., recalled in his memoirs,

> To Moscow, Humphrey certainly was preferable to Richard Nixon, who had founded and built his career on opposing communism and was considered profoundly anti-Soviet. Our leadership was growing seriously concerned that he might win the election. As a result the top Soviet leaders took an extraordinary step, unprecedented in the history of Soviet-American relations, by secretly offering Humphrey any conceivable help in his election campaign – including financial aid ... I received a top-secret instruction to that effect from [Andrei] Gromyko [the Soviet Minister of Foreign Affairs] personally and did my utmost to dissuade him from embarking on such a dangerous venture, which if discovered certainly would have backfired and ensured Humphrey's defeat, to say nothing of the real trouble it would have caused for Soviet-American relations. Gromyko answered laconically, "There is a decision, you carry it out."
>
> Shortly afterward, I happened to be at breakfast at Humphrey's home. Naturally, we talked about the election campaign, so I tried to take advantage of that to carry out my instructions as tactfully as possible. I asked him how his campaign was going, and then I moved the conversation diplomatically to the state of his campaign finances. Humphrey, I must say, was not only a very intelligent but also a very clever man. He knew at once what was going on. He told me it was more than enough for him to have Moscow's good wishes which he highly appreciated. The matter was thus settled to our mutual relief, never to be discussed again.
>
> This story has never been told before. The Politburo always watched American presidential elections closely for their potential effect on Soviet-American relations and usually had a preference but rarely expressed it or took sides by offering diplomatic or other help. To my knowledge this was the only time Moscow tried to intervene directly to help a favored candidate – and it got nowhere.[54]

But according to the KGB documents, despite Humphrey's refusal to accept the Soviet financial aid in his election campaign of 1968, following the recommendation of the Soviet leadership, the KGB administration still tried to use him as another "useful asset" for Soviet politics inside the USA. According to the confession of Benjamin Reid, an executive secretary at the US Department of State, to the KGB agent as early as January 1969, in a confidential conversation with Humphrey Soviet Ambassador Dobrynin promised to him the official invitation from Alexei Kosygin, a Chairman of the USSR Council of Ministers, to visit the USSR, "where they could meet non-officially." As a result, in July of 1969 Humphrey did visit the Soviet Union, and on July 12–13, 1969, he visited Kyiv with the US secretaries Benjamin Reid and E. Watson, and his personal friend Dwayne Andreas, went sightseeing in Kyiv and the near-by agricultural enterprise "Kyivskyi." They had the non-official meetings with the representatives of the Soviet government and the KGB agents, and Humphrey "characterized positively a progress made in [the USSR] and praised [Kosygin] as a man of high culture and brilliant intellect."[55] As the KGB agent reported, Reid emphasized that the non-official meetings between Soviet and American politicians were much better and efficient than the official ones, and they "contributed to the improving of the relations between two states." The KGB administration reminded the Soviet leadership in July of 1969 about the importance of the support of Humphrey because of his intentions to run as a candidate in the elections of the US President again. Therefore, the KGB still considered Humphrey as a "useful asset" for the interference in the US politics.[56]

The KGB even used a special operation, targeting another American visitor, who was close to Humphrey. This American was John Peter Grote (1931–2012), who drafted the original Peace Corps legislation, and invented the name for this organization in 1960. At the same time he worked as Foreign Relations Adviser and Speech Writer for Senator Hubert H. Humphrey; a year later, in 1961, he was appointed Deputy Director of the U.N. Division of the U.S. Peace Corps. Grote visited Kyiv during June 27–July 2, and July 7–July 14, 1968. Suspecting Grote's connections to the CIA and knowing about his connections to Humphrey, the KGB followed him and tried to influence him during his visit, helping him and Humphrey in their political struggle against candidate Nixon. Grote confessed to a KGB agent that "Humphrey had more chances to become the next US President," winning over Nixon, whom he considered a "dishonest man."[57] After analyzing their surveillance material on Grote in Kyiv (including his previous visit to the USSR in 1962), the KGB reported to the Soviet leadership about his and Humphrey's "friendly feelings towards the Soviet people" and about their plans to extend "the cultural and scientific cooperation between the USSR and the USA." Grote openly declared that his study of 550 American tourists, who visited the USSR, demonstrated that 52% of those tourists changed their opinion about the Soviet Union in "the positive direction": "they liked the Soviet realities and cheerfulness of the Soviet people, a wide scope of the construction projects, achievements in various spheres of science, industry and the arts." Only 32% of the Americans did not change their views after visiting the USSR; approximately 16% of them were hesitant. The KGB agents did all their best to influence Grote (and Humphrey through him) "to create the beneficial to us impression from his trip to the Soviet Union [and use it for our best interests]." Grote, like Humphrey, could be the "useful assets" for the needs of the KGB inside the US politics.[58]

Through the entire 1970s and the 1980s, the specially trained KGB agents approached various US official delegations visiting Soviet Ukraine, trying to influence in positive "pro-Soviet direction" those members of those delegations who demonstrated "a possibility of dialogue with the Soviet administration." Those representatives of the US Congress, or the American judges, or the US governors became the targets of the special KGB operations, which sometime resulted in the "positive (for the Soviet side) decisions" in the US politics.[59]

Another element of the meddling with overall Western political life, and especially the US politics, was the KGB support (including its financial funding) of various "progressive" (meaning pro-Soviet) political movements and parties in "capitalist West." Almost every year, the KGB files provided the information about the special KGB assistance to the numerous anti-war movements in the West and to the "friendly communist parties" in the West, especially to the communists in the USA and Canada. Even the organization of the Black Panther Party, which started in 1966 in Oakland, California, attracted the KGB attention, because it was "a dynamic negro organization which posed a serious threat to America's ruling classes." According to the official KGB report of 1970, there was "a discernable tendency among the 'Black Panthers' to increase cooperation with progressive organizations [including communists] which are opposed to the existing system in the USA." Therefore, the KGB administration as early as 1970, suggested to the Soviet political leadership the special KGB "active measures" regarding this organization:

> Because the rise of negro protest in the USA will bring definite difficulties to the ruling classes of the USA and will distract the attention of the Nixon administration from pursuing an active foreign policy, we would consider it feasible to implement a number of measures to support this movement and assist its growth … Employing the possibilities of the KGB in New York and Washington, to influence the "Black Panthers" to address appeals to the UN and other international bodies for assistance in bringing the US government's policy of genocide toward American negroes to an end … It is likely that by carrying out the abovementioned measures it will be possible to mobilize public opinion in the US and in other countries in support of the rights of American negroes and thereby stimulate the "Black Panthers" into further activation of their struggle.[60]

The representatives of the Ukrainian KGB took an active part in these operations by using and influencing the Afro-American followers of this organization in the KGB interests.

The KGB agents in the USA always targeted the "historically black colleges and universities" especially in Washington, D.C. area. They tried to find "the most radicalized" Afro-American students, who supported the "Black Panthers" movement, and use them for various pro-Soviet actions, including the "anti-Vietnam war demonstrations" with participation of the students from Howard University during the 1970s. The most successful operations by the KGB agents on Howard University's campus were devoted to various actions against the American Ukrainian meetings and demonstrations in the Washington, D.C. Usually, "the KGB agitators" engaged Howard University's students in these actions by disseminating the leaflets and various literature about "the racist" and "fascist" origins of the Ukrainian diaspora in America, "ideologically discrediting" and portraying all American Ukrainians as "the militant anti-Afro-American and Neo-Nazi group," which was "a real threat to all Afro-Americans and Jews" in the US. In some cases, the KGB managed to involve the "Black Panthers" followers from Howard University to disrupt and disperse the American Ukrainians' demonstrations in downtown D.C. The most famous attempt to provoke a physical conflict between the Howard University's students, engaged by the KGB "agitators," and American Ukrainians in downtown Washington, D.C. was prevented by the local police on September 16, 1984. The KGB agents tried to discredit the anti-Soviet actions of the American-Ukrainian activists at Taras Shevchenko monument in Washington, DC, on September 16, 1984, to mark the 20th anniversary of its official opening in the USA against "the forceful Russification of Ukraine." American Ukrainians planned even to attract the Afro-American students of Howard University, spreading among them the information about friendship between a Ukrainian poet and artist Taras Shevchenko (1814–1861), and American black actor Ira Aldridge (1807–1867). Eventually, the KGB succeeded in disruption of those plans, using disinformation about the so-called Fascist and racist nature of "Ukrainian nationalists," spreading various leaflets and pamphlets about the Ukrainian "white racists" among the black college students in their dorms. As a result of this KGB operation, the Black Panthers became involved in this conflict with the alleged Ukrainian racists and Fascists in America and prevented the anti-Soviet meetings of American Ukrainians in downtown Washington, D.C.[61]

At the same time, the KGB administration in Kyiv tried to monitor any political elections in both the USA and Canada which involved the representatives of the Ukrainian diaspora in America, and try to "create a political influence for pro-Soviet candidates." On July 15, 1968, the KGB agents in Canada informed their administration in Kyiv that they "focused their operation on the elections of members of the Canadian parliament," when seven Canadian Ukrainians were in the list of possible candidates. These agents "checked the background and ideological positions of each of those candidates," and promised to "monitor thoroughly all of them to use them in the future in the interests of Soviet Ukraine." The KGB agents reported to their Kyiv administration that they "became especially interested in influencing and supporting" the Ukrainian Canadian businessman Mark G. Smerchanski (1914–1989), from the Liberal Party of Canada, Province Manitoba, "who was loyal to Soviet Ukraine, and assisted materially" the Ukrainian Canadian Congress and Ukrainian Orthodox Church.

Smerchanski visited the USSR in 1967, and the KGB noticed his "good behavior without any public demonstration of the anti-Soviet feelings." They noted that "he expressed his strong interest in maintaining good trade relations between Canada and the Soviet Union."[62]

Since 1968, the KGB representatives had continued their monitoring of all elections in both Canada and the USA, trying to influence the "pro-Soviet inclined politicians" and promote their political careers all the time.[63] During the summer of 1972, the KGB agents in Canada promoted in American and Canadian mass media the information about the Canadian Prime Minister Pierre Trudeau's comparison of the Ukrainian nationalists with the French separatists in the Province of Quebec. Through the entire 1970s, any "bad and negative description of the Ukrainian diaspora in America" by Canadian politicians was disseminated by the KGB representatives in various American media with purpose of discredit "anti-Soviet inclinations" of American Ukrainians.[64]

The KGB managed to recruit and infiltrate the numerous agents (eight in only one year of 1973) in various Ukrainian Canadian organizations, "the Ukrainian nationalistic newspapers," and Canadian universities in the cities of Winnipeg, Montreal, Ottawa and Toronto, using them for triggering the campaigns to discredit those Canadian politicians, like a former Canadian Prime Minister John Diefenbaker, who supported the anti-Soviet slogans of the Ukrainian diaspora in Canada.[65]

The KGB agents focused on strengthening the split between the radical Ukrainian nationalists ("*banderovtsy*" in the KGB documents) and a more moderate part of the Ukrainian diaspora in America. These agents supported and helped to publicize all over America a moderate "pro-Soviet" position of the Ukrainian American intellectuals, such as O. Pritsak, a director of the Harvard Ukrainian Research Institute, B. Krawchenko, one of the leaders of the Canadian Institute of the Ukrainian Studies, Yu. Darevich, a Physics Professor at the University of Toronto and Yu. Gaetskii, a Professor of History at the University of Chicago. They "rejected to participate in the political actions of *banderovtsy*," "opposed their attitudes directed on boycott of the scientific and cultural connections with Soviet Ukraine." "In contrast to *banderovtsy*," they "demanded directing the activities of the Ukrainian emigration to a preservation of the Ukrainian language, culture, and strengthening its cultural role in the social life of the country of their residence."[66]

Besides the political careers of American politicians, the KGB administration in Kyiv tried to influence even academic careers of some American/Canadian teachers, who brought their students on the study tours to Soviet Ukraine. In one month alone, in July of 1968, the KGB operatives sent twice the official requests to punish via *Inturist*, the Soviet organization of international tourism, and the Soviet Embassy in Washington, D.C. such American teachers – professors from the American colleges, who came with their students to visit Kyiv. For these requests, the KGB officers collected the "discrediting material" about the anti-Soviet actions of those American college professors, who (during their visits) "spread anti-Soviet propaganda and tendentious rumors in public, trying to persuade Soviet citizens in the advantages of the American way of life over the Soviet one, attempted to pit Soviet people against Soviet government, trying to divide Soviet citizens into the hostile groups, which were fighting each other." The KGB requested to extradite those American professors from Soviet Ukraine and cancel "their Soviet visas forever," looking for various means "how to affect negatively their academic careers in the US."[67] In its official report, the KGB administration especially focused on the group of the American students from the University of Wisconsin, who were "led by their professors Robert Schacht (born in 1915) and Michael Petrovich (born in 1922)." These two professors "prepared the special teaching program, in which those students were enrolled." Before their trip to Soviet Ukraine, the American students "studied the classical works of Marxism-Leninism, conducted the conversations based on those works, organized the special discussions for better and more efficient learning of this material, and during their tour in the USSR and other countries of the socialist camp they were making a comparison of the Marxist-Leninist theory with the reality, existing in these countries." The KGB complained that Professor Petrovich organized a special tour for his students to Babyn Yar [a location of the mass killing of Soviet Jews by the Nazis during WWII in Kyiv]. During this visit, Professor Schacht "organized the ideological demonstration, trying to attract the attention of Soviet people" to this location, "shouting anti-Semitic slogans." The KGB officers filed an official report about the "anti-Soviet behavior" of Schacht and Petrovich, and as a result, the Soviet administration denied their future applications for the entry visa into the Soviet Union.[68]

Sometimes, the KGB administration organized the special operations trying to discredit and compromise those American tourists, who expressed their anti-Soviet views in public, visiting Soviet Ukraine. During his tourist visit on May 19–21, 1981, Ivan Koropetskii, the American Professor of the Ukrainian origin from Temple University in Philadelphia, who traveled with his wife, and communicated with Soviet Ukrainians, telling them that "Ukraine had to be independent" from Russia, criticized the national politics of the Soviet state, "declaring that the Ukrainian culture was in decline" due to Russification of Soviet Ukraine. Moreover, the KGB agents discovered in Koropetskii's personal papers a text of his lecture about "advantages of capitalism over socialism," which this American professor planned to deliver in various universities and colleges of Kyiv, Kharkiv and Odesa during his touristic visit. "To prevent the hostile anti-Soviet actions of Koropetskii," the KGB organized a "special operation of provocation" in Kharkiv, where Koropetskii and his wife tried to buy the old Ukrainian Christian icons from the city "black marketers." During the day of this "illegal deal," Koropetskii was arrested by the local policemen who filmed the entire scene of this transaction as a proof of Koropetskii's crime. Eventually, the KGB confronted Koropetskii and his wife and demanded about their immediate departure from Soviet Ukraine. The KGB administration used the story of the illegal transaction of American Professor in Kharkiv not only for a denial for the future entry visa for Koropetskii and his wife, but also for compromising his academic career in the USA, sending the information to Philadelphia about his behavior in Ukraine and promoting publications in Soviet and international media, characterizing him and his wife "as anti-Soviet greedy people, trying to steal and cheat," who were forbidden to visit the USSR for their illegal "criminal" transactions with the criminals.[69]

Another typical case of the KGB operations against the Americans, which involved the meddling into "the clerical affairs" of the Western Christian Church, also targeted the American and Canadian tourists, visiting Soviet Ukraine. Using the official representatives of the Ukrainian Greek Catholic (Uniate) Church from the US, who visited Soviet Ukraine as the "regular foreign tourists," the KGB agents tried to divide and destroy the remnants of this church on the territory of Soviet Ukraine. In 1967–1968, the KGB provided the special information to a cardinal Josyf Slipyj, a leader of this church abroad, in Rome, Italy. This information sent for Vatican characterized in "the unpleasant light" the activities of the leaders of "illegal Uniate church" in Ukraine, portraying them as "the corrupt and greedy" priests. Cardinal Slipyj (1892–1984), a legendary leader of the Ukrainian Greek Catholic Church since 1944, who suffered persecution by the Soviet administration and incarceration in Soviet prisons during 1944–1963, became a symbol of the resistance to the Soviet atheistic regime for thousands of his followers in Western Ukraine. The KGB knew that Slipyj played the important role in mobilizing this "Ukrainian Uniate Church" and inspiring the Ukrainian Christians for their "silent resistance" to Soviet administration. That was why the KGB planned to discredit the followers of this church in Ukraine, using the American priest, whom Slipyj sent to Soviet Ukraine in the late 1960s. As the KGB agents found out, in May 1968 cardinal Slipyj asked a Uniate priest from the USA to travel as his representative to Lviv to investigate the church affairs there, "pretending to be an ordinary tourist from America." This American priest, Dmytro Blazheyovskyi (1910–2011), who presented himself as a high school teacher in the official documents, played a role of "the secret envoy from Vatican" for collecting the information about the situation among the followers of the Ukrainian Greek Catholic Church in the Western Ukrainian regions. The KGB agents met Blazheyovskyi in Lviv and playing the role of "the pious Ukrainian Christians," provided him with the information, which discredited all leaders of the "Uniate Church" in Ukraine, confirming the bad rumors about their "very corrupt behavior." Eventually, all this KGB "disinformation" provided by the KGB for Blazheyovskyi contributed to "the weakening of the connections" between Vatican and the Ukrainian Greek Catholic Christians in Soviet Ukraine. As one contemporary of those events noted, this KGB operation was part of "the regular Soviet meddling in the Vatican politics, using American priests, to divide and suppress the remnants of the Catholic influence in Soviet Ukraine."[70] In 1973 the similar operation to discredit and compromise Reverend Mstislav Skrypnyk, a head of the Ukrainian Autocephalous Orthodox Church in USA was organized by the KGB as a response to his criticism of "Soviet repressive regime." The major goal was to discredit also the church, whose leaders, such as Skrypnyk, allegedly collaborated with the Nazis during WWII.[71]

The KGB Operations against US Consulate and US Diplomats in Kyiv

Political détente and an improvement of the Soviet-American relations became a serious challenge for the KGB operatives in Soviet Ukraine. These so-called détente problems were not only connected to the civil rights of Soviet Ukrainians, which Soviet administration promised to protect and respect according to the Helsinki Agreements of 1975, but also to an opening of the US Consulate in Kyiv in 1974–1980, and to an increase of various activities of the American diplomats in Ukraine.[72]

After the summit meeting of Brezhnev and Nixon in 1972, when the decision about the opening of the US Consulate in Kyiv, a capital city of Soviet Ukraine, was made, the US officials began their preparatory work in Kyiv.[73] Starting at the end of 1974, the KGB reported almost monthly about such a work. The first inspection for a location of the US consulate in Kyiv by American representatives took place in April of 1975. On June 1–3, 1975, the American official delegation went to Kyiv and inspected more buildings on the streets of Lenina, Reiterskaia, Chkalova and Florentsii, which were offered by the city administration for the American inspection. This delegation selected the buildings for the offices and residences of the diplomatic personnel, waiting for the final approval of the American administration.[74] Eventually, on November 19, 1975, the special representatives of the US Department of State visited Kyiv for an inspection of the buildings selected for the US Consulate. Together with representatives of Kyiv city administration and the Ministry of Foreign Affairs, the KGB officers followed the American delegation, which checked the building structures on the streets of Chkalova, Streletskaia and Kruglouniversitetskaia. Eventually, the Americans selected a building on Chkalova Street, 9. During 1976, Americans requested more apartments in different houses on the streets of Gorkii and Streletskaia for the US personnel, working for the Consulate. As a result, in two years, the Americans created a vibrant and growing community of the American diplomats in downtown Kyiv.[75]

The frequent visits of American officials in 1974–1976, which were related to the opening of the US Consulate in Kyiv, activated various forms of the US intelligence work in Soviet Ukraine. The KGB operatives who followed the US diplomats noted how they visited the Ukrainian countryside and studied the situation in the Ukrainian agriculture, comparing "the harvest situation in the local collective farms and availability of the agricultural products in the city's food stores and prices for these products." The KGB agents who retrieved the personal notes of the American diplomats in March of 1974 about their visits to the Ukrainian countryside, were surprised how "methodically the Americans explored the preparation for harvesting" in Ukraine, and how they "reported in detail about this to their administration in Washington." As the KGB administration realized, the US diplomats' regular reports were about "the problems in Ukrainian agriculture" and "the serious crisis in distribution of agricultural products in Soviet Ukraine." Some KGB officers who followed the US diplomats in 1974 were so impressed by the Americans' knowledge and expertise in agricultural developments and by their recommendations for the Soviet officials that they suggested the Ukrainian government officials "to take to consideration what Americans study in our Ukrainian land." As one officer noted, "if our Soviet bureaucrats studied the real Ukrainian agricultural situation, like Americans did, we could have avoided the agricultural crisis of the mid-1970s."[76]

According to the KGB reports, the US diplomats collected the secret information about "58 objects of the defense branches of industry in Ukraine." By monitoring the actions of US diplomats, who were involved in the functions of the new offices of the US Consulate, the KGB agents could steal "American classified information" and prevent "American intelligence's actions against Soviet Ukraine." As a result of the successful KGB operation in August of 1976, the KGB operatives thwarted the attempts of the US diplomats from Kyiv to use the city of Kharkiv "for collecting the intelligence information during their official travels in southern Ukraine."[77]

The KGB operations especially targeted Ralph C. Porter, a "head of American mission (*rukovoditel' peredovoi gruppy*), who was in charge of organizing the US Consulate" in Kyiv. The KGB officers collected the secret information from his personal papers about the "strengthening of political intelligence" in Soviet Ukraine, which were recommended by the CIA and the US Embassy.[78] The major themes for Porter's collecting of this intelligence included the following: "goals and plans of the Kremlin regarding the further development of the Soviet society; mutual relations between the regime and the Soviet realities of life; the Soviet reality and the new five-year plan (of the economic development)." These instructions stressed on the necessity to raise the "nationality question" in discussions with Soviet citizens during the US diplomats' travels in Soviet Ukraine. This information, especially about "the Jewish question and the human rights," should "reflect the influence of those [nationality] issues on the US politics regarding the diplomatic relations and cultural exchange [between the US and the USSR]." The recommendations of the US Embassy for the American diplomats in Kyiv also included a reminder about the establishing of the human contacts with the people of Soviet Ukraine, visiting the offices of the Ukrainian government and colleges, the editorial offices of the Ukrainian media, using not only American diplomats, but also American exchange scholars. A group of the US officials headed by R. Porter organized the visits of various US scholars, especially the experts in "the nationality question," to Kyiv State University, to various research institutes of the Academy of Science, to the editorial office of *Vsesvit* magazine, etc. R. Porter and his colleague Robert H. Mills visited also the local collective farms near Kyiv, "trying to figure out the college students' reaction to government's decision to send them in the countryside for participation in the agricultural work there." At the same time, the American officials visited various clerical leaders in Soviet Ukraine, including a head of the Evangelical Christian Baptists and the leadership of the Jewish community in Kyiv. The KGB agents were especially surprised "how much time Porter and Mills spent in the farmers market and at various industrial and food stores" during their visit to a city of Chernigov in December of 1976. When these KGB agents stole the US diplomats' notes after Americans' visit to Chernigov, they realized that by "studying an availability of the goods and products, the existing demand and prices," the Americans "attempted to make their conclusions about the difficulties in the industrial and agricultural production, the state of supply of the urban population and the mood of the masses."[79]

During the night of December 30, 1976, the KGB operatives illegally penetrated in the offices of the US Consulate and made photos (more than 400 pictures) of the secret American documents about the connections of American diplomats with the Soviet citizens (including various Soviet dissidents), data of the US personnel, the analytical study of the Soviet media and description of the political and economic situation in Soviet Ukraine, etc. Eventually all this information will be used by the KGB to persecute any critic of the Soviet regime for his or her connections to the US Consulate. Since December of 1976 until the closing of the US consulate in Kyiv in February of 1980 under a US President Jimmy Carter, such secret KGB operations against the official US diplomats were organized on the regular basis, providing the Soviet intelligence with precious information not only about the CIA activities, but also about the civil rights movement and national (Ukrainian, Jewish, Tatar) and religious (Protestant and Catholic/ Uniate Christian, Judaism, Muslim) activists in Soviet Ukraine. The secret collection of American documents from US Consulate reached a peak under Porter's successors, when the KGB tried to get even the technological details from the American companies like the Occidental Petroleum Corporation and his owner Armand Hammer, connected to the CIA.[80]

As the former KGB officers joked, "Unknowingly, the US Consulate provided the KGB with the excellent information about all important Ukrainian dissidents; our operatives got more precious materials from this consulate's papers than from the active measures against the anti-Soviet activists (from the Ukrainian nationalists and Zionists to Crimean Muslim Tatars) in Ukraine."[81] In 1978 and 1979, using the US Consulate information, the KGB successfully completed its special operation against the attempts of American diplomats to collect the information about persecutions the Ukrainian followers of the Christian sect of Pentecostals. In December 1978–January 1979, the KGB agents not only prevented the meetings of the American diplomats with "the most extremist activists" of this sect, but also stopped the emigration of Pentecostals from Ukraine to the USA. As a result of KGB operation, by the end of 1979, from 651 families of Pentecostals (3,296 people), who had submitted already their documents for emigration, 353 families of sectarians (1,748 people) withdrew their applications.[82]

During one "KGB raid" in the US Consulate at the end of 1976, the KGB operatives discovered the papers with a proof of the direct connections of the American officials with Soviet dissidents; they made photocopies of all those documents about these connections between Americans and local dissidents. Plus, the KGB officers obtained the American lists of the Ukrainian, Russian and Jewish political prisoners, "who needed the American support"; a list of those "Ukrainian activist-nationalists," who belonged to so-called BLOC organization; and a list of those Ukrainian intellectuals, who had the direct contacts with American diplomats in 1975–1976, including Soviet Ukrainian Americanists such as Leonid Leshchenko and Arnold Shlepakov, who also had their own direct connections to the KGB.[83]

At the same time, the KGB agents, especially those with technical education and skills, tried to study the new technical equipment, used by the American personnel in the US Consulate in Kyiv, to photograph it, and to transfer all available information about this equipment to the special KGB departments responsible for the industrial and technological espionage. Simultaneously, the KGB experts in engineering and electronic technology not only supervised "the hidden technological espionage" at the US Consulate, but also on the premises of the American firm *Norton* in Zaporizhie in February–March 1978.[84]

According to the materials of the KGB raids on the US Consulate in September 1977, March 1978 and May 1978, the KGB administration was interested more in the analytical intelligence studies and the information about the "anti-Soviet activists" collected by the US officials and "systematized" in their offices at the Consulate, than in the technical innovations of their colleagues from the US intelligence. On June 5, 1978, the KGB administration reported to Volodymyr V. Shcherbytskyi, a leader of the Communist Party of Soviet Ukraine, that the KGB operatives organized "a secret search of the chancellery at the US Consulate in Kyiv" on May 23. According to this report, which contained an analysis of the "KGB secret search," the Americans kept "the targeted collection of the political and economic information in Ukraine by processing the republican and central press for their analysis, evaluation and forecasting of the internal political situation in the [Ukrainian] republic according to the interests of the intelligence of the adversary." Besides the political and economic issues, the

US officials also added a section on the dissidents, registering all critical publications in the Ukrainian media about the "migratory and nationalistic inclined persons." Following the classification system of the analytical material, collected by the US intelligence, the KGB officers noted such sections like "Kiev" about the city transport and problems of housing construction, or section about "the difficulties in Ukrainian agricultural production." A section "Environment" contained the information about the Ukrainian experts in "the cleaning of hazardous production waste," including L. A. Kul'chitskyi, a director of the Institute of colloidal chemistry of the Ukrainian Academy of Sciences. It was noteworthy that the American Consul R. Porter paid more attention to the environmental problems of Kyiv and Ukraine, than Soviet administration did. Porter sent Kul'chitskyi and other Kyiv's officials "the recent [Western] scientific literature about a protection of environment." The KGB operatives also noted a special section "The Relations of Ukraine with Eastern Europe" which recorded all trade and economic agreements, cultural exchange, the official contacts of politicians and other forms of diplomatic links between Soviet Ukraine and its Eastern European neighbors.[85]

Again, the KGB collected the new information about 38 "anti-Soviet dissidents" [who had been already incarcerated by the Soviet authorities or "were monitored by the foreign nationalistic press"] from the special "informative cards" composed by the US intelligence officers as a reminder about "the useful contacts for American diplomats." According to the personal papers of the Consulate's official R. Mills, retrieved by the KGB, the Americans tried to "strengthen their contacts with the Tolstoy Foundation, which helped the Soviet citizens" to get the official invitations from the US to obtain the US visas and emigrate to America. Using this information, the KGB operatives began monitoring all actions of those dissidents who "expected" the foreign assistance (including the Tolstoy Foundation connections) for their future emigration from Ukraine. Eventually, until 1989, the KGB managed to prevent any attempt for an emigration of all those people, whose personal information was presented in the US Consulate's "secret papers."[86]

The special section of the KGB information from the US Consulate was about how the Americans used the American exchange scholars for "the subversive activities against" Soviet Ukraine. One case, which attracted the KGB attention, was about the American exchange student Mikhail Bakalets from the Lviv Music Conservatory. On April 23, 1978, Bakalets asked R. Mills to help his Soviet friend "to flee from Soviet Ukraine" via Hungary "by requesting the political shelter in the US Embassy in Budapest." Using Bakalets' letters to Mills "with the detailed political information about the life" in Ukrainian city of Lviv, the KGB demonstrated how even an American music student could be used "by the CIA for collecting intelligence information" in Soviet Ukraine. It is noteworthy that the immediate KGB reaction after finding these Bakalets' papers was to report to the Soviet political leadership about this music student's "involvement with the US intelligence" and then to request his extradition from Soviet Ukraine.[87]

On the regular basis, the KGB administration submitted their detailed reports to the Ukrainian communist party leadership about the personnel of the US consulate, emphasizing the important role and influence of the US intelligence in the everyday life of American diplomats. According to these reports, in January of 1979, six from eight official members of the US Consulate's personnel "were directly connected to the CIA."[88]

Paradoxically, from 1975 until 1980, the US Consulate's papers retrieved by the KGB became the major KGB source of the important information not only for the anti-American operations and monitoring the US diplomats and other American officials, who visited Soviet Ukraine, but also for various active measures against various anti-Soviet dissidents, who tried to establish the personal contacts with the citizens of the country of "the main adversary."[89] Moreover, the KGB raids in the US Consulate provided the important material, which helped the KGB agents in their operative work in Canada and the USA. Thus, as a result of one of those raids, the KGB administration obtained in July of 1978 the proof that the Ukrainian diaspora in Canada had already arranged the official invitations for a visit to Canada for some Soviet Ukrainian intellectuals, who were the well-known "anti-Soviet nationalists," and had sent those invitations through the US Consulate in Kyiv. In the special operation against Ukrainian Canadians in Toronto, the KGB agents *Yadviga* and *Visla* collected the special compromising material against those Soviet Ukrainians, who were just invited to visit Canada. These letters of invitation inside the US Consulate, which were found by the KGB operatives during their raid in Kyiv, justified and confirmed the information reported by the KGB agents *Yadviga* and *Visla* from Toronto, which led to canceling all travels to Canada of the "nationalistic Soviet Ukrainians" after July of 1978.[90] Even during the last year of US Consulate in 1980, the KGB operatives, using their stolen information from the Consulate building, established the contacts with eight scientists from the USA and NATO countries, blackmailed them, "compromising" them. As a result, those scientists provided the KGB agents with the secret information in radio-electronics, computer and space science. The same year, using the official US documents from the Consulate, the KGB managed to recruit five new agents among the international graduate students who took classes in the Ukrainian colleges and universities "with perspective of sending them to the USA for collecting the scientific-technological information in America."[91]

During the détente, especially after 1972, numerous official delegations of American politicians and businessmen visited Kyiv on the regular basis. So, besides spying on the US diplomats, the Ukrainian KGB operatives became involved in the new operations of collecting precious information from the American official guests. Usually, playing the role of the official Soviet interpreters, the KGB agents led the personal conversations with US

Congressmen, US Governors, the representatives of the US Department of State, the American scholars and the Americans of the Ukrainian dissent, who took the special courses of Ukrainian language at Kyiv State University, with the American and Canadian experts in the international relations, economy and politics, who officially visited a capital city of Soviet Ukraine. Sometimes these conversations looked like the specialized interviews about the US-China relations, the arms and space race, the recent development in the "corporate capitalism," the war in Afghanistan, the evaluations of various American and Soviet politicians, even about the details of everyday life in the US and Canada. During the 1970s, almost every month the KGB administration provided the Ukrainian Communist party leadership with the information the KGB agents obtained from the American official visitors in Kyiv.[92]

At the same time, dealing with the official American delegations, the KGB operatives in Kyiv developed one model of the active measures against the Americans, which had been used all the time until the end of the 1980s. According to this model, it was necessary (1) to create the very positive and attractive representation for the Americans about the situation [they came in Soviet Ukraine to criticize and expose 'the situation with the Jews,' 'the persecution of the civil rights activists,' etc.], (2) to take their time and distract their attention as much as possible, and restrain their actions, aimed at the implementation of the unwanted and provocative [anti-Soviet] acts."[93] Years later, monitoring a visit of 12 US district attorneys to Odesa in September 1978, the KGB administration took the same approach, while dealing with the official US delegation: "organizing the measures of the politically beneficial influence on the Americans and preventing them from collecting biased information [in Soviet Ukraine] during their visit."[94] Using their numerous agents in August of 1980, the KGB operatives tried to influence the American official guests in Kyiv, especially if they were part of the US anti-war pacifist organizations, and re-direct their attention from the conversation about the civil rights' situation in the USSR to a discussion of the problems of disarmament and of the Ukrainian Nazi's collaborators who settled in the US.[95]

Still, the most problematic for the KGB operations were not the official US delegations or American and Canadian politicians, visiting Soviet Ukraine, but the actions of American personnel from the US Consulate. The KGB administration complained to the Soviet leadership on the regular basis about the US Consulate's connections to all major "anti-Soviet groups" in Soviet Ukraine: the "Ukrainian nationalists," the "Jewish Zionists," and the "Christian sectarians" such as the Baptists, the Adventists and the Pentecostals. The KGB worried about "the justification of these groups' anti-Soviet behavior and the moral and material support by the Americans provided to these groups via the US Consulate."[96] When the relations between the US and the USSR deteriorated in the beginning of 1980, the US administration of the President Jimmy Carter decided to close the US Consulate in Kyiv, and the US Consul left Kyiv for good on February 27, 1980.

This affected the entire strategy of the KGB anti-American operations in 1980. The US administration closed all mutual Soviet-American industrial projects, which had already existed in Soviet Ukraine. Due to this process of the closure, the KGB had to protect such projects from "destroying them by the Americans," when the American engineers and workers were leaving the location of Soviet-American enterprises.[97] At the same time, in 1980, the KGB intensified its operations against the US diplomats, visiting Ukraine, to compromise and to discredit them.

Among numerous anti-American KGB operations, which targeted the US diplomats, the most impudent case involved two representatives of the American military-naval attaché from the US Embassy in Moscow, who visited Kyiv and Kherson in July 1970. When these American visitors tried to use their video cameras on the board of Soviet plane during their flight from Kyiv to Kherson for videotaping the allegedly strategic objects (the secret missile formations and the factories of defense industries) from the air, the KGB agents interfered and prevented the Americans from doing this.[98] A peak of the anti-American operations in 1980 included more than 100 so-called active measures acts against American journalists (allegedly the CIA agents), who tried openly to approach the local dissidents and collect the information about their persecutions by Soviet authorities and the violations of the civil rights in Soviet Ukraine.[99] Comparing to an average 40–50 of such cases in the KGB reports during 1972–1975, this rise of the number of the KGB operations in Soviet Ukraine against American media, demonstrates the real deterioration of Soviet-American relations in 1980, a year of the American boycott of Soviet Olympic games.[100] At the same time, the KGB operatives recorded the positive and "pro-Soviet" feelings of some official American visitors to Soviet Ukraine during 1980. In the personal conversations with the KGB agents in June of 1980, these Americans, such as Thomas Watson, US Ambassador in Moscow, criticized the politics of US President Carter and supported the "peaceful efforts of the Soviet leadership."[101]

******

As the former KGB officers, who lived through the détente, described this period as one of "the lost opportunities and the forgotten hopes." On the one hand, the intelligence officers from the US and Soviet Ukraine began their first mutual attempts to collaborate and protect their political leaders, engaging in the friendly acts of "trying to understand and respect each other." On the other hand, "the old Stalinist trends of spying and cheating on the enemies," were revived and they "shaped the entire domestic and foreign politics of the USSR," which not only undermined the attempts of any reforms, but contributed to a decline of the Soviet politics and economy, and eventually, led to the collapse of the Soviet civilization, protected by the KGB.[102]

The détente offered the unique opportunity of cultural dialogue and mutual understanding to both countries, the USSR and the USA, and to their intelligence service. Unfortunately, after 1979, following the traditional politics and ideology of confrontation, Soviet political leadership rejected this opportunity and this affected the entire strategy and tactics of the KGB operations as well. The international dimension of the politics of confrontation took the conservative turn in domestic policy as well, when the new front of cultural consumption and the youth culture attracted the more efforts from the KGB to stop the influences of the main adversary, the USA, inside the Soviet society.

Notes

1 Anatoly Dobrynin, *In Confidence: Moscow's Ambassador to America's Six Cold War Presidents (1962-1986)* (New York: Times Books, 1995), 358.
2 See the official documents, especially "Document 106: Memorandum of Conference with President Eisenhauer, August 5, 1959," in *Foreign Relations of the United States, 1958-1960*, vol. X, part 1, p. 382. Compare with the American version of these events in E. Bruce Geelhoed, *Diplomacy Shot Down: The U-2 Crisis and Eisenhower's Aborted Mission to Moscow, 1959-1960* (Norman: University of Oklahoma Press, 2020), see especially pp. 181, 185, 217, 243, 210.
3 SBU, f. 16, op. 1, spr. 931, ark. 8–15, 181–182.
4 Ibid., 181; 183–193. The retired KGB officers, whose supervisors were in charge of this "security" operation, emphasized a term "professional security" and especially "isolating/protecting" an American important guest from various anti-Soviet dissidents in Kyiv. See an interview with Stepan Ivanovich K., a retired KGB officer, Kyiv, February 12, 2019.
5 Ibid., 188; 181–182; interview with Stepan Ivanovich K.
6 Ibid., 181–182; 183–193.
7 See my interview with Stepan Ivanovich K. Compare with a new study by Serhii Plokhy, *Nuclear Folly: A History of the Cuban Missile Crisis* (New York: W.W. Norton, 2021).
8 Anatoly Dobrynin, *In Confidence*, 42.
9 Walter LaFeber, *America, Russia, and the Cold War 1945-2006*: The 10th Edition (Boston: McGraw-Hill, 2008), 211.
10 See in details about Soviet preparations of this visit in Anatoly Dobrynin, *In Confidence*, 212ff., especially 213–225, 228–264 and in Raymond L. Garthoff, *A Journey through the Cold War: A Memoir of Containment and Coexistence* (Washington, DC: Brookings Institution Press, 2001), 243–276. Compare with Walter LaFeber, Op. cit., 281–284. About a Nixon's visit to Kiev in 1972 see a published collection online: Richard Nixon: 1972: Containing the Public Messages, Speeches, and Statements of the President. Nixon, Richard M. (Richard Milhous), 1913-, United States. President (1969–1974: Nixon), United States. Office of the Federal Register.
11 SBU, f. 16, op. 1, spr. 1026, ark. 279, 299, 141.
12 Ibid., 284–286, 310–303, 312–314, 320–322, 360–362.
13 SBU, f. 16, op. 1, 1045, ark. 29–31. In this report, a KGB agent described a meeting of Nixon in Los Angeles with "a US student of Ukrainian origin, Starosolsky Vladimir Yurievich, whose father was a famous Ukrainian nationalist, but now a lawyer, and his grandfather was killed by Stalin's regime in Lviv," and he also reported about Nixon's support of Ukrainian emigrants' demands. The KGB administration in Kyiv was afraid that the American Ukrainian nationalists would use a reputation of Starosolsky's family to resume

anti-Soviet attacks, blaming the Soviets in breaking the rules of civility, and human rights violations. "Nixon demonstrated a good knowledge of Ukrainian history in a conversation with Starosolsky."

14 See in SBU, f. 16, op. 1, spr. 1045, ark. 24-28, 32–35, 29–31, especially ark. 29.
15 Ibid., 29.
16 See my interview with Stepan Ivanovich K. in Kyiv.
17 SBU, f. 16, op. 1, spr. 1045, ark. 19–23.
18 Ibid., 24–28.
19 Ibid., 32–35.
20 Ibid., 132–135.
21 Ibid., 148–149. The arrested US students asked police not to publicize that incident, and the KGB supervisors supported this request, punishing only one organizer of this "photo session" by cancelling his visa.
22 Ibid., ark. 164.
23 F. 16, op. 1, spr. 1046, ark. 51.
24 Ibid., spr. 1045, ark. 182–183.
25 Ibid., ark. 167.
26 Ibid., ark. 184.
27 Ibid., 190.
28 Ibid., ark. 191.
29 Ibid., ark. 192, 193–194. The KGB followed the American Ukrainian publications to evaluate Dobriansky's role in American politics as well. They used the article such as "President Confirms Détente, Not Acquiescence," in *The Ukrainian Weekly. Svoboda: Ukrainian Daily*, August 5, 1972, p. 1.
30 SBU, f. 16, op. 1, spr. 1045, ark. 211.
31 Ibid.
32 Ibid., ark. 188.
33 SBU, f. 16, op. 1, spr. 1041, ark. 232.
34 Ibid., 160–162.
35 SBU, f. 16, op. 1, spr. 1046, ark. 76.
36 SBU, f. 16, op. 1, spr. 1046, ark. 77–78.
37 Ibid., spr. 1045, ark. 178–179.
38 Interview with Leonid K., the retired KGB officer, Kyiv, February 5, 2019.
39 Ibid., ark. 177. During the same time, the KGB worried about a visit of another American scientist of the Ukrainian origin to Kyiv, who "openly expressed anti-Soviet views." He was "a visiting Ukrainian American exchange scientist Petryshyn Vladimir, who had a relative of OUN member who worked for English intelligence and was arrested" by the KGB. See in SBU, f. 16, op. 1, spr. 1045, ark. 65–66.
40 Ibid., 245–247.
41 Ibid., 214–217.
42 F. 16, op. 1, spr. 1046, ark. 52–56.
43 Ibid., ark. 54-55.
44 Ibid., ark. 78.
45 Ibid. All former KGB officers whom I interviewed, recalled how friendly and open were both Americans and their Soviet hosts during those meetings in 1972.
46 Ibid., ark. 80–81. See also a popular explanation of the KGB notion of the useful "asset" in Craig Unger, *American Kompromat*, 37–48.
47 SBU, f. 16, op. 1, spr.1046, ark. 90–93, 102–106. On July 6, 1972, the official US delegation visited the Academy of Sciences of the Ukrainian SSR, including its Institute of Cybernetics and the Institute of the Theoretical Physics, and discussed the future academic exchanges between American and Soviet Ukrainian scientists. See in SBU, f. 16, op. 1, spr. 1051, ark. 40–41.

48 Interview with Leonid K., the retired KGB officer, Kyiv, February 5, 2019. Compare with the KGB operations against the American officials, involved in a preparation of the Nixon's visit in SBU, f. 16, op. 1, spr. 1046, ark. 86–89, 90–93.
49 SBU, f. 16, op. 1, spr. 1046, ark. 227–228.
50 The KGB officers, participants of the events, used those words. Interview with Leonid K., the retired KGB officer, Kyiv, February 5, 2019.
51 Quoted from the KGB officers' report: SBU, f. 16, op. 1, spr. 1046, ark. 321, 323, 324.
52 SBU, f. 16, op. 1, spr. 1055, ark. 323–328, 335. I quote also my interviews with Leonid K., the retired KGB officer, Kyiv, February 5, 2019.
53 I quote all three officers who were active in Kyiv during 1972: Stepan Ivanovich, Leonid K., and Igor T.
54 Anatoly Dobrynin, *In Confidence*, 176. Dobrynin devoted the entire chapter of his book to this story: "Humphrey Declines Moscow's Secret Offer to Help His Election," pp. 174–176.
55 SBU, f. 16, op. 1, spr. 990, ark. 67.
56 Ibid., ark. 68.
57 SBU, f. 16, op. 1, spr.974, ark. 158–159.
58 Ibid., ark. 159–160. Another KGB case, related to Humphrey, involved a visit to Soviet Ukraine of Teddy Row-Mansfield, a US Senator from the Democratic Party, in April 1968. The KGB knew that he was a Democratic candidate for the post of the US Secretary of State in the future elections. During his travels in Ukraine, the KGB agents managed to photo his personal diaries, which had "the honest descriptions of Soviet realities." See ibid., ark. 99, 100–126. This diary became an object of interest for numerous post-Soviet journalists who had worked in the SBU archive in Kyiv, Ukraine since 2015. Compare with Eduard Andrushchenko's material in Russian in: https://www.currenttime.tv/a/soviet-diary/30581678.html. See also the similar material in English translation: https://www.forumdaily.com/en/amerikanec-posetil-sssr-a-spustya-polveka-prochital-chto-o-nem-pisali-v-kgb/
59 See numerous KGB reports about those operations targeting various US delegations, such as SBU, f. 16, op. 1, spr. 1053, ark. 26–29, 240–241 (1972); spr. 1092, ark. 135–136 (1974); spr. 1111, ark. 27–32, 33–34 (1975); spr. 1172, ark. 275-279.
60 I quote the special KGB report to the Central Committee of CPSU on April 28, 1970 from Vladimir Bukovsky, *Judgment in Moscow: Soviet Crimes and Western Complicity*, Translated by Alyona Kojevnikov, ([California]: Ninth of November Press, 2019), 28. I follow the original orthography of the document, published by Bukovsky in his book.
61 I quote information about "the real threat" from my interview with Stepan Ivanovich K., a retired KGB officer, Kyiv, February 12, 2019. The best description of such KGB operations, involving Howard University's students, is in SBU, f. 16, op.1, spr. 1218, ark. 265.
62 SBU, f. 16, op. 1, spr. 974, ark. 54–55.
63 Interview with Leonid K., a retired KGB officer, Kyiv.
64 SBU, f. 16, op. 1, spr. 1051, ark. 189-190. Compare with my interview with Leonid K., a retired KGB officer, Kyiv.
65 SBU, f. 16, op. 1, spr. 1077, ark. 188-195.
66 SBU, f. 16, op. 1, spr. 1185, ark. 272–273. See similar report from the US in ibid., spr. 1192, ark. 47.
67 SBU, f. 16, op. 1, spr. 944, ark. 135–136, 137–138.

68 Ibid., ark. 137–138. As some former KGB officers noted, this entire story was an example of misunderstanding from the part of the KGB operatives, who filed their request "to punish American educators." The same situation happened in July of 1980 with the American students and faculty from Georgetown University and Dartmouth College, who visited Zaporizhie and Kharkiv, led by Mark Von Hagen and Richard Sheldon. The KGB threatened to punish American tourists of this group for their "anti-Soviet actions." See SBU, f. 16, op. 1, spr. 1171, ark. 195–196.

69 SBU, f. 16, op. 1, spr.1184, ark. 116–117.

70 SBU, f. 16, op. 1, spr. 974, ark. 19–21. Dmytro Blazheyovskyi became the famous Catholic scholar and collector of the embroidered icons. I refer also to my interview with Leonid K., a retired KGB officer in Kyiv, March 2, 2019.

71 SBU, f. 16, op. 1, spr. 1077, ark. 330–331.

72 Alexander J. Motyl, "The Foreign Relations of the Ukrainian SSR," *Harvard Ukrainian Studies*, March 1982, Vol. 6, No. 1, 62-78. The KGB connected the CIA activities in Ukraine directly to this opening of the US Consulate in Kyiv. See SBU, f. 16, op. 1, spr. 1116, ark. 210–212.

73 SBU, f. 16, op. 1, spr. 1111, ark. 162–164.

74 SBU, f. 16, op. 1, spr. 1106, ark. 185–186. All these buildings were "100%" monitored by the KGB.

75 Ibid. The city administration provided the American officials a list of buildings, approved by the KGB, of course. See also the documents of August 1976 in SBU, f. 16, op. 1, spr. 1122, ark. 116–119.

76 SBU, f. 16, op. 1, spr. 1089, ark. 329–333. I quote my interview with Leonid K. He referred to a crisis in production and distribution of the agricultural produce in Ukraine during the same time.

77 SBU, f. 16, op. 1, spr. 1127, ark. 81–82. One of the major sources of information for the Americans about those "secret defense factories" came from their former Soviet workers, who emigrated to Israel and the US (between 1967 and 1975, at least 313 of these [Jewish] "emigrants had been employed on those regime objects.")

78 Compare with the KGB analysis of Porter's behavior in SBU, f. 16, op. 1, spr.1124, ark. 204–207.

79 Ibid., spr. 1127, ark. 151–153.

80 Ibid., ark. 186–187. About Hammer visit to Soviet Ukraine in 1978 see ibid., spr. 1146, ark. 105–107.

81 Both Leonid K. and Stepan Ivanovich used the similar phrases, describing this situation.

82 SBU, f. 16, op. 1, spr. 1150, ark. 46–47, 325–326; spr. 1151, ark. 198–199.

83 SBU, f. 16, op. 1, spr. 1128, ark. 157–158, 159–167, 168–182. The KGB administration used a special name of "Bloc" for all groups of the Soviet Ukrainian patriots who tried to establish relations with the Ukrainian Diaspora (especially in America). About Leshchenko and Shlepakov see a chapter 4 of this book.

84 Ibid., spr. 1128, ark. 292–293; ibid. spr. 1142, ark. 86–87, 128–130.

85 SBU, f. 16, op. 1, spr. 1141, ark. 380–381.

86 Ibid., spr. 1141, ark. 381. The Tolstoy Foundation was established in 1939 in New York State by Aleksandra Tolstaya, youngest daughter of the Russian writer Leo Tolstoy and by her friend Tatiana Schaufuss to help the refugees from the former Russian imperial geo-political space to settle in the West.

87 Ibid., ark. 382. The KGB used the US Consulate's papers to investigate a case of Soviet high school students from Lviv, who participated in the Ukrainian patriotic movement and wrote essays criticizing Soviet politics in Ukraine.

American diplomats tried to help those students to establish relations with the Ukrainian Diaspora and publish their "anti-Soviet pamphlets" in the Ukrainian daily newspapers abroad, such as *Svoboda*. Using Consulate's documents, the KGB operatives figured out the name of one of those students from Lviv. It was Markian Kulyk, born in 1961, a student of 10th grade at Lviv high school. See ibid., 382.

88 SBU, f. 16, op. 1, spr. 1151, ark. 152–155.

89 The last time the KGB secretly photocopied US Consulate's materials in Kyiv was on January 16, 1980. See SBU, f. 16, op. 1, spr. 1164, ar. 115–118.

90 SBU, f. 16, op. 1, spr. 1146, ark. 210–212.

91 SBU, f. 16, op. 1, spr. 1178, ark. 321 and my interview with Leonid K. in Kyiv.

92 Among the numerous KGB reports see SBU, f. 16, op. 1, spr. 1142, ark. 194–196, 302–304; spr. 1146, ark. 105–107, 118–122, 251–254, 270–272; spr. 1150, ark. 26–29, 45–47, 84–88.

93 SBU, f. 16, op. 1, spr. 1106, ark. 86.

94 SBU, f. 16, op. 1, spr. 1146, 253–254.

95 Ibid., spr. 1171, ar. 198–199.

96 SBU, f. 16, op. 1, spr. 1150, ark. 26–29, 46–47, 84-88; spr. 1151, ar. 109–112, 130–132, 198–199, 226–227; spr. 1164, ark. 115–118, 137–138.

97 SBU, f. 16, op. 1, spr. 1167, ark. 35–38. When the industrial factory [*proizvodstvennoe ob'edinenie*] *Azot* (in Severodonetsk, Voloroshilovograd Region) constructed by the American firm *Lummus Corporation* stopped, following the order of American administration in February 1980, the KGB operatives received an order to protect the factory from the alleged sabotage by 15 American engineers who were left on the premises of the *Azot* factory.

98 SBU, f. 16, op. 1, spr.1171, ark. 130–132.

99 Ibid., spr. 1178, ark. 214–217. See a description of KGB operation against the American correspondents of *The Washington Post* and *The Financial Times* in December of 1980, who tried to interview Aleksei V. Nikitin in the city of Donetsk, and collected the "anti-Soviet" information prepared by Nikitin for them.

100 Interview with Stepan Ivanovich T. See also about the counter-intelligence measures of the KGB against a group of the tourists from the USA who specialized in "Journalism and the Arts", which visited Kyiv during September 15–18, 1980, in SBU, f. 16, op. 1, spr. 1172, ark. 145–148.

101 SBU, f. 16, op. 1, spr.1169, ark. 296–298. Compare with anti-Soviet declarations of another US official visitor to Kyiv in October 1980 in ibid., spr. 1172, ark. 275–279.

102 I paraphrased my old interviews with Igor T. in Dnipropetrovsk and Leonid Leshchenko in Kyiv.

Part III

The KGB of Soviet Ukraine in the Cultural Cold War against Capitalist America

The KGB operations reflected a variety of spheres of life, interests and practices of Soviet society. With an opening of the Soviet society to Western influences during the Khrushchev's Thaw, the KGB became more and more involved in the real cultural Cold War with American influences inside the Soviet society. The new leadership of the KGB under Andropov reflected this new situation of cultural openness, noting that "the enemy has shifted his ideological tactics so as not to break Soviet law." Therefore the KGB tried to challenge the new fronts of their war with capitalist America – in culture and ideology, including a variety of the forms of cultural consumption – from reading of literature to listening of music and watching movies. As a result, the KGB's Fifth Directorate, devoted to the fight against ideological subversion, was established in summer of 1967, and the Third Department of the Fifth Directorate for preventing student unrest was added later the same year.[1]

Two chapters of the third part of this book will focus on those KGB operations, which targeted the American influences in the culture of Soviet Ukraine after Khrushchev, when the Western, mostly American, influences not only spread throughout the entire Soviet society, affecting all its social groups, but also led to the massive commercialization of Soviet youth culture, shaping the values and interests of the new young generation of Soviet consumers, including the young KGB officers as well. On September 20, 1978, the KGB administration in Kyiv prepared special report about the youth in Soviet Ukraine for Communist Party leadership. In this report, besides the traditional information about the "dangerous youth engagement" in activities of Ukrainian nationalists, Zionists and religious sectarians, the KGB analysts pointed out the new important sphere of their operations – "protection of the young people of Soviet Ukraine from the poison of Western, especially American, mass culture" which was "consumed by immature youth" through various media, such as radio, films, music records and audio tapes. This consumption contributed to the "hostile anti-Soviet attitudes" of the Soviet youth. For the KGB, this sphere became their major "domestic" front of the international cultural Cold War, elaborating their special measures to "protect young people from and fight with Western influences."[2]

DOI: 10.4324/9781003212522-10

8 KGB Special Operations, Cultural Consumption and the Youth Culture in Soviet Ukraine

One retired Ukrainian KGB officer has noted that

> Since 1945 until the collapse of the USSR, capitalist America was the main real adversary of the Soviet leadership and the KGB. But after the opening of Soviet Ukraine to various Western influences under Khrushchev, and especially under Brezhnev, this adversary, the U.S.A., created a new front inside Soviet society, affecting the Soviet youth culture. After 1945, enduring Ukrainian nationalism, Zionism, and religious sects became traditional targets of KGB operations in Soviet Ukraine. Since 1968, after the massive participation of Czech youth, influenced by American imperialist propaganda, in the events of the Prague Spring, a new object had emerged for KGB active measures and special operations. This object was Soviet Ukrainian youth culture, which was shaped by alien Western, especially American, influences.[3]

This former KGB officer and other colleagues of his emphasized an importance of the KGB operations, targeting the Soviet youth cultural practises. For them, so-called Americanization of those practices created the serious problem, because, suddenly, the massive consumption by young people of the pop cultural products led not only to a creation of the various political alternatives to the traditional political Soviet structures, such as Komsomol, but also, sometime, to the obvious anti-Soviet actions.

So this chapter explores KGB active measures and special operations against Americanization/Westernization of Soviet youth culture which is analyzed here through the prism of cultural consumption in Soviet Ukraine. The first persecutions of "mass alien" groupings of college students who imitated American hippies in 1968 and campaigns against high school student neo-Nazi punks during the Andropov era is the focal point of this archival research. Through an analysis of declassified KGB documents, this study adds depth to prior attempts to analyze KGB operations targeting the youth culture in Soviet Ukraine during late socialism.[4]

In 1968, KGB officials expanded the scope of their special operations in Soviet Ukraine. Besides the perpetrators of Ukrainian nationalism, Jewish

DOI: 10.4324/9781003212522-11

Zionism and religious sects, the KGB concentrated on the problems of youth culture and American influences which, in the KGB's view, were associated with the old issues of dissident activities in Soviet society. Targeting Western influences on Soviet youth, KGB operations became an important part of active measures.

These KGB activities began during the World Youth Festival in 1957 in Moscow, when Soviet youth were exposed to contacts with Western guests. As early as June 1956, Ukraine's KGB ordered the formation and special training of a group of special operatives, undercover KGB agents, to be sent to the World Youth Festival in 1957 in Moscow as official members of the delegation from Soviet Ukraine. According to official lists, composed by the KGB in Kyiv, more than 60% of the representatives of Soviet Ukrainian youth in Moscow were undercover KGB agents.[5] The KGB administration in Kyiv continued the same strategy for the future World Youth Festivals. As early as January 1959, they ordered "to prepare the specially trained agents to visit Austria for Youth Festival there, to neutralize Ukrainian nationalists abroad, preventing them from spying and provoking Soviet tourists" in Austria.[6]

At the same time, the Ukrainian KGB analysts acknowledged that both Soviet ideologists and the police lost their control over Soviet youth, especially during and after the Youth Festival of 1957. The "American cultural influences" produced not only the new sub-culture of few Americanized *stiliagi*, but also mass imitation of the American fashions by the young people, living in the cities of Soviet Ukraine. All such international venues as the World Youth Festivals became the channels of all "dangerous American influences," which could result in the "unexpected anti-Soviet behavior" of young Soviet Ukrainians. The KGB analysts "established the fact that foreigners, especially Americans, during the Youth Festival studied Soviet young people in Moscow and Kyiv in 1957," and these foreigners tried to establish "personal connections with them and use them for collecting secret information"; some foreigners "dealt with them in anti-Soviet spirit, and bringing them to the active anti-Soviet activities." After their analysis, the KGB administration admitted their failure in the fight with these Western/American influences. In their report to the Ukrainian Communist leadership in January 1959, the KGB officers complained that they "did not work efficiently [with foreign influences]," and they "lost the information about those connections between foreigners and Soviet people." Now they needed "to strengthen control over foreigners: and as one of measures would be to establish control over correspondence (mail) of foreigners from capitalist states for 4–6 months to find any suspicious activities."[7]

Since 1959 until 1968, the KGB administration and Soviet ideologists in Kyiv still emphasized the main goal of all their actions, regarding the Soviet youth, which was "a protection of the young people of Soviet Ukraine from the ideological provocations from the West, especially from capitalist America." Until 1968, the KGB operatives had not anticipated any kind of the massive "politicization" of Soviet youth culture in "a direction of the anti-Soviet actions" and a creation of the alternative cultural and political practices to Komsomol among the young citizens of Ukraine without a direct presence of the "foreign agents."[8]

The events of the Prague Spring of 1968, which involved the mass participation of Czechoslovak youth in politics, contributed to the KGB's anxieties about political and ideological stability in the USSR. On March 21, 1968, during the CPSU Politburo meeting in Moscow, the Ukrainian Communist Party leader Petro Shelest, frightened of "American dangerous ideological influences" being spread from Czechoslovakia to Ukraine and to the "entire socialist camp," proposed to suppress those developments immediately. Supported by Yuri Andropov, the KGB's new head, Shelest emphasized that, although it was "essential to seek out the healthy (pro-Soviet) forces in Czechoslovakia more actively," immediate "military measures" there would also be necessary. This was especially important for prevention of similar developments elsewhere, especially in Soviet Ukraine.[9]

As a result, Ukraine's KGB directed its efforts on special operations against its main enemy, capitalist America, and its influences on young Ukrainians. In the 1970s, Ukrainian nationalism in both capitalist America and socialist Ukraine was still a major concern of KGB operatives (20% of all cases). Jewish nationalism/Zionism followed suit (20%). Various Christian sects continued to be a serious problem for the KGB in Ukraine (20%). A rising problem was Crimean Tatar nationalism/Muslim activism (10%). Western intelligence in various forms, including espionage, was among the aforementioned targets of the Ukrainian KGB leadership (10%). Perceived as the US' creation and inspiration, the Helsinki Accords of 1975 and the Soviet human rights movement posed a new threat for the KGB. A special KGB operation codenamed "BLOC" was designed to curtail the political activism of Ukrainian intellectuals, constituting approximately 10% of the KGB's counterintelligence operations.[10] Finally, a new and serious problem for the KGB campaigns, "the threat of westernization" of Soviet youth, constituted the major focus of approximately 10% of all criminal and "prophylactic" cases in the 1970s, and nearly 20% of all cases in the 1980s.[11] KGB analysts realized that "capitalist America" became not only the main, but also the "seductive adversary," creating political forms, cultural products and practices, attractive for young Soviet consumers.[12]

The Prague Spring, College Students and Soviet Hippies

While observing the events in Czechoslovakia in 1967–1968, KGB officials emphasized the active involvement of Czechoslovak youth and college students in the Prague Spring.[13] In this context, KGB analysts realized an urgent necessity to seriously investigate various youth social groups in the Soviet Union. According to former KGB officers and archival documents, the most volatile, ideologically unreliable, and susceptible to Western (especially American) influences was the group of college students,[14] a notion that was consistent with the Czech trends of 1967–1968. As early as May 1967, immediately after Yuri Andropov was appointed the head of the KGB, the intelligence analysts initiated a series of research projects to study various Soviet college student groups. The KGB realized that the official sociological data provided by Komsomol ideologists and researchers from various departments of social sciences and humanities in Soviet universities (i.e., History of the Communist Party, Marxist-Leninist Philosophy, Political Economy and Scientific Communism) were extremely orthodox, cautious and, overall, unreliable. Therefore, the KGB administration decided to employ various non-orthodox sources of information that provided them with necessary information.

The KGB operatives selected the most articulate representatives of the college student community who were ready to share their sociological analyses with the state police. They prepared special reports/surveys of Soviet college student groups, which the KGB sent on to the Communist Party leadership. The KGB department in Kyiv sponsored a special study involving Odesa college students, which was disseminated in 1968 among all KGB officers and the party leadership as a "model" survey of a college group in Soviet Ukraine.[15] Interestingly, the most controversial and shocking observation of this 1968 survey, emphasizing the apolitical and cynical character of the students and their gradual distancing from the communist ideology, were used by the KGB in their active measures to counter the "dangerous ideological influences" in Soviet youth culture through the entire decade of the 1970s.[16] Many trends in youth behavior noted by that KGB survey of college students in 1968 survived throughout the 1980s and spread to other more numerous and much younger categories of Soviet Ukrainian youth, a phenomenon that required much more sophisticated and diverse active measures to eradicate it.

This official survey of 1968 showed the growth of political indifference, apathy and the unscrupulous attitude toward life among Soviet college students.[17] Those students demonstrated openly their scepticism toward a leadership of the communist party and Komsomol, membership in which they used mainly for promoting their career in college and on the job market.[18] According to this survey, the students' "encounters with party/Komsomol leadership at the colleges produced an impression that the communist party/Komsomol organizations were led by completely ignorant people who hopelessly lagged behind the modern requirements of life." As the author of this survey noted, "[c]ollege communist party leadership's ignorance of the fashionable music, of the views of favorite heroes of the youth, of the youth demands from their senior colleagues, the lack of deep culture among the communist leaders – [all this] leads to the result that these college communist/Komsomol leaders looked to their students like the dogmatists and the reactionaries."[19] At the same time, college students demonstrated their own shocking ignorance of not only Marxism-Leninism, but also of the modern trends in Western philosophy, culture and political science. They tried to compensate for this by listening to the broadcasting of Western radio stations and by reading the available literature and discussing this with their classmates, during their drinking parties either in the dorms or in the bars. As a result of this experience, the students developed their own notions of the communist party as "the only one ruling corrupt political organization," which constantly "re-produces the Soviet bourgeoisie."[20] Soviet students were already ready to accept the Western propaganda's clichés about "the degeneration of the communist party" in the Soviet Union. Their favorite phrase was "there are no real communists anymore." The very word "communist" had already been discredited among the Soviet youth.[21] Komsomol had lost the ideological control over college students and "its prestige and attractiveness to young people." The main reasons of Komsomol ideological failure were its inability to find the new forms of work with the youth, and its complete dependence on institutional, communist party, and trade union administration.[22] Students were sceptical about the anti-capitalist propaganda on official Soviet television and radio, and tried to avoid watching and listening to any kind of the ideological shows with criticism of the Western way of life.[23]

Overall, the college students in the cities of Eastern and Southern Ukraine, such as Odesa and Dnipropetrovsk, demonstrated their complete Russification. They "called Ukrainian language 'kolkhoz tongue' and its usage in public considered to be ridiculous and caused bewilderment." According to the survey of 1968, the college students from East Ukrainian cities "consider[ed] knowledge of Ukrainian language unnecessary," because this was "a rural obsolete language, the language of ignorant and poorly educated people." As the author emphasized, "even the rural [Ukrainian-speaking] students in [the city] turned to Russian language because they wanted to look more cultured and civilized." At the same time, those college students were against a process of "Ukrainization" of the East Ukrainian cities, like Odesa, and demonstrated their very negative attitude towards Kyiv "as a city and a national center, where the [Ukrainian] nationalists settled down."[24]

The most shocking revelation in this survey for the KGB officers was its detailed and convincing description of massive commercialization and "Americanization" of the youth culture in cities such as Odesa. For those students, a bench-mark of all economic and social development was the USA and "an expression 'made in the USA' was a sign of good quality." The main opinion of those students was that Soviet economic conditions did not allow using the economic talents of Soviet people to be the real organizers of socialist enterprise and the active participants of socialist market. As the survey's noted, "everybody insist[ed] on the necessity of a competition in the economy [like in the USA], which would not allow [a production of] the low quality of the products." Students loved freedom of opinion, which they thought existed only in the West, "in America." In their mind, the main criterion of "human success was defined by the level of his/her personal material prosperity (well-being), like in America."[25]

It is noteworthy that on the eve of the September 1968 Plenum of the CPSU, devoted to the problems of transition to the new system of planning with the "elements of socialist marketing," the city youth discussed the revival of the private entrepreneurship in light industry and in the sphere of service. The college students demonstrated an obvious propensity to commercialization in their activity, spending more time on the black market, etc. Their typical joke was "the Americans [we]re the wise people, and that is why they have no ruling communist party, [but only a market]."[26]

Besides the commercialization, the second channel of penetration of the American ideals in the consciousness of the Soviet youth, according to the 1968 survey, was a cult of hero:

> Modern young boy and girl needed the real hero (as a role model), but our cinema showed them either unusual people in the unusual situations, or the personalities who were so dull and boring, that they could not be an example for imitation. On this background, the heroes of the western films, who solved their problems by the punch of their fist, these strong handsome characters became the involuntary models for emulation. After watching the movie *The Magnificent Seven*, a half of the college male students developed a walking style of Chris (a major character of the film).[27] The youth love the strength; that was why a body-building fashion, which came from the West and was mainly criticized at the beginning by our ideologists, achieved an unprecedented scope in the country. Regarding this cult of strength, it is noteworthy that we witness the surprising rise of sympathy towards Fascism among some students. Agreeing with its blunders (like an annihilation of the Jews), students admire its attractive appearance of the tall, physically fit, and handsome Arians (*ariitsy*), parading in the military marches ...[28]

According to the KGB documents, paradoxically, everyday anti-Semitism and racism (especially toward African college students) also became the feature of the collective portrait of college students from Odesa, who, on the one hand, expressed their preferences for American jazz and beat-music and openly showed their solidarity with Czech students during the Prague Spring, but, on the other hand, participated in the physical attacks on students from Africa, calling them "black-ass people (*chornozhopye*)."[29]

In other East Ukrainian cities, besides such cases of racism, idealization of Fascist leaders and anti-Semitism, the KGB noted the rise of Ukrainian nationalism and Zionism among college students as well. In some Russian-speaking cities of Eastern Ukraine, such as Kharkiv and Dnipropetrovsk, the KGB officers recorded the frequent cases of "Ukrainian nationalism." As KGB reports noted, the rise of Ukrainian nationalism in Dnipropetrovsk was the result of demographic and political developments after 1956.

According to a KGB decision, former political prisoners who had been indicted for "Ukrainian bourgeois nationalism" and had served their prison terms in the Gulag were released after the Twentieth Party Congress but were not allowed to return to their homes in Western Ukraine. These prisoners, called *banderovtsy* in official documents, were either members or supporters of the Ukrainian Insurgent Army (UPA), the Organization of Ukrainian Nationalists (OUN) and/or members of the Ukrainian Greek-Catholic Church (Uniate or the Ukrainian Greek-rite Catholic Church) from the Trans-Carpathian and Galician regions of Western Ukraine.[30] When the Soviet army suppressed these patriotic and anti-Soviet movements after 1945, thousands of adherents were sent into exile far from Ukraine – to Siberia and Kazakhstan. KGB officials tried to prevent any contacts between these former political prisoners and their homeland in Western Ukraine. By the mid-sixties, many of these ex-prisoners settled in eastern, more Russified regions of Ukraine. KGB officials tried to control the movement of these "Ukrainian nationalists" there and isolate them among the more diverse, and less Ukrainian, population of Dnipropetrovsk and Donetsk regions. By 1967, 1,041 former political prisoners who were labeled "Ukrainian nationalists" from Western Ukraine had settled in the region of Dnipropetrovsk alone.[31] This posed a danger to ideological and political control of the region because they lived not only in the countryside, but also in strategically important cities such as Dnipropetrovsk. Eventually, a combination of these influences with a cultural influx of the college students from Western Ukraine to the Dnipropetrovsk region created a serious international scandal, involving a group of the local young patriotic Ukrainian-speaking poets, who complained about the "official politics" of Russification in Eastern Ukraine. They sent their "Letter from the Creative Youth of Dnipropetrovsk," in which they documented the KGB's suppression of Ukrainian patriots and massive Russification of Soviet Ukraine, to various offices of communist party, Komsomol, and Soviet organizations and colleges in Kyiv and Dnipropetrovsk in September–December 1968. Eventually, it reached not only the political leaders of Ukraine, but also Ukrainian émigré centers abroad. The following spring, the foreign radio stations like Liberty included a text of this letter in their broadcasts.[32] In 1969–1970, the KGB managed to supress this group of young Ukrainian patriots.[33] But until 1990, the cases of "Ukrainian nationalism" had always been connected to the activities of college students in Soviet Ukraine. Another type of "dangerous connection," which worried the KGB officers, was the so-called Americanization of the youth of Soviet Ukraine, which was shaped by the new forms of every day consumption of Western (in many cases, American) cultural products, especially by popular music from "capitalist America."

For the KGB, the most dangerous example of such "Americanization" was a case of hippies in Soviet Ukraine, which became "directly related to the political threat of American influences on Soviet youth."[34] The Ukrainian KGB focused on this hippie movement as early as 1968. The first official KGB report about "a so-called movement of 'hippies' … among part of the Soviet youth" was submitted to the communist party leadership in Kyiv on May 20, 1969. According to this report, the followers of this movement were found in Kyiv, Simferopol', Luhansk, Odesa, Lviv, Rivne and other cities of Soviet Ukraine. These people were boys and girls of 17–20-years-old, mainly students of high schools and college students. As this report noted, those "hippies" were seeking to imitate the Western lifestyle in everything: "Some of them, using various pretexts, try to avoid military service, criticize Soviet order, lead amoral way of life, use drugs, systematically establish contacts with foreigners, are involved in the black market proceedings (*fartsovka*) … Gatherings of hippies are held in the private apartments, and as a rule, are accompanied (by parties) with drinking alcohol, with listening to the new releases of foreign jazz music and frequently ended in orgies." They established contacts with like-minded people everywhere in and outside the republic. To explain better to the communist leadership the essence of this hippie phenomenon, which had begun in the USA and was imitated by its young Soviet followers, the KGB analysts added the excerpts of the analytical article about American hippies, written by the American psychologist from Yale University Kenneth Keniston and published in Russian translation in US magazine *America* (No. 150, April 1969).[35] Soviet leadership immediately demanded special active measures from the KGB regarding this new phenomenon of youth culture.

As a response to these demands, the KGB officials submitted another, more detailed, report to the party leaders on February 16, 1971 with a description of the active measures to stop this movement.[36] The first time, the KGB located the centers of the origin of this "social current" in 1968 in major industrial college cities of Ukraine: Kyiv, Kharkiv, Lviv, Dnipropetrovsk, Odesa, Donetsk, Voroshilovograd, Zaporizhie, Simferopol, Rivne, Poltava, Kirovograd, Sumy and Chernivtsy. The members of these groups called themselves "the followers of 'hippies' movement, which became widely spread in some western countries, especially in England and the USA." Two social groups: (1) *fartsovshchiks* (black marketers) and (2) *bitlomans*, the fans of "beat-music" (Anglo-American rock-n-roll) provided the social basis for this movement.[37] The KGB analysts worried that "in contrast to *fartsovshiks* and *bitlomans*, hippies have their own ideological platform. If hippies in the West protest against the rules of bourgeois society, their imitators in our country argue for revision of the moral-ethical norms of the socialist way of life, for formation of their own norms of morality. In addition, they doubt the revolutionary traditions of the past and the spirit of "the conservative fathers' legacy."[38]

The KGB operatives discovered that the college students (including college dropouts) were the "initiators" of this movement. At the same time, they acknowledged that those leaders were "the much older people than the regular college students," who tried to explain an emergence of "hippies" in the USSR "by the political motives, present themselves as the articulators of the ideological opposition in a specific form and formulate for them a program of their activity." To illustrate the political danger of such leaders, they quoted "one of the authorities" among the Kharkiv hippies, A. L. Kleshcheiev, who explained to the KGB officer:

> ... We speak for a degree of democracy, freedom of moralities (*nravov*), free speech, freedom of creative activity, freedom of propaganda of own ideas, free demonstrations, free love, disengagement in behavior, not limited by moral. A society should not interfere in a (development of) personality: I do what I want to do, if I do not impede people, – I can sit and lie down, where I want; if there is a possibility to live without work – I avoid working, because our demands are minimum; I want to be dressed in what I like, even if I want to go naked without dress; I want to spend the night, where I like, travel where I like. Because we have no such things, I and my friends think that our (Soviet) powers do the wrong things, what is incorrect, and we have no complete freedom and democracy; and people, who have power to do all this, are the (culturally) limited (narrow-minded) and do not understand our demands. We make a conclusion, that at this stage, under this political system (in the USSR), we hardly can implement our ideas in everyday life therefore, it seems to us that the West is more progressive and democratic than our (political) regime ...[39]

According to the official KGB reports to Petro Shelest, "hippie behavior (in public) has, as a rule, ugly forms. There were widely spread among them drinking, gambling, drugs, *fartsovka*, sexual perversions, procurement, etc. Meeting at restaurants, cafes, city square parks and other places for socializing, they create an obscene environment there, trying to attract attention of the public by their indecent appearances and behavior." Some of them attempted "to avoid a military draft, do not participate in socially useful work, lead wandering life, and express traitor's mood." A significant part of young people, "counting themselves as hippies, took the ideologically harmful positions as a result of the systematic listening to broadcasting of foreign radio stations."[40] The major KGB concern was to prevent "the development of the tendency to a creation of the stable connections among the groups of hippies of different cities, and their organizational unification," as their representatives in Kyiv, Odesa, Kharkiv and Voroshilovograd "tried to organize in 1969 the first republican, and then all-Union, congresses for solving the organizational questions about uniting all hippies in one centralized organization, which would spread the products of literature and art, reflecting the ideas of 'hippies'." The KGB operatives used their agents to infiltrate those groups and undermine them from the inside and stop those "attempts to unify."[41]

As a result of "prophylactic actions" against hippies in 1970, the KGB officers could draw the typical picture of the genesis of such groups, using two hippie organizations in Kharkiv as a model for their investigation. According to this KGB analysis, the initial impulse for the gathering of these 20 "hippie imitators" came from "their passion (enthusiasm) for the worst patterns of western (rock) music," when in 1968, on the initiative of 2 students (A. Soloviev, A. Makarenko) and one dropout (Yu. Shatunovskii) from Kharkiv State University, they created "the amateur club of fans" of rock music. The first action of those amateurs of rock music in 1968–1969 was an organization of "the numerous so-called psycho-concerts at the private apartments, in the basements and on the stairways of public houses." They included in their concerts "the compositions of foreign music stars and the songs of obscene content, doubtful in a political and artistic sense. Under a signboard of this 'club,' they planned to unite up to 2,000 people." Using this form (of the amateur club), they composed a program, considering at the first stage the purely illegal character of the activity of this club, introducing the rights and duties of its members. This conspiratorial club "Society of Fighters for the Flaming Heart of Danko" ("Bortsy za ogon-tolchki v obshchestvo Danko) was named after Danko, a character from Maxim Gorky's *Old Izergil*, who sacrificed himself, saving his people with his flaming heart. The club members adopted a song "House of the Rising Sun" performed by the the British rock band "The Animals" as its hymn.[42]

In October 1969, Makarenko and Shatunovskii made an attempt to organize a demonstration of their followers on the Dzerzhinskii square in downtown Kharkiv, during which "they intended to express in public their demands to local administration, regarding the official recognition of 'hippie' organization." The KGB used their agents in the special operations of stopping this demonstration and arresting ten Kharkiv hippie activists on the spot.

The same happened in April of 1970 in Voroshilovograd, when nine participants of the local hippie group were arrested for using drugs in public. A hippie group from Zaporizhie in April 1970, "with a goal of popularization of their ideas," organized a special march in the city, "like a demonstration, under a form of protest against American aggression in Vietnam." In December of 1970 in Lviv, 22 local "hippies" who composed "a constitution (*ustav*) of the hippie club" planned a similar action. In April 1971, 30 hippies from Ivano-Frankivsk planned an "action (rock) concert" on the central square in the city downtown. On the evening of June 18, 1971, in Chernivtsi, the local 17 hippies, "carrying the hand-made banners with portrait of Paul McCartney, one of the leaders of *Bitly* (the Beatles)," organized a demonstration to celebrate his birthday, and completely paralyzed the downtown. Eventually, after the numerous arrests, the KGB prevented a repetition of these public actions.[43] But despite the KGB active measures, this movement kept growing, especially in the capital city of Kyiv.

By the end of 1969, in the city of Kyiv, the KGB discovered more than 170 people who called themselves hippies. Their "president" was S. Baiev, another dropout from Kyiv pedagogical institute, who demonstrated his leader's role in the "attempts to unite and consolidate the movement." He "openly contacted the foreign tourists and kept the active correspondence with foreign journalists," especially with Americans; in public, Baiev "criticized the socialist way of life, told about his desire to escape abroad." He and his followers "condemned sending the Soviet troops to Czechoslovakia" and "criticized communism as a pure utopia without any material basis."[44] Despite various KGB active measures – the numerous arrests, expulsions from Komsomol and colleges, prophylactic interrogations of the participants and their parents, – the hippie groups in Kyiv survived. In 1974, another leader of those hippies, Oleg Pokal'chuk, a student from the Department of Biology, Kyiv State University, not only revived the movement, but emphasized the religious (spiritual) dimension in the life of Ukrainian hippies. Pokal'chuk offered the "Buddhist commune" as a new hippie model for his followers. During 1974–1975, the KGB discovered the active interactions of Ukrainian hippies not only with Orthodox Christian and Baptist communities, but also their involvement in the growing Krishnaite movement in Soviet Ukraine, which eventually led to the contacts with their foreign co-religionists[45] (Figures 8.1 and 8.2).

On October 11, 1979, in his official report to Volodymyr Shcherbytskyi, Vitalii Fedorchuk, head of the Ukrainian KGB, acknowledged the KGB

Figure 8.1 Oleg Pokal'chuk before arrest.

Figure 8.2 Oleg Pokal'chuk after arrest.

failure to stop the *"hippisty"* movement in Ukraine. According to his statistics, the KGB recorded 80 criminal cases launched against those "who imitated Western hippies" in various regions of Ukraine: Lviv 48, Donetsk 6, Crimea 5, Poltava 5, Zaporizhzhia 5, Dnipropetrovsk 4, Kyiv 2, Kherson 2, Ternopil 2 and Chernihiv 1. Among them, 65 people were between 16 and 25 years of age, and 15 people between 26 and 30 years of age; 64 were males, and 16 were females.[46] Thirteen of them had been "targets of active KGB measures;" 10 were "involved in ideologically harmful actions;" 3 were indicted for criminal offences; 8 were arrested for manufacturing and selling drugs; 27 were arrested for using drugs; 15 were receiving medical treatment in mental institutions; 10 were "arrested for avoiding military service; and approximately 50% of all Ukrainian hippies did not study or work."[47] As late as April 1987, the KGB still noted the existence in Ukraine of the "hippies-pacifists," who called themselves *"Sistema."* Overall, there were 60 hippies in the republic (mainly in Dnipropetrovsk, Lviv, Odesa and Simferopol), and 30 in Kyiv.[48]

In their reports, the KGB officers noted in 1979 the new attempts of the creation "new hippie connections" by some hippie enthusiasts, who organized "the special weddings," inviting all major hippie groups from all the Soviet Union to Crimea and Lviv. In September of 1979, the similar massive meeting was planned to "pay respect to a memory of the American guitarist [Jimmy] Hendrix, one of the leaders of hippies in the West."[49]

Another attempt of hippies to reach their followers was by using popular music to attract the young rock music fans. A "group of the imitators of hippies" created the "amateur vocal-instrumental [rock music] group 'Vuiky'" in Lviv in 1977. According to the KGB report, these musicians were touring in Lviv and Crimea, spreading the ideas of hippies among their audiences. Hippies also used religion to attract people to their meetings. This happened in August of 1978, when 60 Soviet hippies met in the city of Riga, Latvia, for their meeting, where they spread "the ideologically dangerous religious literature" among their followers. One of this meeting's organizers was a former acolyte of the Orthodox Christian Church from Moscow. He called on "uniting all the youth [followers of hippies] in Christ." As the KGB agent, infiltrated in a group of the Ukrainian hippies, reported, such organizers praised these All-Union meetings as a movement toward "the meaningful and not spontaneous protest to the authorities, using democracy of the Soviet laws." At the same time, these hippie activists "called on to collect the facts of 'oppression' of the imitators of hippies by the Soviet authorities for the subsequent transfer of these materials to the West."[50]

In August 1979 in Crimea, a KGB agent met another hippie activist who was a participant of "The Christian Seminar on the Problems of the Religious Revival", which published illegal religious-philosophical journal *Obshchina (Community)*. This "seminar" was also engaged in the process of involvement of the new members, first of all, those who were "the imitators of original hippies." According to calculations of those KGB officers who were in charge of monitoring the groups of Soviet Ukrainian hippies, at least 60% of all arrested representatives of this "subculture" in Soviet Ukraine admitted their "association with some kind of Christianity" during the 1970s. Later on, around 30% of them belonged to so-called Eastern Asian sects, who followed teachings of Buddha or Krishna.[51]

The KGB documents provided Communist leadership of Ukraine with a relatively good sociological analysis of the hippie movement, which was used for all KGB active measures from 1969 until 1987. According to such an analysis, based on the interviews with former hippies,

> The group of hippies was characterized by such a contrast. On the one hand, there were young people, who (due to their young age) were aspiring to something unusual, romantic, having read a certain type of literature, which somebody provided them with more than enough information; and those people being too young, did not see in this more serious reasons, and took this for granted, were keen on their crazy ideas and colorful clothes and on something unusual, (which allowed them to stand out among their peers). On the other hand, there was another group of young people who understood very well an incompatibility of the ideas of hippies with Soviet system, and, nevertheless, they joined the movement consciously. In this very group you could more often meet people, who made money using this movement, i.e. traded

clothes (*"fartsuiut barakhlom,"*) drugs, and other things. In this very group you could more often meet people, who criticized (*"khaiut"*) all the Soviet things, calling this *"sovdela"* (Soviet stuff), who wanted to escape to the West, and moreover, they incited others to do the same. It was noteworthy that many of them maintained connections with the people living abroad, wrote and sent letters abroad, they had relatives or friends there, or established the contacts with foreigners in the city on regular basis ... In their milieu, they propagandized "free love", freedom of behavior and actions, parasitism and reluctance to obey (Soviet) laws and moral norms, calling this coercion ... They insisted that we had no democracy if we had only one ruling political party, and that people had to enjoy their life rather than waste it for the state ...[52]

For the KGB, the major threat of the hippie movement was a "politicization" of Soviet youth, a creation of a dangerous alternative to the traditional Komsomol structures and political practices, which they called the "institutionalization" of Soviet hippies. The KGB operatives noted a creation of the "underground hippie clubs" in all major industrial cities. In Kirovograd, in February 1971, the local hippies organized an anti-Komsomol "Union of Free Youth," which had 20 members. Using their active measures, including infiltrating this hippie organization, the local KGB office managed to prevent the massive demonstration of the "free youth" of Kirovograd, which had a goal to mobilize all young people for a collective fight for "freedom of speech, free love, and freedom of demonstrations."[53]

As the KGB officers, participants of these events, explained, the KGB always tried to justify their special operations against the youth culture by raising an issue of its connections to Fascism. For the Soviet Ukrainian KGB official strategies, Fascism always was a sign of the Ukrainian nationalism and the Ukrainian nationalists' collaboration with Nazis during WWII. Such a narrative, which likened any Ukrainian patriotic movement with Fascism, became a justification of all major active measures and operations of the KGB against so-called Ukrainian bourgeois nationalism in Soviet Ukraine. The KGB administration used the same narrative dealing with hippies in Soviet Ukraine as well.[54]

According to the KGB analysis, which attempted to connect the youth movement in the Prague Spring to Neo-Fascism, "hippies were the active collaborators of the counter-revolutionary [pro-Fascist] elements in Czechoslovakia in 1968." The similar hippie groups in socialist Hungary were arrested "for collection of intelligence information for one Western diversion spy center." And finally, the KGB operatives provided information that "Soviet followers of hippies [in major cities of Ukraine] spread the ideas of Fascism" as well. In 1971, one Ukrainian hippie, Aleksandr Balykin, a student from Nikolaev ship-building institute, declared that "the ideas of Hitler are similar to the ideas of modern youth, which discarded such notions as conscience, shame and morality." Some of Ukrainian hippies, like a group from Lviv, demonstrated in public "their black ties, which were decorated with swastikas and crosses."[55]

As I mentioned before, after WWII the KGB administration always interpreted "a massive expression of the Ukrainian patriotic feelings in public" as a Ukrainian nationalism, which in their interpretation was always related to Fascism. By the beginning of the 1980s, the KGB operatives in Kyiv and Lviv were struck by the fact that even the representatives of the Americanized "subcultures of hippies" among Soviet Ukrainian college students used the images and poetry of Taras Shevchenko, a national icon of the Ukrainian culture, to identify themselves "as the Ukrainians, as a separate (from Russia) nation." During the 1980s, the KGB reported that numerous young followers of "the hippie system" and another "subculture of Indianists" (imitators of North American Indian [indigenous] culture) among Soviet Ukrainian youth not only demonstrated publicly their respect for Taras Shevchenko, but also "identified themselves with the Ukrainian nationalistic symbols such as 'fascist' trident."[56] In this way, the KGB tried to present the Ukrainian hippies as a version of the Ukrainian nationalism, which in the KGB narratives was always associated with the Fascist symbols such as a trident and swastika. Thus, the KGB directly connected the political activism of Ukrainian youth to Fascism, which eventually justified ideologically all KGB active measures against hippies in Soviet Ukraine (Figure 8.3).

Figure 8.3 Ukrainian hippies and Indianists with a sign of Trident (a state symbol of independent Ukraine) in 1989.

Clearly, the Czech youth political activities in 1968 forced the KGB to think about the Ukrainian hippies' political activism in similar terms. The commercialization of Soviet youth culture and disco music that became extremely popular among Soviet youth seemed innocent in comparison with political statements made by the hippies and their attempts to organize. The KGB arrested hundreds of Ukrainian imitators of American hippies and expelled them from universities and the Komsomol all over Ukraine. Ukrainian punks who were similarly portrayed as neo-Nazi presented the same threat to the Soviet system, the Soviet Ukrainian culture and the Soviet identity of Komsomol members.

The KGB documented two massive, organized youth movements in Soviet Ukraine after Stalin, which challenged the very existence of the Komsomol, an official Soviet youth organization, and offered the venues for anti-Soviet activities in which thousands of Komsomol members participated in the 1960s–1980s. The hippie movement emerged first, followed by the punk "imitation" movement. At the beginning, the members of both movements had some cultural fixation with Western cultural products, mainly rock music and films, but by the 1980s their cultural practices evolved embracing neo-Nazi ideas, processes that were documented by the KGB. These practices became more prominent, and even radical, especially among Soviet imitators of Western punks.[57] Moreover, in contrast to the Ukrainian followers of hippies who were older and more college educated, adopting American cultural practices of pacifism and non-violence, the Ukrainian punks were much younger, with only high school education, and they adopted more radical, violent, and sometimes explicitly neo-fascist models informed by the neo-fascist movements that emerged in Italy, Germany and Britain after 1945.

The KGB Anti-fascist Campaign

In the fall of 1982, in their letters to the Communist leadership of Soviet Ukraine, the KGB officers demonstrated their concern about "the obvious expressions of Neo-Nazism and Fascism" among Soviet Ukrainian youth. "Since 1979," they reported in September 1982, "in the city of Chernivtsy, the unknown persons left the numerous pictures of Fascist swastika on sidewalks, the walls of public buildings and telephone booths."[58] The KGB established the identity of at least five former students from the local technical schools (all of them were 17–19 years old), who were engaged in those "Neo-Fascist acts." All of them were under the serious influence of American popular culture, listening to American "beat-music, known as punk, and worshipping American pop-idols."[59]

According to the KGB description of their prophylactic measures, it turned out that after watching an Italian movie *San Babila – 8 PM* (in Italian: *San Babila ore 20: un delitto inutile*), "a film about the outrages of Fascist youth [in Italy]," those young people "demonstrated the strong interest in Fascist ideology, symbols and paraphernalia."[60] Eventually, the KGB experts realized that this Italian feature film of 1976 was directed by an Italian film director Carlo Lizzani. It was entered into the 10th Moscow International Film Festival in 1977. The movie was inspired by the events of violence that occurred in Piazza San Babila in Milan in 1975, where groups of neo-fascists and communists were the protagonists. Four Milanese boys were part of a fascist group, claiming with all sorts of violence a new order based on the ideas of the fascist movement of *"squadrism"* of Benito Mussolini. The boys were fighting with the institutions and against the youth group of the communists and the anarchists, and often collided during the protests, with violent outcomes. One day the leader of the fascist group asked Franco, the most insecure boy of the brigade, to perform a violent and demonstrative act against a randomly chosen communist boy, in order to redeem his "honor." So one night in Piazza San Babila the boys met a couple of lovers, dressed in red (they are believed to be communists), and the group's madness pushed the boys to chase them, and to stab them. Franco was shocked and ran away from home, denouncing assault to the police. Eventually, all group of these young fascists was arrested and persecuted by the police. The KGB officer, who investigated a group of Chernivtsi punks, fans of Carlo Lizzani's film, realized that young Ukrainian imitators of Italian Neo-Fascism were especially influenced by the images of modern fashionable dress and behavior models of the young Neo-Fascist heroes from this Italian movie.[61]

The young Ukrainian imitators of Italian Neo-Fascists organized their meetings at Chernivtsi downtown café, listened to punk rock music and "being under influence of the foreign radio stations, they used to listened at home, they pronounced in public the apparent anti-Soviet judgements" about Soviet politics.[62] Two of those students, leaders of that group, "openly spoke out about a necessity of the replacement of political system in the USSR, transfer of political power to 'the military regime' and applying in state management of the fascist methods of political rule." As the police discovered, these students demonstrated in public the large images of a swastika. They were suspected of the public burning of the state Soviet banner on the façade of one public building in downtown Chernivtsi on May 10, 1981. During the KGB interrogation, it turned out that those Chernivtsi's students "were brainwashed by the Italian and American propaganda to change their Soviet Ukrainian image into a Western Neo-Fascist."[63]

In October of the same, 1981 year, the KGB administration reported about a creation of the so-called Fascist Party in Novebelichi residential area in Leningrad district of Kyiv. The founders of this group were five adolescent students from one high school and a neighboring technical school (*uchilishche*), age of 15–17 years old. Ivan O. Bleichik, a leader of this group, which was created in December of 1980, proposed a special title for this formation: "The Pupils of the Great Reich [*Raikh*]." This group was meeting on the regular basis at one of the housing projects, where Bleichik lived. For this organization, Bleichik offered a special banner from white cloth with a big sign of red Fascist swastika and a major program slogan for their organization in Ukrainian "Let the Independent Ukraine Live! (*Khai zhyve samostiina Ukraina!*)" Eventually Bleichik and his friend S. Kostin not only made a big flag with swastika, but also painted an emblem of their "Fascist Party" with a portrait of Adolf Hitler. During the meetings of their "party" Bleichik "eulogized" a personality of Hitler, telling various biographical stories from his life; justified the actions of Nazi troops in Europe during WWII and praised a life of Stepan Bandera, a legendary symbol of Ukrainian nationalism. During the winter of 1980–1981, the participants of this group attacked numerous times other young people, Komsomol members, and with shouts "hit the Komsomol members! (*bei komsomol'tsev*)" beat them up.[64] The police arrested members of this "Fascist Party" in Kyiv, but they could not stop the growth of this strange "Neo-Fascist movement." The similar groups of young Neo-Fascists spread all over Soviet Ukraine after 1981. It turned out that another group with the name of "Neo-Nazi Party," organized by the high school student fans of Anglo-American punk rock music, posted the leaflets with criticism of Soviet political system in downtown Kyiv by April 22, 1981. According to the KGB officers, who witnessed this rise of Neo-Fascism among Ukrainian high school students, all arrested "Neo-Fascist hooligans" called the Soviet state "a Mafia state."[65]

This was a new phenomenon for the KGB operatives. Traditionally, "the anti-Soviet criminals," who were arrested for the public demonstration of swastika and other fascist signs, tended to be much older. V. Bubnov, who put a large flag with swastika on the eve of May 9, 1979, on a water tower in the city of Konotop, the region of Sumy, was 28-year-old. A. Maliovanyi, who put a sign of swastika with anti-Soviet slogans on a Lenin monument at the center of the town of Vatutino, the region of Cherkasy, on the eve of November 7, 1980, was 27-year-old.[66] Now much younger people, the adolescents of 15–17 years old, demonstrated this strange "Neo-Fascist madness" all over the Soviet Ukraine.

As it turned out, almost every group of this "madness," which was recorded by the KGB documents, was organized under influence of two different kinds of cultural consumption among the Soviet youth. One direct influence came from an Italian movie *San Babila – 8 PM*; another cultural product, which inspired the imitators of Neo-Fascists in Soviet Ukraine, was Anglo-American rock music, especially punk rock.

Moreover, the KGB officers discovered the similarities of these Ukrainian students' imitations of Neo-Fascists with "those pro-Nazi imitators of English punks in Poland and Yugoslavia," which were presented in the special "classified" informational bulletins about a situation in the socialist East Europe in 1981. Both Soviet ideologists and the KGB administration asked the Soviet cultural administration to stop showing in Soviet Ukraine the Italian movie by Carlo Lizzani, due to its "ideological threat."[67] As we see, this case of fascination of the Ukrainian students with the Italian movie, and their imitation of the Italian young neo-Fascists' behavior, became a representation of the global cultural Cold War, which connected the cultural product from capitalist Italy, Anglo-American punks and Soviet Ukrainian high school students together in one cultural phenomenon.

As the KGB found out also, these Ukrainian students referred to the Soviet political system as "Mafia State," which had to be replaced with the strong authoritarian power of the Fascist state. The police discovered that all groups of young Soviet imitators of Neo-Fascism in major Ukrainian cities compared the Communist party system to "Mafia rule." And again, all the arrested Ukrainian Neo-Fascists emphasized an influence of the Italian films on them.[68]

Soviet Notions about Mafia

Traditionally, the KGB connected the notions of Mafia as "the capitalist organized crime" to the US, arguing that this was a purely American "social-political phenomenon." But the realities of cultural consumption "on the ground" demonstrated again the Italian, rather than American, influences on Soviet youth.[69] Among Soviet audiences, the first images of organized crime in the capitalist West and notions about the Mafia came from the movie screen, from the political films, directed by the Italian film director Damiano Damiani.[70] Two of his best films about organized crime were popular in the Soviet Union in the early 1970s. Soviet ideologists and the KGB officers considered them as a serious alternative to other Western films about crime. Damiani's first film about the Italian Mafia was an adaptation of Leonardo Sciascia's novel *The Day of the Owl*. In this film, released in 1968, the young police inspector Bellodi (Franco Nero) began his investigation of Mafia crimes in Sicily but encountered a wall of silence and isolation. As a result, all his efforts to discover the truth about these crimes failed. This film was released in the Soviet Union in 1969 under the title *Sova poiavliaetsia dniom* (The Owl Appears in Day Light). From the first days of the film's release, Soviet ideologists used it as their counter-propaganda to the Western style of life.[71]

The most successful and impressive political film about the Mafia was Damiani's 1971 movie, *Priznanie komissara politsii prokuroru respubliki* (Confessions of a Police Captain). According to Howard Hughes, this movie "remains Damiani's best and most controversial film." In this film, Italian movie star Franco Nero plays Traini, "a young district attorney assigned to investigate an assassination attempt with police captain Bonavia (Martin Balsam)."[72] Eventually, Traini discovered that his supervisors, representatives of the elite of Italian jurisprudence, were connected to the Mafia. All information about the new facts of Mafia criminal activities, which a captain Bonavia had submitted to the young district attorney's office, became known to Mafia leaders. Bonavia realized that he was powerless in the struggle with the Mafia because even his bosses were part of the same system of the organized crime. In an act of despair, acting alone he shot and killed a leader of the Mafia group. Bonavia was indicted for premeditated manslaughter and sent to prison. The final scene is the most tragic and heart-rending in the film. In this scene a bleeding Bonavia is dying in a prison movie theater after being stabbed in the prison dining room by the criminals who had worked for the Mafia. Everybody is laughing at the jokes of a comedy film in the prison movie theater. Nobody pays attention to the former police captain who was silently dying in his theater seat.

Confessions of a Police Captain was shown for the first time in the Soviet Union as part of the program of the Seventh Moscow International Film Festival during the summer of 1971. Even traditionally conservative Soviet film critics who covered the Moscow Film Festival praised Damiani's film as "an important contribution to a progressive humanistic tradition of the Western filmmakers."[73] Soviet ideologists in Ukraine immediately followed this positive evaluation of Damiani's film. They promoted the release of this film all over Ukraine during the fall of 1972. *Confessions of a Police Captain* reached Ukrainian cities at the end of September of 1972 and immediately became a blockbuster in local movie theaters.[74] Moreover, this film became a real box-office success all over the Soviet Union. According to the All-Union readers' survey of *Sovetskii ekran*, *Confessions of a Police Captain* was the most popular foreign film of 1972 in the USSR after the British movie *Romeo and Juliet* which beat all the records of foreign film releases in the country.[75]

Soviet ideologists in Ukraine were always more cautious and conservative than their colleagues in Moscow. Conservative attitudes influenced the Ukrainian Soviet *apparatchiks* who were responsible for the release of foreign films in the republic. The positive evaluations of Moscow about Carlo Lizzani's film about Italian Neo-Fascist youth also influenced the Ukrainian Communist ideologists, who ignored critical remarks of the Ukrainian KGB officers about an "ideological threat of the Italian movies."[76]

During the 1970s, the Italian films about the Mafia became the most important ideological tool for diverting young filmgoers from their favorite westerns and foreign adventure films. On the one hand, Soviet ideologists tried to use Damiani's films to discredit the popularity of the West in the popular imagination of the local filmgoers. On the other hand, they tried to stop a rise in crime among the local youth. Instead of the films about the French fictional criminal Fantomas, or Japanese martial arts, or Hollywood Westerns, which triggered various forms of criminal activities, Soviet ideologists promoted Italian anti-Mafia films. The official promotion of Damiani's films did not stop the rise of the crime among the Ukrainian youth. Instead, more and more young filmgoers began using the term "Mafia" in their description of the local everyday realities of corruption in Soviet organs of power – which had failed to prevent a catastrophic growth of crime in Ukrainian cities. And the most articulate consumers of the Italian anti-Mafia films were the young Ukrainian imitators of Neo-Fascism, who applied the Mafia model to realities of Soviet domestic politics.[77] At the same time, the police discovered another unusual source of inspiration for the young Ukrainian Neo-Nazis. It was Anglo-American rock music, known under such alien names as "punk" and "heavy metal."[78]

The KGB Campaign against the Punks

In Soviet Ukraine, the KGB campaign against the young imitators of Neo-Fascism converged with the old ideological campaigns against the "ideological dangers of Western popular music." This campaign, which started in the 1960s as a struggle against "beat music" of the Beatles and Rolling Stones and their hippie imitators, reached a peak in 1980–1981 as a new campaign against "Fascist punks." This campaign was a reaction, to some extent, to confusing information in the central Soviet periodicals, where such new cultural phenomenon as British punks was presented as Neo-Fascists, as "skinheads." Therefore, all Western music, which was associated with the punk movement and used fascist symbols had to be prohibited for mass consumption in the Soviet Union. According to Soviet music critics, the periodicals' description of punks as fascists confused and disoriented thousands of Communist ideologists in provincial cities of Soviet Ukraine:

> The only thing anyone knew about punks was that they were "fascists" because that's how our British-based correspondents had described them for us. Several angry feature articles appeared in the summer and fall of 1977 with lurid descriptions of their unsavoury appearance and disgraceful manners, including one that quoted sympathetically a diatribe from the *Daily Telegraph*. To illustrate all this, a few photos of "monster" with swastikas were printed ... The image of punks as Nazis was established very effectively, and in our country, as you should understand, the swastika will never receive a positive reaction, even purely for shock value.[79]

The KGB and Komsomol activists thought punk and fascist were the same. All Komsomol propagandists and people in charge of discotheques in Soviet Ukraine received special notices about punk ideology with Russian translations of British punks' phrases. This information was reprinted in many publications by Ukrainian journalists who covered this anti-punk campaign. The journalists of the youth periodicals quoted the punk slogans:

> Live by today's day only! Do not think about tomorrow! Do not give a damn about all these spiritual crutches of religion, utopia and politics! Forget about this. Enjoy your day. You are young, and do not hurry to become a new young corpse.

Ukrainian journalists usually added their comments about the anti-human essence of the "fascist punk music": "These were slogans of punks, preachers of bestial cynicism and meanness, who were the real spiritual mongrels of the twentieth century."[80]

The first public scandal, which involved both "fascist music" and the display of "fascist symbols," took place in Soviet Ukraine in the city of Dnipropetrovsk during the fall of 1982. The city police arrested two college students, Igor Keivan and Aleksandr Plastun, who had their own collections of Western music records with "fascist symbols" and who demonstrated their "Neo-Nazi" behavior in downtown Dnipropetrovsk. These students were dressed in T-shirts with images of Kiss and AC/DC which attracted the policemen who interpreted such images as the "fascist" ones. After the arrest of Kievan and Plastun and the confiscation of their "fascist" records, the police sent information about these students' anti-Soviet behavior to their colleges. In December of 1982 the entire city and region of Dnipropetrovsk experienced the beginning of the anti-Fascist and anti-punk campaign. Dnipropetrovsk City Committee of CPSU approached Nadezhda A. Sarana, an old Communist, a member of the anti-fascist resistance group during WWII, to write a letter about the dangerous fashion of "Fascist punks." On December 22, 1982, they staged an open public meeting with participation of all Communist and Komsomol activists in downtown Dnipropetrovsk. During this meeting all activists supported Sarana's letter against punks and "declared war on punk movement" in Soviet Ukraine. Later, under KGB pressure, the local ideologists organized a special public trial of Keivan, Plastun and another young punk Vadim Shmeliov who were expelled from Komsomol and their colleges in January of 1983. The KGB officers were especially outraged about an attempt by Keivan and Plastun to "interpret" this punishment as a violation of their human rights. From this time on, all Komsomol organizations of the region began to purge Komsomol members who were suspected of unusual enthusiasm for the forbidden music.[81]

During the early 1980s, every issue of the local newspapers contained material which portrayed the ideological danger of the Western music consumption.[82] Local journalists were so intimidated by the anti-rock music campaign that they rejected any public demonstration of preferences for Western cultural products as an act of betrayal. Therefore, they took an active part in a campaign against a Leningrad rock band, *Zemliane*, during the spring of 1984. It was the second concert of this band in Dnipropetrovsk in 1984. During the first time, in January of 1984, local journalists applauded the band.[83] But during the spring a situation changed. To advertise their concert in Dnipropetrovsk, Leningrad rock musicians used a photograph of Igor Romanov, their lead guitarist, who was dressed in a T-shirt with the US flag on it. Moreover, according to the local journalists, during their concert in the closed city, *Zemliane* played songs of "forbidden fascist and punk bands." As a result, the Dnipropetrovsk Komsomol newspaper organized an anti-*Zemliane* campaign, accusing Leningrad musicians of "a betrayal of socialist principles of music performance." Despite readers' support of the popular Leningrad band, the journalists, together with local KGB officials, insisted on punishment for rock musicians for their low ideological level and for promoting "capitalist standards of anti-human mass culture." In April 1984, the administration of "Leningrad Concert," an organization responsible for *Zemliane*'s concert tours, punished the rock musicians; their concerts were banned, and they had to re-write their repertoire. After this scandal about the *Zemliane*'s concert, Dnipropetrovsk officials stopped inviting "suspicious" rock bands from Moscow and Leningrad.[84]

The same happened with a concert tour of the Estonian hard rock band Magnetic Bend in Ukraine, which visited such Ukrainian cities as Zhitomir, Lutsk, Vinnytsa and Lviv in September of 1982. The KGB witnessed the expressions of "Fascist punk" behavior during this tour by Ukrainian fans of this Estonian band. Komsomol ideologists who organized this tour were punished and demoted according to the official KGB complaints. More than 90 fans who demonstrated pro-punk and anti-Soviet behavior were arrested by the police and *"prophylactirovany"* by the KGB.[85]

This anti-punk campaign especially affected the Ukrainian fans of heavy metal. When in 1983 Dnipropetrovsk police arrested ten students from the local vocational school for "acts of hooliganism," they discovered various symbols of Nazism and the American KKK used by those students. As it turned out, Sergei Onushev, Aleksandr Rvachenko and their friends made special white robes, put the letters KKK on them and tried to "imitate acts of this American fascist organization."[86] The leader of this "fascist" group was Sergei Onushev, who "used to play at home the music tapes of bands which belonged to the pro-fascist movement – Kiss, Nazareth, AC/DC, Black Sabbath." Local ideologists established a direct connection between fascism in Onushev's group and this music. According to them, Kiss provoked the Soviet students to commit inhuman fascist acts.

> What kind of art, a journalist commented, did the musicians of Kiss represent? They tear apart live chickens and vomit in public during their performances. This band Kiss is a group of four hooligans, who selected SS Nazi symbol as the symbol of their band. Nevertheless, the show businessmen transform them into the idols of the contemporary youth and proclaim them as "trendsetters" in popular culture.[87]

Another case that attracted the attention of local journalists concerned Dmitrii Frolin, a student from the Department of Philology at Dnipropetrovsk University. As a result of the anti-punk and anti-fascist campaign, Frolin was arrested by the police in 1983 and expelled from both the Komsomol and the university in 1985 for "propaganda of fascism." According to the local ideologists, Frolin's activities were the direct result of "intensive listening" to the music by "fascists bands" such as Kiss and AC/DC.

Our Soviet books paradoxically co-existed with fascist and racist slogans on Frolin's book shelves, wrote one local journalist. These slogans were written in Gothic script in both English and German languages with phrases such as "Only for Whites" etc. Over his bed, Frolin put a fascist cross and a poster with distorted in non-human grimaces and ugly decorated faces of members of the band Kiss. (Frolin paid forty rubles for this Kiss poster on the "black market.") In addition, he had a variety of audio tapes with music of Kiss and AC/DC. Just press a button of his tape recorder and you will hear this music.

And then a journalist made his own ideological comments:

Let's think about all this! They, musicians of AC/DC, call themselves the devil's children. Their song "Back In Black" became an anthem of the American Nazi Party. During a Komsomol meeting Dmitrii justified his behavior, "I do not consider my collecting of such things a crime. This is just a mere collecting. It does not matter what is a subject of this collection. These items reflect a certain period of history of the people. I consider that a listening to my favorite music, collecting and listening to music records are part of my private life. And I have a right to protect my privacy according to Soviet and international laws."[88]

In December of 1983 the local youth periodical published the results of sociological analysis among Dnipropetrovsk youth compiled by the Komsomol scholars. According to this publication, in many student dorms in Dnipropetrovsk colleges, the special Komsomol raids discovered images of the American band Kiss, "on which any observer could easily find without any difficulties the SS symbols and Nazi signs." Moreover, a majority of the student population in Dnipropetrovsk "preferred T-shirts with the signs of the US military and insignia of the capitalist countries, the political and military enemies of the Soviet Union." Dnipropetrovsk students bought these T-shirts on the black market and wore them even during their classes while in college.[89]

According to KGB officers, "a youth culture of fascist music" was also connected to an idealization of Hitler and Ukrainian nationalist leaders during World War II, such as Stepan Bandera. In 1983 and 1984 the police arrested members of "a fascist Banderovite group" who were students of the Dnipropetrovsk agricultural college. These students – Konstantin Shipunov and his five followers listened to "fascist rock music," organized their own "party" and popularized the ideas of Nazi leaders and the Ukrainian nationalist politicians. They criticized the Russification of cultural life in Ukraine, emphasized the necessity of Ukrainian independence from the Soviet Union and insisted on protecting the national rights of all Ukrainian patriots.[90]

All over Ukraine, many young punk rock fans not only openly criticized Soviet political system and Russification of Soviet Ukraine, but also worshiped Stepan Bandera and other Ukrainian patriots who were persecuted by the Soviet authorities after WWII. In January of 1983, the KGB officers in the city of Novovolynsk discovered the hand-written text about "Ukrainian patriot Bandera" by the local students of the technical school (PTU), who were listening the American radio broadcasts on the regular basis. As a result of this practice, these students were especially interested in those American radio shows, which covered history of the Ukrainian nationalism; and they made their notes about the Ukrainian patriotic movement OUN-UPA, which they tried to spread among their classmates in late 1982. All these Nonovolynsk young "Ukrainian nationalists" were also enthusiastic fans of Anglo-American "fascist" heavy metal and punk rock.[91]

The criminal cases of Ukrainian "fascist" heavy metal fans revealed the surprising connections between different forms of cultural consumption in Soviet Ukraine during 1982–1984. The arrested members of Onushev's and Shipunov's groups confessed that they were inspired by the images of "clean, intelligent and civilized" Nazi officers portrayed in the Soviet TV series *Seventeen Moments of Spring* (1973). Based on the novel by Yulian Semenov, a famous Soviet writer of the mystery and spy novels, this TV movie about Stirlitz (Viacheslav Tikhonov), a Soviet agent posing as a Nazi officer in Hitlerite Germany in the spring of 1945, during the final months of WWII, became a real blockbuster during the 1970s and early 1980s in the USSR. Many "fascist" heavy metal fans and local "punks" tried to imitate dress and behavior of the Nazi characters from this old Soviet TV film. Numerous members of those groups also referred to Carlo Lizzani's film about Milanese Neo-Fascists.[92]

As early as December of 1983, the secretary of the Dnipropetrovsk regional Komsomol committee O. Fedoseev reported to the Komsomol Central Committee in Kyiv that in February–March of 1983, local ideologists encountered the rise of the punk movement in the city of Dnipropetrovsk, but they successfully mobilized all activists and "Soviet patriots," organizing special counter-propaganda events all over the city and the Dnipropetrovsk Region. As a result, they managed to curtail this "fascist movement." The Dnipropetrovsk regional Komsomol organization developed political measures on "how to fight fascist punks," which became a model for the entire republic. The KGB administration approved those measures.[93]

However, between 1982 and 1985, the KGB and the police identified twenty five new groups of neo-fascists/punks in Ukraine who had hundreds of followers. Arrested by the police and interrogated by the KGB, the members of these groups employed various fascist symbols and paraphernalia, painted their faces "in punk fashion," and shaved their temples.[94] Only a few of them, however, had anything to do with the Nazi ideology or fascism.

Still, during 1982–1985, the KGB analysts and special KGB lecturers toured through the entire Ukraine, lecturing to various audiences, blaming all major youth subcultures of Soviet Ukraine, such as hippies and punks, to be a "product of American propaganda and American pop culture." At the same time, these KGB lecturers emphasized "the **obvious Fascist** character of the behavior of all young imitators of American hippies and punks." So-called **pro-fascist ideology** of Soviet young rock music fans "was fed by ideologically dangerous, but **emotionally attractive and seductive cultural** products of the capitalist America."[95]

*****

As the KGB analysts reported to the Communist party leadership, the major reasons for the "getting on the criminal path" of young people in Soviet Ukraine were "their regular listening to foreign anti-Soviet radio broadcasts, the contacts with the foreigners on the basis of '*fartsovka*' and participation in groups of hippies and punks." The major conclusion of the KGB analysis was that all the "Ukrainian followers of the American hippies and punks" represented the "dangerous category of people with [their] anti-Soviet, anti-social and massive amoral manifestations," and the very fact of an emergence of hippies and punks in Soviet Ukraine "had to be appraised as a result of sabotage (*diversii*) of the ideological centers of our adversary," the United States of America.[96]

Moreover, the KGB connected these provocations of American ideological centers to two major international political crises in the Soviet bloc: a phenomenon of "hippies" had a "direct link" to the events Prague Spring of 1968 in socialist Czechoslovakia; and a "movement of punks was triggered" by the Solidarity events in socialist Poland in 1980. In the KGB analysis, these Soviet imitations of the Western youth subcultures were the "products" of ideological and political provocations of the American intelligence centers, which tried to "undermine the socialist society from inside, using various forms of the American mass culture, starting in more Westernized countries of Warsaw pact (*dogovora*), such as Czechoslovakia and Poland, and then targeting non-Russian republics of the USSR, such as Ukraine."[97]

The KGB's anti-hippie, anti-fascist, and anti-punk campaigns in Soviet Ukraine were intended to weaken young Ukrainians' fascination with the products of Western (especially American) popular culture, such as films and pop music, and their idealization of Western neo-fascist images and culture. However, the results of these campaigns were contrary to what had been expected. The campaigns contributed to the immense popularity of forbidden Western cultural products among young consumers. Ironically, these campaigns amplified the interest in Western culture among the transgressors' ideological supervisors who were supposed to erase it from the imagination of the Soviet youth.

Yet, there was another surprising and dangerous outcome of the anti-punk campaign in Soviet Ukraine, accentuated by KGB officers and local propagandists. During 1982–1984, the KGB active measures targeting "fascist punks" and the authorities' hostile and coercive actions against disobedient youth encouraged young people to think about the state in political terms, and to openly criticize the Soviet political system, identifying it as a mafia state.[98] Since 1968 and the anti-hippie campaigns in Soviet Ukraine, the KGB feared the potential "politicization" of cultural consumption by local youth. The drastic difference between the peaceful and relatively a-political Soviet hippies' behavior and that of the Ukrainian "fascist punks" inspired by Italian films and Anglo-American rock music exacerbated the KGB's fear. The political behavior of young Komsomol members became a dangerous cultural phenomenon. Their political programs, adopting neo-fascist cultural practices, challenged the Soviet political system that had to be replaced by a "more efficient, honest and stable" authoritarian system. Worse, many Ukrainian punks demanded the "liberation of Ukraine from Russian exploitation."[99] The cultural trends among young Soviet Ukrainians analyzed in this chapter – the mixture of popular culture and political nationalism – survived the KGB persecution, foreshadowing the distinct signs of revival in post-Soviet contemporary Ukraine.

Notes

1 See about this in detail in Christopher Andrew and Vasili Mitrokhin, *The Sword and the Shield: The Mitrokhin Archive and the Secret History of the KGB* (New York: Basic Books, 1999), 150ff.

2 SBU, f. 16, op. 1, spr. 1146, ark. 219–232, see especially about special measures on ark. 224–232.

3 Interview with Stepan Ivanovich T. in Kyiv, February 20, 2019. He referred to the "active measures" that were defined by Vladimir Bukovsky as "[a]ctions of political warfare conducted by the Soviet and Russian security services (Cheka, OGPU, NKVD, KGB, FSB) ranging from media manipulation to outright violence." See Vladimir Bukovsky, *Judgment in Moscow: Soviet Crimes and Western Complicity*, trans. Alyona Kojevnikov (Westlake Village, CA: Ninth of November Press, 2019), 629.

4 I refer to the pioneering study by William Jay Risch, "Soviet 'Flower Children': Hippies and the Youth Counter-Culture in 1970s Lviv," *Journal of Contemporary History,* July 2005, Vol. 40, No. 3, 565–584, and his book, *The Ukrainian West: Culture and the Fate of Empire in Soviet Lviv* (Cambridge, Mass.: Harvard University Press, 2011), esp. 237–244. Juliane Fürst has recently published a book about Soviet hippies: Juliane Fürst, *Flowers through Concrete: Explorations in Soviet Hippieland* (New York: Oxford University Press, 2021). Gleb Tsipursky and I also addressed some issues of Soviet youth culture. See especially Gleb Tsipursky, *Socialist Fun: Youth, Consumption, and State-Sponsored Popular Culture in the Soviet Union, 1945–1970* (Pittsburgh: University of Pittsburgh Press, 2016) and my book: Sergei I. Zhuk, *Rock and Roll in the Rocket City: The West, Identity, and Ideology in Soviet Dniepropetrovsk, 1960–1985* (Baltimore, MD: Johns Hopkins University Press & Washington, D.C.: Woodrow Wilson Center Press, 2010). All those authors (excluding Juliane Fürst) did not use the KGB documents from the Archive of SBU in Kyiv. In this chapter, I try to compensate this with the new KGB documents and my interviews with the former KGB officers.

5 SBU, f. 16, op. 1, spr. 919, ark. 60–61.

6 Ibid., spr. 927, ark. 17–19.

7 Ibid., ark. 27–28.
8 Interview with Stepan Ivanovich T., a retired KGB officer, January 30, 2019, Kyiv, Ukraine.
9 Rudolf Pihoia, "Chekhoslovakia 1968 god (Part 1)," *Novaia i noveishaia istoriia*, no. 6 (1994): 24–28. See also Mark Kramer, ed., "Ukraine and the Soviet-Czechoslovak Crisis of 1968 (Part I): New Evidence from the Diary of Petro Shelest," *Cold War International History Project Bulletin*, no. 10 (1998): 234–247; Andrew and Mitrokhin, *The Sword and the Shield*, 251.
10 Vitalii K. Vrublevskii, *Vladimir Shcherbitskii: zapiski pomoshchnika: slukhi, legendy, dokumenty* (Kyiv: Dovira, 1993), 167–168.
11 It is based on my calculations of criminal cases from 1971 (SBU, f. 16, op. 1, spr. 1017) to 1989 (spr. 1271). An analysis of various official KGB reports to Ukraine's Communist Party leadership has confirmed the preliminary calculations (spr. 1056, ark. 1–311; spr. 1115, ark. 5–310; spr. 1115, ark. 25–301; spr. 1209, ark. 25–290).
12 SBU, f. 16, op. 1, spr. 1249, ark. 147–149. On the Soviet youth's fascination with American jazz and rock music as early as September 1964, see especially the September 1964 KGB report in SBU, f. 1, op. 1, spr. 1567, ark. 151–152.
13 See the material about the KGB operations and Prague Spring in Andrew and Mitrokhin, *The Sword and the Shield*, 247–261.
14 The author's interview with Igor T., a KGB officer, May 15, 1991, Dnipropetrovsk, Ukraine.
15 SBU, f. 16, op. 1, spr. 977, ark. 253–288.
16 This survey was submitted to the KGB on September 13, 1968. See "Obzor: Odesskoe studenchestvo. 1968 god" ["The Odessa College Students (1968)"] in SBU, f. 16, op. 1, spr. 977, ark. 255–88.
17 Ibid., 258–259.
18 Ibid., 275, 276.
19 Ibid., 275.
20 Ibid., 273.
21 Ibid., 274.
22 Ibid., 275.
23 Ibid., 274.
24 Ibid., 277–278. See in detail about such Russification of the Ukrainian speakers from the country side in the city of Dnipropetrovsk in Sergei I. Zhuk, *Rock and Roll*, 176ff.
25 Ibid., 281, 263.
26 Ibid., 280–281.
27 See about the cult of this movie among Soviet youth in Sergei I. Zhuk, *Soviet Americana: The Cultural History of Russian and Ukrainian Americanists* (London and New York: I.B. Tauris, 2018 [London and New York: Bloomsbury Publishing, 2019]), 138–140.
28 Ibid., 281–282.
29 Ibid., 282–283, 281.
30 *Banderovtsy* was derived from the name of Stepan Bandera, a leader of the OUN radical branch. His name became a symbol of the Ukrainian national course in the Western Ukraine since the end of the 1940s. See in Serhy Yekelchyk, *Ukraine: Birth of a Modern Nation* (New York: Oxford University Press, 2007), 125–128, 141–151.
31 Derzhavnyi arkhiv Dnipropetrovskoi oblasti (hereafter – DADO), f. 19, op. 52, spr. 72, ark. 9.
32 See an English translation of this letter in *The Ukrainian Review*, 1969, vol. XVI, No. 3, 46–52. As a result of international publicity of this case, the first scholarly

analysis of these events appeared in English in: Kenneth C. Farmer. *Ukrainian Nationalism in the Post-Stalin Era*, 158–159. Compare with Ludmila Alexeyeva, *Soviet Dissent: Contemporary Movements for National, Religious, and Human Rights*, Transl. by Carol Pearce and John Glad (Middletown, CT: Wesleyan University Press, 1985), 40. See also SBU, f. 16, op. 1, spr. 977, ark. 367–371.

33 See in detail about this in Sergei I. Zhuk, *Rock and Roll in the Rocket City*, 48–64. Compare with the KGB criminal cases of Ivan Sokul'sky, a leader of Dnipropetrovsk group of young Ukrainian patriots in SBU, f. 16, op. 1, spr. 988, ark. 290–293 (1969) and spr. 1167, ark. 252–257 (1980).

34 See the first time, when the KGB documents about Soviet hippies were quoted in the famous book by a prominent Soviet dissident as early as 1996: Vladimir Bukovsky, *Judgment in Moscow*, 136.

35 SBU, spr. 974, ark. 114–115. Those hippies planned to participate "in the All-Union congress during this summer (1969) either in Riga, or Tallinn." Even the recent graduates of high schools demonstrated the similar behavior in 1969-70. Some of them organized the secret society of "Koka-Kola" in the city of Slaviansk (Donetsk Region) "expressing their protest against the existing political order." See in Ibid., spr. 1009, ark. 167–168.

36 Ibid., spr. 1011, ark. 81–92 (with a hand-written note by a party secretary "Personally report the measures" on ark. 81). See the second copy of the same report in spr. 1009, ark. 317–328.

37 See about those groups in detail in Sergei I. Zhuk, *Rock and Roll in the Rocket City*, 79–92, 97–105.

38 SBU, f. 16, op 1, spr. 1011, ark. 81.

39 Ibid., 82.

40 Ibid., 85.

41 Ibid., 84. "In April 1970, more than 100 hippies from different cities of the USSR, including Lviv, met in Vilnius, where they had non-official festival of natural music."

42 SBU, f. 16, op. 1, spr. 1011, ark. 85–86. The third part of Gorky's *Old Izergil* entitled "The Flaming Heart of Danko" was an obligatory reading in Russian literature classes in Soviet high schools. Writing the report, a KGB officer, by mistake, presented the British rock band "The Animals" as American. ("Amerikanskii modernistskii ansambl 'Zhivotnyie'" in the original, ark. 86).

43 SBU, f. 1, op. 1, spr. 1011, ark. 87–88; spr. 993, ark. 358–361; spr. 1015, ark. 325.

44 SBU, spr. 1011, ark. 88–89

45 About Pokal'chuk see spr. 1095, ark. 182–185; about hippie engagement with Orthodox Church in Kupiansk see spr. 1089, ar. 321; about a massive growth of Krishnaites in Ukraine see spr. 1175, ark. 132–134, and spr. 1184, ark. 36–37. On April 14, 1974, fifty hippies in Kupiansk, Kharkiv Region, not only organized a demonstration with the slogans "Freedom to the Youth!" near the local Orthodox Church, but also tried to join a procession to celebrate Christian Easter. See also in detail about this in Sergei I. Zhuk, *Rock and Roll*, 200, 201, 205. See especially DADO, f. 19, op. 60, spr. 85, ark. 7, 17. Some police officers reported that the hippies had publicly displayed various religious symbols, such as Christian crosses and icons, as well as "portraits of Krishna and Buddha."

46 SBU, f. 16, op. 1, spr. 1162, ark. 126.

47 SBU, f. 16, op. 1, spr. 1162, ark. 128.

48 Spr. 1249, ark. 147.

49 SBU, f. 16, op. 1, spr. 1162, ark. 126. All these reports were based on the information provided by the special agents infiltrated in the groups of Ukrainian hippies.

50 Ibid., 126–127.

51 Ibid., ark. 127–128. I used calculations from my interview with Leonid T., a retired KGB officer in Kyiv.
52 Spr. 1011, ark. 90. The KGB officers, who studied the local hippies, distanced themselves from the "ideological nonsense" of Komsomol periodicals, which wrote that "American hippies was a satanic sect with a mixture of palmistry, astrology and black magic, and that hippies were looking for a virgin girl for their devilish black mass ritual and can't find such girls among themselves." See Interview with Stepan Ivanovich T. He referred to Mykola Solomatin, "Zhertvy chornoi magii," *Ranok,* 1974, January, No. 1, 18–19.
53 Spr. 1015, ark. 324–325.
54 See my interviews with Stepan Ivanovich and Leonid K., the retired KGB officers. Some Western scholars dismiss this interpretation of Fascism used by the KGB for the Ukrainian hippies. See, e.g., a good study by Juliane Fürst, *Flowers through Concrete,* 80–82, 176–177, 198–199.
55 Spr. 1015, ark. 323. See also Juliane Fürst, Op. cit., 198–199.
56 See Sergei I. Zhuk, *Soviet Americana: The Cultural History of Russian and Ukrainian Americanists* (London and New York: I.B. Tauris, 2018 [London and New York: Bloomsbury Publishing, 2019] [paperback: September 2019]), 193. The KGB operatives often connected the Ukrainian symbol of trident (*tryzub*) with fascism.
57 Zhuk, *Rock and Roll,* 102, 103, 170–171, 267–279.
58 SBU, spr. 1200, ark. 68.
59 Ibid., Interview with Stepan Ivanovich T., a retired KGB officer, January 30, 2019, Kyiv, Ukraine.
60 SBU, f. 16, op. 1, spr. 1200, ark. 68. In the original KGB report, they described the movie as story about "*beschinstvakh fashistvuiushchei molodiozhi.*"
61 Interview with Stepan K., retired SBU/KGB officer, Kyiv, Ukraine, February 2, 2019.
62 SBU, f. 16, op. 1, d. 1200, p. 68.
63 Ibid.
64 SBU, f. 16, op. 1, spr. 1192, ark. 47–48.
65 SBU.f. 16, op. 1, spr. 1182, ark. 212–213. See a case of young Neo-Nazis in a town of Novovolynsk in 1983 in SBU, f. 16, op. 1, spr. 1205, ark. 224–225. Compare with my interview with Leonid K., a retired KGB officer, Kyiv, Ukraine, May 4, 2019, who called this phenomenon "Neo-Fascist madness."
66 SBU, f. 16, op. 1, spr. 1162, ark. 149; spr. 1184, ark. 120–121.
67 SBU, f. 16, op. 1, spr. 1192, ark. 47–48.
68 Interview with Stepan K., retired SBU/KGB officer, Kyiv, Ukraine, February 2, 2019. See about these Italian films in Sergei Zhuk, *Rock and Roll,* 145–148.
69 Interview with Leonid K., a retired KGB officer, Kyiv, Ukraine, May 4, 2019.
70 See the Westerner opinion in Howard Hughes, *Once Upon A Time in the Italian West: The Filmgoers' Guide to Spaghetti Westerns* (London, England, 2004), 105.
71 See information in *Dneprovskaia Pravda,* October 5, 1969. Some contemporaries argued that the original images of Mafia came from an American book and American movie The Godfather. See Sergei I. Zhuk, *Soviet Americana,* 146–148.
72 Hughes, *Once Upon A Time in the Italian West,* 105.
73 G. Kapralov, "Utverzhdenie istiny, razoblachenie mifov," *Iskusstvo kino,* 1971, 11: 2–18.
74 *Dneprovskaia Pravda,* September 30, 1972.
75 See the results of the readers' survey in *Sovetskii ekran,* 10 (1973): 12.
76 See the KGB alarming calls about the ideological danger of the Western cultural products in their official reports to the communist leadership of Soviet Ukraine: SBU, f. 16, op. 1, spr. 1011, ark. 87–88; spr. 993, ark. 358–361; spr. 1015, ark.

325. Compare with G. Bogemskii, "Franko Nero: Ot "zvezdy" k bortsu," *Sovetskii ekran*, 2 (1974): 14–15. Valerii Baranovs'kyi, "Buty 'lidynoi chesti' ...," *Novyny kinoekranu*, 5 (1978): 12–13. See also an interview with Igor T., retired KGB officer from Dnipropetrovsk, April 2, 2002, who confirmed the Ukrainian KGB concerns about a threat of those movies.

77 Interview with Vitalii Pidgaetskii at the Department of History, Dnipropetrovsk University, February 10, 1996. Even in 1984 "Mafia films" were still popular in Dnipropetrovsk. See *Dnepr vechernii*, 1984, December 8, 4. Compare with the KGB report in: SBU, f. 16, op. 1, spr. 1200, ark. 68–69.

78 SBU, f. 16, op. 1, d. 1200, pp. 199, 236–237, 267–268.

79 Artemy Troitsky, *Back in the USSR: The True Story of Rock in Russia* (London: Omnibus Press, 1987), 42–43.

80 Even during *perestroika* the local journalists and KGB officials still used these materials. They reprinted some British punks' declarations for a use of Komsomol ideologists. See in L. Gamol'sky, N. Efremenko, V. Inshakov, *Na barrikadakh sovesti: Ocherki, razmyshlenia, interviu* (Dnipropetrovsk, 1988), 139. Author interview with Igor T., KGB officer, Dnipropetrovsk, May 15, 1991; Author interview with Mikhail Suvorov, June 1, 1991. See also about Hungarian situation in Anna Szemere, *Up from the Underground: The Culture of Rock Music in Postsocialist Hungary* (University Park, Pa.: The Pennsylvania State University Press, 2001).

81 See a letter of a CPSU veteran Nadezhda Sarana against local punks under a title "We declare war to everybody who interfere in our life and work!": "*Boi tem, kto meshaet nam stroit' i zhit'!" Dnepr vechernii*, December 23, 1982, p. 3, and A. Liamina and L. Gamol'skii, "Grazhdaninom byt' obiazan," ibid., about a public trial that took place on December 22, 1982 in Dnipropetrovsk. Compare with a reaction of activists in "Iz vystuplenii uchastnikov sobrania," ibid., 1982, December 3, p. 3. See also L. Vasil'eva, "Takim ne mesto sredi nas!" *Dnepr vechernii*, January 10, 1983. See also my interview of Mikhail Suvorov, June 1, 1991.

82 A majority of the publications in the local youth periodicals demonstrated an obvious incompetence and ignorance of the Komsomol journalists in the Western music. See the typical essays about an ideological danger of the foreign music for the Soviet youth in: Yu. Lystopad, "Ideologichna borot'ba i molod' (Notatky z oblasnoi naukovo-praktychnoi konferentsii)," *Prapor iunosti*, December 17, 1983, p. 2; S. Mykytov, "Khto zamovliaie rok-rytmy, abo pogliad na suchasnyi show business," *Prapor iunosti*, February 7, 9 and 11, 1984, p. 4; M. Pozdniakov, "Piraty vid muzyky (v tumani antymystetstva)," *Prapor iunosti*, June 14, 1984, p. 3; O. Razumkov, "Prestyzhni detsybely," *Prapor iunosti*, November 27 and 29, 1984, p. 4. Some of these publications were reprinted in a special collection of ideological material during *perestroika*. See reprint of the old newspaper articles in a collection: L. Gamol'sky, N. Efremenko, V. Inshakov, *Na barrikadakh sovesti*, especially 133–137.

83 Igor Tishchenko, "Poiot VIA "Zemliane"," *Dnepr vechernii*, 1984, January 21, p. 4.

84 O. Rozumkov, M. Skoryk, "Komu zemliaky 'Zemliane'? (Rozdumy pislia kontsertu)," *Prapor iunosti*, 1984, March 15, p. 4; M. Skoryk, "Komu zemliaky 'Zemliane' (Rozdumy nad poshtoiu), ibid., 1984, April 17, p. 4; ibid., 1984, April 24, p. 3.

85 SBU, f. 16, op. 1, spr. 1200, ark. 267–268.

86 L. Gamol'sky, N. Efremenko, V. Inshakov, *Na barrikadakh sovesti*, 133.

87 L. Gamol'sky, N. Efremenko, V. Inshakov, *Na barrikadakh sovesti*, 134. Some university students suffered persecutions for posters of the British band Black

Sabbath in 1984–85. See my interview of Oleksandr Beznosov, Department of History, Dnipropetrovsk University, July 19, 2008.

88 And journalists continued: "Let's think again! There is no justification for collection of the Nazi regalia! Many people in the West understand this. And Leon Rappoport, an American professor from the University of Kansas, was absolutely right, when he sincerely declared: "Collecting of Nazi relic is certainly one of the forms of fascist propaganda." L. Gamol'sky, N. Efremenko, V. Inshakov, *Na barrikadakh sovesti*, 135–136. See about Frolin's phrase in Mikhail Suvorov's interview as well.

89 Yu. Lystopad, "Ideologichna borot'ba i molod' (Notatky z oblasnoi naukovo-praktychnoi konferentsii)," *Prapor iunosti,* December 17, 1983, p. 2.

90 L. Gamol'sky, N. Efremenko, V. Inshakov, *Na barrikadakh sovesti*, 137.

91 SBU, f. 16, op. 1, spr. 1205, ark. 224–225.

92 See about this film and similar cases during perestroika in Richard Stites, *Russian Popular Culture: Entertainment and Society Since 1900* (New York: Cambridge University Press, 1992), 152, 168, 170. Igor T., retired KGB officer, Dnipropetrovsk, May 15, 1991 mentioned the Italian movie's influences in his interview as well.

93 Tsentralnyi Derzhavnyi Arkhiv Hromadskykh Ob'ednan Ukrainy (TsDAHOU), f. 7, op. 20, spr. 3087, ark. 43 ("Otchet Dnepropetrovskogo OK LKSMU ot 23 dekabria 1983 g.").

94 SBU, f. 16, op. 1, spr. 1197, ark. 30–31, 68–69; spr. 1200, ark. 236–237; interview with Igor T., a retired KGB officer, 15 May 1991, Dnipropetrovsk, Ukraine.

95 See the KGB report about these lectures in March 1983 in SBU, f. 16, op. 1, spr. 1206, ark. 105–128, esp. 109, 112.

96 SBU, f. 16, op. 1, spr. 1055, ark. 340.

97 I quote my interview with Igor T., a retired KGB officer in Dnipropetrovsk. See also my book, Sergei Zhuk, *Rock and Roll in the Rocket City*, 3, 41, 43, 103, 170, 267.

98 On how Soviet young consumers used films about the Italian mafia by Damiano Damiani to criticize the USSR as a mafia state, see Sergei I. Zhuk, "'The Disco Mafia' and 'Komsomol Capitalism' in Soviet Ukraine during Late Socialism," in *Material Culture in Russia and the USSR: Things, Values, Identities*, ed. Graham H. Roberts (London and Oxford: Bloomsbury Publishing, 2017), 173–195.

99 SBU, f. 16, op. 1, spr. 1192, ark. 68–69, and spr. 1199, ark. 49.

9 "American Influences" in Forbidden Literature, Non-traditional Religions, Music, Video and Sex

The American cultural influences on the Soviet youth during détente became the major goal for the KGB operations all over the Soviet Union. Through rock and roll, disco and foreign films the new and very attractive forms of the "Americanized" popular culture, from jeans to audio cassette players, came to Soviet Ukraine. All these forms became incorporated in everyday life of the millions Soviet young people. But the Ukrainian case of "Americanization" was more complicated with involvement of the "Ukrainian nationalist elements," connected to the Ukrainian diaspora from America. Even an imitation of the American hippies in Soviet Ukraine involved the dangerous elements of the "Ukrainian nationalism" with "Fascist overtones," reminiscent of the traditional KGB stereotypical view of the "Ukrainian nationalists as Nazi collaborators."[1]

Non-traditional Religions from America

Besides these "Fascist overtones," another serious concern for the KGB was another set of cultural practices, connected to the hippies' experience in Soviet Ukraine. In their reports the KGB operatives called them "the Ancient Eastern religious mystical teachings and the attempts of the youth groupings on that foundation." The KGB agents noted that those teachings "such as worshiping an Indian deity Krishna" attracted the young people who imitated the American hippies. According to the KGB administration, the "ideological harm of those teachings consist in a fact that they are built on mysticism, they preach social passivity and individualism, oppose an individual personality to a society." The KGB analysts emphasized that these mystical religions were "promoted by American imperialism in the countries of Warsaw Pact to undermine and dissolve the ideological unity of the youth in those socialist countries."[2]

Various missionary organizations of Krishnaism in the USA, such as the "International Society of Consciousness of Krishna" and "Teaching of Jiddu Krishnamurti," sent their representatives to Soviet Ukraine as well to spread their ideas among Soviet youth. In August of 1978, using their cars, two American "auto-tourists" Kenneth Valpei (born in 1950) and Philip

DOI: 10.4324/9781003212522-12

Murphy (born in 1952), students of Columbia University, who were sponsored by the "International Society of Consciousness of Krishna," drove to Ukraine and arrived in Kyiv "to organize propaganda of Hinduism among the Soviet youth." They brought film projector, three films about their religion, special dress and ritualistic accessories. They "took part in two meetings with local youth in Kyiv at the personal apartments, showed their films to participants in these meetings, recited their prayers and performed various rituals [of their religion]."[3]

When the KGB officers began their investigation of these American Krishna missionaries' trip to Kyiv in 1978, they discovered that this Asian religion of Krishnaism had been already spreading among the Ukrainian followers of hippies and *bitlomans* (Soviet Beatles fans) since the late 1960s. This popularity was connected to the "cult of George Harrison" from the Beatles among the Soviet youth. Harrison was a well-known follower of the Indian religions, who even played the Indian music [Hindu-raga] with the Beatles. The KGB operatives informed their supervisors that the foreign religious organizations, such as the "International Society of Consciousness of Krishna" and "Teaching of Jiddu Krishnamurti," could be used by the American intelligence not only for "smuggling in the USSR an alien ideology, but also for other subversive goals." The KGB found in Kyiv 30 young people who joined these groups of the "mystic teachings," who also "allowed to express in public the ideologically harmful and anti-social manifestations [of their religion]."[4]

As it turned out during the KGB investigation of 1978, a majority of those people had nothing to do with the groups of hippies' imitators. They became seriously engaged in their own religious activities. Seven older members of those groups became their "spiritual teachers and mentors." The KGB administration was afraid of "the growing anti-Soviet mood" of those followers of Krishna in Ukraine, who "doubted a possibility of communism built in the USSR," criticized "the realities of socialism," trying to establish their relations with other Krishna groups in Ukraine and other republics of the USSR. According to the KGB reports, in 1979–1980, the representatives of the movement of "Consciousness of Krishna" from Moscow, Leningrad and Riga, so-called authorities (*avtoritety*) of this movement, visited Kyiv on the regular basis, spreading the special religious literature among their followers in Soviet Ukraine, reaching other cities such as Lviv, Dnipropetrovsk, Odesa and Donetsk, targeting mainly young people with college education, trying to involve them in Hare Krishna movement.[5]

The KGB tried to prevent a creation of the All-Union relations among various groups of those young followers of Krishna, who began influencing the educated youth in the big Ukrainian cities. Both Soviet ideologists and the police warned about the anti-social and anti-Soviet position of those followers who "preached about a detachment from the world, individualism, and asocial worldview."[6] On May 7, 1981, in Kyiv the KGB operatives detained four so-called missionaries of this movement, which after 1980 was defined in the official KGB documents as the "religious-mystical Hindu teaching 'Hare Krishna'." As it turned out these missionaries arrived from Moscow to Kyiv, and one of them was a native of Dnipropetrovsk V. P. Yaroshchuk (born in 1956), a student of one technical college in Dnipropetrovsk. These Krishna teachers had connections with their Kyiv followers who arranged their lecture in the dormitory of Kyiv Pedagogical Institute. The official title of this lecture was *Culture and Philosophy of Ancient India: The Methods of Yoga*. The real text, obtained by the KGB agent, was an explicit propaganda of Hare Krishna teachings, far from the announced title of that lecture. But an interference of the KGB officers prevented this lecture, by arresting their organizers. The police confiscated the materials brought by those missionaries: the typewritten and hand-written texts, audio tapes with prayers, the books about Krishna, published in India. Eventually, the KGB released arrested Hare Krishna leaders, and next day, on May 8, 1981, they were sent back to Moscow "under the control of the local KGB officers."[7] Despite the efforts of the KGB to stop a popularity of Hare Krishna, followers of this religion appeared in all major industrial cities of Soviet Ukraine. Almost every year during the 1980s, the KGB documents recorded the cases of the Southern Asian mystical religions such as Hare Krishna and Buddhism among various groups of Soviet Ukrainian youth. And until the 1990s, the most popular religion among Ukrainian youth was Hare Krishna.[8]

Another Asian "religious" practice, which attracted the KGB attention, was Buddhism related to the cult of Japanese karate martial arts among the Soviet youth. During 1981 in Kyiv, the KGB operatives discovered this connection in the existing 60 non-official sections "for a study of karate techniques" with 10–15 members in each group (more than 600 participants all together). The "teachers" and founders of these sections preached to their young pupils "Buddhism, ancient Chinese philosophy and various religious-mystical teachings."[9] One of such teachers composed a statute for this karate school, which prescribed "a strict adherence to conspiracy and unquestioning the will and the orders of the teacher." Another teacher from another karate section, O. V. Pivovar (born in 1949), an official teacher of physical education from a technical school (GPTU No. 12), was arrested in the wooden area of Kyiv's outskirts while teaching his 18 students various karate techniques with cold steel weapons (self-made swords, knives and sticks). As it turned out, Pivovar manufactured all those swords and knives and sold them to his own students. Moreover, Pivovar wrote a book *Kung Fu in a Mirror of Secret Sciences*, published its text and sold it, charging 10–15 rubles per copy. In his book, based on a Russian translation of the American martial arts textbooks, Pivovar denied Darwin's theory of evolution, promulgated mysticism and other popular Asian religious teachings in America. Pivovar and other "tea-chers" of "Chinese and Japanese religions through martial arts" were arrested for "engaging in private business (*zaniatie chastnopreprinimatel'skoi deia-tel'nost'iu*)" and spreading "ideologically harmful teachings among the Soviet youth." It is noteworthy that the KGB analysts called the cases of the spread of Krishnaism and Kung Fu/karate in Soviet Ukraine "the American ideological poison." Later, in 1984–1987, the police found that the illegal forms of the Asian martial arts spread all over Ukraine, using a massive popularity of the illegal video tapes with American martial arts feature films, demonstrating Bruce Lee's Kung Fu skills.[10]

Besides the exotic religious cults and teachings from capitalist America, such as Hare Krishna and Kung Fu, the KGB encountered also more familiar forms of the American religious influences through various evangelical Protestant Christian sects. Only in June of 1980, the numerous missionaries of "non-Orthodox Christian sects from the West," mainly from the US and Canada were detained by the KGB officers in all major industrial cities of Soviet Ukraine. All of these missionaries came to Ukraine as regular tourists. The overwhelming majority of them were the American college students, who brought religious literature, trying to spread it through various communities of the Pentecostals and "schismatic Baptists" all over Ukraine.[11] The new "American charismatic" Christian sects became another target for the KGB operations. One of the most persecuted religious groups in Soviet Ukraine by the KGB was a sect of Jehovah's Witnesses.[12]

The KGB administration knew that the Brooklyn Center of Jehovah's Witnesses in New York City was actively involved in providing the religious literature and the material assistance to their 16,000 followers in Soviet Ukraine. Every year this sect used the American auto-tourists for bringing in Ukraine and distributing of "the forbidden religious books and magazines in Russian translation" there. In early 1975, the KGB operatives received information from the Brooklyn Center of Jehovah's Witnesses that the "leadership of this American sect announced about the beginning of Armageddon and the end of the world, the beginning of the Millennium for all humankind" during the fall of 1975. According to this information, during this event of Armageddon, "all atheists and people of other religions, including Christians, would perish; and only the true followers of Jehovah's Witnesses would survive."[13]

Using this information, the KGB administration decided to organize a special operation (a complex of active measures) against this "America's religious sect" inside Soviet Ukraine in the fall and winter of 1975. The major goal was to discredit this sect and undermine its influence on the Ukrainian co-religionists. The KGB analysts noted that "a preparation for the end of the world" spread mostly among Jehovah's Witnesses in Zakarpatska, Chernivtsy, Volyn, Crimea and Khmelnytskyi regions of Ukraine. Many sectarians returned to their homes "to be ready for this event; and they began selling out their expensive dress, refrigerators, etc." Some preachers of this sect began massive baptism rituals for the sectarians' children to prepare them for Armageddon.[14]

Meanwhile, the KGB agents among sectarians began spreading the rumours that the Brooklyn Center merely invented the fact of approaching of

Armageddon; that the American leaders of Jehovah's Witnesses manipulated the biblical interpretation of the events and they gave the incorrect time for the "end of the world," etc. The KGB strategy worked, and by December of 1975, many sectarians expressed publicly their mistrust in the American leaders of their sect and doubted the decisions of the Brooklyn Center. Some of them even declared that if "Armageddon wouldn't happen they quit the sect and burn their bibles." Some preachers of the sect were afraid that "more than a half of their sect would stop believing in God in a case of an absence of Armageddon." Engaging the local mass media, television and radio, in December of 1975, the KGB also organized a massive campaign of criticism of the American Brooklyn Center of Jehovah's Witnesses, which had triggered "the action of manipulation and lies" about the approaching the end of the world to attract more followers in Soviet Ukraine.[15] As a result of this KGB operation against Jehovah's Witnesses, the sectarians began losing their members in 1976; moreover, the KGB managed publicly to discredit the American leadership of the Ukrainian sectarians, and undermine their influence in Soviet Ukraine.[16]

For the KGB administration in Kyiv, the more dangerous from the ideological point of view was a combination of religious propaganda and Ukrainian nationalism, especially when the American religious missionaries, who visited Soviet Ukraine, were of the Ukrainian origin, planning to use "God's word" to "liberate Ukraine from the Russian occupation." The most famous criminal case, reported by the KGB, was about the missionary's activities of Roman Strotsky, who was born in 1948 in the USA, in a state of Oregon, in the family of the Ukrainian nationalist A. Strotsky, who fought against the Soviet Army in the Division *SS Galician* (14th Waffen Grenadier Division of the SS) during WWII.[17]

From the early age Roman was an active participant of the Ukrainian nationalist organizations in America, such as the Ukrainian Youth Association, studied the Ukrainian folk music and dance, and at the same time was involved in the anti-Soviet demonstrations in the US, demanding a liberation of all arrested in the USSR "the Ukrainian nationalists." Later, living in Clifton, Oregon, Roman Strotsky joined the Christian charismatic "Path" Church in a neighboring small town, where he was trained as a missionary minister of this "Path" church. According to the KGB investigation, in 1982, using the international system of cultural exchange between the USSR and the USA, Roman visited Kyiv and joined the Pavlo Virsky Ukrainian National Folk Dance Ensemble for the entire year "to take the folk dance classes." Fulfilling his religious mission of the American "Path" Church, Roman used his time in Kyiv not only for his dance study, but also for a creation of the group of young people from the Kyiv's residents, his followers, "for spreading his religious teaching of the politically harmful orientation among the Soviet youth."[18]

According to the KGB information, Roman Strotsky organized the regular meetings of his Ukrainian followers for the public listening of the audio tapes with his recorded religious lectures and sermons in Ukrainian. Members of his audience helped him with re-recording and distributing of his lectures and sermons about the Divine Path. Meanwhile, during his meetings with his Ukrainian followers Strotsky told them about "the violent Russification of Ukraine," about the artificial hunger (Holodomor) in Ukraine in 1933, "induced them to emigrate from Ukraine to America"; declared that the "God's Word" brought by him in the original Ukrainian national language to Soviet citizens, "would transform, eventually, the entire Soviet Union [changing it in a Christian direction]."[19] The KGB operatives realized a double danger of the preaching by this American missionary: Roman Strotsky combined both Protestant Christian religion and Ukrainian nationalism, trying to create "*gilochka*" (a branch) of the American charismatic sect "Path" with the "Ukrainian nationalist twist" in Kyiv in 1982–1983.

While using his cultural exchange opportunities and time, being associated with Virsky Ukrainian National Folk Dance Ensemble, Strotsky not only spread the influences of his "non-traditional Christian sect" with the "Ukrainian nationalist twist" among the young residents of Kyiv, but also involved his young wife, L. Popovich (born in 1961), who was a student of dance affiliated with Virsky Ensemble, in his "ideologically harmful activities." After his marriage to Popovich in 1982, Strotsky began employing his wife as a new missionary of his "Path" Church in Kyiv.[20]

The KGB administration decided to use Popovich in their new operation against Strotsky, trying to prevent his creation of the branch for the American charismatic Christian sect in Ukraine, "incriminating him un-lawfulness of his actions, taken by him to create illegal group, and the facts of his ideologically harmful nationalistic indoctrination of Soviet citizens." So when Strotsky left Ukraine for the US in 1983, the KGB operatives approached Popovich, blackmailed her, and persuaded her to agree to "dissolve her marriage" with Strotsky. Moreover, under a pressure from the KGB, Popovich revealed in public, before the invited Soviet journalists, about all "the illegal anti-Soviet actions of her former husband." So, when Strotsky returned to Kyiv on May 5, 1984, he was confronted by the KGB operatives, who acting undercover as the officials of the Kyiv tourist organization *Inturist* and using the public testimony of his wife, blamed him not only in the attempt to create a branch of the American charismatic sect "Path" with the "Ukrainian nationalist twist" in Kyiv, but also in the "direct connections" with two US intelligence officers from the US Embassy in Moscow, who "personally directed and coordinated his anti-Soviet activities." After the long "prophylactic" conversations with the KGB officers on May 14–15, 1984, Strotsky admitted in public his guilt. Eventually, using the materials of KGB operation against Strotsky, the Soviet administration announced about "the official expulsion [of American tourist Strotsky] from the Soviet Union for his illegal actions" and about "a visa closure for his entry to the USSR in the future." Next day, on May 16, 1984, Roman Strotsky left

Kyiv for good.[21] In this way, the KGB operation prevented the American religious missionary's attempts to use a combination of "the non-traditional Christianity with Ukrainian nationalism" in promoting "the ideologically harmful American influences" among the youth of Soviet Ukraine.

Forbidden Literature and Films from America and Forbidden Sex in Ukraine

The KGB analysts realized that the "American ideological poison" reached the Soviet audiences not only through zealous American or "home-made" "religious missionaries," but also through the legal official sources, and spread through the offices of Soviet government in Soviet Ukraine. During the détente, following the Helsinki agreements of 1975 on the exchange of books, various international publishing houses, including famous American publishers, sent the copies of their books in English to Soviet Ukraine. Almost every year the KGB censors checked those American books, received by the Soviet centers for international book trade in Kyiv, such as *Kievknigotorg* [Kyiv Book Trade], and they realized "an obvious ideological danger" of this kind of literature for the Soviet, especially young, consumers of foreign books. In November of 1979, the KGB administration reported "the discovery by our operatives of a whole slew of foreign publications received by *Kievknigotorg* that contained malicious slander against the Soviet government and our social order, and [those books] also propagandized cruelty, violence, and pornography."[22] Among those publications the KGB agents discovered in *Kievknigotorg*, there were 100 copies of the autobiographical book, written by an American writer John Steinbeck, *Journal of a Novel: The East of Eden Letters*. The KGB administration interpreted this book as "malicious attacks on the Soviet Union." Steinbeck wrote that the Soviet Union was doomed to collapse and would likely disintegrate into several mutually antagonistic ethnic states. "In the author's opinion," the KGB reported, "Western countries must remember that the Kremlin regime, sensing danger, might launch a world war in a bid to save itself."[23]

The KGB also explained the "ideological harm" of two other American books, sent by the American publishers to Kyiv: in May of 1979, 70 copies of *The Day of The Jackal* by Frederick Forsyth, and in March of 1979, 10 copies of *A Clockwork Orange* by Anthony Burgess. For some reason, a KGB analyst, who read the text of the Burgess' book and contributed his interpretation of this book into the official report, presented it as a description of England in the future "with the triumphant communism, when brutality and violence reigns everywhere."[24]

Among foreign books, which were considered as "part of the ideological diversion and provocation," the KGB operatives found also various sex guides, which were "explicit pornography." In August of 1979, Kyiv book store received an American book with a title about "the penis songs" with the descriptions of various scenes of "sex pathology."[25] As a result of the findings in *Kievknigotorg*, by November of 1979, the Ukrainian KGB administration organized a special "anti-American" operation not only in Kyiv, but also in all major cities of Soviet Ukraine, targeting the chain of book stores *Inostrannaia kniga* (*The Foreign Book*), which received and distributed "the American forbidden literature" in English during 1977–1979. As a result of this operation, the KGB operatives discovered that this "forbidden ideologically harmful literature" from the American publishers became the source of the lucrative book business in the Ukrainian cities' black markets, where one American book from a store *Inostrannaia kniga* could be sold for 350–500 rubles.[26] Numerous book store managers and *fartsovshchiks* (black marketers) were arrested and hundreds of the "American books" were confiscated by the police in 1979. But eventually, this KGB operation failed, and the "American books' business" survived. Through the entire period of perestroika, this business merged with the music business in the black market, resulting in the growing profits of the young *fartsovshchiks* in big industrial cities, such as Dnipropetrovsk, Odesa and Lviv.[27]

The special object of the KGB operations against "the American books" was the erotic literature, pornography and various sex guides. A part of those operations targeted not only the consumers of such literature (mainly young people), but also its young practitioners. On May 10, 1974, E. N. Gol'tsev, an editor-in-chief of the regional newspaper *Cherkas'ka Pravda* in the city of Cherkasy, caught his colleague, a young chair of the editorial department from the same newspaper, who, using the newspaper copying equipment, tried secretly to copy "the sexual-pornographic brochure *Tekhnika sovremennogo seksa* (*Modern Sex Techniques*) by R[obert] Street, published in England." Gol'tsev immediately confiscated this book and "reported about this scandal" to a Cherkasy office of the KGB.[28]

As a result, the local KGB operatives organized the "special raid" in the editorial board of *Cherkas'ka Pravda*, where they realized that the text of the scandalous English book had already spread all over the city of Cherkasy. After this special operation, the KGB officers confiscated 11 type-written copies of this book, and "also three brochures *Entsiklopedia polovoi zhizni* (*Encyclopedia of Sex Life*) by W. Hargins (USA)." It turned out that the original American editions of those books, which were professionally written sex guides, had been brought to Cherkassy in 1971 by a guest from Moscow, and in 1972 by a visitor from Kyiv. The KGB operatives discovered that at least 37 people, Cherkasy residents, were involved in a process of type-writing and distributing those "American pornographic materials." Many of those people worked at the communist party and government offices in Cherkasy and they used their offices' typewriters "for a dissemination of those scandalous books among their friends and colleagues." Officially, the operation of "confiscation and annihilation" of the "American pornographic literature" was finished by the KGB operatives by the end of 1974.[29]

But in a real life, numerous "American sex guides," including the old (first published in 1959) Robert Street's book, survived the KGB operation of 1974. Those "scandalous" books were circulating "non-officially" all over the Cherkasy region among the groups of close friends. Even in the summer of 1976, as a recent graduate from the local high school in a town Vatutino, Zvenigorodka district, Cherkasy region, I, together with my classmates, learned English, reading Robert Street's brochure (of course, secretly from my mom). Moreover, when, next year, in 1977, now as a freshman at Dnipropetrovsk State University, looking for the fresh rock and roll music records, I visited the black market in downtown Dnipropetrovsk, I was surprised that the "scandalous" American sex guides circulated there and were available for local customers as well.

During the 1970s and the 1980s, the KGB discovered that the youth of Soviet Ukraine not only read forbidden American pornography, but also practiced sexual experimentation. In November of 1981, the KGB officers of the city of Khmel'nitskyi received the information about such erotic practices and sexual experiments among the senior students of Khmelnytskyi Technological Institute of Consumer Service (*bytovogo obsluzhivaniia*), about "their incorrect interpretation of the role of family in Soviet society and calls for moral licentiousness."[30] The leader of this student group and the main author of their "program documents" was V. E. Pasiutin (born in 1957), a junior (a third year) student from the Mechanical Department of that institute. "Bowing to the western lifestyle, and sharing the views of Sigmund Freud and other western scholars" about freedom of sex, Pasiutin composed "theses" and so-called program of Khmel'nitskyi Party of Sexual Democrats. In these texts, he put "an appeal to free love" and to an abolition of family institute (*instituta sem'i*)." He began his theses with epigraph "A ghost roams Europe – a ghost of the sexual revolution," and he finished his text with the words: "Sexual democrats of all countries, unite, we have nothing to lose except our clothes." In his program, Pasiutin "put forward a task to liberate a woman by abolishing a family as a social institute, eradicate adultery by creating the state brothels." Six students joined Pasiutin to "establish" a new party of "free love."[31] And again this idea was triggered by their reading of various American books about sex life, which reached Khmel'nitskyi students through their Kyiv friends, who got those books in the official Kyiv book store at the end of 1970s. A few other groups of "free love" were discovered among college students in big industrial cities of Soviet Ukraine in the 1970s and the 1980s, including the communes of "imitators of hippies." But after the preventive actions, including the long conversations with the KGB operatives, the students, who tried sexual experimentations, quit, and their groups were disbanded.

Another source of "inspiration" for sexual experimentation and "debauchery" among the youth of Soviet Ukraine was also related to the traditional forms of cultural consumption, promoted by the Soviet state during the détente: watching the American feature films and dancing to the American disco music in the legal Soviet venues. As the KGB investigated, during 1976–1979, in the House of Cinema in downtown Kyiv, a Moscow film critic Yuri Sher on the regular basis delivered his lectures about the American films. Moreover, Sher showed (as illustrations to his lectures) "the forbidden for public demonstration in the USSR" the American movies such as *The Godfather* (1972), *Great Gatsby* (1974), and *Straw Dogs* (1971), which were "preaching violence, pornography and propagandizing the Western style of life." During the days of demonstration of those films in the House of Cinema, "'the [young] anti-societal [anti-Soviet] elements' crowded the streets around this place; some of them penetrated inside [bribing] the officials of the House of Cinema."[32] According to the KGB officers, during the end of the 1970s and the 1980s, some young consumers of those American films in Kyiv and Dnipropetrovsk were caught by the police for possessing and disseminating "American" pornography. After 1984, in both Kyiv and Dnipropetrovsk, various private parties of foreign videos' showing included the frequent demonstrations of American video films such as *Straw Dogs* and numerous "soft porn" movies.[33]

The KGB operatives continued to control "the ideological level" of various disco clubs and dance parties in the cities of Soviet Ukraine during the 1970s. Beside the traditional complaints about a domination of foreign, mainly Anglo-American, popular music in the dance programs of all discotheques, the KGB officers discovered the facts of various forms of sexual orgies and debauchery at some disco clubs. The most famous criminal case of 1979 was connected to the music and "sexual" practices of A. Kharchuk (born in 1951), one DJ from Maliovanskyi House of Culture in the city of Zhitomyr. On a regular basis, using "American jazz music" Kharchuk seduced his young female followers and organized "disco sex orgies" at his apartment. These followers and participants in Kharchuk's orgies became the active organizers of the official disco in Zhitomyr, where they also "abused alcoholic beverages and committed various lecherous acts." Eventually, the KGB officers arrested Kharchuk, and he was officially indicted "for satisfaction of sex passions in perverted forms, for involvement of minors in criminal activities, for maintenance of dens of debauchery and procurement (pimping)," and he was "sentenced to five years term in prison."[34]

According to the KGB reports, the dancing floor of various restaurants and disco clubs became the location where the young customers demonstrated "the obvious eroticism and imitated the sexual acts in public." On November 17, 1979, in the city of Odesa, in the restaurant *Khadzhibei*, inspired by the American music, 4 drunken half naked girls performed so-called *tanets zhivota* periodically demonstrating their naked breasts to the public. In March-April of 1979, after the official closing of the restaurant *Vezha* in Lviv, every night, the "selected customers" watched three American pornographic films on the upper floor, and then were allowed to have sex in underground cellar (for the additional payment).[35] In 1979–1985, in many disco clubs and video salons, there was the regular watching of the "illegal pornographic video films" after dances, followed with the sexual orgies, which imitated the American movies "with a sexual content."[36]

Through the entire period of so-called Westernization and Americanization of the Soviet youth culture after the Khrushchev's Thaw, the KGB administration tried to prevent this ideologically dangerous phenomenon by controlling various forms of cultural consumption in Soviet Ukraine. They established control over what the young people read, listened to, danced and watched. The KGB coordinated their anti-American operations against American cultural influences inside Soviet Ukraine with Soviet ideologists and the government officials.[37] They arrested, expelled from Komsomol and various colleges, fired from the job positions, and sent to jail thousands of the "Americanized" young people of Soviet Ukraine. But at the end, they failed their mission.[38] By the end of the 1980s, millions of young people in Soviet Ukraine still demonstrated Americanization of their culture and everyday behavior.

Taras Shevchenko, Americanization and Ukrainization of Cultural Consumption (Instead of Conclusion)

Moreover, Americanization of millions of young Soviet Ukrainians co-existed with their gradual "Ukrainization" in a process of cultural consumption. Even reading the classic Ukrainian literature, like the poetry of Taras Shevchenko, demonstrated these dangerous ideological trends of Ukrainian nationalism.[39] And again Shevchenko's poems and his figure as a founder of the Ukrainian national literature became involved in the cultural Cold War between the Soviet KGB and the Ukrainian diaspora in America. Both Soviet ideologists and the KGB organized the special campaigns, emphasizing the crucial role of Taras Shevchenko in a creation of Soviet Ukrainian culture contrasting it with the American Ukrainians' "bourgeois nationalistic" interpretation of Shevchenko. Even the celebration of the 100th anniversary of Taras Shevchenko in 1964 became the symbolic ideological duel between the Soviet (good) Ukrainians and the American (bad) Ukrainians.

Among many symbolic actions, including a publication of the complete collections of Shevchenko's works, Soviet administration prepared a creation of the poet's statue in downtown Moscow, near Hotel *Ukraina*, in 1964. Paradoxically, the Ukrainian diaspora in America planned the similar event: a building of Shevchenko's memorial in Dupont Circle in Washington, DC in 1964. As Markian Dobczansky noted, these two Taras Shevchenko's statues "were unveiled within weeks of each other in June 1964, but they're linked by more than that simple fact. Both memorials are embedded in a transnational argument over Shevchenko's legacy, which in this case served as a proxy for a broader argument over the fate of Ukrainian culture under Soviet rule."[40] Using Shevchenko memorial in Washington, DC, American Ukrainians often organized the patriotic demonstrations for independence of Ukraine, criticizing Russification and repressions against civil rights activists in Soviet Ukraine. The KGB agents, who operated in the US, always reacted against these "anti-Soviet provocations," initiating the special operations targeting the Ukrainian diaspora in America, trying to discredit

American Ukrainians as "the fascist collaborators" and "the traitors of old humanitarian tradition, represented by a great Ukrainian poet Taras Shevchenko." Almost every year, after 1964, the KGB agents organized the "special actions" in support of Soviet Ukraine near Taras Shevchenko memorial in Washington, DC.[41]

For the KGB, the consumption and "nationalistic" interpretation of Taras Shevchenko's lyrics by the college students inside Soviet Ukraine had also created a serious problem from the early 1960s.[42] As the KGB agents reported, Taras Shevchenko and his poetry united together all "nationalistically inclined" college students from both Western and Eastern Ukraine. Students from the Western Ukrainian Universities became the targets of the KGB special operations, or "active measures," during the officially sponsored literary/theatrical/music campaign in March of 1981, which was approved by the Soviet administration to commemorate the 120th-anniversary of Taras Shevchenko's death. Using the line from Shevchenko's poetry, the Ministry of Culture of Soviet Ukraine called this massive campaign "*In the family of nations, which is free and new ...*" The students from the Department of History from Chernivtsi State University in Western Ukraine, under a leadership of two friends V. Oliinyk and I. Mytskaniuk, using the university discussion club *Verax* (which meant "speaking the truth" in Latin), organized a special concert and series of public actions on March 6, 1981, in memory of the "Great *Kobzar*, a Unifier of the entire Ukraine." Those students collected more than 100 roubles "for their organizational needs." They planned the special student demonstration to put flowers at the Shevchenko bust in the nearby city park, a concert of Ukrainian music and the special "music-poetic funeral repast" (*pominki*) to pay a tribute to Taras Shevchenko. The Chernivtsi students invited the students-historians from Lviv and Ivano-Frankivsk Universities to participate in those events as well. The KGB operatives discovered that all students-organizers and their guests, such as S. Skrypnyk, a student-historian from Lviv State University, had been already suspected in the "Ukrainian nationalistic activities." Being afraid that those students would use those events as a pretext for the public "expressions of nationalism," the KGB banned the "Taras Shevchenko's events" in Chernivtsi and engaged "all Communist Party and Komsomol activists" (with 80 local communist party apparatchiks as their leaders) "to act on the streets" to prevent any pro-Shevchenko public actions, organized by the students. Eventually, under the KGB supervision, Komsomol leaders of Chernivtsi State University re-wrote the entire script for the Shevchenko's concert removing "an ideologically dangerous thesis" about "a Great *Kobzar* as a Unifier of Ukraine."[43]

Taras Shevchenko became the symbol of resistance to Russification and the oppression by Moscow for all Ukrainians all over Ukraine. This symbol not only united people of Western and Eastern Ukraine in one nation, but also strengthened the self-awareness of Ukrainian identity for representatives of the Ukrainian diaspora in America, who participated in the ritualistic pilgrimage, visiting Taras Shevchenko's memorials in Soviet Ukraine on the regular basis since the opening Soviet Ukraine to the foreigners' visits by Nikita Khrushchev.

These new regular visits of American and Canadian Ukrainians to Soviet Ukraine created the real problems for the KGB operatives, especially in the 1960s and the 1970s. In May of 1973, the KGB agents arrested an American student from the University of California, Sandra Olden, who tried to organize a demonstration of American Ukrainians and the local Ukrainian college students in Kyiv near Taras Shevchenko's monument to commemorate his contribution to Ukrainian culture.[44] In March of 1974, the KGB agents prevented the public action of 162 Canadian-Ukrainian tourists (mainly high school students and their teachers), who intended to put the national blue and yellow flag of independent Ukraine at the Taras Shevchenko's monument in Kyiv. The KGB officers surrounded this group of Canadian tourists, persuaded them to return to their hotel and confiscated a blue and yellow flag of the Ukraine' People Republic of 1918.[45]

Despite the numerous operations against "using Taras Shevchenko as a symbol of Ukrainian nationalism," the KGB and Soviet ideologists in Cold War's Ukraine not only failed to stop such cultural practices, but paradoxically also strengthened the symbolic significance of Taras Shevchenko in the resistance of the Ukrainian patriots to Russification and in their struggle for independence of Ukraine. Despite all KGB efforts, Taras Shevchenko's poetry, ideas and images **did unify and consolidate** both Western and Eastern Ukraine by the end of the 1980s, and **did contribute to a formation of a common Ukrainian identity** during perestroika in Soviet Ukraine, preparing the road to its political independence.

Notes

1 I quote my old interview with Igor T., retired KGB officer, Dnipropetrovsk, August 12, 1991.
2 Interview with Leonid Leshchenko in Kyiv, May 12, 2012; SBU, f. 16, op. 1, spr. 1175, ark. 132.
3 Ibid.
4 Ibid., spr. 1175, ark. 133–134; spr. 1169, ark. 337–338.
5 Ibid., spr. 1169, 337–338.
6 SBU, f. 16, op. 1, spr. 1184, ark. 36.
7 SBU, f. 16, op. 1, spr. 1184, ark. 36–37.
8 See also Sergei I. Zhuk, *Rock and Roll in the Rocket City*, 200, 201.
9 Ibid., ark. 166.
10 See also Sergei I. Zhuk, *Rock and Roll in the Rocket City*, 141, 144–145. The most popular Bruce Lee's film (on video tapes) among Soviet Ukrainian karate's fans was *Enter the Dragon* (1973).
11 SBU, f. 16, op. 1, spr. 1171, ark. 96–99.
12 See a Soviet and Post-Soviet history of Jehovah's Witnesses in the best study of this sect: Emily B. Baran, *Dissent on the Margins: How Soviet Jehovah's Witnesses Defied Communism and Lived to Preach About It* (New York: Oxford University Press, 2016).

13 SBU, f. 16, op. 1, spr. 1111, ark. 182–183. See about the Christian notion of Millennium among the similar sects in Sergei I. Zhuk, *Russia's Lost Reformation: Peasants, Millennialism and Radical Sects in Southern Russia and Ukraine, 1830–1917* (Baltimore, MD: Johns Hopkins University Press & Washington, D.C.: Woodrow Wilson Center Press, 2004), 129–136.

14 Ibid., ark. 183.

15 Ibid., ark. 184.

16 Interview with Stepan T., retired KGB officer, in Kyiv.

17 SBU, f. 16, op. 1, spr. 1217, ark. 195–197.

18 Ibid., ark. 196.

19 Ibid.

20 Ibid., ark. 196–197.

21 Ibid., ark. 197.

22 SBU, f. 16, op. 1, spr. 1162, ark. 164. See also a description of this document in Eduard Andryushenko and Robert Coalson, "Inside The Soviet KGB's Secret War on Western Books", April 21, 2019, see a link: https://www.rferl.org/a/inside-the-soviet-kgb-s-secret-war-on-western-books/29894541.html

23 SBU, f. 16, op. 1, spr. 1162, ark. 164.

24 Ibid. The report characterized Forsyth's book as "a practical handbook for any maniac wishing to carry out a terrorist act," and Burgess' novel as "fundamentally anti-communist, mostly because the roaming gang of ruffians in the book speaks in "a semi-Russian language."

25 Ibid., spr. 1162, ark. 164. In original it was written in Russian: «поступила книжка американского автора Р. Купера 'Песни полового члена и мысли о нем' с описанием всевозможных сексопатологических сцен.»

26 Ibid., spr. 1162, ark. 165, 166.

27 See about this process in Dnipropetrovsk in Sergei I. Zhuk, *Rock and Roll in the Rocket City*, 121–123.

28 SBU, f. 16, op. 1, spr. 1092, ark. 83.

29 Ibid., ark. 83–84.

30 SBU, f. 16, op. 1, spr. 1192, ark. 68.

31 Ibid., spr. 1192, ark. 69.

32 SBU, f. 16, op. 1, spr. 1162, ark. 195.

33 See interview with Igor T. and Sergei Zhuk, *Rock and Roll in the Rocket City*, 295–298.

34 SBU, f. 16, op. 1, spr. 1162, ark. 192.

35 SBU, f. 16, op. 1, spr.1164, ark. 132–135.

36 Ibid., spr. 1271, ark. 235–236.

37 See how KGB and the Soviet government tried to control the system of radio broadcasting in the republic in a document of January 1981: SBU, f. 16, op. 1, spr. 1179, ark. 112–114.

38 See about this failure in Sergei Zhuk, Op. cit.

39 See about this in detail in Sergei Zhuk, Op. cit., 34–36, 49.

40 Markian Dobczansky, "Dueling Shevchenkos: An Episode in the Transnational Ukrainian Cold War," *Harriman Magazine*, Spring 2019, 27–33. Citation is from p. 28.

41 SBU, f. 16, op.1, spr. 1218, ark. 265.

42 See about this in Sergei Zhuk, *Rock and Roll in the Rocket City*, 34–35.

43 SBU, f. 16, op. 1, spr. 1181, ark. 158–159.

44 SBU, f. 16, op. 1, spr. 1070, ark. 214–215.

45 SBU, f. 16, op. 1, spr. 1095, ark. 180–181.

Epilogue: "Learning from the Main Adversary" and Returning to the Soviet Anti-American and Anti-Fascist Scenario

Through the entire history of post-Stalin (late) socialism in Soviet Ukraine (1953–1991), for the Ukrainian KGB, their main enemy was "capitalist America." Despite three attempts of opening of the Soviet society to the western influences and starting a dialogue with the "capitalist" West: during Khrushchev Thaw, Brezhnev détente and Gorbachev perestroika – the KGB in Soviet Ukraine considered and treated the US and Canada as its major enemies, which were behind, triggering and funding Ukrainian nationalism, Jewish Zionism, Christian sectarianism, Crimean Tartar, civil rights (Helsinki) activism and finally, various forms of the youth movement, from hippies to punks. At the same time, during détente of the 1970s, the new trends appeared in the KGB attitudes toward America. Besides traditional forms of collecting the intelligence information, meddling in the American politics, and fighting the espionage efforts of the US intelligence and the ideological influences of "capitalist way of life" inside the Soviet society, the KGB began adjusting to the western (in many cases, American) forms of financial and technological activities.

As I had already mentioned this before, from the early beginning, during the détente, the academic exchanges between the US and the USSR were used for infiltration with the "KGB people."[1] These "people" included a wide variety of the experts – from the ranked KGB officers to various scholars and scientists, who collaborated with the KGB and provided those "directing organs" not only with intelligence information and necessary "informal" contacts in academic and diplomatic circles, but also with the very important expertise in such different fields of knowledge as the functions of the US Department of State, computer science or banking system. Many Soviet participants recalled how their KGB supervisors requested them to provide information about the different functions of US banks "to use this experience for organization of the Soviet foreign banks, working abroad."[2] According to former Soviet KGB officers, who participated in these exchange programs, this information about banking and financial service in the West would be used for future financial operations in post-Soviet Russia and Ukraine.[3]

During the same period of détente, the KGB operatives in Soviet Ukraine and the US intelligence officers began their collaboration in 1972, trying to protect their political leaders, during the official visit of the US President Richard Nixon to Kyiv. The KGB and CIA officers helped each other, exchanged the classified information, combined their efforts, targeting all terrorist attempts on the life of Soviet and American political leaders. Unfortunately, this period of friendly cooperation between the state security service of two states did not last long enough. During the 1970s, while permitting the Americans to open their Consulate office in Kyiv, Soviet administration sanctioned simultaneously the series of the KGB active measures and espionage operations against the same US Consulate in a capital of Soviet Ukraine.

Even Gorbachev's perestroika, the last attempt to open the Soviet Union to the West (including the US and Canada), did not change priorities in the KGB treatment of their main adversary – the capitalist America. The Ukrainian office of the KGB in Kyiv still targeted the USA and Canada as the main enemies of Soviet Ukraine. At the same time, during perestroika two new factors, produced by the political center of the Soviet administration in Moscow, brought a significant confusion in the "anti-American" operations of the KGB in Soviet Ukraine. The first factor was the Chernobyl catastrophe of 1986, which not only discredited the central political leadership in Kremlin, but also led to the tragic loss among the Ukrainian KGB personnel.[4] For some Ukrainian KGB officers, it started "their own national awakening," contributing to their growing national awareness, especially in a situation of keeping secret and protecting the information about the nuclear accident from the very Americans and Canadians, who sincerely expressed their readiness to help the Ukrainian population. The second factor, which contributed to a confusion of the KGB administration in Kyiv, was a process of glasnost, sanctioned by the Soviet leadership, and public criticism of Stalinism and political repressions in Soviet history. In the context of such criticism and revision of the relations with the Ukrainian diaspora in America, many goals of the KGB "anti-American operations" began looking obsolete and required the new approach in the spirit of New Thinking concept, offered by Mikhail Gorbachev. As one former KGB officer, who lived through this period of the KGB transformation in Ukraine, noted, "it was a complete mess: on the one hand, the leaders in Moscow still required from us the same operations against American intelligence and the American influences in the society of Soviet Ukraine; on the other hand, they recommended us a strategy of cultural dialogue and mutual understanding with our traditional opponent – imperialist America." In this situation, he continued, "many young KGB officers tried to adjust to these confusing requirements of confrontation and dialogue with Americans, and they began borrowing various elements from the American style of living and introducing them in their practices of 'American commercialization' and American technologies: they began making money, trading their precious secret information, using their KGB connections."[5] As another contemporary of those developments called this process "a phenomenon of learning from our main enemy, America, how to make profit from the information and new technologies."[6]

During the 1980s, at the beginning of perestroika, the KGB operatives collected and implemented new financial and technological experiences of their American opponents, which became useful for opening of the new banking system [and other financial and technological practices] in late Soviet and post-Soviet geopolitical space [all KGB reports in 1989–1991 discuss such information and practices on regular basis].[7] Using its previous American experience and connections with "useful" Americans, the KGB administration, including its Ukrainian office, founded a series of financial organizations in the West, especially in the US, which became important venues for various banking and other financial operations of the KGB.[8] During the end of perestroika, the KGB office in Kyiv stopped discussing the dangers of "capitalist America" and all the evils it produced, such as Ukrainian nationalism, Jewish Zionism and the products of American mass culture. Instead, after 1989, the more KGB documents concentrated on various lessons of the American economy, politics and security service, which should be used in Soviet Ukraine. The Ukrainian KGB not only recommended the political leadership in Kyiv to learn from the American experience, but began participating in various commercial deals, bringing to Ukraine and trading there so-called *org tekhnika* from America, which included the foreign computers, various technological devices for intelligence service, etc.[9] Paradoxically, the KGB operatives in Soviet Ukraine (like their colleagues in other parts of the Soviet space) used their main enemy – "capitalist America" – as their main teacher for their own survival in the critical conditions of post-Soviet market economy and adopting various practices of the American intelligence service to the rise of post-Soviet capitalism.

******

Historically, the KGB (and all its predecessors [NKVD, OGPU] and successors [FSB, SBU] in the Soviet space) in their operations reflected (and still reflect) the major developments in political ideology of the political regimes they served. Therefore, all their operations against "the American adversaries" such as the US and Canada had become the reflections of their regimes' changing attitudes toward America since the beginning of the Soviet political police. During the Soviet period of history, especially after Stalin, the KGB operations were the reflections of the political implementation of the Marxist-Leninist ideology of the ruling Communist party. After 1991, the successors of the KGB, especially in Russia and Belarus, became the police tool of the ruling political elites, which after the Maidan Revolution of 2013–2014 in Ukraine, took an anti-Western, anti-American position. If the Ukrainian successor of the Soviet KGB, SBU, became ready for a dialogue with the West and for a cooperation with the American intelligence after 2014, the Belarusian KGB and the Russian FSB (Federal Security

Service) still follow the old Soviet models for anti-American active measures. Besides the traditional intelligence and counter-intelligence operations against America, Russian and Belarusian security service still use anti-American active measures such as collecting the compromising material (*kompromat*); dividing and weakening the American society from inside; meddling in the American politics by supporting pro-Russian politicians; stealing the American technological and industrial information.[10]

At the same time, both Russian and Belarusian political police use the traditional Soviet propagandist scenario of the KGB operations blaming America in every problem of the domestic and international politics: from the economic crisis in post-Soviet Russia and Belarus to the so-called coloured revolutions in Georgia and Ukraine, and recently (in January 2022) in provoking the anti-government protests in post-Soviet Kazakhstan. Especially, FSB and Belarusian KGB focus their attention on the contemporary cultural consumption and the youth culture, which became, in the KGB imagination, the object of "Americanization," the direct result of American cultural and ideological influences.

The KGB/FSB ideologists in Russia, like Andranik Migranian, blame Americans in "creating" all domestic and international problems for the Russian state.[11] Another Russian ideologist, Vyacheslav Nikonov, served an Executive Director of Russkii Mir Foundation from 2007 to 2012, taking publicly anti-American position, criticizing the Orange Revolution and Maidan Revolution in Ukraine as "American conspiracy against Russia." In his textbook, whose publication was funded by Russkii Mir Foundation, Nikonov presented the US as the major geo-political enemy of Russia. He interpreted all events in Georgia, Moldova, and Ukraine since the collapse of the Soviet Union as a result of "US expansionism." According to Nikonov, the major goal of the US is to "weaken" and to "punish" Russia, using the recent developments in Ukraine and Russia. Moreover, Nikonov supports the Russian expansionism, Russian annexation of Crimea and Russian military presence in eastern Ukraine. He justifies the Russian war in Ukraine by the "historical mission" of Russian state to "defend" its state national interests against "American imperialism" in Eastern Europe, in post-Soviet geopolitical space.[12] Other Russian ideologists also follow Nikonov in their criticism of US "public diplomacy" criticizing Americans in "masterminding" "Ukrainian revolutions." They accuse US politicians in the attempts to "take out" Ukraine from the Russian sphere of influence in Eastern Europe as early as 2003. According to them, US "public diplomacy" focused its efforts on pro-Western Ukrainian youth, trying organized so-called Orange and other anti-Russian revolutions in Ukraine. These Russian ideologists repeat the old Soviet concepts about "American anti-Russian conspiracy." They emphasized that since 2003 "the USA were able to create [in Ukraine] a solid human potential, oriented to the West."[13]

Another old Soviet concept, used by the KGB and restored by the Russian FSB and Belarusian KGB today, is a connection of anti-Russian nationalism in Ukraine and Belarus to fascism, neo-Nazism. Even post-Soviet youth culture, including the consumption of rock and hip-hop music, is targeted by the KGB successors in Russia and Belarus as the American ideological provocation, which is linked directly to the old ideological threat – to fascism. This threatening fetish of fascism and neo-Nazism is present today not only in the everyday Russian media propagandist criticism of the youth participation in the Ukrainian and Belarusian events, but also in FSB various operations against "the American/Western intrusion" in the domestic politics of Ukrainians and Belarusians, including the recent escalation of the Russian and Belarusian military troops on the borders of Ukraine in 2022. As Russian President Vladimir Putin wrote recently: "Radicals and neo-Nazis were open and more and more insolent about their ambitions [in post-Soviet Ukraine. -SZh.]. They were indulged by both the official authorities and local oligarchs, who robbed the people of Ukraine and kept their stolen money in Western banks, ready to sell their motherland for the sake of preserving their capital. To this should be added the persistent weakness of state institutions and the position of a willing hostage to someone else's geopolitical will." Putin blames the West and, first of all, America for the Ukraine's anti-Russian position today.[14]

As we see, after the long period of learning from their main and "seductive" adversary in the 1970s and 1990s, the Russian successor of Soviet KGB and its ideologists, such as Putin, gradually returned now to the old Soviet scenario of blaming "the Americans" and "neo-Nazi radicals" for all main problems in the post-Soviet geo-political space. Unfortunately, this "Anti-American" scenario shapes nowadays not only international, but also domestic politics in both Russia and Belarus. And the KGB successors there play the important role in an implementation of the old Soviet practices of this "Anti-American" and "Anti-Fascist" scenario in every day politics in post-Soviet states.

Notes

1 Sergei I. Zhuk, "The 'KGB People,' Soviet Americanists and Soviet-American Academic Exchanges, 1958-1985," *The Soviet and Post-Soviet Review*, 2017, vol. 44, No. 2, 133–167.
2 Interview with Nikolai Bolkhovitinov, March 23, 1991, Moscow.
3 See Oleg D. Kalugin, *Spymaster: My Thirty-Two Years in Intelligence and Espionage Against the West* (New York, NY: Basic Books, 2009), 424.
4 See in detail about this in the study based on the archival research at the SBU archive in Kyiv: Serhii Plokhy, *Chernobyl: History of a Tragedy* (New York: Penguin, 2019).
5 Interview with Stepan K., former KGB officer, March 3, 2019, Kyiv.
6 Interview with Leonid Leshchenko, May 12, 2010, Kyiv.
7 See, e.g., in SBU, f. 16, op.1, spr. 1271, ark. 21–25; spr. 1295, ark. 52–54, 83–85 ff.
8 See about a creation of hundreds of front companies by the KGB in the 1980s in the US and Canada in Craig Unger, *House of Trump, House of Putin: The Untold Story of Donald Trump and Russian Mafia* (New York: Penguin, 2019), 70–71,

144–145; see about KGB recruiting useful Americans, so-called American assets on pp. 28–29, 46–47.

9 See SBU, f. 16, op. 1, spr. 1295, ark. 197, 199.

10 Among the growing number of the recent studies of the Russian FSB, and other successors of the Soviet KGB activities, inside the USA after the collapse of the Soviet Union, see especially *The Kremlin's Malign Influence inside the US*, Edited by Michael Weiss (Washington, DC: Free Russia, 2021). See also a link: https://www.4freerussia.org/wp-content/uploads/2021/08/TheKremlinsMalignInfluenceInsidethe US.pdf

11 Andranik Migranian, "Putin Triumphs in Ukraine," *The National Interest*, March 6, 2014. See about a role of Andranik Migranian as an advisor of both Presidents Yeltsin and Putin in Eugeniusz Górski, *Civil Society, Pluralism and Universalism (Polish Philosophical Studies, VIII)* (Washington, DC: The Council for Research in Values and Philosophy, 2007), 57, 58, 61.

12 V. A. Nikonov, *Sovremennyi mir i ego istoki* (Moscow: Izd-vo Moskovskogo universiteta, 2015), esp. 302–304.

13 N. A. Tsvetkova, "Publichania diplomatiia SSHA: ot kholodnoi voiny k novoi kholodnoi voine," in *Rossiia i SShA: poznavaia drug druga. Sbornik pamiati akademika Aleksandra Aleksandrovicha Fursenko*, Ed. by Vladimir V. Noskov (Saint-Petersburg: Nestor-Istoriia, 2015), 82–97, citations are from pp. 92 and 93.

14 Citation is from Vladimir Putin's article "On the Historical Unity of Russians and Ukrainians," published on the official Kremlin site on July 12, 2021. See a link: http://en.kremlin.ru/events/president/news/66181.

Selected Bibliography

The Most Important Interviews

Interview with Bohdan Josypovych K., a retired KGB/SBU officer, February 9, 2019, Kyiv, Ukraine.
Interview with Nikolai N. Bolkhovitinov, January 4, 2004, Moscow, Russian Federation.
Interview with Igor T., a retired KGB officer, May 15, 1991, Dnipropetrovsk, Ukraine.
Interview with Ivan Grigorovich K., a retired KGB officer, February 3, 2019, Kyiv, Ukraine.
Interview with Leonid K., a retired KGB officer, March 3, 2019, Kyiv, Ukraine.
Interviews with Leonid Leshchenko, June 23, 2012, and June 25, 2013, Kyiv, Ukraine.
Interview with Stepan Ivanovich T., a retired KGB officer, January 30, 2019, Kyiv, Ukraine.
Interview with Vitalii Pidgaetskii at the Department of History, Dnipropetrovsk University, February 10, 1996, Dnipro, Ukraine.
Interview with Arnold Shlepakov, August 29, 1991, Kyiv, Ukraine.

Archival Sources

Arkhiv Nathional'noi Akademii Nauk Ukrainy [Kyiv, Ukraine], Opys 1-L, Otdel kadrov, Files of Shlepakov, Arnol'd; Leshchenko, Leonid, etc.
Derzhavnyi arkhiv Dnipropetrovs'koi oblasti, Dnipropetrovs'k, Ukraine.
Fond 17, Dnepropetrovskii Gorkom LKSMU (Komsomola Ukrainy).
Fond 18, Dnepropetrovskii Gorkom KPU (Kommunisticheskoi partii Ukrainy).
Fond 19, Dnepropetrovskii Obkom KPU (Kommunisticheskoi partii Ukrainy).
Fond 22, Dnepropetrovskii Obkom LKSMU (Komsomola Ukrainy).
Fond 9870, Dnepropetrovskii Obkom KPU (Kommunisticheskoi partii Ukrainy). Otdel: Osobyi sector. Sektor: Sekretnaiu chast'.
Galuzevyi Derzhavnyi Arkhiv Sluzhby Bezpeky Ukrainy (The Branch State Archive of the Security Service of Ukraine [SBU]), Kyiv, Ukraine.
Fond 1, The Second Main (Counterintelligence) Directorate of the KGB.
Fond 16, The Secretariat of GPU-KGB of Ukraine.
Tsentral'nyi derzhavnyi arkhiv vyshchykh organiv vlady ta upravlinnia, Kyiv, Ukraine.
Fond 5116, Ministerstvo kul'tury URSR.

Tsentral'nyi Derzhavnyi Arkhiv Gromads'kykh Ob'ednan' Ukrainy, Kyiv, Ukraine.
Fond 7, Tsentral'nyi Komitet LKSMU.
Viddil kul'tury.
Viddil Propagandy i agitatsii.

Newspapers and Journals

Pravda Ukrainy
Iskusstvo kino
Izvestia
Molod' Ukrainy
Prapor iunosti
Pravda
Ranok
Sovetskii ekran
Telegram
The Ukrainian Weekly
Vokrug sveta
Vsesvit
Zhyttia i slovo

Secondary Sources

Ludmila Alexeyeva, *Soviet Dissent: Contemporary Movements for National, Religious, and Human Rights*, Transl. by Carol Pearce and John Glad (Middletown, CT: Wesleyan University Press, 1985).

Christopher Andrew and Vasili Mitrokhin, *The Sword and the Shield: The Mitrokhin Archive and the Secret History of the KGB* (New York: Basic Books, 1999).

Jan-Hinnerk Antons, "Displaced Persons in Postwar Germany: Parallel Societies in a Hostile Environment," *Journal of Contemporary History*, Vol. 49, No. 1 (January 2014), pp. 92–114.

Emily B. Baran, *Dissent on the Margins: How Soviet Jehovah's Witnesses Defied Communism and Lived to Preach About It* (New York: Oxford University Press, 2016).

Olga Bertelsen, "Political Affinities and Maneuvering of Soviet Political Elites: Heorhii Shevel and Ukraine's Ministry of Strange Affairs in the 1970s," *Nationalities Papers: The Journal of Nationalism and Ethnicity*, Vol. 47, No. 3 (2019), pp. 394–411.

Olga Bertelsen, "The KGB Operation 'Retribution' and John Demjaniuk," in *Russian Active Measures: Yesterday, Today and Tomorrow*: Edited by Olga Bertelsen (New York: ibidem Press and Columbia University Press, 2021), pp. 93–136.

Joseph L. Black, *Canada in the Soviet Mirror: Ideology and Perception in Soviet Foreign Affairs, 1917–1991* (Ottawa: Carleton University Press, 1998).

Vladimir Bukovsky, *Judgment in Moscow: Soviet Crimes and Western Complicity*, trans. Alyona Kojevnikov (Westlake Village, CA: Ninth of November Press, 2019).

Francesco A. Cacciatore, *"Their Need Was Great": Émigrés and Anglo-American*

Intelligence Operations in the Early Cold War (Ph. D. diss, University of Westminster, March 2018).

Jolanta Darczewska and Piotr Żochowski, "ACTIVE MEASURES: Russia's key export," *Point of View*, June 2017, Number 64 (Warsaw: Center for Eastern Studies), pp. 5–71.

Viktor M. Danylenko, *Ukrainav mizhnarodnykh naukovo-tekhnichnykh zv'iazkakh (70-80-i rr.)* (Kyiv: Instytut istorii Ukrainy. Instytut ukrais'koi arkheografii, 1993).

Markian Dobczansky, "Dueling Shevchenkos: An Episode in the Transnational Ukrainian Cold War," *Harriman Magazine*, Spring, 2019, 27–33.

Anatoly Dobrynin, *In Confidence: Moscow's Ambassador to America's Six Cold War Presidents (1962–1986)* (New York: Times Books, 1995).

Juliane Fürst, *Flowers through Concrete: Explorations in Soviet Hippieland* (New York: Oxford University Press, 2021).

Leonid Gamol'sky, Natalia Efremenko, and Viktor Inshakov, *Na barrikadakh sovesti: Ocherki, razmyshlenia, interviu* (Dnipropetrovsk, 1988).

Raymond L. Garthoff, *A Journey through the Cold War: A Memoir of Containment and Coexistence* (Washington, DC: Brookings Institution Press, 2001).

E. Bruce Geelhoed, *Diplomacy Shot Down: The U-2 Crisis and Eisenhower's Aborted Mission to Moscow, 1959–1960* (Norman: University of Oklahoma Press, 2020).

Michael Hanusiak and Sam Pevzner, *Lest We Forget* (New York: The Ukrainian American League, 1973).

John E. Haynes, Harvey Klehr, and Alexander Vassiliev, *Spies: The Rise and Fall of the KGB in America* (New Haven: Yale University Press, 2009).

Howard Hughes, *Once Upon A Time in the Italian West: The Filmgoers' Guide to Spaghetti Westerns* (London, England: I.B. Tauris, 2004).

Seth G. Jones, *A Covert Action: Reagan, the CIA, and the Cold War Struggle in Poland* (New York: W.W. Norton, 2018).

G. P. Kalantaevska, N. N. Prokopenko, S. V. Voropai, "Literary Environment and Literary Situation in Ukraine in 60–70's of XX Century in the Context of the Correspondence of B. Antonenko-Davydovych," *Philologichni traktaty*, Vol. 10, No. 4 (2018), pp. 94–104.

G. Kapralov, "Utverzhdenie istiny, razoblachenie mifov," *Iskusstvo kino*, Vol. 11, (1971), pp. 2–18.

Allen H. Kassof, "Scholarly Exchanges and the Collapse of Communism," *The Soviet and Post-Soviet Review*, Vol. 22, No. 3, (1995), pp. 263–274.

Sergei N. Khrushchev, *Nikita Khrushchev and the Creation of a Superpower* (University Park, PA: The Pennsylvania State University Press, 2000).

John Kolasky, *Education in Soviet Ukraine: A Study in Discrimination and Russification* (Toronto: Peter Martin Associates, 1968).

John Kolasky, *Two Years in Soviet Ukraine: A Canadian's Personal Account of Russian Oppression and the Growing Opposition* (Toronto: Peter Martin Associates Books, 1970).

John Kolasky, *The Shattered Illusion: The History of Ukrainian Pro-Communist Organizations in Canada* (Toronto: Peter Martin Associates Books, 1979).

Mark Kramer, ed., "Ukraine and the Soviet-Czechoslovak Crisis of 1968 (Part I): New Evidence from the Diary of Petro Shelest," *Cold War International History Project Bulletin*, No. 10 (1998), pp. 234–247.

Petro Kravchuk, *Bez nedomovok: Spogady* (Kyiv: Literaturna Ukraina, 1995).

Petro Kravchuk, *Ukraintsi v Kanadi: Statti, narysy, pamflety* (Kyiv: Dnipro, 1981).

Peter Krawchuk, *Our History: The Ukrainian Labour-Farmer Movement in Canada, 1907–1991*, Translated from Ukrainian by Mary Skrypnyk, Edited by John Boyd (Toronto: Lugus, 1996).

Taras Kuzio, "U.S. Support for Ukraine's Liberation during the Cold War: A Study of Prolog Research and Publishing Corporation," *Communist and Post-Communist Studies*, Vol. 45 (2012), pp. 51–64.

Walter LaFeber, *America, Russia, and the Cold War 1945–2006*: The 10th Edition (Boston: McGraw-Hill, 2008).

Stanislav Lazebnyk, *Zakordonne ukrainstvo: vytoky ta siogodennia* (Kyiv: Istyna, 2007).

Stanislav Lazebnyk and Olha B. Havura, *Rozdumy na mostu z dvobichnym rukhom* (Kyiv: Etnos, 2004).

Rósa Magnúsdóttir, *Enemy Number One: The United States of America in Soviet Ideology and Propaganda, 1945–1959* (New York: Oxford University Press, 2019).

Mykhailo H. Marunchak, *The Ukrainian Canadians: A History* (Winnipeg/Ottawa: Ukrainian Free Academy of Sciences, 1976).

Kevin N. McCauley, *Russian Influence Campaigns Against the West: From the Cold War to Putin* (North Charleston, SC: CreateSpace Independent Publishing Platform, 2016).

Edward Mickolus, *The Counterintelligence Chronology: Spying By and Against the United States From the 1700s Through 2014* (Jefferson, NC: McFarland & Company, Inc., 2015).

Simo Mikkonen, "Soviet-American Art Exchanges during the Thaw: From Bold Openings to Hasty Retreats," in *Art and Political Reality*, Edited by M. Kurisoo. Proceedings in the Art Museum of Estonia, Vol. 8 (Tallinn: Art Museum of Estonia – Kumu Art Museum, 2013), 57–76.

Alexander J. Motyl, "The Foreign Relations of the Ukrainian SSR," *Harvard Ukrainian Studies*, Vol. 6, No. 1 (March 1982), pp. 62–78.

Wojciech J. Muszyński, "The Polish Guards Companies of the U.S. Army After World War II," *The Polish Review*, Vol. 57, No. 4 (2012), pp. 75–86.

Na skryzhaliakh istorii: Z istorii vzaiemozv'iazkiv uriadovykh struktur i hromads'kykh kil Ukrainy z ukrains'ko-kanads'koiu hromadoiu v drugii polovyni 1940–1980-ti roky, Edited by P. Tron'ko a. o. (Kyiv: Instytut istorii Ukrainy NANU, Fundatsiia ukrains'koi spadshchyny Al'berty, 2003).

Pavel Palazchenko, *My Years with Gorbachev and Shevardnadze: The Memoir of a Soviet Interpreter* (University Park, PA: The Pennsylvania State University Press, 1997).

Michael Parrish, *The Lesser Terror: Soviet State Security, 1939–1953* (Westport, CT: Praeger Publishers, 1996).

Curtis Peebles, *Twilight Warriors: Covert Air Opera tions against the USSR* (Annapolis, MD: Naval Institute Press, 2005).

Rudolf Pihoia, "Chekhoslovakia 1968 god (Part 1)," *Novaia i noveishaia istoriia*, no. 6 (1994), pp. 24–28.

Serhii Plokhy, *The Man with the Poison Gun: A Cold War Spy Story* (New York: Basic Books, 2016).

Serhii Plokhy, *Chernobyl: History of a Tragedy* (New York: Penguin, 2019).

Serhii Plokhy, *Forgotten Bastards of the Eastern Front: American Airmen behind the Soviet Lines and the Collapse of the Grand Alliance* (New York: Oxford University Press, 2019).

Serhii Plokhy, *Nuclear Folly: A History of the Cuban Missile Crisis* (New York: W.W. Norton, 2021).

Re-Imagining Ukrainian Canadians: History, Politics, and Identity, Edited by Rhonda L. Hinther and Jim Mochoruk (Toronto: University of Toronto Press, 2011).

William J. Risch, "Soviet 'Flower Children': Hippies and the Youth Counter-Culture in 1970s Lviv," *Journal of Contemporary History*, Vol. 40, No. 3 (July 2005), pp. 565–584.

William J. Risch, *The Ukrainian West: Culture and the Fate of Empire in Soviet Lviv* (Cambridge, MA: Harvard University Press, 2011).

Russian Active Measures: Yesterday, Today and Tomorrow, Edited by Olga Bertelsen (New York: ibidem Press and Columbia University Press, 2021).

Arnold M. Shlepakov, *Ukrains'ka trudova immigratsiia v SShA i Kanadi (kinets' XIX – poch. XX st.)* (Kyiv: Naukova dumka, 1960).

Mykola Solomatin, "Zhertvy chornoi magii," *Ranok*, 1974, January, No. 1, 18–19.

Richard H. Shultz, and Roy Godson, *Dezinformatsia: Active Measures in Soviet Strategy* (New York, NY: Pergamon-Brassey's International Defense Publishers, 1984).

Richard Stengel, *Information Wars: How We Lost the Global Battle against Disinformation & What We Can Do About It* (New York: Atlantic Monthly Press, 2019).

Anna Szemere, *Up from the Underground: The Culture of Rock Music in Postsocialist Hungary* (University Park, PA: The Pennsylvania State University Press, 2001).

William Taubman, *Khrushchev: The Man and His Era* (New York: W. W. Norton, 2003).

The Kremlin's Malign Influence inside the US, Edited by Michael Weiss (Washington, DC: Free Russia, 2021).

Artemy Troitsky, *Back in the USSR: The True Story of Rock in Russia* (London: Omnibus Press, 1987).

Benjamin Tromly, *Cold War Exiles and the CIA: Plotting to Free Russia* (New York: Oxford University Press, 2019).

Gleb Tsipursky, *Socialist Fun: Youth, Consumption, and State-Sponsored Popular Culture in the Soviet Union, 1945–1970* (Pittsburgh: University of Pittsburgh Press, 2016).

Douglas Tuttle, *Fraud, Famine and Fascism: The Ukrainian Genocide Myth from Hitler to Harvard* (Toronto: Progress Books, 1987).

Craig Unger, *House of Trump, House of Putin: The Untold Story of Donald Trump and Russian Mafia* (New York: Penguin, 2019).

Craig Unger, *American Kompromat: How the KGB Cultivated Donald Trump, and Related Tales of Sex, Greed, Power, and Treachery* (New York: Dutton, 2021).

Dmitrii Vedeneiev, *Ateisty v mundirakh: Sovetskie spetssluzhby i religioznaia sfera Ukrainy* (Moscow: Algoritm, 2016).

Vitaliy K. Vrublevskiy, *Vladimir Shcherbitskiy: zapiski pomoshchnika: slukhi, legendy, dokumenty* (Kyiv: Dovira, 1993).

Serhy Yekelchyk, *Ukraine: Birth of a Modern Nation* (New York: Oxford University Press, 2007).

Sergei I. Zhuk, *Russia's Lost Reformation: Peasants, Millennialism and Radical Sects in Southern Russia and Ukraine, 1830–1917* (Baltimore, MD: Johns Hopkins University Press & Washington, D.C.: Woodrow Wilson Center Press, 2004).

Sergei I. Zhuk, *Rock and Roll in the Rocket City: The West, Identity, and Ideology in Soviet Dniepropetrovsk, 1960–1985* (Baltimore, MD: Johns Hopkins University Press & Washington, D.C.: Woodrow Wilson Center Press, 2010).

Sergei I. Zhuk, *Soviet Americana: The Cultural History of Russian and Ukrainian Americanists* (London and New York: I.B. Tauris, 2018).

Sergei I. Zhuk, "The 'KGB People,' Soviet Americanists and Soviet-American Academic Exchanges, 1958–1985," *The Soviet and Post-Soviet Review*, Vol. 44, No. 2 (2017), pp. 133–167.

Sergei I. Zhuk, "'Academic Détente': IREX Files, Academic Reports, and 'American' Adventures of Soviet Americanists during the Brezhnev Era," *Cahiers du monde russe*, Vol. 54, No. 1–2 (Janvier–juin 2013), pp. 297–328.

Sergei I. Zhuk, "'The Disco Mafia' and 'Komsomol Capitalism' in Soviet Ukraine during Late Socialism," in *Material Culture in Russia and the USSR: Things, Values, Identities*, Edited by Graham H. Roberts (London and Oxford: Bloomsbury Publishing, 2017), 173–195.

Index

Printed in the United States
by Baker & Taylor Publisher Services